Marcel Proust in the Light of William James

Marcel Proust in the Light of William James

In Search of a Lost Source

Marilyn M. Sachs

LEXINGTON BOOKS
Lanham • Boulder • New York • Toronto • Plymouth, UK

Published by Lexington Books
A wholly owned subsidiary of Rowman & Littlefield
4501 Forbes Boulevard, Suite 200, Lanham, Maryland 20706
www.rowman.com

10 Thornbury Road, Plymouth PL6 7PP, United Kingdom

British Library Cataloguing in Publication Information Available

Library of Congress Cataloging-in-Publication Data
Library of Congress Cataloging-in-Publication Data Available
ISBN 978-0-7391-8162-1 (cloth : alk. paper)
ISBN 978-0-7391-8163-8 (electronic)

∞™ The paper used in this publication meets the minimum requirements of American National Standard for Information Sciences Permanence of Paper for

Printed in the United States of America

Contents

Acknowledgments vii

Introduction: Seeing Proust in a New Light ix

1 Text in Context: Points of Contact and Circles of Acquaintance 1

2 The Jamesian Stream and the Proustian Art of Consciousness 53

3 Parallels in the Penumbra: Tracking James's Psychology in Proust's Novel 103

4 From Jean to Je: Experience in the First-Person Singular 171

5 Patterns of Palimpsest: James's Theories and Proust's Prose in the Purview of Neuro-Cognitive Science 231

Afterword 265

Appendix 271

Works Cited or Consulted 281

Index 295

About the Author 311

Acknowledgments

An inspiration, mentor, and friend, my thanks go first to Elyane Dezon-Jones, who shared with me the depth of her expertise and introduced me to France's community of Proust scholars. I am also most grateful to Pascal Ifri for his thoughtful advice and continued encouragement. I owe many thanks to Tedi Macias and to St. Louis's Pioneers literary society for introducing me to Prof. Dezon-Jones and for providing a wider avenue for my interest in Proust. I am particularly thankful to the staff of Washington University's Olin Library and especially the Interlibrary Loan group, without whom my research would not have been possible. Several members of the William James Society were generously willing to share their scholarship. And for their enthusiastic encouragement and editorial and technical advice over the years of my involvement with this book, I want to thank my husband, Alan, my sons, David and Stephen, and my daughter-in-law, Amanda.

IMAGE CREDITS

The photograph of William James is in the public domain and is reproduced with the assistance of Houghton Library at Harvard University. The photograph of Marcel Proust is from a private collection at the Archives Charmet and is reprinted with the permission of the Bridgeman Art Library. The two figures illustrating "association" and "reasoning" found in chapter 3, figures 1 and 2, are from volume 2 of the Henry Holt edition (1890) of William James's *Principles of Psychology* and are no longer under copyright. These figures also appear, however, in *The Works of William James* published by Harvard University Press in 1981 and are reprinted here with permission.

William James's name is found in a letter Marcel Proust wrote to Lionel Hauser on May 2, 1918 and in the annotations to a letter he wrote to Gaston Gallimard on September 2, 1920, edited by Philip Kolb and published by Éditions Plon, Paris, France. Although still under copyright, these are reproduced in the appendix with permission.

Introduction

Seeing Proust in a New Light

It has been nearly one hundred years since the day in 1913 when Bernard Grasset released *Du côté de chez Swann*, the first of the seven-volume masterwork *À la recherche du temps perdu* by Marcel Proust, a writer few then realized would come to exemplify the literary modern. In the introduction to *Proust in Perspective*, millennial tribute to Proust's place at the crest of twentieth-century literary production, Katherine Kolb and Armine Kotin Mortimer take note of this writer's durable presence in mainstream awareness that they term "the popular imagination."[1] And the trend continues—hardly a week goes by without mention of Proust somewhere in the American media. An international critical commentariat continues to mine the riches of his text at conferences and colloquia, in articles and books. Added to this tidal wave of Proust study are recent forays in cognitive science labs to unravel the mysteries of mind and memory his novel made manifest. Wave after wave of readers feel as if *they* have been psychologically scanned and exposed. Proust's language—so complex yet compellingly beautiful—has drawn us into his world and him into ours: we identify with his hero's experience, reading into it our own.[2]

Many attempts have been made to ascertain just why this is so. Proust's originality and his "sources" are plentiful quarry for researchers. Some have positioned Marcel Proust side by side with fellow novelist Henry James. In 1964, Bruce Lowery undertook a detailed comparison of these two writers.[3] Roughly contemporary,[4] both wrote dense prose, showed similar interest in probing the wiles and minutiae of human consciousness and perception, and utilized the point of view of a character within the story. In the background of his comparison, however, Lowery often mentions Henry's older brother, William James, professor at Harvard University, public lecturer, and author of many articles and books that in their time captured the public's imagination and continue to find an appreciative audience today. A number of scholars, including Lowery, have pondered the relationship between the James brothers; a few have noticed certain commonalities between William James and Marcel Proust, as he has. But no close examination of Marcel Proust's prose has yet been undertaken in the light of William James's writings.

In his day, William James held a central place among the philosophers and psychological researchers charting the course of theory about man's capacities and his place in the world around him. Masterful and independent, James grappled with the fundamental issues of psychology and philosophy. Today, his readers continue to extol the freshness of James's prose and the challenging resilience of his thought. His understanding of the plumbing and performance of the human mind, at the forefront of neuro-cognitive science in the early years of the twentieth century, still resonates at the frontiers of today's neurobiology.

Using his broad array of connections on two continents, James gathered and examined the psychological research and philosophical arguments then current. As he brought his own ideas to public and professionals alike, he altered assumptions and stimulated his contemporaries to contend with a new view. Perhaps in a less direct but more starkly visible way, his work opened new vistas of the "modern" for painters and novelists to explore.

The vast majority of William James's work was published before his death in 1910, much of it already available in French translation. Although the initial volume of Proust's novel reached the public in 1913, it was not until after World War I ended and the French printing industry resumed normal activity that the bulk of his work came to public attention. When Proust died on November 18, 1922, the novel was not yet published in its entirety. During his lifetime, Marcel Proust was recognized as a great and original writer and was awarded the Prix Goncourt in 1919. But his book was seen as difficult to understand and hard for the public to embrace. His readership was narrow and determined, intrigued by the resemblances between the characters and the author's social contemporaries. By 1923, when the *Nouvelle Revue Française* published a special edition in tribute to his memory and Jacques Rivière delivered a series of four lectures at l'École du Vieux Colombier entitled *Quelques progrès dans l'étude du coeur humain* [*Current Advances in the Study of the Human Heart*][5] on Sigmund Freud and on Marcel Proust,[6] William James had been eclipsed from the cultural environment of which he had been so integral a part fifteen years before. His work must have seemed quaint and old-fashioned in comparison with the power of Freud's theories then being translated into French and found so promising an explanation of the profound psychological mysteries of Proust's novel.[7]

In my view, however, it was the thought of William James—physician by training, psychologist by interest, religious thinker and philosopher by disposition—that actually played a pivotal role in Marcel Proust's development into the writer we know. Proust's novel illustrates certain basic mental mechanisms and twentieth-century philosophic perspectives that ring universal, stimulating our continued interest. Reading Proust in close comparison with William James reveals much that derives from this unexpected source and bestows a greater appreciation of *À la recherche du temps perdu* and its modernity.

To produce his *Principles of Psychology*, James began with what was then known about the physiology of the brain. He studied the psychology common to us all and touched on the pathological and paranormal. In the course of his twelve-year project, he evaluated the best in the research and theory of the time. For James, the thinking self was central, and thought streamed in transitional flights between substantive perchings with fringes of felt relation surrounding the objects of focus. Attention was selective, purposeful, and subject to the vagaries of our physical nature (our senses, passions, habits, memory).

As his philosophical career developed, James held that consciousness was not an entity but played a functional role in *experience*, which had affective richness and felt continuity. He argued that truth was attained in the making, and that culture evolved through participation. He embraced the idea of the energized individual able to choose and act in the face of uncertainty in a world where individual temperament informed outlook, "novelty" nudged "essence," and "interest" impelled behavior, where the "vague" gray areas were fertile and the possibilities multiple. "Belief" in man's affective connection with the streaming real, in his willful ability to ride its bucking possibilities and participate in its facts and practical outcomes, as well as in his capacity to encounter the spiritual potentialities of a mysterious beyond were paramount features of his writing.

Although for a time the notion of "influence" wavered in consequence for evaluation of literary texts, more recently the term has been cleansed of critical disavowal and has assumed a resurgent role in interpretation. Neither eschewing the notion completely nor relying upon it unduly seems to provide the best understanding of the potential for relationship.

Direct literary influence, noted Billy Collins,[8] occurs within a writer's own genre: novelist to novelist or poet to poet. It is generally propelled by envy. This is the prompt accounting for the anxiety Harold Bloom has associated with originality,[9] the compulsion to surpass what others have done so very well already. Proust's self-announced ability to hear the musicality distinguishing writers one from another, his studied efforts to honor, mock, and comprehend their talent in the close imitation of pastiche would have been thrust to paper then by his desire to supersede their success, to eliminate the persistent tunes of other writers and find the voice and timbre of his unique style.

Indirect influence has no such clear and obvious derivation. Coming from outside the artist's specific genre, it can be had from almost anywhere. It can result from an active search for information or inspiration, or it can be had passively from the ambient atmosphere of the moment. By way of example, Collins noted the influence of Warner Brothers cartoons on his own poetry, and as he widened the limits of influence to include almost anything occurring on an artist's intellectual horizon or in the various planes of his history, he brought to mind what those influences might have included in the Paris of Proust's time.

Proust was a voracious consumer of literature and news,[10] enmeshed in the social and cultural matrix of his time, familiar with the major currents of activity and the practitioners. William James held a notable place in the ambient intellectual mix, the lively scientific, religious, and philosophical discourse taking place in Proust's Paris.

Julie Lambilliotte's efforts to use Proust's letters to document what he read and to ascertain how what he read affected what he wrote focus primarily on literary sources but do not exclude other types of reading such as the casual daily glance at newspapers and journals that might have mentioned James and his works. Her analysis, resting on Proust's use of quotations often deformed beautifully to express his own voice rather than that of the original writer, is limited by her ready assumption that these sources will be identifiable.[11]

Along similar lines, Anka Muhlstein uses Proust's writings and his correspondence, as well as analyses done by other critics, to trace the vestiges of his literary models. She identifies authors he admired (and those he disparaged) who in her view swayed his pen and were absorbed into the construction of his novel.[12]

Although few would venture so far as to say that Proust "channeled" James as a model, opportunities existed for Proust to absorb and *poeticize* what James had *theorized*. Despite his disavowals of outside influence in *Contre Sainte-Beuve* and his contention that an artist's work is crafted in the profound isolation of the self using only "le son vrai de notre cœur"[13] [the authentic sound of our own hearts], Proust's work was not immune to the scientific information, the bias and attitudes permeating the cultural background common to many. The historical fact of potential encounter is the first subject that must be tackled, and so I explore the surrounding cultural context and the points of contact bringing James and Proust together.

Two references to William James appear in Proust's correspondence, both in letters written late in his life and both mentioning Pragmatism.[14] Beyond these there is no direct proof that Proust knew the man or read his works, although many of the publications Proust mentions printed or reviewed James's articles and books. A comparison of Proust's novel with James's writings underscores the echoes of similar interests and the resemblances of shared imagery and intimates that Proust was familiar with their contents, revealing the profoundly seminal effect of James's theory on Proust's literary creativity and on the substance of his novel.

"L'originalité de Proust semble incontestable," wrote Elizabeth Czoniczer. "Seulement toute originalité n'est en fin de compte qu'une combinaison nouvelle d'éléments existants, déjà connus"[15] [Proust's originality is indisputable. . . . But ultimately originality consists of a new alignment of existing, familiar elements]. It is incontrovertible that in Proust's day the latest writing on psychology, religious experience, and metaphysics—"l'air du temps" [the spirit of the times]—included William James. Distilled from this background noise, a unique form of novel gestated.

Reiteration and transformation are literary constants, the intertextual theorists tell us. Comparative analysis can clarify a text's meaning and reveal the reprises and relations apparent or covert. Sometimes the surrounding discourse contemporaneous with a given work will give a reader all the interpretive tools necessary to understand and appreciate it. At other times, a work is so original, so unexpected, so different from other works of its time that years will go by before readers develop the interpretive maturity to make sense of it, as Proust himself noted,[16] and the judgmental perspective to see the connections it had to its time and appreciate the relations it bears to its sources.

James's message was relevant, and his style, erudite yet personal, was contrived to appeal to academic readers as well as in a lecture hall—and it did. Within his professional arena there was little anxiety of subsequence: scientists and philosophers referred to James's work, took issue where they disagreed, and made clear their own theories without much trepidation, just as he did with theirs. Colleagues seemed to relish pointing out each other's "mistaken" ideas. And in the course of so doing, they helped publicize James and his views.

Proust's articulated intention was to find within *himself* the work of art he would put forth, rendering in words a subject as obscure and unique as an individual.[17] Yet Proust denied that critics could—or should—expect to read the meaning of an author's work as code produced from the facts of his life. If, as Cahier 59 suggests with regard to Bergson, Proust wished to keep at least some of his "sources" to himself, it is not unlikely that he would conceal and even deny those influences that might reveal too much about his "originality." But the elimination of other writers is never total. In his attempt to express the emotional and psychological experience of his narrator's self, Proust had enriched his own vision with what was most current in contemporary psychological thinking.

Scholars often look at stance and word usage permeating a literary text and see the stamp of style that Proust himself described in a letter to Anna de Noailles (June 12 or 13, 1904) as "une espèce de fondu, d'unité transparente où toutes les choses [. . .] sont [. . .] pénétrées de la même lumière"[18] [a type of infusion, a transparent unity in which everything is permeated with the same light] and wrote about in *Contre Sainte-Beuve*: "C'est quelque chose de vague et d'obsédant comme le souvenir. C'est une atmosphère"[19] [It is something nebulous and persistent like a memory. An ambiance]. This was beyond the purview of will or reason, a watermark of the temperament and views of the individual experience that created it, a notion with affinities to the importance of meaning and values in James's radical empiricism and his desire to reinstate the relevance of flux and ambiguity so essential to Proust's development of his own characteristic voice.

"A man's vision," wrote James in *A Pluralistic Universe*, "is the great fact about him."[20] It must be apprehended, he advised a student, "by an act of imagination."[21] For Proust, an artist's style—that individual imaginative component at the basis of aesthetic production—reveals the unique vision at its core.

> Le style n'est nullement un enjolivement comme croient certaines personnes, ce n'est même pas une question de technique, c'est—comme la couleur chez les peintres—une qualité de la vision, la révélation de l'univers particulier que chacun de nous voit et que ne voient pas les autres.[22]
>
> [Style is not merely a beautification, as certain persons may think, it is not even a question of technique, it is—like color for painters—a quality of the vision, the revelation of the private universe that each one of us sees that others do not.]

Why is Proust referred to so often in the highly specialized lecture halls of neuro-cognitive scientists? What accounts for his appeal to researchers interested in understanding the intricacies of the human mind? The answer has to do with his depiction of who we are as sentient beings that scientists are drawn to scrutinize as they study how our conscious existence and the facts of our behavior are wired. Scientific investigations of how the brain works using the latest in technological tools are finding the accuracy of James's theories. Their work elucidates the combination of memory and current experience described by James as personal vision that was formulated as aesthetic theory and fashioned so magnificently into literature by Proust.

Exemplifying James's theory, the narrator-hero "Je" [I] in Proust's novel explores the way the mind works, the way experience feels, the way we behave consciously and unconsciously, how we are trapped in our very selves and how that self is construed, how every thought brings with it an array of associated thoughts, the way our attention flits and leaps, stops intermittently to dwell and focus in detail on an event or desire or the penumbra of awareness surrounding it, how we create our reality by means of our very desires and actions, the way emotions are in play and guide our everyday actions, how our experience unfolds pragmatically as we go along, the way moments of "religious" elevation lead to greater understanding. He searches for essential truth in a world of shifting, relative, pragmatic truths where language and interpretation create substance and effect, where misperception arises from the potentially faulty narrative thread that temperament weaves into reading what is seen.

To illuminate and preserve events and feelings from the fog of reality, Proust focused a lighthouse beam in *Jean Santeuil* on those moments worth fictionalizing. These became the objects of the beam of attention related as if in real time by the narrator of *À la recherche du temps perdu*. The truths of human psychology and behavior described by William James are made fictional flesh in Proust's rendition of lived experience, and without reading James it is difficult to fully value Proust. James is indeed present, hidden in the shadows of Proust's prose.

NOTES

1. *Proust in Perspective*, ed. Armine Kotin Mortimer and Katherine Kolb (Urbana: University of Illinois Press, 2002), 2.
2. Alain de Botton, *How Proust Can Change Your Life: Not a Novel* (New York: Pantheon, 1997): "It should not be Illiers-Combray that we visit: a genuine homage to Proust would be to look at our world though his eyes, not to look at his world through our eyes" (196).
3. Bruce Lowery, *Marcel Proust et Henry James: une confrontation* (Paris: Librairie Plon, 1964).
4. William James, 1842–1910; Henry James, 1843–1916; Marcel Proust, 1871–1922.
5. Translations from the French are the author's unless otherwise indicated.
6. *Hommage à Marcel Proust (1871–1922), La Nouvelle Revue Française* XX, 10.112 (January 1923): 337. Tomoko Boongja Woo, "Lecture de Proust, à travers Freud, par les premiers critiques," *Bulletin Marcel Proust* 58 (2008): 69–79, 70. For Rivière's four lectures, see Jacques Rivière, *Quelques progrès dans l'étude du coeur humain* (Paris: Gallimard [Cahiers Marcel Proust 13], 1985): 77–189.
7. Woo, 75.
8. Poet laureate of the United States, 2001–2003. "Cartoons and Poetry," narr. Billy Collins, commentary Marc Sanchez, *Weekend America*, American Public Media, radio broadcast on KWMU St. Louis, September 20, 2008. Poems originally appeared in "Porkface," 1977.
9. Harold Bloom, *The Anxiety of Influence: A Theory of Poetry*, 2nd ed. (New York: Oxford University Press,).
10. "Proust avait [. . .] tout lu," noted Gabriel de la Rochefoucauld, "Souvenirs et Aperçus," *Hommage à Marcel Proust (1871–1922), La Nouvelle Revue Française* XX, 10.112 (January 1923): 69–76, 69. Also in Cahiers Marcel Proust, 1, 63.
11. Julie Lambilliotte, "La Bibliothèque de Marcel Proust: De la lecture à l'écriture," *Bulletin d'informations Proustiennes* 30 (1999): 81–89.
12. Anka Muhlstein, *Monsieur Proust's Library* (New York: Other Press, 2012).
13. Marcel Proust, "La Méthode de Sainte-Beuve," *Contre Sainte-Beuve*, éd. Pierre Clarac et Yves Sandre (Paris: Éditions Gallimard [Bibliothèque de la Pléiade], 1971): 219–232, 224 (hereafter *CSB*).
14. One mentions James outright. In the other, only Pragmatism is mentioned; the editors refer to James in the notes. Marcel Proust, Letter to Lionel Hauser, 2 May 1918, *Correspondance*, XVII, *87*, 227–231, and Marcel Proust, Letter to Gaston Gallimard, 2 September 1920, *Correspondance*, XIX, *213*, 437–440. See Appendix.
15. Elizabeth Czoniczer, *Quelques antécédents de À la recherche du temps perdu* (Genève: E. Droz, 1957), 11.
16. Marcel Proust, *À la recherche du temps perdu*, 4 vols. (Paris: Éditions Gallimard [Bibliothèque de la Pléiade], 1987–1989), II, 623–624 (hereafter *RTP*).
17. Marcel Proust, "Contre l'obscurité," *La Revue blanche* (15 juillet 1896), repr. *Essais et articles, Contre Sainte-Beuve* (Paris: Éditions Gallimard [Bibliothèque de la Pléiade], 1971): 390–395, 390: "le pouvoir de réduire un tempérament original aux lois générales

de l'art, au génie permanent de la langue," and Antoine Compagnon, *La Troisième République des lettres, de Flaubert à Proust* (Paris: Éditions du Seuil, 1983), 216.

18. Marcel Proust, *Correspondance*, éd. Philip Kolb, 21 T. (Paris: Librairie Plon, 1970–1993), IV, *81*, 156 (hereafter *Corr*.).

19. "Gérard de Nerval," *CSB*, 242.

20. William James, *A Pluralistic Universe* (Cambridge: Harvard University Press, 1977), 14.

21. William James, *The Letters of William James*, ed. by his son Henry James,. 2 vols. (Boston: The Atlantic Monthly Press, 1920), II, 355.

22. Elie-Joseph Bois, "Variétés Littéraires: *Á la recherche du temps pesder* (1913)," *Le Temps* (November 1913). Repr. Cahiers Marcel Proust 3: *Textes Retrouvés*. éd. Philip Kolb (Paris: Éditions Gallinard, 1971) 285-291, 290.

ONE

Text in Context

Points of Contact and Circles of Acquaintance

"Ils ont fait classique," Proust wrote to Paul Morand, commenting on painters Courbet, Manet, and Renoir, "parce qu'ils ont voulu faire nouveau"[1] [They created a classic . . . because they wanted to fashion something new]. Like Proust, Antoine Compagnon has suggested that a classic lasts beyond its time because it is so startling and dazzling in its time. But disjunctive and innovative as a classic work may be, isn't it also anchored to its moment, reflecting or refuting that ether and melody, as much a salvo to its era as an impress of its author? Or is a classic work timeless, experienced solely in the "present" it "share[s]" with its readers,[2] completely divorced from "le moi et le monde"[3] [the self and the world] that created it?

Tying the work to its season, surveying the linkages and ruptures, is not new. In 1800 Mme. de Staël practiced and proclaimed the historical analysis of literature in *De la littérature*.[4] Her aim was to see the work in its place in the surrounding culture and to examine its effects. In her wake, literary study has become an annex of history, a way to show how great works, those that are truly new, relate to their moment but carve a gash, confiding to posterity a mysterious contradiction of continuity and defiance.[5]

Ever since it was first published in 1913, *À la recherche du temps perdu* has been examined from every imaginable angle; its ties to its time and to Marcel Proust's biography have been well explored. Yet, to understand Proust's evolution and innovation as an artist we must no longer neglect William James and the place his thought and writings occupied in Proust's Paris, because their sweep and legacy reverberate in the power of Proust's novel.

William James called consciousness "a witness to happenings in time."[6] For Proust, writing his masterwork with all the intensity he could muster[7] would be to witness and meld the events, thoughts, and theories of an individual conscious life into a novel ardent with passions and latent with introspection, tumbling with the characters, scenes, and the erudition amassed in the drama of turn of the century Paris. Proust would shape "la réalité en soi" [reality itself], as he wrote in his notebook in 1908,[8] into a work of fiction in the guise of the autobiography of a conscious mind. Proust prospected through "ce qui se présente obscurément au fond de la conscience"[9] [what arises obscurely in the depths of consciousness], the penumbra of streaming psychological awareness, to write a story of individual experience in time, using—intentionally or not—tenets of the psychology and philosophy expounded by William James.

The first-person saga Proust created for his narrator bears great similarity to experience as it is depicted in James's radical empiricism—a mental residue of physical events—and described in the lecture James delivered in French at the Fifth International Congress of Psychology in Rome on April 30, 1905: "des manières rétrospectives de nommer le contenu lui-même, lorsqu'on l'aura séparé de tous ces intermédiaires physiques, et relié à un nouveau groupe d'associés qui le font rentrer dans ma vie mentale, les émotions par exemple qu'il a éveillées en moi, l'attention que j'y porte, mes idées de tout à l'heure qui l'ont suscité comme souvenir"[10] ["retrospective ways of naming the content itself, after separating it from all those physical intermediaries and connecting it to a new group of associates which make it re-enter my mental life, for instance the emotions it has aroused in me, the attention I am paying to it, my ideas of a few minutes ago which gave rise to it as a memory"[11]].

Ultimately for James, the physical and the psychological, the subject viewing and the object viewed, blend together in personal experience. The fleeting minutes spent listening to his lecture become ephemeral fragments of each auditor's biography. If they survive as memories, as part of the mind's life, they will have an emotional cast, perhaps pleasant, incorporating into each listener's private thread of awareness and singular personal history the physical facts of sitting in the hall and the intellectual stimulation of the talk.

The diaphanous, ephemeral nature of what James calls experience, sparkling with sensation, leavened by the caprices of emotion and the seemingly random floating insertions of memory bubbling to surface awareness from the depths of a murky and mysterious unconscious, captivated those who experimented and theorized in the new science of psychology toward the end of the nineteenth century and at the beginning of the twentieth, drawing into its thrall the fiction writers who would themselves experiment with this new science of the individual mind. Beginning with Edouard Dujardin in France and continuing with

Marcel Proust, James Joyce, Dorothy Richardson, and Virginia Woolf, writers would attempt to render in a fictional text the experience of individual experience.

For his student Horace Kallen, James was the "spokesman for the whole age that passed with the Great War," his philosophy "the peer of the arts and sciences."[12] Like his psychology and Proust's narrative, James's philosophy was a new way of *looking*; it spread, in Kallen's terms, a "transforming power upon the stuffs and dimensions of the world."[13]

Proust's literary innovations brought James's thought to fiction. His text reads like the stream James had depicted as the rhythm and structure of conscious life itself. The "flights and perchings" of attention in Proust's fictional fabric, the emotive and associative "fringe of relations" infusing names and images and informing their imaginative content—where Proust found "beauty" and which Virginia Woolf characterized as "the astonishing vibration and saturation and intensification that [Proust] procures"[14] —have origins in James. Proust's narrator delivers a tale developing out of his own mind and motives, one not directed by any rational system but guided simply by his own varied reactions and multiple interpretations of the world around him. For James, the systems by which we live and explain our existence are contingent, dependent upon the feelings and thoughts of those who create them. James saw the tenebrous ambiguities of daily life and did not attempt to diminish the importance of the free and accidental, the erratic, the mistaken, and the inexplicable. The explanations of Philosophy may change with succeeding generations, its constructs acknowledged to be as much a fiction as fiction. But the doctrines James espouses are those "which we rely on when we take experience at its face value as it comes, radically, in its living fullness."[15] This is the stuff of Proust's prose.

According to Dorrit Cohn, Proust's narrator ventures well beyond the fictional device of "interior monologue" to embody more of what she terms William James's "mind stuff."[16] His continuous stream of awareness, like James's stream[17] of consciousness, approaches that underlying level of basic apprehension that is close to extinguished in the heavy sleep following rigorous bodily activity, those moments when we are returned to the deepest, darkest recesses of our physical being—the locus where earliest memories subsist.

What could Proust have known of William James and how might he have encountered his ideas? How had James become such an integral part of the intellectual mix in Proust's Paris between 1889 and 1911 that there were multiple opportunities for Proust to espy his name and become familiar with the content of his works? This first chapter points out the mutual acquaintances and direct connections through the news media that would allow Proust to absorb James's insights into his novel in basic and formative ways.

James's transatlantic training and his position at Harvard University lent credibility to his position at the center of discoveries, theories, and controversies of the moment. His *Principles of Psychology* summarized the latest in the scientific and philosophical trends in psychology and referenced the work of most everyone renowned in the field. It was widely reviewed and accessible to the curious. James knew or was known to those individuals who directed the journals and reviews, and they were willing and eager to promulgate his prodigious body of articles and books. Gregarious and enthusiastic, James welcomed friendships with colleagues. He was a popular "philosopher" who earned needed money from public lectures and participated eagerly, his health permitting, in international conferences. He made frequent visits to Paris and maintained ongoing relationships with scholar-philosophers, researchers, and the medical-psychological establishment, many of whose members were known to the Proust family. His name well known, his ideas—debated or refuted—managed to seep into the culture of his time, to permeate and influence the most basic ways people saw themselves and their world, to direct discussion and shift the paradigm.

WILLIAM JAMES IN EUROPE

William James was born on January 11, 1842, and died August 26, 1910. There is no shortage of biographical studies of a figure so eminent in his time, and much has been written about James's very international background and education,[18] the amount of time he spent in Europe, and the extent of his circle of acquaintance there.

James's father had inherited sufficient wealth to free himself from becoming rooted professionally and his family from being settled geographically. His Swedenborgian thinking, conversing, and writing could be done almost anywhere, as could conversations with such luminaries as family friends Emerson and Carlyle. Where he wanted to go depended in large degree on the educational compass most suitable in his view for raising his children. And that often involved traversing the Atlantic. Henry James the father "maintained with his children an intimacy of contact" and permitted greater latitude in their career choices than was typical of his era.[19] William was first-born, clearly bright and talented. His lifetime of energetic travel began with the first of this family's many decampments to Europe when he was only two years old. Given Henry Senior's unorthodox ideas and the fact that he maintained a certain disregard for organized schooling of any sort, William's education was decidedly fitful, taking place in bits and pieces spread from New York and Newport to London, Paris, Boulogne, Geneva, and for one short summer, Bonn. Henry's educational priority was to provide the most broadening exposure possible. The goal was not so much to encourage the accumulation of skills for use in some specified profession, but rather to make men of William and his three brothers[20] and delay their choice of career until they had grown into themselves and could choose wisely. The effect of this conviction was a peripatetic, disjointed, ultimately almost irrelevant schooling. William's natural intellectual curiosity was encouraged; he tried what appealed to him and was in many ways self-taught.

William's youthful sojourns in Europe were frequent and prolonged. So much of his limited formal schooling took place there that Ralph Barton Perry remarked: "Europe was nearer than were the Ohio and Mississippi valleys,"[21] and Horace Kallen noted that James's intellectual formation was more European than American.[22]

After flirting with the idea of becoming a painter, James abandoned art for science and entered Harvard's Lawrence Scientific School in 1861. Harvard connected James with the writers and editors of such august publications as *The North American Review*, *The Nation*, and *The Atlantic Monthly* (a journal created to cover content from both sides of the ocean). It was a community of the distinguished who "belonged to the European as well as to the American world of letters. They frequently visited Europe themselves, and were in turn visited by distinguished travelers from abroad,"[23] observed Perry. James was comfortable in the cosmopolitan environment of Cambridge and Boston. When he began to write articles and reviews, no doubt his contact with the Boston literati enhanced his access to their well-known journals: "[H]is career as a writer was greatly facilitated by the fact that he lived among the editors, and numbered [many among his friends]." At that time as well, the scientific community at Harvard was an environment that could give James access to current thinking from abroad. Although the United States was isolated geographically and inward looking, embroiled for the moment in the Civil War, Harvard was "stirred from provincial sluggishness by winds from abroad."[24]

With his education in medicine and his interest in the cutting-edge research his European counterparts were doing in their laboratories, James was hired by Harvard to teach physiology at a point when the university was committing itself to modernizing. He summarized his career trajectory in the following, which is often cited to describe his evolving interests: "I originally studied medicine in order to be a physiologist, but I drifted into psychology and philosophy from a sort of fatality. I never had any philosophic instruction, the first lecture on psychology I ever heard being the first I ever gave."[25]

James began his international publishing career in 1867. Persistent ill health and "neurasthenia" led him as a young man to try rest cures in Europe. Early trips to Switzerland and Germany provided a certain familiarity with German, but during the longer stays, living with families, learning in the laboratories, seeking treatment at the bathing spas, he expressly sought to perfect his ability to interact with the physiologists and psychologists who were to teach him the techniques and the questions he chose to pursue in becoming one of their colleagues. The spas and baths he visited in France and Germany throughout his life did not help to cure, or in many instances even relieve, persistent physical discomfort, but the enforced leisure of these sojourns allowed him the chance to read widely, including many of the same authors whose work would also captivate Proust. James became familiar with the best and most recent in European thought and discovery, often attended by contact with the men who were on the forefront of the fields of interest to him. Thus, his serious back pain complicated by persistent depression and doubts about the direction his career would take eventually had some beneficial side effects. It made it difficult for James to pursue physiological laboratory work and contributed to his growing interest in the more observational science of psychology then in its infancy in German laboratories. It also gave him occasion to review for the American press some of the European books and articles he was reading.

In 1868, when he was twenty-five years old, during a stay in Europe intended to combat the pain, depression, and moral anxiety that plagued him, James's first published article appeared. It was an unsigned review of a novel by Herman Grimm, which he wrote for *The Nation*.[26] The following year, to earn a little pocket money, he published his first reviews (again unsigned) of articles on medical topics that had appeared in French publications.[27]

In a letter to his brother, Henry, written while at a spa in Divonne, France, in August 1868, James described what he had been reading: "I have read several novels lately, some of the irrepressible George Sand. . . . But the things which have given me the most pleasure have been some traveling sketches by Théophile Gautier. . . . [T]he delicious *Capitaine Fracasse*."[28] Proust described *Le Capitaine Fracasse*, a childhood favorite, as "l'ami à qui on pense sans cesse, dont la société rend délicieuses les heures où on en jouit"[29] [the friend you think of continually, whose company makes the hours spent together so delicious]. Surprisingly, both authors used the same tasty adjective to describe their reactions!

In addition to a certain predilection in literature, James and Proust shared the common experience of suffering from physical ailments and questions of will. Without early and definite professional direction, both were unsure of their future orientation. Both became writers whose personal experiences had great impact on the direction that writing took.

Twenty-nine years his junior, Marcel Proust was student at lycée Condorcet when James published his "Theory of Emotions" in 1884.[30] In 1890, when James published *The Principles of Psychology*,[31] Proust was happily fulfilling his yearlong military obligation and (to please his father) planning to study law and political science at the end of his term of service. Between 1895 and 1900, Proust worked on *Jean Santeuil* and then abandoned this first effort to create a novel, for lack, according to

William Carter, of "plot, point of view and structure,"[32] elements of fictional composition that would ultimately be assisted by what Proust could learn from James. He was looking for a publisher for his translation of Ruskin's *Bible d'Amiens*[33] when James published *Varieties of Religious Experience* in 1902. As the controversy over James's *Pragmatism* (1907) raged in the European press, Proust was publishing short pieces, some presaging passages in *À la recherche du temps perdu*. In 1909, James's *Principles of Psychology: Briefer Course* was published in French translation,[34] and Proust began the serious business of his masterwork.[35]

James's world as an adult was as international as his childhood. He crossed the Atlantic as readily as we do today and more often. At times he felt almost "dépaysé": "One should not be cosmopolitan," James wrote to Carl Stumpf in 1894, "one's soul becomes 'disaggregated,' as Janet would say. Parts of it remain in different places, and the whole of it is nowhere. One's native land seems foreign."[36]

His intellectual life took place on two continents. It has even been said that he was "more widely known and his ideas more attended to in Europe than in the United States."[37] If the most important thinkers in his field were in England, France, Germany, Italy, it was with them that he debated his theories as readily as with his colleagues at Harvard and other American universities. Of the formative relationships accruing over his lifetime, many were with the scholars, psychologists, and philosophers in France. Some critics, Eliza Jane Reilly among them, contend that James's "discovery" as a philosopher belongs almost more to France than to America.[38]

So much of his schooling had taken place in France that French was really a second language for James. He wrote easily, corresponded, and published articles in French. French phrases pepper his books and letters, and he was sufficiently fluent to deliver papers and lectures in French. Although it would be challenging to document all the instances James's writings were cited by his European associates, it is important to consider how his works came to be so well embedded.

James and his colleagues lived in a period of burgeoning science and technological advancement in communication and transportation. They were well educated, versed in a number of languages, eager to participate in international debate and exchange. The journals and newspapers of the time purposefully carried articles and reviews in special sections devoted to publications in the foreign press. James's books and articles were reported and analyzed because there was an interested international marketplace for his ideas. His work was notable for its novelty of thought, its comprehensive analysis of current issues, its very personal and colorfully metaphorical almost conversational style. His writing in psychology was encyclopedic and foundational; his thought on religion was emblematic of his time; his radical empiricism and pragmatic philosophy were new ways of looking at the world; and his work had a transformational effect on aesthetic expression.

Journals known to Proust and read continuously over his lifetime carried many articles devoted to James's works. Since Proust acknowledged awareness of James in only two of his letters, the potential influence of these limited references might easily be dismissed were it not for the prevalence of publicity surrounding James, the degree to which his views were integrated into European intellectual discussion, and the scope of his acquaintances and friendships in Proust's Paris.

Several of James's major early articles were first published in the British journal *Mind*, some subsequently included as chapters in *The Principles of Psychology*.[39] This highly influential and foundational text was among the first compendia of experimental psychology, reviewing and commenting on the approaches to psychology then current. It became the main textbook used in psychology courses in America "and in Europe,"[40] notes Ignas Skrupskelis, for many years to come and provided its author with a steady income. It served as basis for the discipline's transition from philosophical discussion of mental faculties to a methodologically scientific pursuit, as James's purpose was to demonstrate the function of thoughts and feelings in acquisition of knowledge and to connect them with activity in the brain. James's intent would be to limit his discussion to the here and now, to what would be demonstrable based on observation, experimentation, and introspection.

In the two volumes of his *Principles of Psychology*, James cited the work of contemporary scientists and philosophical theoreticians in a most readable, almost entertaining style. The book, observed Perry, "revealed the author's genius for catching the elusive and fugitive states of human experience and transfixing them with a telling phrase. It was daring in its humor, in its use of colloquial speech, and in its picturesqueness of metaphor and illustration; so that though many doubted whether anything so interesting could possibly be scientific, nobody ignored it."[41] In 1892 and 1893, Léon Marillier wrote "a very detailed analysis" of James's psychology for the *Revue Philosophique*.[42]

The controversy later sparked by James's philosophy of Pragmatism—a methodological doctrine, the notoriety of which spread over Europe like a conflagration during the first decade of the twentieth century—was so widespread and heated that it was covered in many mainstream newspapers as well as in academic journals and was the subject of refutation in one of Emile Durkheim's courses at the Sorbonne.[43] It would have been difficult for anyone involved to any extent in European intellectual life, particularly in Paris, to avoid William James's name and his contributions. In fact, notes Eliza Jane Reilly, a hefty proportion of the New York Public Library's holdings of works on James's philosophy—and on Pragmatism in particular—had been published by foreign presses, particularly in Western Europe.[44]

James's Swiss friend and long-time correspondent Théodore Flournoy wrote in 1907 regarding the spread of James's thought in French-speaking parts of Switzerland:

> [T]he enlightened public is each day becoming better acquainted with your thought [. . .]. There is, moreover, a clear and odd affinity between our temperament and your mental processes generally: our public finds in you something that it needs and which it finds neither in French nor in German philosophers of the present day.[45]

With his brother, Henry, living most of his adult years in England, William James participated readily in international conferences and used the occasions of professional trips to visit with European colleagues, friends, and relatives. Before popular and academic audiences, James drew crowds at home and abroad. He was honored to be asked to deliver the prestigious Gifford lectures at the University of Edinburgh in 1901–1902, published as *The Varieties of Religious Experience* in 1902, and the Hibbert Lectures at Manchester College, Oxford, in 1908–1909, published as *A Pluralistic Universe* in 1909.[46]

When he died in 1910, eulogies in the form of books were dedicated to his memory by several of Europe's most prominent philosophers who had known and loved James as one of their own. These eulogy texts include one written by James's long-time friend Flournoy and one by his more recent but equally close friend Émile Boutroux. In addition, Henri Bergson wrote the Préface to the French translation of James's *Pragmatisme* published in 1911. There are many other examples of books of philosophy, psychology, and university curricula in Europe that referred to James's ideas and suggest the extent to which his thought had been incorporated into European intellectual life. They attest to which individuals were his contacts and friends. At the time of James's death, George Santayana, a fellow Harvard professor, noted that "until the return wave of James's reputation reached America from Europe, his pupils and friends were hardly aware that he was such a distinguished man."[47]

More recently, there has been another resurgence of interest in William James in France. Scholars are eager to revive and translate James's works and to explore the extent of their influence. Among these are Mathias Girel and David Lapoujade,[48] who have published recent works on James's Radical Empiricism and Pragmatism. Henri Bergson's *Correspondances*, published in 2002, reveals the depth and extent of Bergson's friendship and collegial relationship with James.[49]

CHARLES RENOUVIER INTRODUCES JAMES TO FRANCE

James did not at first suspect that a publication he described in a letter to his father on October 5, 1868 would be a turning point in his life. He wrote from Europe about discovering the philosophy of Charles Renouvier: "I got a little book by a number of authors, '*L'Année 1867 philosophique*,' which may interest you if you have not got it already. The introduction, a review of the state of philosophy in France for some years back, is by one Charles Renouvier, of whom I have never heard before."[50] The discovery of Renouvier would have long-lasting implications. James subsequently felt that he owed much to the relationship that developed between him and the French philosopher who would become his colleague, his friend, and his editor at the journal *La Critique Philosophique*.

Upon returning home, James completed his medical studies and received his degree in 1869. He continued to read the French journals and newspapers he had been reading overseas, including *La Revue des Deux Mondes* and others on science and religion. But a severe struggle with depression culminated in a "spiritual crisis" and an "ebbing of the will to live."[51] He ascribed his recovery to reading "part of Renouvier's second *Essais*" [*sic*]:[52] the cure would be to "choose" his thoughts, and his "first act of free will" would be "to believe in free will."[53] From this point on, James never ceased taking the pragmatic initiative to create his life and writing to document his thought and to grapple with the thinking of his colleagues.

The first article by James published in France appeared in 1878 in Charles Renouvier's *La Critique Philosophique*. According to Ralph Barton Perry, Renouvier "appended a highly appreciative note," indicating (given the mixed nature of the disciplines at that time) that James was already received in Europe "as a philosopher" even before he was recognized as a psychologist.[54]

From that time on, James's articles were reviewed promptly in the European press, and many were translated for publication if not originally written in French. When he became Assistant Professor of Philosophy at Harvard, James taught a course on Renouvier, and correspondence between the two continued for over twenty-five years. Because Renouvier enjoyed great stature at the time, and because France was then open to philosophical thinking from beyond its borders,[55] James's ideas gained the attention of the French. Articles by James in English as well as in translation were disseminated in *La Critique Philosophique*, including several that later became chapters in *The Principles of Psychology* but were published here well before the text itself was completed in 1890.[56] This relationship continued until *La Critique Philosophique* ceased publication in 1889. When François Pillon resumed publication under the name *L'Année Philosophique*, James's work appeared there, and he became friends with Pillon.

The early relationship with Renouvier had "secured his entrée into French philosophical discourse,"[57] noted John B. Allcock. James was forever grateful to this early mentor for the impetus he had provided and dedicated the last of the works assembled during his lifetime to Renouvier's memory.[58] Renouvier had given James credibility and voice before the French public.

The importance of other of James's early articles[59] was not lost on the European philosophical and psychological establishment. Footnotes referring to them and to *The Principles of Psychology* once published were legion in texts written by French scientists and scholars.

Théodule Ribot's journal *Revue Philosophique de la France et de l'Étranger* had been founded in 1876, its very title indicating the intended purpose to cover breaking research and theory from many sources. Each issue listed and reviewed foreign works and published in translation several pieces originally written in English and German, including works by James (who became good friends with Ribot). *La Revue de métaphysique et de morale,* founded by Alphonse Darlu and edited subsequently by Léon Brunschvicg, Élie Halévy, and Xavier Léon, Darlu's former students and classmates of Marcel Proust, also covered James. *Le Journal des Débats Politiques et Littéraires* printed commentary.

With time James's reputation grew and any lag between publication of his books in English and their translation into French diminished. And over the years, James had developed close affiliations with a wide circle of academics in France and even closer friendships with several among them. As his books found translators in France, his friends (most notable among these, Émile Boutroux and Henri Bergson, who were well known to Proust and had ties to him and to others in his family over a long period of time) happily wrote prefaces to introduce and publicize James's major works to the French reading public. It should also be mentioned that James's practice of gathering his lectures and articles together in subsequent book form served to reiterate his thought before the public, making it all the more evident.

It was almost an anomaly for an American to enjoy such popularity in France. But the educated community interested in these topics was relatively small, very international. His following in France widened as James's popular style, the lectures, articles, and books as well as frequent reviews in the scholarly and popular press encouraged assimilation of his ideas into the public mind. By the time the Fifth International Conference of Psychology was held in Rome in 1905, where James presented "La Notion de Conscience" in French, the paper was considered the "highlight,"[60] and James was delightfully surprised to find himself a celebrity.[61]

CONNECTING JAMES TO PROUST

Abnormal Psychology in France

William James was immersed "in virtually every philosophical controversy from the 1870s until his death in 1910," wrote John J. McDermott.[62] He was fascinated by the potential for psychical phenomena, as he held the wider view that abnormal conditions—including the concept of split or "dissociated" personality being studied by Pierre Janet and others—were worthy of investigation, holding the possibility of explaining psychological behavior beyond disease. According to Robert D. Richardson, James "tended to look on the subconscious as something not pathological but normal, though different from our daylight consciousness."[63] Perry notes that this interest developed during a stay in England (1882–1883) and was sparked by his colleagues Frederick Myers, Edmund Gurney, and Henry Sidgwick. Sidgwick had founded the Society for Psychical Research in England in 1882. James joined in 1884 and maintained his membership to the end of his life. He served eighteen years as a vice president and was president from 1894 to 1896. James was a founder of a similar American society in Boston in 1884 and served as president.

James consistently appreciated the potential for the supra-normal and the effects of hypnotism, but he maintained a certain skepticism that kept the boundaries in view. He allowed for the human being's desire to believe in such phenomena along with the idea of life after death and the "mother-sea" of consciousness in which individual minds might participate.[64] His interests evolved to include the role of the subliminal in religious experience—those privileged moments of unanticipated life altering feeling accessible to anyone and evident in personal testimony of conversion experiences.

His interest in psychopathology was of long standing. In 1868, just before leaving Europe for home, he bought his first book on abnormal psychology. At the time there was not yet a split between the study of abnormal and paranormal psychology; the study of hysteria and psychical research were not yet clearly divided branches. James felt that research on the abnormal mind was an integral part of any functional understanding of the interacting mind-body system. In this area, he was quite aware of the work being done in France and acquainted with most of those doing the research.[65] He was interested in Charcot's work on hypnotism, and it was while attending Charcot's lectures on the hypnotism of "hysterical" patients at the Salpêtrière in Paris in 1882 that James was informed that his own father was deathly ill.

Jean-Martin Charcot, along with Théodule Ribot, had founded the Société de psychologie physiologique in 1885, serving as president and bringing hypnotism into the fold of official medical academia. They were joined by other eminent "philosophers" of the day.[66] International interest in the subject of the society's activities was burgeoning, and discoveries were moving from speculation to observations and experimentation in hospitals and academic laboratories. When Pierre Janet based his experimental work with patients suffering from "automatisme psychologique" on hypnotic techniques, physiological psychology became the observational and experimental arm of hypnotic theory. The two were officially wed when *La Revue de l'Hypnotisme*, directed by Dr. Edgar Bérillon, added *Revue de psychologie physiologique* to its name to commence with its fourth year of publication (1890). Bérillon and his review helped inspire and reported on the first international gathering and exchange of ideas on the subject that took place in Paris in August 1889, among the many celebrations to commemorate the centennial of the Revolution. At the time of the conference the revue had been publishing for three years. James was the American representative.

And that was how a tantalizing opportunity for a James-Proust connection occurred in 1889. This opportunity was close to home, almost personal.

During the month of August, Paris was abuzz with scientific conclaves. "[U]ne animation scientifique vraiment extraordinaire" [An extraordinary level of scientific excitement] was how the 1889–1890 issue of the *Revue de l'Hypnotisme expérimental et thérapeutique* described it.[67] This first international conference consisted essentially of a series of conclaves on related topics: "le premier Congrès de Psychologie physiologique, le Congrès de l'Anthropologie criminelle," and "le premier Congrès de l'Hypnotisme expérimental et thérapeutique" [The first Congress of Physiological Psychology, the Congress of Criminal Anthropology, and the first Congress of Experimental and Therapeutic Hypnotism].

Ian Hacking mentions a "mental medicine congress [. . .], [that] ran 4–10 August." "The assembly was an international Who's Who of psychology, hysteria, and hypnotism."[68] As president of la Société de psychologie physiologique, Charcot served nominally as President of the Congrès; but he did not appear, and the Congrès opened instead with an address by Ribot. The *Revue* counted many of its subscribers among the registrants and described the proceedings in detail.

G. Ballet, later the co-author with Adrien Proust of *L'Hygiène du neurasthénique*[69] (an American term for "symptoms of physical and mental exhaustion" described in a quasi-financial frame as "nervous bankruptcy" and originally applied solely to men[70]), was listed among the members of the Congress.[71] He was not an official presenter but spoke, giving his views on the issues involved in the controversy dividing the Salpêtrière school of thought from that of Nancy,[72] according to an article covering the conference in the *Revue de l'Hypnotisme*.[73] The same issue of the *Revue* included an article by Adrien Proust, Marcel's father. The article was entitled "Automatisme ambulatoire chez un hystérique"[74] [involuntary ambulation in a hysterical patient] and associated automatic behavior with hysteria rather than with epilepsy, as did Charcot. In it A. Proust recounted the story of Émile X, a case of multiple personalities (two).

The term "automatisme ambulatoire" [involuntary ambulation] had been coined by Charcot in 1888 and used in his Salpêtrière lectures. The article's relevance to the publication and to the subjects covered during the conference were in areas of "automatisme" [unconscious involuntary behavior]—multiple personality hysterias caused by spontaneous reversion to an alternate personality state, explained by and curable using hypnotic technique—and the determination of criminality for patients who commit crimes while in an alternative personality state. A footnote to the article indicates that Adrien Proust delivered it (actually something similar) as an address to the Académie des sciences morales et politiques[75] (followed by publication in the *Bulletin Médical* in 1890[76]). This article itself did not appear as an address in the proceedings of the Congress, but the topic was clearly germane. In the address read to the Académie, Adrien Proust refers specifically to "M. le professeur Charcot" [Professor Charcot] and work he and other researchers present at the Congrès had done with patients suffering from "automatisme ambulatoire" resulting from cerebral trauma or, in the case of Charcot's patients, from epilepsy. Émile's case had been presented to Adrien Proust by J. Luys, the attending physician who treated Émile at the Charité hospital. G. Ballet had served as an expert witness at one of Émile's trials.

Adrien Proust had known Charcot for a long time. At the Faculté de Paris, when Proust defended his thesis on lung disease for the degree of Doctor of Medicine on December 29, 1862, Charcot was an intern at the Faculté de Médecine in Paris; he, too, had written a thesis on lung disease (chronic pneumonia).[77] In 1866, A. Proust received honors for his doctoral thesis on neurological and brain disease for what was essentially an interpretation of work done under Charcot at the Salpêtrière.

Adrien Proust was evidently interested in the topics covered at this first international conference, and the timing of his publications is remarkably coincidental with it. They were intended for a readership and audience made up of those most likely to have attended the conference. Therefore, it is certainly possible that Adrien Proust was among the four hundred registrants ("the majority naturally French") noted by William James in his factual and delightfully entertaining description of the conference written for the Notes section of *Mind* in October 1889.[78]

In 1897, when Adrien Proust added the volume on neurasthenia to the series of texts published under his direction on various medical topics, it was apparent right at the beginning of the book that he followed developments described in medical literature in America, England, and Germany as well as in France. Co-authored with G. Ballet, the volume on neurasthenia began with a preface citing the truly "fondamentale" [fundamental] and most complete work on the history, diagnosis, and treatment of neurasthenia done by Beard of New York. The disease syndrome was named in America and referred to a condition of "nervous exhaustion."[79]

Dr. Proust's book is medical in nature and examines the condition from the point of view of a medical practitioner dedicated to treating his patients and providing technical information to others in the profession. He cites another American article, one written by Weber in the *Boston Medical Journal*, in his description of symptoms of "névrose vasa-motrice" [autonomic nervous dysfunction affecting the blood vessels].[80] Also included among Dr. Proust's sources is Charcot's work at the Salpêtrière and specifically his lectures, some of which were attended by James. Was the purpose of the book to attempt to understand and treat the various medical complaints and sexual conditions specific to his elder son? It provides not only a medical backdrop for understanding Marcel Proust's life at the time but also serves almost as a template for some of the thematic material that appears later in *À la recherche du temps perdu*.[81]

As discussion of split or dissociated personality ignited in the scientific and medical communities, the literary potential of these disorders captivated writers who undertook more detailed and finer exploration of multiple personality. The creative possibilities of an alternative self "oublié et enfoui" [buried and forgotten] exposed by experimental psychology in France between 1874 and 1914, and in Adrien Proust's article on Émile in particular, may have inspired Marcel Proust, according to Edward Bizub.[82]

Many works written early in the twentieth century evoke "the polypsychic structure of the human mind," and any list of writers who palpated the scientific discourse for literary use would surely include Marcel Proust, notes Henri Ellenberger, who cites Proust's mention "during idle talk in Madame Verdurin's salon" of "the case of an honest man who, in his secondary personality, turned into a scoundrel."[83] He, too, is referring to the story of Émile X, published and presented by Marcel's father "as a significant psychopathological case." Ellenberger goes on to describe Proust the novelist's "[indefatigable analysis of] the multiple shades of personality within us," the way we are altered by our surroundings and our companions, by events, by reminiscences, by our cultural milieu—what we read or hear in conversation. Ellenberger changes William James's metaphor but refers nonetheless to the "fluidity in the mind," which James described as the "stream" of human consciousness. Ellenberger attributes this "fluidity" to "these metamorphoses of personality," which he finds curious, given that the available influences on Proust could not yet have included Freud or "other representatives of the new dynamic psychiatry." Proust could only have drawn from "academic sources [that] went no further than Ribot and Bergson," drawing a literary "treatise on the mind" before psychiatric sources did, in Ellenberger's view.

Acknowledging James's contributions to notions of "dissociation" and the subconscious, as Ellenberger does, allows for the possibility that William James's descriptions of consciousness and self may also have been interpolated into the backdrop of Proust's depictions. In *The Principles of Psychology*, James includes an analysis of an instance of multiple personality characterized by amnesiac ignorance by one personality of the presence of the other, much like the case Proust's father reported at about the same time. Ellenberger refers to this case as "[o]ne of the first reliably recorded instances of mutually amnestic personalities,"[84] and he suggests that "the psychology of William James" was among the greatest influences on "the dynamic psychiatry of Pierre Janet."[85]

Pierre Janet had presented his thesis on "automatisme" [unconscious involuntary behavior] at the International Congress in Paris in 1889 where James was a participant, and only thereafter began medical studies and research at the Salpêtrière. James found Janet's subsequent work with hysterics to be extremely valuable in understanding the mind. Perry points out James had spoken on psychopathology in one of his Lowell lectures in 1896, identifying the works of Freud and Janet as pointing to useful "discoveries."[86] James wrote to his friend Stumpf in Munich in 1900 that with regard to the study of "dissociation" (hypnotism, hysteria, trance, etc.), the French were "doing the best psychological work these days."[87]

Also in 1900 James became a member of the Institut Psychologique Internationale founded by Janet to replace the Société de Psychologie Physiologique, which had foundered after Charcot's death in 1893. James was seamlessly integrated into the European scholarly establishment. He wrote to President Eliot of Harvard during his sabbatical stay in Europe that year, while composing the Edinburgh Gifford lectures, that he and his family were staying most comfortably at the chateau in Hyères owned by his friend, physiology professor Charles Robert Richet, who, like Proust's father, was a member of the Faculté de Médecine in Paris and shared some of James's interests in psychical phenomena. He, too, had been present at the First International Congress in 1889.

Émile Boutroux

Problems encountered by potential translators in arranging French publication of *The Principles of Psychology* left James uncomfortable, even skeptical, about prospects for translations of his works, and he often objected to taking responsibility for them. Although his friend Théodore Flournoy had generously offered to translate *The Varieties of Religious Experience* himself, James did not want to burden his friend with the task and, ironically, felt this work was more specialized and would only appeal to a "smaller public."

James and Flournoy had become acquainted at the 1889 International Congress of Physiological Psychology in Paris. Flournoy was a professor of experimental psychology at the University of Geneva and reviewed *The Principles of Psychology* for the *Journal de Genève*. The two men shared many interests and became very close friends. James opposed the diversion a translation would represent from Flournoy's own work, but apparently Flournoy did begin one. Frank Abauzit, a Swiss scholar like Flournoy, was selected to complete the task with James's approval. Abauzit approached Henri Bergson for the Preface, but Bergson declined for reasons of health (although it was possible that he had some reservations about the translation itself). Émile Boutroux agreed to write it.

In 1905, the book was published in French under the title *L'Expérience religieuse: Essai de Psychologie descriptive*, following excerpts that had been printed in French in *Les Annales de Philosophie Chrétienne* in 1903 and in the *Revue de Philosophie* in 1905, also translated by Abauzit. In November 1905, James wrote to Boutroux, thanking him for his "long and highly sympathetic" approach in the Preface.[88]

Boutroux was professor at the Sorbonne from 1888 to 1902 and subsequently director of the Fondation Thiers. Although correspondence between James and Boutroux had begun some years earlier, they first met in person at the "Moral Education Congress" held in England in 1908. James wrote to Flournoy that he had found Boutroux "very *sympatico*."[89] Boutroux serves not only as a link between James and French philosophy, but also as a potential connection between James and Marcel Proust.

In his book *Alphonse Darlu*, Henri Bonnet notes that Marcel Proust, uncertain about his future career or perhaps torn as to how best to pursue his interest in writing while satisfying his family's desire that he choose a serious profession, was a student of philosophy at the Sorbonne during the academic year 1894–1895. He was studying under Egger, using materials by Boutroux, and taking private tutorials from his lycée philosophy instructor Darlu. Bonnet notes the following: "[observation du professeur Egger sur un devoir dans ce même carnet]: 'S'est servi de Boutr. (Note 1: Boutroux, bien entendu), ms aussi d'autres et a tout compris'"[90] [(observation by prof. Egger on an assignment in the same notebook): Used Boutr (Note 1: Boutroux, of course), but also others and (he) understood everything].

Boutroux's philosophical approach was a blending of science and religion that had exposed him to interaction with James's ideas and made him an ideal candidate to write the preface to the French translation of *The Varieties of Religious Experience*. He was elected a member of the Académie des sciences morales et politiques in 1898 and became a member of the Académie française in 1912. Boutroux was a popular philosopher at a time when philosophers were not confined to academia but, like James and Bergson, offered public lectures and published in well-read journals, including the *Revue Philosophique* and the *Revue de Métaphysique et de Morale*. When it was released in 1907, James sent Boutroux a copy of his new book, *Pragmatism*. In 1908, Boutroux published an article entitled "William James et l'expérience religieuse"[91] [William James and Religious Experience] later incorporated as a chapter in his book *Science et religion dans la philosophie contemporaine*[92] [*Science and Religion in Contemporary Philosophy*], in which he commented on James's religious doctrines and views on the relationship between religion and science.

Once the two men met, Boutroux and James became extremely close personal friends. Correspondence between them was frequent. Boutroux read James's newest books as soon as they were published. In 1909, Boutroux was invited to give the Hyde lectures at Harvard to take place in March of the following year. In January 1910, Boutroux became president of the Académie des sciences morales et politiques, giving him the delightful opportunity to announce that James had been elected a foreign associate. (This is the same group that Marcel Proust's father, Adrien, had very much wanted to join at the apogee of his public health career, albeit unsuccessfully.[93]) Although we do not know if Marcel Proust was aware of the honor thus accorded James, there are indications in his *Correspondance* that he paid attention to who was being nominated and elected to honorary societies.

Arriving in Cambridge to deliver the Hyde lectures, Boutroux resided in the James home for more than two weeks. James summed up this visit in "A Great French Philosopher at Harvard," published in the *Nation*,[94] and Boutroux followed it with an address before the Académie chronicling his "observations on his voyage to America"[95] and with a subsequent article for *Le Journal des Débats politiques et littéraires* about Harvard and his sojourn in the James home.[96]

James described his relationship with Boutroux as "one of the pleasantest episodes of my life" as he bid him adieux in one of his final letters.[97] In 1911, Boutroux wrote what was essentially a eulogy of James's life and work. Translated into English in 1912, its attempt to ally James with the French tradition has been considered more a tribute than an exact interpretation of James's philosophy. The book most likely did serve to extend the reach of James's ideas on French soil, since it included in its first footnote a listing of James's most important works with their dates of publication and whether they had appeared in French translation.[98]

By virtue of their warm friendship, Boutroux acted as a personal champion for James; the endorsement bestowed by so prominent a member of French academic society furthered dissemination of James's ideas.

Émile Boutroux was also a significant point of contact in the circle of acquaintances connecting William James and Marcel Proust. He had long been known to the Proust family. His name first appears in Proust's correspondence in a letter to Marcel from his mother written on April 23, 1890.[99] The letter excitedly informs Marcel that his younger brother Robert is going to attend (without fail!) Boutroux's course. The editor notes that at a certain point in his life Proust admired this professor of philosophy at the Sorbonne almost as much as he admired Darlu, calling the two men "mes héros dans la vie réelle"[100] [my real-life heroes].

Several other references to Boutroux in Proust's letters indicate that Proust was familiar with his writings and throughout his life maintained a continuing respect and admiration for Boutroux.[101] Along with Boutroux and Henri Bergson, among other notables, Proust was asked to sit on a jury designated to award the Blumenthal Prize for French literature and poetry.

Boutroux's name appears twice in *Sodome et Gomorrhe II*. The first mention is in a conversation at the Verdurin's, in which the "philosophe norvégien" [Norwegian philosopher] (based on Algot Ruhe, Swedish translator of Bergson's works) mentions that he has a meeting to go to the next day at which Boutroux will be speaking about "des séances de spiritisme"[102] [séance to commune with spirits]. (Coincidentally, in 1916 Ruhe translated William James's *Pragmatism* into Swedish.[103]) We can ponder whether the "séances de spiritisme" might really refer to James, known in part for his *psychical* interests, rather than Boutroux, well known for his *spiritualist* views (in the sense that man is endowed with spirit and not simply subject to science's materialistic determinism) and for his religious philosophy.

Henri Bergson

Proust's second reference to Boutroux in *À la recherche du temps perdu* concerns a purported conversation between Boutroux and Bergson about sleep, drugs, and memory.

The narrator is not certain about whether this conversation ever took place because the Norwegian who reports it has difficulty with the French language and might have misunderstood. The editors indicate that a similar actual conversation might have taken place when Proust, Boutroux, and Bergson were together for the Blumenthal jury, or the source might have been Bergson's *Le Rêve*.[104]

Henri Bergson had been Boutroux's student at the Sorbonne in 1885.[105] Like William James, Bergson was a philosophical personality and "popularizer."[106] While Bergson's public stature was considerable, it is the important professional as well as personal relationship he had with William James and the private family (and perhaps mentoring) relationship he had with Marcel Proust that are of interest here. Bergson was Proust's cousin by virtue of his marriage to Louise Neuberger, daughter of one of Marcel's mother's first cousins. Henri Bergson married Louise on January 7, 1892, and Marcel was "garçon d'honneur" [best man] at the ceremony. The extent and intimacy of Proust's relationship with Bergson has been subject to debate. In Proust's *Correspondance*, letters that include references to Bergson shortly follow the marriage bringing Bergson into the extended family. On November 7, 1892, Marcel invited Fernand Gregh, then a philosophy student, to dine with Bergson.[107] A letter to Marcel from his mother written in 1895 confirmed that Bergson was to send him a copy of a speech.[108] On December 7, 1900, Proust sat in on the first lecture of the course Bergson was teaching at the Collège de France.[109] In the letters mentioning him, a certain degree of familiarity and comfort with Bergson, if not a sense of intimacy, is definitely implied. Bergson presented a synopsis of Proust's translation of Ruskin's *Bible d'Amiens* at the Académie des sciences morales et politiques on May 28, 1904.[110] In a letter to Georges de Lauris written in April 1908, Proust mentions his high regard for Bergson and how good Bergson has always been to him.[111]

Whatever the links critics may think they identify between Bergson's ideas and Proust's aesthetic or philosophy, Proust does not indicate that he read Bergson's works avidly. The letter to George de Lauris written in April 1908 mentions familiarity with "la parabole de sa pensée" [the arc of his thought] if not with specifics of Bergson's latest works.[112] In a letter to Henri Ghéon of January 6, 1914, Proust categorically denies any purported linkage of his work to Bergson's, saying, "Jamais je n'ai eu une idée pareille!" [Never would I have such a thought!] He goes on to declare that his intention was to "faire avec ce que j'ai senti, et à tâcher de le convertir [. . .] en idées claires, sans chercher à mettre en roman la philosophie de M. Bergson!"[113] [work with what I have felt and try to convert it . . . into clear ideas without attempting to turn Mr. Bergson's philosophy into a novel].

On November 8, 1913, Proust had granted an interview to Élie-Joseph Bois of *Le Temps*. His purpose was to publicize and explain the forthcoming *Du côté de chez Swann* in an attempt to enhance public acceptance of what was going to be a strange new reading experience. The text of the printed interview is based, despite Proust's protestations to the contrary, on something Proust himself had written the previous year in a letter to Antoine Bibesco. In other words, it was largely a set piece prepared in advance by the author.[114] In the interview, Proust publicly repudiated Bergson's influence, saying that while literature of every period has connections to current philosophical ideas, what he has written is actually "contradictory" to what Bergson's philosophy holds:

> À ce point de vue, continue M. Proust, mon livre serait peut-être comme un essai d'une suite de 'Romans de l'Inconscient' : je n'aurais aucune honte à dire de 'romans bergsoniens', si je le croyais, car à toute époque il arrive que la littérature a tâché de se rattacher—après coup, naturellement—à la philosophie régnante. Mais ce ne serait pas exact, car mon oeuvre est dominée par la distinction entre la mémoire invo-

lontaire et la mémoire volontaire, distinction qui non seulement ne figure pas dans la philosophie de M. Bergson, mais est même contredite par elle.[115]

[From this point of view, continues Mr. Proust, my book would perhaps be like an attempt at a series of "Novels of the Unconscious": I would not be ashamed to say 'bergsonian novels' if I thought they were, because in every period literature has tried to emulate—after the fact, of course—the philosophy in vogue. But this would not be truthful, because my work is dominated by the distinction between involuntary memory and voluntary memory, a distinction that not only does not appear in Mr. Bergson's thought but in fact contradicts it.]

The quest to identify Proust's provenance has been in process for the near century since he began composition of *À la recherche du temps perdu*. For much of that time, Henri Bergson has indeed been considered a likely source. However, many specific and significant differences between the two were identified in 1932 by Charles Blondel[116] and have been pointed out more recently by Joyce Megay in areas that are very basic to the originality of each.[117]

In Cahier 59, Proust makes it very clear that he plans to allow only "les étincelles" [sparks] of philosophy to shimmer in *À la recherche du temps perdu*. He wants his work to be a work of fiction, not a treatise. And clearly we can assume an interest on Proust's part in taking credit for the integrity of his work as wholly his own, for not attributing any part of it to outside sources. But given the wide availability and familiarity of James's works in France at the time, his very public persona, and the parallels between his text and Proust's, no one can discount "les étincelles" of James's thought that pepper Proust's book.

In 1896 Bergson published his second major work, *Matière et mémoire*[118] [*Matter and Memory*, translated in 1911]. A footnote cites James's *Principles of Psychology* in a discussion of the psychophysiology of attention.[119]

Much has been made of the question of which of these two writers had priority over the other. In fact, James was older and had published first, his earliest articles widely disseminated. Reporting on the Fifth International Congress of Psychology held in Rome in 1905, an article in the *Revue philosophique de la France et de l'étranger* by G. Rageot attributed to "the Americans" (i.e., James) a significant early influence on the work of France's "eminent philosopher" Henri Bergson. Bergson summarily wrote an indignant letter in response. He claimed that his *Essai sur les données immédiates de la conscience* [English translation *Time and Free Will*, 1910] owed little to others. He admitted being aware at the time of writing (between 1883 and 1887) of James's articles on effort and emotion. But he categorically denied any knowledge of James's concept of the "stream of thought" described in the 1884 article "On Some Omissions of Introspective Psychology," and stressed that although the terms may sound similar, the approaches sourcing the concepts "stream of thought" and "durée réelle" [duration and change] were fundamentally very different.[120] James's ideas were of psychological origin, Bergson claimed, while his own were derived from a response to the mathematical notion of "homogeneous time."[121]

André Lalande did not shy away from suggesting, denied vehemently by Bergson, that the French philosopher "received his primary impulse from Mr. James."[122]

Bergson was fluent in English (his mother was English, and he spent the first six years of his life in England). Depending on the language of his correspondents, he chose to write some of his letters in English. When William James's son Henry was collecting his father's correspondence for publication, Bergson sent the originals and his own translations of his letters for inclusion in the American work. As evidenced in his letters, throughout his life Bergson maintained warm, respectful, and admiring feelings for William James. Bergson advised James on translation of his works into French and had even recommended individuals well suited to the task. He wrote many letters to James demonstrating a strong personal bond in addition to the parallels in their professional interests.

When writing *The Principles of Psychology*, James refers to having read Bergson's *Données immédiates de la conscience* right after its publication in 1889, but the text seems to have had no significant impact on him at the time. Bergson sent James an autographed copy of *Matière et mémoire* upon publication in 1896, and again the same reaction prevailed. However, in 1902 James reread both books—this time with great admiration. James wrote to Bergson on December 14, 1902, with praise and to describe the stimulating effect the books had had on his own thought. He forwarded to Bergson copies of "Human Immortality" and *The Varieties of Religious Experience*. Thus, their correspondence and friendship began.

Bergson responded from Paris on January 6, 1903, and included in his letter the following statement: "If you have had occasion during the last ten or twelve years to talk with French students visiting Cambridge, they must have told you that I have been one of your admirers from the beginning, and that I have lost no opportunity of expressing to my hearers my great sympathy for your ideas."[123] Might Bergson himself have served as vector for James's ideas to Proust?

Bergson continues his letter with a request that James inform him in advance of his next trip to France so that the two men can arrange to meet. According to the editors, at the time he was writing, Bergson had in his possession copies of a number of James's works.[124]

James replied and sent a copy of the syllabus for Philosophy 3 summarizing his philosophical outlook at the time: "[I]t will show you the sort of lines upon which I have been working."[125] Theirs was going to be an intensely personal intellectual engagement.

On May 28, 1905, in Paris, where James had gone in large part for that purpose, he and Bergson first met face to face. James documented the rendezvous in his diary, referencing his colleague as "Beautiful Bergson."[126] It was definitely an auspicious start to a significant relationship for both men. James followed his increasing penchant for creating his own metaphysical philosophy, one leaning in the same general direction as Bergson's.

In the letter James wrote to Bergson setting the date for their meeting, James mentions having been invited by Léon Brunschvicg to the Société française de philosophie and asks Bergson not to reveal their plan to anyone. James did not feel well enough to attend the Société gathering and did not want the group to know he was meeting with someone else. It is noteworthy that the invitation came from Léon Brunschvicg, then a professor of philosophy at the Sorbonne, former classmate of Proust's at the lycée Condorcet, and founder—along with Alphonse Darlu—of the *Revue de métaphysique et de morale.* By this time, James was clearly annexed to Parisian intellectual society.

Whereas James's interests in the first half of the 1890s, after the publication of *The Principles of Psychology* and *The Principles of Psychology: Briefer Course,* had tended toward the abnormal and paranormal in psychology, his publications during the second half of the decade leaned toward moral philosophy and the psychology of belief. His major works at this time include *The Will to Believe and Other Essays in Popular Philosophy,*[127] *Human Immortality: Two Supposed Objections to the Doctrine, Talks to Teachers on Psychology: and to Students on Some of Life's Ideals* (1899),[128] culminating in 1902 with *The Varieties of Religious Experience: A Study in Human Nature.* These works were in large part collections and expansions of addresses James had made to popular as well as scholarly audiences. The works were personal in tone, colorful in delivery, and in places touch on themes that will resonate for Proust.

On August 26, 1898, James presented an address to the Philosophical Union of the University of California on the religious application of a topic first referred to as "Pragmatism" (or "Pragmaticism") by Charles Peirce twenty years before. This initial lecture was translated into French for publication in 1906[129] and developed into a series of lectures James delivered at the Lowell Institute in Boston in 1906 and to a standing-room-only audience at Columbia University in New York in 1907. Although by this time James's works had been available to French readers for some time, with publication of *Pragmatism* in 1907 it was the press itself that occasioned much of James's celebrity and notoriety.

On June 13, 1907, James congratulated Bergson on his newest work, *L'Évolution créatrice.*[130] Reading the work left James feeling "rejuvenated"; although he readily admitted that "younger men" might more easily tangle with the "development of detail." "I feel at bottom we are fighting the same fight" [against Intellectualism], noted James. With this letter

James sent a copy of *Pragmatism.*[131] Bergson's reply calls James "the thinker who has so powerfully contributed to the refashioning of the soul of the new generations."[132] Was this Proust's generation to whom he was referring?

James devoted one of his Hibbert Lectures (Oxford, 1908) to "The Philosophy of Bergson."[133] Letters were exchanged in an effort to arrange a meeting somewhere in Europe. On October 4, 1908, just before James sailed for home and while Bergson was in England visiting relatives, the two men met once again. No nearer to a clear understanding of Bergson's ideas, James definitely felt closer to the man. James published this series of lectures in 1909 under the title *A Pluralistic Universe.* In the chapter entitled "Bergson and his Critique of Intellectualism," James states that searching for immutable laws, for structural connectors, does not assist in understanding the way experience itself is shaped. "Our intellect casts, in short, no ray of light on the processes by which experiences *get made.*"[134]

James next traveled to Paris in the spring of 1910 and met twice with Bergson during this final visit. "It is clear from the record of these meetings that each enjoyed the other's company as much as his philosophy."[135]

Bergson agreed to write the Preface for the French translation of *Pragmatism* published in 1911, shortly after James's death. He reviewed all of James's works in preparation, and the depth of his regard for James is evident. In a letter to Mrs. James written on June 21, 1911, Bergson admits that he was unable to avoid expressing his feelings for James: "Quoique j'aie tâché de faire de cette introduction un travail absolument impersonnel, je n'ai pu m'empêcher de laisser percer, dans les dernières lignes, quelque chose du sentiment que j'éprouve à l'égard de la mémoire de William James lui-même"[136] [Although I tried to remain completely objective in writing this introduction, it nevertheless reflects something of my feeling for the memory of William James himself]. Bergson later wrote the Preface to the French translation of *The Letters of William James* published in English by William's son Henry in 1920.[137]

Each man was nearly completely versed in the other's written product and intimately familiar with every twist of thought and theory. The relationship was close, and long lasting for Bergson, who mentioned James in correspondence throughout his life. The most striking example of the depth and duration of Bergson's regard for James appears in a heart-rending letter he wrote to United States President Franklin Roosevelt in the spring of 1940 as Germany marched over Europe. He offers as witness to the credibility of his views that they come from someone so close a friend to William James that he keeps a picture of James on his desk: "Il fut l'ami presque intime de William James, qu'il tient pour un des plus grands penseurs de tous les temps, et dont il a le portrait devant lui quand il travaille"[138] [someone so nearly an intimate friend of William James, whom he considered on the of great thinkers of all time, that he keeps a portrait of James in front of him when he works]. Ultimately, the question we must ask is whether there were implications for Proust in the intellectual intimacy between Bergson and James. *Pragmatism* brings James into Proust's ken in the two letters[139] that form the only direct link.

Why was James so well received in France, and in what ways did his friendship with Henri Bergson contribute to his popularity? In the preface to Durkheim's *Pragmatism and Sociology,* John B. Allcock identifies the same scientific and publishing interconnections we have described and reminds us of the effect of James's style on his wider audience. James's works were often composed originally for oral delivery, and so were written in "prose of almost startling vividness,"[140] marked by a very personal oral-expository style. Each listener and each reader feels that James is speaking directly to him. He wrote in the manner of a lecturer weaving a colorful web of argument to entice and hold his audience; his style drew the greatest thinkers of his time to engage in the disputes of the moment. His friendship with Bergson enhanced his position in the public mind, because Bergson was a public intellectual whose own lectures became tourist events. According to Allcock, "Jamesian pragmatism was closely associated with the thought of this highly influential and popular figure."[141]

And, in addition, it was a very cosmopolitan time: educated men and women (like Proust's mother) were conversant and literate in languages beyond their own, particularly in English, French, and German (some even in Italian), which were the languages of discovery and political power. The elements of James's thought on experience, relativity and chance, the stream of consciousness, attention, habit, memory, the various schools of the scientific psychology, the unconscious, mystical experience became so enmeshed in the way of looking at the world that grew out of the early twentieth century that they were absorbed into literature, art, and culture, and shaped a perspective still considered modern. In France at the time of Proust, it was very hard to avoid becoming aware of William James.

But before looking more specifically at journalistic coverage of *Pragmatism* in France and at Bergson's Preface to the translation, there is yet another possible Proust-James connection to consider.

Dr. Paul Sollier

A paragraph in the *Cahier de 1908* highlights a procedure Proust chooses to use in his novel: "approfondir des réminiscences"[142] [amplify the recollections]. Rather than the philosophical or intellectualist *conceptions* that intelligence uses to disentangle and sort out aspects of experience, Proust notes an intention to elaborate on memory. A point of common interest to James and to Bergson, this topic was also central to a late

James article entitled "A Suggestion about Mysticism"[143] and was a method of treatment utilized by Dr. Paul Sollier.

After his mother's death in September 1905, Proust was in a state of emotional and physical disarray. In December he entered Dr. Paul Sollier's clinic in Boulogne-sur-Seine for treatment and a brief respite: "Proust s'est fait soigner en décembre 1906—janvier 1907 [*sic*] chez le docteur Sollier, à Boulogne-sur-Seine, dans son sanatorium pour les maladies du système nerveux"[144] [In December 1906 and January 1907, Proust received treatment for nervous disorders in Dr. Sollier's sanatorium located in Boulogne-sur-Seine].

He found the treatment unsatisfying and unsuccessful, and he remained in the sanatorium for a period some say was just short of a month,[145] while others recount that his stay lasted about six weeks, from December 6, 1905, until the last week in January 1906.[146]

Dr. Sollier had written a number of works on hysteria and emotional abnormalities as well as works on memory and association. Two are of particular interest. In 1905 Alcan published *Le Mécanisme des émotions*,[147] a collection of course lectures delivered by the author in Brussels in 1903. In these, there are no fewer than thirty-five references to William James, including many specific references to *La Théorie de l'émotion*, translated from the English by G. Dumas and published by Alcan in 1903. Sollier took issue with much of the substance of the James-Lange theory of emotion and proposed his own interpretations of emotivity and brain function in emotional expression. His 1907 book on association, *Essai critique et théorique sur l'Association en psychologie*,[148] was derived from lectures given in Brussels in 1905. Once again his work refers frequently to William James, this time taking issue with James's interpretation of association as occurring between "choses pensées"—things thought—rather than between some sort of abstractions called "ideas." Sollier critiques what James has to say but references James as one would someone who laid the groundwork in the field and served as point of departure for further research. Sollier evidently had an intimate familiarity with William James's work and likely had copies of James's books on hand or, at the very least, a copy of *La Théorie de l'émotion* since he refers to it so specifically. It is certainly possible that he referred to James's ideas in his consultations and treatment programs, whether subscribing to or refuting them, whether naming them outright or not. James's ideas were the benchmark against which others could elaborate their own theories, including Sollier.

Recently, Dr. Paul Sollier is enjoying a renaissance in publications on Proust, memory, and emotion. While acknowledging Proust's desire to minimize any benefit from his stay at Sollier's clinic, O. Walusinski and J. Bogousslavsky[149] cite Sollier's method of eliciting "reviviscences" from his patients and compare this to Proust's use of moments of involuntary memory to structure his novel. They describe Sollier's early work on the neurophysiology of memory,[150] placing him in the context of his French contemporaries Charcot, Ribot, and Richet, but they omit any mention of William James.

In his article "Proust et le docteur Sollier: les 'molécules impressionnées'"[151] [Proust and Dr. Sollier: the etched traces[152]], Edward Bizub discusses the "enregistrement" or recording of experience in Proust's novel. He likens the word "sillon" used by Proust's narrator for the imprint of an impression on his sensibility to the channels or grooves pressed into a phonographic cylinder or transmitted to a disk. The recording device was a technological innovation of the time, noted by Bergson, and Bizub finds reference to it in the work on memory written by Dr. Paul Sollier. According to Bizub, Sollier's cure involved resurrecting past memories from the depths of the unconscious. He implies that Proust owed a great deal to Sollier's influence but chose to remain silent about how he had benefitted, a contention shared by Walusinski and Bogousslavsky. Sollier, however, was not the only possible medical source for Proust's thoughts on impression and memory, nor is it likely that he was the only medical or psychological influence *not* mentioned by the author. Sollier's connection with the neuroscience of his time will be revisited.

CONNECTING PROUST TO JAMES: PROUST'S PHILOSOPHICAL EDUCATION AND LITERARY INTERESTS

Given the late dates (1918 and 1920) of the references to James in Proust's letters, can a case be made for an earlier connection between William James and Marcel Proust? While Bergson was family and Boutroux a respected professor, Proust also had a demonstrably long-standing passion for philosophy (including Americans such as Emerson), interest in literature by English and American authors, familiarity with the reputation and perhaps the work of Henry James, and shared certain mutual acquaintances with the James family.

Paul Bourget was friends with Proust and with Henry James and dedicated his book *Cruelle Énigme* to Henry James. Jacques-Émile Blanche, neighbor to Proust in Auteuil when they were young, painted Proust's celebrated portrait in 1895, and also painted a portrait of Henry James. Citing Blanche's book *Mes modèles*, Bruce Lowery shows great interest in the possibility that, friendly with Proust and with Henry James, Blanche "sert de révélateur de James [Henry] à Proust" [revealed Henry James to Proust]. Apparently, Proust asked Blanche to compare Henry as a writer to George Meredith and Thomas Hardy.[153]

Blanche begins his contribution to the NRF's *Hommage à Marcel Proust*, "Quelques Instantanés de Marcel Proust" [Homage to Marcel Proust: Some Snapshots of Marcel Proust], with the fact that he was in the country reading Henry James's correspondence when he received the shocking news of Proust's death. He remarks on the contents of a letter Henry James wrote to his brother, William, who was clearly not an unknown in their common milieu.[154]

Lowery states that "Georges de Lauris nous affirme que Proust *voyait* toujours les revues principales, mais il estime qu'il ne lisait que ce qui l'intéressait" [George de Lauris asserts that Proust always *looked at* the most important journals but only read those that interested him]. Lowery speculates that Proust, like other members his family—his mother in particular—was most literate, subscribed to many journals, and was likely to be "au courant" [155] [up to date].

Raised by such an extremely cultivated and well-educated mother, who was able to read Latin and Greek as well as German and English, Marcel Proust shared her passion for reading and showed his talent for writing early. According to André Ferré in his book about Marcel Proust's school years, early exchanges of letters mention books borrowed from a "cabinet de lecture" [reading room or private library], including classics and new works, but Ferré does not specify whether this material was composed of fiction only or included nonfiction as well.[156] Given the scientific interests of Professor Proust and his younger son, Robert, and the fact that Mme. Proust was able to read English, it is not impossible that works by James may have passed through the family library.

Ferré does specify a few of the books Proust read as a child, mentioning Théophile Gautier's *Le Capitaine Fracasse*, noted above as an interest shared with James. Ferré is convinced that bits of writing Proust did during his school years, and that have survived, demonstrate that Proust's psychological approach and awareness of the "vérités aux faces multiples" [many-sided truths] existed in his primal style.[157] It is hard to base this kind of judgment on such a scant quantity of early fictional writing, although it is clear that Proust sensed his vocation and enjoyed a certain continuity of interest, retaining certain elements of style throughout his life.

More significant is the long-standing interest in philosophy Proust developed during his school years. Proust studied under Darlu in 1888 and 1889, and his parents hired Darlu to tutor Marcel at home as well. Whether this was, as Ferré suggests, in place of more typical after-school lessons in sports or piano, or to make up for Proust's frequent bouts of illness and absence from classes, does not really matter. What matters is Proust's passion for the subject and his sincere regard for the teacher. We think it unlikely, although it is impossible to know for certain, that any of William James's articles were discussed in class or in tutorial.

Later, after his year of military service, and after passing examinations in law and political science on the second attempt in 1893, Proust continued to pursue his interest in philosophy, this time at the Sorbonne for a year. Proust received his "licence" [degree] in Philosophie in 1895. Again, whether James's work—much better known by this time—was part of the curriculum is not known. It was during this period that other of Darlu's former students were soliciting articles and reviews for their newly founded *Revue de métaphysique et de morale*.

Proust wrote his examination for the "licence" [degree] in part on a psychological subject that would continue to preoccupy him: the unity of the self, a central topic in James's psychology. Bonnet indicates that Janet was examiner for the first part, and Boutroux for the second part on Descartes, but whether this meant that James's ideas might have been covered is not known.

Proust's year of philosophy represented a path he might have followed but that perhaps was not really his calling; his talent and his future lay more likely in literature. Darlu had inspired strong admiration in the young Proust, who later outgrew the need for this mentor. At the time he was translating Ruskin's *Sésame et les Lys*, he greatly admired Darlu and attributed much influence to him. But as of 1907, Darlu's name disappears from Proust's correspondence, and in the Carnet of 1908 Proust characterizes his great influence as detrimental. Is this Proust the writer revisiting and rejecting his earlier personal passion for philosophy? Is it a judgment about Darlu's philosophical stance and a repudiation of any echoes that might taint Proust's future writing? Or is this a test of a topic for his novel, the narrator's "je" speaking in a voice that will only pemit "étincelles" of philosophy to glint through his words?

While Ferré and H. Bonnet choose to read Darlu's influence in *À la recherche du temps perdu*, it is more likely that Proust had decided to move the "philosophie infinie" [comprehensive philosophy] he might have wanted to write at an earlier point in his life into the background, to use the hunt for reality's hidden essence to provide texture under the fictional turf. Philosophy held appeal because of its invitation to think and exercise the intellect, to experiment with logic, to seek answers, explanations, structure, truths, so fulfilling in days before Proust realized that the thrust of his fiction would require that he exorcize a conceptual or intellectually systemic stance, instead coloring his plot and giving it depth using memory—and desire and the emotions it engenders—the thinking man as feeling man thinking about the way his experience "feels." Perhaps this, too, can be viewed as originating[158] in the work of a "philosopher"—William James.

Proust's interest in English and American literary works has been well documented. Many references appear in his *Correspondance* and in *À la recherche du temps perdu*. Lowery cites a letter from Proust to Robert de Billy[159] to that effect. This interest is further evidenced by P.-E. Robert in *Marcel Proust, lecteur des Anglo-Saxons*.[160] Robert underscores the fact that Proust had never studied English nor was he proficient in the language: "Les connaissances de Marcel Proust en littérature anglo-saxonne étaient très supérieures à sa connaissance de la langue et il était obligé d'utiliser des traductions, sauf pour Ruskin, puisqu'il n'en existait pas"[161] [Marcel

Proust's knowledge about English-language literature was far superior to his knowledge of the language; he was obligated to use translations except for Ruskin, because there were none]. Robert suggests that Proust's prolonged intense work on the translation of Ruskin helped to improve his English, but notes that Proust himself parodied his own ability or lack thereof in one of his pastiches.

Although Proust was aware of Henry James's reputation, it is unlikely that the two ever met face to face despite assertions of a possible contact between Proust and Henry at the home of Mme. Straus. This would have taken place during Henry's stay in Paris in 1888–1889. They did share a number of other acquaintances including Mr. and Mrs. Schiff, Charles Du Bos, Walter Berry, and Douglas Ainslie. Several of Henry James's books were available in French translation. Walter Berry has indicated that Proust was particularly interested in the point of view used by Henry James for the character Maisie in *What Maisie Knew*.[162] P.-E. Robert suggests that Proust imitated the Anglo-Saxon writers' utilization of a philosophical basis, or moral compass, for the art of their fiction; but it was his encounter also with the aesthetic influence of the Anglo-Saxon authors, Ruskin among them, that allowed for the emergence of Proust's own aesthetic ideas.

In the chapter entitled "Proust's English World" in his book *Proust's English*,[163] Daniel Karlin reiterates that Proust's ability to *speak* or comprehend *spoken* English was decidedly limited. Apparently, Proust had tried to learn English at one time, but only written English, as he blamed his asthmatic condition for preventing him from learning pronunciation and oral comprehension. Karlin delves into the atmosphere of Anglomania in which Proust's social and aesthetic worlds were steeped. He mentions Proust's friendship with Willy Heath and lists other of Proust's acquaintances with at least some connections to England. Among these are Robert d'Humières, who translated Kipling and helped Proust with his work on Ruskin; Reynaldo Hahn's cousin Marie Nordlinger, who was in large part responsible for assisting Proust with the Ruskin translation; Robert de Montesquiou; and Oscar Wilde.

Michael Murphy's *Proust and America*[164] reflects on the presence of Americans in Europe and France's awareness of America's increasing world power and influence during Proust's lifetime. Murphy's book suggests Proust's exploitation of the imaginative power of America's passion for invention, mechanization, and speed. It describes the integration of a bounty of American words, including slang into *À la recherche du temps perdu*, in addition to the tempo of America's "nervousness" and the cultural impress of its writers and artists. These included painter James McNeill Whistler, philosopher Ralph Waldo Emerson, writer Edgar Allen Poe, and the above-mentioned neurologist George Beard, but no mention of William James.

Given the sizable circle of English and American diplomats, artists, heiresses, and expatriates living in Paris in Proust's time and the degree of international scientific and philosophical cross-pollination, there were many avenues by which Proust could have become aware of James. The English and American writers who interested Proust were often the ones excerpted or otherwise covered in the many newspapers and journals he read that also covered William James.

Coincidentally only, Carlyle and Emerson, whose works were of significant interest to Proust, were great friends of William James's father and frequent guests in the James household.

CONNECTING THROUGH THE MEDIA

Proust himself noted the power of the press to affect the opinions of the young in a letter to Georges de Lauris on July 29, 1903. He wrote about the separation of the Church from the state and growing anticlericalism and secularity. With the exception of those who go on to higher education and are committed to the philosophy of their instructors (and here he mentions Boutroux specifically), it is not the teachers who create opinion but what the media spreads that has the greatest effect, he surmised.

James's *Pragmatism* was responsible in large part for its author's celebrity in the last years before his death. The controversy it aroused has occasioned entire bibliographies.[165] Even before the book was translated into French, articles raged all over Europe, and a symposium on Pragmatism was held in 1908 coordinated by the Société française de philosophie [French Philosophical Society]. Philosophy was serious business in Europe, and all the philosophical heavyweights of the time participated in the slugfest. Although James was decidedly not the only American pragmatist, he was largely responsible for the notion's arrival in France and for the warm and wild welcome it received. According to John R. Shook, whose annotated bibliography of pragmatism in France covers the period from James's first mention of the word in his address in California in 1898 through 1940, the French never interpreted pragmatism exactly the same way as James and lost interest in pragmatism shortly after his death. Durkheim went so far as to lecture in 1913 on "le Pragmatisme" with the purpose of discrediting it in relation to his concept of sociology.[166]

Was the French press kind to pragmatism?

To set the tempest raised by *Pragmatism* into its historical context in Paris, we must recount at least in part its journalistic history. As a theory of truth, pragmatism was viciously attacked in the press, often in the religious press, as relativistic and utilitarian. The response was a storm of public media controversy much like the flurry of contravening opinion that was unleashed in the Querelle de l'Hystérie [dispute over pathological nervous hysteria].

The controversy was lively and engendered much coverage. According to Shook's bibliography, pragmatism received the most attention between 1907 and 1911. Léon Brunschvicg, Émile Boutroux, and Henri Bergson participated. Even Paul Sollier wrote two articles in 1909. In 1910, the year of his death, James's name appears fifteen times, as reviewers remembered his contributions. While some of the articles were printed in specialty journals devoted to specific philosophical or religious questions, many appeared in journals aimed at a broader reading public. Proust's Paris was steeped in pragmatism.

In Shook's bibliography, the word "pragmatism" first appears in the titles of two articles published in 1905. One by C. Dessoulavy was printed in *La Revue de philosophie*'s July issue and one by George Tyrrell was included in the *Annales de philosophie chrétienne*. André Lalande wrote an article including pragmatism in a review of current trends in philosophy entitled "Philosophy in France (1905)" that appeared in *The Philosophical Review* in May 1906.[167] The first word is "pragmatism." The previous February, he had authored an article for *La Revue philosophique* with the title "Pragmatisme et pragmaticisme."[168]

Did Proust know of Lalande? In his *Correspondance, La Revue philosophique* is mentioned on March 14, 1919, in an explanatory footnote the editors have added to a letter to Walter Berry. Proust is responding to Berry's mention of Ribot, director of that journal and denigrated here by Proust as a low-level philosopher. This occurred, obviously, years after Lalande's articles on pragmatism were published.

The content of Lalande's work is interesting in that it seems to have set the stage for the French reception of pragmatism. In "Philosophy in France (1905)," Lalande finds that pragmatism has taken up a position "in the air" of the times and credits Charles Peirce for first using the term and James for popularizing it. He describes a French version of pragmatism, in moral, spiritual, and religious contexts, citing Maurice Blondel's claim to have "created [it] anew" as early as 1893. According to Lalande, William James had outlined the basic principles of his theory of pragmatism in *The Varieties of Religious Experience* to demonstrate experience as self-correcting, verifying, and amplifying original assumptions.

Lalande distinguishes between James's notion of pragmatism as supporting "social discourse" and Bergson's idea in *Les Données immédiates de la conscience* that experience is "ineffable and unique," inexpressible in language. For Bergson, according to Lalande, "The word is stable, brutal, banal, common: to name experience is to falsify it and make it a dead thing."[169] This is very different from James's stress on the "vague" fringe effects and cataclysm of perception perceived through language and fictionally explored by Proust.

Lalande's article "Pragmatisme et pragmaticisme" quotes extensively from a variety of James's works, highlighting direct experience of the concrete, determination of truth based on consequences, risk-taking, and evaluation, the importance of the affective (desires, emotions, interests, judgments), the engaged first person. Much of this will find its way into Proust's themes and technique in *À la recherche du temps perdu*.

In Lalande's opinion, the reason that pragmatism stormed into philosophical consciousness during the first decade of the twentieth century was due in part to James's ability to popularize the theory even before publishing his book *Pragmatism* in 1907: "Il conçoit le pragmatisme beaucoup moins comme une doctrine que comme un mouvement d'esprit contemporaine" [He conceives of pragmatism less as a doctrine than as a contemporary spiritual movement], creating by 1906 what Lalande called "toute cette effervescence intellectuelle"[170] [all this intellectual effervescence].

From 1789 to 1944 *Le Journal des débats politiques et littéraires* was published in Paris, first weekly and then daily. As they were released, William James's books were announced in the *Débats*'s listings of recent publications, and the controversies those books engendered received significant editorial attention and commentary.

The first reference to *Les Débats* in Proust's *Correspondance* occurs in 1889. On around the May 15, signing anonymously as "un élève de philosophie" [a philosophy student], he wrote to Anatole France about an article written by Henri Chantavoine that Proust had found unjustly critical of France's *Balthasar* and which had appeared on page 3 of that day's *Journal des débats*. On February 16, 1892 and March 1, 1893, *Les Débats* reported on Dr. Adrien Proust's presentations on foreign public health questions and on cholera. The last reference to *Les Débats* in Proust's *Correspondance* is in a letter written about December 10, 1921. He writes to Daniel Halévy about an article Halévy had authored that appeared on page 3 of the *Débats* dated the eleventh (available the night before) and that also mentions another article by Halévy that had appeared on February 14, 1920. From the dates of these letters mentioning *Le Journal des débats* and from the many references to it in letters written in between, it is evident that Proust was a reader of that paper for most of his adult life.

In *À la recherche du temps perdu* Proust includes mention of the journal several times; specifically referred to five times in volume I of the 1987 Pléiade edition, it appears in conjunction with several of the novel's important themes.

The narrator mentions *Le Journal des débats politiques et littéraires* for the first time in *Du côté de chez Swann*. It is a snowy day. The narrator is certain Gilberte will not come to the Champs-Élysées to play. He sees a woman of a certain age, who is always on the avenue no matter the weather, always dressed in the same elegant dark costume, keeping an eye on her grandchildren, reading what she refers to as "mes vieux *Débats*"[171] [my good old *Débats*]. The same woman reappears a few pages later as "la vieille lectrice des *Débats*" [the elderly reader of the *Débats*], this time on a day when Gilberte does appear.[172] The woman is among the privileged circle the narrator so intently wishes to penetrate, those who know Gilberte and her family. His obsessive desire for Gilberte has stimulated his imagination; he glamorizes anyone in her social aureole. This, however, turns out to be a serious misperception that causes him an embarrassed blush, when, correcting his initial mental picture of the woman, his mother describes her own maneuvers to avoid her at "gymnastique" [exercise] class: "Mais elle est horrible [. . .] elle voulait venir me parler sous prétexte de me dire que tu étais 'trop beau pour un garçon'" [Why, she is perfectly horrible . . . she was always trying to get hold of me . . . to tell me that you were "too beautiful for a boy"].[173] The topic of equivocal sexuality has been broached. Nothing good or socially desirable can be said about this woman—or about her acquaintance with Mme. Swann.

Le Journal des débats is mentioned for the last time at the start of *À l'ombre des jeunes filles en fleurs*. Here, the narrator describes "qui était le marquis de Norpois" [the background of the marquis de Norpois]. Norpois was one of the capable aristocrats serving in foreign missions, even under radical cabinets. He was "contrôleur de la Dette, en Égypte" [held a high financial position] and was considered a statesman in the pages of *Les Débats*. The responsibility of representing France in this way added luster to his name, which the political affiliation of the appointment could not tarnish.[174]

When James's books appeared in French translation, they were publicized in the general press, including *Les Débats*. Under the heading "Quelques publications à signaler" [works worth mentioning], *Le Journal des débats politiques et littéraires* of April 22, 1910, listed *La Philosophie de l'expérience*, the French translation of *A Pluralistic Universe* published in New York and London the year before, consisting of James's Hibbert Lectures delivered at Manchester College, Oxford, in 1908 and 1909. Future commentary by J. Bourdeau was promised.[175]

Also included in the April 22, 1910 issue of the *Débats* was the three-page article submitted by Émile Boutroux entitled "Les Conférences de M Émile Boutroux en Amérique" describing his impressions of America and of Harvard and the twelve-lecture series he had delivered at the invitation of William James.[176] He gave an account of the congenial hospitality offered to him by James and his wife at their home on Irving Street and reported that James had attended every one of the lectures.

Jean Bourdeau authored a sequence of articles on pragmatism that were printed in the *Débats*, and Proust was familiar with his name. It appears on several occasions in Proust's *Correspondance*, suggesting that Proust was aware that Bourdeau wrote for the *Débats* and indicating that Proust had read at least some of Bourdeau's articles.

Proust's first reference to "J. Bourdeau" occurs in a footnote to a letter he wrote to Constantin de Brancovan on about September 20, 1899. A letter to Reynaldo Hahn written on August 1, 1907 also mentions M.

Bourdeau. A note explains that Bourdeau lived from 1848 to 1928 and was a "publiciste et philosophe" [publicist and philosopher] who published a serial ("feuilleton") in *Le Journal des débats*.[177]

More significant still in terms of timing is a letter Proust wrote to Robert Dreyfus on about the November 21, 1910, shortly after James's death. Proust comments about "savantes bêtises" [erudite stupidities] written by Bourdeau in an article on Tolstoï that had appeared in the *Débats* that day. The letter confirms that Proust was reading the *Débats* during the period when James's name was prominent in the paper.

The series on pragmatism that Bourdeau wrote for *Les Débats* was collected and reprinted with the addition of a few other essays[178] in his book *Pragmatisme et modernisme*.[179]

The book was intended to present to the young and to the curious amateur significant lines of current thinking—including an exposé of pragmatism, the new method for interpreting experience by submitting it to verification in practice. In the preface, he suggests that in the French context, always enamored of theoretical explanation, the pragmatism of Peirce and James presents a breath of fresh air and directs attention to center on what an individual feels: "soumettre les idées à l'expérience personnelle, les agir pour les connaître, les *vérifier* par les résultats pratiques"[180] [compare ideas to personal experience, use them to understand them, verify them by their practical results]. The articles definitively place James by name at the center of a topic being hotly debated in the news of the day and available in French for Proust to read.

William James, wrote Bourdeau, "a le plus contribué à répandre le pragmatisme américain"[181] [has contributed the most to spreading American pragmatism]. James's 1898 lecture to the University of California Philosophical Union was cited as reprise of Peirce's 1878 article in *Popular Science*, and there is a reference to Lalande's summary in Ribot's *Revue philosophique* of February 1906 and to the 1906 French translation. "Le pragmatiste explore ces voies contraires qu'on lui propose, constate où elles le mènent et ne se fie qu'à ce qu'il a lui-même éprouvé"[182] [The pragmatist explores the contrary paths presented, states where each leads, and only trust what he himself has experienced]. It is a philosophy based on "l'observation et l'expérience"[183] [observation and experience], corresponding to the vagaries and mutating truths of a life viewed from the individual's personal perspective, the view through the eyes of a "je."

The occasion of William James's death on August 26, 1910 was a media event in Paris that could only have brought his thought more directly to the public mind at the time Proust was thinking about and composing his novel. He was mourned privately by his family, friends, and colleagues, and publicly in many newspaper obituaries. Many of the publications Proust was familiar with ran long articles eulogizing James and describing and/or disagreeing with the major tenets of his thought. The great respect felt for him in France was demonstrated at the time of his death, wrote former student John Elof Boodin, when "all the great French papers came out in black borders."[184]

Les Débats published an obituary on September 2, acknowledging James's role in the Society for Psychical Research and mentioning the fact that he had left messages for his colleagues to compare to what he might reveal from "the great beyond."[185] Today it is difficult to determine just how seriously to take this, but clearly it was noteworthy at the time of James's death.

The tone of the obituary in *Les Débats* is straightforward, serious, and respectful, careful to fit James into a French context:

> L'Amérique vient de perdre en William James son plus grand philosophe et le monde savant de toute l'Europe regrettera sa disparition. William James s'était concilié en France particulièrement beaucoup de sympathies.[186]
>
> [In William James, America has just lost its greatest philosopher, and the educated world all over Europe will miss him. William James had developed a great many admirers in France.]

James was remembered as a member of L'Institut de France with important connections there; also indicated are his "affinités" with the ideas of Renouvier, in whose journal he had published many articles, with Émile Boutroux, who had brought him to public attention, and with Henri Bergson, by whom he had been embraced with enthusiasm. James was particularly well received in France, the article continues ("son influence a été si rapidement sentie") [his influence so rapidly felt], because his style and clarity of thought were so very compatible with that of French writers, and his subject matter accessible to nonprofessionals. His observations and vivid descriptions of consciousness and "la vie de l'esprit" [the life of the mind], combined with "les notions, les images, les sentiments [. . .] tirés de l'expérience" [the notions, images, feelings . . . drawn from experience] were often delivered in published lectures, written as if by a friendly and instructive preacher. Snippets of James's philosophical and religious thought were included in the obituary:

> Ainsi par une analyse approfondie et complètement sincère de l'expérience, William James a fait rentrer dans le champ de la sensibilité et de la pensée humaine beaucoup d'éléments essentiels que l'analyse intellectualiste avait voulu dissoudre.
>
> [Thus by his profound and completely honest analysis of experience, William James returned to the study of feeling and human thought many of the essential elements that intellectualist analysis had wished to remove.]

James's was not an unfamiliar voice in the Paris of the first decade of the twentieth century; he was recognized as belonging within ongoing debates.

On September 3, 1910, Émile Boutroux, the society's president, delivered a funeral eulogy for William James before the Académie des sciences morales et politiques.[187] The speech was subsequently published in the *Séances et travaux de l'Académie* in 1910,[188] as "Décès de M William James: Paroles de M Boutroux, Président."[189] The address is noteworthy for the stress placed on James's view of the world from inside the self, where reality is palpable for each individual, as it will be for Proust's narrator. Boutroux reviewed the highlights of James's career and the fact that he was not imprisoned by his medical training; his academic interests and pedagogical position expanded from physiology into psychology and philosophy, remaining grounded in ways the self could experience emotion, consciousness, and the religious and subliminal possibilities that might exist beyond consciousness. Even more notable is the impact Boutroux attributes to James's books:

> [S]es *Principes de Psychologie* (1890), ouvrage classique en tout pays et traduit dans toutes les langues, et ses *Variétés de l'Expérience religieuse* (1902), transition entre la psychologie et la métaphysique, peut-être actuellement le livre de philosophie le plus lu qui soit au monde.[190]

> [His *Principles of Psychology* (1890), a classic work known in every country and translated into every language, and his *Varieties of Religious Experience* (1902), a transition between psychology and metaphysics, perhaps the most widely read book of philosophy of our day.]

Boutroux eschews understatement when he alludes to the extraordinarily wide readership of James's *Variétés de l'Expérience Religieuse*—the philosophical best-seller of its day—calling it a hybrid of psychological and religious thought. Boutroux points out James's *Talks to Teachers* (1899, translated as *Paroles aux Maîtres* in 1900), *Immortalité humaine, La volonté de croire* [*sic*]. According to Boutroux, these works highlight James's fine-tuned ability to describe individual conscious experience as the actual living thing we know, depicting the sense of reality lived, of interior life unfurled that will prove to be so important in Proust's novel:

> [A]nalyser les phénomènes avec la plus grande finesse, sans pour cela détruire leur originalité concrète et leur vivante unité, James déroule devant nous la conscience elle- même [. . .]. Il nous donne la sensation de ce qu'il y a d'unique et de foncièrement réel dans la vie intérieure.[191]

> [With his fine analyses of phenomena and without destroying its concrete and living unity, James unfurls before us consciousness itself. . . . He gives us a sense of what is unique and deeply authentic in the life of the mind.]

James conveyed a fundamental sense of the centrality of feeling in human life, the importance of free will, the substantive nature of experience, and man's creative ability to affect it all, wrote Boutroux. With respect to pragmatism, James made the word and the philosophy it designated all his own, Boutroux acknowledges, and used it to signify an epistemological methodology ("sa méthode de philosopher") focusing on individual experience:

> [L]'expérience concrète et personnelle, le fait proprement dit, est le seul point de départ qu'il admette, comme le seul terme qu'il vise, et qu'il mesure strictement la valeur des abstractions à leur rapport avec l'expérience ainsi entendue. Une idée vraie est une méthode d'action qui réussit. Vérité est fonction de réalité.[192]
>
> [Concrete personal experience as felt is the only basis he allows and against which he measures all abstractions. A true idea is a method of action that succeeds. Truth is a function of reality.]

On September 15, 1910, Michel Salomon, who wrote columns that appeared in *La Gazette de France, Le Correspondant, Le Journal de Genève*, and in *Le Journal des débats*, dedicated a short analysis to William James. Summarizing his most celebrated books, Salomon wrote that James's death was a loss for everyone, "en tous pays, l'élite pensant"[193] [in all corners of the intellectual world].

Salomon does not hesitate to criticize James—as one would feel comfortable doing for one of one's own cultural masters—for his pragmatic approach to religion, appreciating nonetheless James's view of the religious psychology of the individual. Salomon points out several images James uses that also appear in Proust's fiction: the water imagery in James's description of the stream of consciousness, the flow of the river around containers that will echo remarkably in Proust's image of crystal beakers in the Vivonne. He compares James's idea of the activity of the subliminal consciousness to bubbles rising through water to the surface of "l'océan ténébreux du moi subliminal"[194] [the shadowy sea of the subliminal self]—that we see in Proust's narrator's memories.

Salomon mentions James's notion that the world is not "un vase clos"[195] [a sealed vessel], but rather a seemingly contradictory "agrégat de réalités"[196] [aggregate of realities] that we will see in the facets of "les jeunes filles" [the young girls] and in Proust's more inclusive use of the "vase" image. James valued the tumultuous and indefinite in human conscious life, the very aspects that stimulate yet make Proust's narrator so anxious when faced with uncertainty and misperception. James examines the thinking, feeling, breathing, conscious individual, wrote Salomon, highlighting elements in James's writing that are very similar to Proust's fiction.

A two-part article entitled "Un dernier mot sur le pragmatisme" [A Last Word on Pragmatism] written by J. Bourdeau appeared in *Le Journal des débats politiques et littéraires* on September 30, 1910 and November 4, 1910.

Here we find a negative critique: M. Mentré's nationalistic criticism of an imported philosophy that ran counter to traditional French rationalism. Perhaps adequate for measuring the effectiveness of religious dogma or the productiveness of machinery, such Anglo-American ideas spun from utilitarianism deserve little place in French thought. The product of the race that originated it, pragmatism is inappropriate to the native elegance and refinement of the French. The energy and action orientation are seen as attractive; however, it is a can-do philosophy that will help break down the limitations of constraining habits, a route to progress, a self-help method for energizing "la volonté"[197] [the will], a system stemming from "temperament," an expression of personality. As such, we find, it can serve as profound discovery for a writer searching for a method of creating a fictional reality in which the "will" to make the fiction happen is key and the temperament that gets in the way drives the action.

As Bourdeau described it, pragmatism is a method for pursuit of truth mediating between the rationalist/idealist desire for a pre-existing supraterrestrial eternal system of [essential] truth and a wild, snarling empirical tangle of fact. Its unique benefit is not to select truth but to assist the evaluations necessary to determine truth; actual experience is the ultimate arbiter.

Like Salomon, Bourdeau comments on James's image of the crystal beaker in flowing water. Floating and tumbling in the current, truth gives it shape, buoyancy, and content. But if psychological factors trump logic in a world of relativity, he asks, what exactly does truth mean if subject to constant modification? This was a question with which Proust's narrator would wrestle. According to James, wrote Bourdeau, personal experience "probant"—asking questions—reveals more primary truth than scientific experiment.[198] Similarly, Proust's narrator will seek clues like an alchemist or spy and will read more by interpretation than in what seems to be in evidence. Truth is more in the affect, the impression, than in the rational. Proust's narrator will live in a post-Jamesian pragmatic world, where, according to Bourdeau's exposition of James's thought, as prisoners of our own temperament, we can never see more than a part of the picture and therefore cannot judge facts and events objectively.

James's pragmatism, as diffused in the press thanks perhaps in part to these articles, seems to prove prophetic for Proust: the development of his narrator's life history with its view from his personal perspective, the effort to attain the essential meaning of things and to find the truth behind events and behavior and express it in a personal philosophy and in a seemingly autobiographical manner, his search for his creative potential and individual voice, the "moi véritable du poète"[199] [true self of the poet] infused with "l'air du temps" [spirit of the times] circulating around him would absorb the author's attention thenceforth. As Bourdeau wrote:

> Chacun de nous, qu'il s'en doute ou non, se fait une philosophie, une conception de l'univers, [. . .] et cette réponse lui est dictée par sa façon de réagir contre la poussée et la pression du monde qui l'environne. Mais la source de notre philosophie doit être cherchée non dans notre intelligence, mais dans notre caractère, dans notre tempérament, dans l'inconscient ou, comme on dit aujourd'hui, dans le subconscient. On peut affirmer que toute philosophie sincère est l'expression d'un tempérament personnel, que les philosophes de profession, en élaborant leurs systèmes, ne font qu'écrire leurs mémoires.[200]
>
> [Each of us, whether he suspects it or not, has a personal philosophy, a conception of the universe . . . and this is dictated by his own reaction to the demands and pressures of the world around him. But the source of our individual philosophy should be sought not in our intelligence, but in our character, in our temperament, in the unconscious or, as it is called nowadays, the subconscious. All sincere philosophy is the expression of a personal temperament, and professional philosophers, in creating their systems, are only writing their memoirs.]

James was the quintessential timeless and transnational practitioner of cultural sharing. He sought answers for his most perplexing philosophical questions in common with the thought of his European counterparts. His argumentation flourished when he could joust with a contrasting opinion or when he seemed to swallow whole a creatively enlightened explanation. And Europe shared equally in the exchange, bringing James into sharp view in Proust's own milieu.

BERGSON WRITES THE PREFACE TO THE 1911 FRENCH TRANSLATION OF *PRAGMATISM*

Because pragmatism is the ostensible topic bringing James into Proust's *Correspondance,* Henri Bergson's preface is significant for any informative role it might have played.[201]

On June 21, 1911, Bergson wrote a letter to James's widow, Alice, thanking her for sending him *Some Problems of Philosophy* and indicating that in preparation for writing his preface to the French translation of *Pragmatism* he had reread James's recent works. He did so, he wrote, with great pleasure. (On June 14, 1912 he wrote to her again to thank her for sending *Essays in Radical Empiricism*. These, he says, he had read when they appeared periodical form;[202] the collection in a single volume, however, brought synergies to understanding the whole.[203])

This attitude permeates his enthusiastic preface to *Pragmatism*. Bergson justified his willingness to write a preface for the French translation[204] in part to counter rampant misinterpretation of a book he called "la clarté même."[205] He declares the work "fascinating," "delightful," an "excellent translation" on a topic already familiar to the public because of the extensive critical attention and commentary it had received in the press. It is hard not to read into his reaction a certain wistfulness about the enthusiasm with which James had embraced him; a sense of reciprocal warmth permeates the Préface. He must have felt some obligation to counter negative criticism that he felt diminished and clouded James's memory.[206] Of course, he was also willingly associating himself with a book already proven to garner a great deal of attention.

He praises James's radical empiricist vision of an "indefinite" reality as a rich variety of experiential flow in which relations signify, as do feelings, perceptions, and religious experience:[207]

> We are absolutely sure only of what experience gives us; but we should accept experience wholly, and our feelings are a part of it by the same right as our perceptions, consequently by the same right as "things." In the eyes of William James, the whole man counts.[208]

To fully express the meaning of the English word, he quotes Boutroux:

> In his study of William James (*Revue de métaphysique et de morale*, November 1910) M. Emile Boutroux has brought out the quite unique meaning of the English verb *to experience*, "which means, not coldly to observe a thing happening outside us, but to undergo, to feel within oneself, to live oneself this or that manner of being."[209]

James's idea of pragmatism incorporates the same mechanism that drives "moments privilégiés" and the intense emotional journey they initiate.[210] In parallel with Proust's later use, they invigorate perception and alter perspective.

Although Bergson seems to nudge James's conception of an idea that works and therefore is deemed true, that is substantiated by subsequent events, toward his own conception of the forward movement of a dynamic force field or "élan vital," we find that aspects of James's original vision of Pragmatism exploited by Proust's narrator are closer in terms and conception to their original Jamesian roots. James had asked, "What would be different if something is true or if it prove false," and stated, "Truth *happens* to an idea. It *becomes* true, is *made* true by events."[211] Bergson's terms of interpretation, however, include his own ideas of "invention" and related technological metaphors such as the introduction of the phonograph, an idea taken up in E. Bizub's recent article noted above. Like James, Proust's narrator will search for truth by testing his interpretations against new information as it becomes available and then reformulating them.

Bergson reiterates James's notions that the hypotheses, assumptions, and the structures of language and manners of expression persist through time.[212] Proust's narrator will evince similar interest in etymology, archaisms, and the fads and linguistic tics typical of particular social groups, one of Proust's own persistent personal interests since youth.

At times, Bergson seems to be using James as a jumping off point to further aspects of his own philosophical positions. And despite enthusiasm, he does maintain a slightly lofty posture and certain "reservations."[213] He ends, as suggested in his letter to Alice James, unable to avoid a touch of personal feeling for James, with a rousing finale and a nod to James's interest in the survival of the soul after death, the possibility of receiving a post mortem communication.

Finally, an odd coincidence joins together James, Proust, and Bergson. In 1913, Bernard Grasset, through the influence of René Blum, agreed to publish *Du côté de chez Swann* at Proust's own expense. The same year, he also published a book of critical essays by René Gillouin.[214] Included among them was an essay on William James. Gillouin's critical essay on James was the only one in that volume not previously published as a journal article. It was a timely addition concentrating primarily on James as a religious philosopher and pragmatist. This focus is not hard to understand, as it was the primary way James had been remembered in the press, and his fairly recent death had been a major press event. Also included among the six pieces in Gillouin's book was an essay on Anna de Noailles, poet and friend of Proust, and pieces on Colette Willy (an editor at *Le Temps* when Proust later sent that revue an excerpt on Mme. Villeparisis), Barrès, Charles Demange, and Moréas.

Previously, Gillouin had written three books on Bergson's philosophy, one of which was also published by Grasset, and later, in 1928, well after Proust's death, he wrote the introduction for the publication of Proust's letters to Mme. Scheikévitch.[215] Had Proust seen this book, it would have constituted yet another opportunity for contact with James's ideas. Although inconclusive in determining a Proust-James relation, the confluence of publisher Grasset with Gillouin, James, Noailles, Bergson, and Proust demonstrates, at the least, the degree to which James was integrated into the literary culture of the moment.

NOTES

1. Proust, *Corr.*, XIX, *90*, 207. Cited by Paul Morand in "Notes," *Hommage à Marcel Proust, La Nouvelle Revue Française* XX, 10.112 (janvier 1923): 91–95, 94.
2. Gao Xingjian, *the case for literature* [*sic*], trans. Mabel Lee (New Haven: Yale University Press, 2006), 36.
3. Compagnon, *Troisième*, 54.
4. Germaine de Staël-Holstein, *De la littérature considérée dans ses rapports avec les institutions sociales*. 2 vols. (Paris: Maradan, 1800).

5. See Antoine Compagnon, *Proust entre deux siècles* (Paris: Éditions du Seuil, 1989), 19.

6. William James, "Does Consciousness Exist?" *Essays in Radical Empiricism* (New York: Longmans, Green, and Co., 1912), 5. Reprinted from the *Journal of Philosophy, Psychology, and Scientific Methods* 1.18 (September 1904).

7. Proust, letter to Robert de Flers, written toward the end of the first week of November 1913: "j'y ai mis toute ma pensée, tout mon coeur, ma vie même" (*Corr.*, XII, *135*, 299) ["I put into it all my thought, all my heart, even my life"].

8. Marcel Proust, *Le Carnet de 1908*, Cahiers Marcel Proust 8, éd. Philip Kolb (Paris: Éditions Gallimard, 1976), 101.

9. Proust, *Le Carnet de 1908*, 102.

10. William James, "La Notion de Conscience," first presented (in French) at the Fifth International Congress of Psychology, Rome, April 30, 1905, *Archives de Psychologie* V.17 (June 1905): 1–12, repr. *Essays in Radical Empiricism* (New York: Longmans, Green, and Co., 1912), 206–233, 214 (hereafter *ERE*).

11. William James, "The Notion of Consciousness," *Essays in Radical Empiricism*, ed. Ralph Barton Perry, repr. with trans. Stanley Appelbaum (Mineola, NY: Dover Publications, Inc., 2003), 113.

12. Horace M. Kallen, *The Philosophy of William James* (New York: The Modern Library, 1953), 3, 4.

13. Kallen, 4.

14. Virginia Woolf, letter to Roger Fry, *The Letters of Virginia Woolf*, ed. Nigel Nicolson and Joann Trautmann, 2 vols. (New York: Harcourt Brace Jovanovich, 1975–1980), 2, 525.

15. Kallen, 8.

16. Dorrit Cohn, *Transparent Minds* (Princeton: Princeton University Press, 1978), 78–80.

17. William James, *The Principles of Psychology*, 2 vols. (Cambridge, MA and London: Harvard University Press, 1981) I, 233.

18. I rely upon Ralph Barton Perry, *The Thought and Character of William James*, 2 vols. (Boston: Little, Brown, and Company, 1935), and *The Thought and Character of William James: Briefer Version* (Boston: Harvard University Press, 1948). Both made extensive use of James's published correspondence in William James, *The Letters of William James*, ed. by his son Henry James, 2 vols. (Boston: The Atlantic Monthly Press, 1920), as well as unpublished letters and James's published writings. Newer biographies by Robert D. Richardson and Linda Simon will be indicated where used.

19. See Kallen, 15.

20. The effect on their sister, Alice, has been documented by Jean Strouse, *Alice James: A Biography* (Boston: Houghton Mifflin, 1980; repr. Harvard University Press, 1999).

21. Perry, *Thought/Character*, I, 205.

22. Kallen, 33.

23. Perry, *Thought/Character*, I, 204.

24. Perry, *Thought/Character*, I, 205.

25. Letter of August 16, 1902, published by A. Ménard, *Analyse et critique des "Principes de la psychologie" de William James* (Paris: Alcan, 1911), 5, note, cited in Perry, *Thought/Character*, I, 228, note 2.

26. Unsigned review by William James of *Unüberwindliche Mächte*, by Herman Grimm, *Nation* 5 (1867): 432–433.

27. Unsigned reviews by William James of *Du Sommeil et des États analogues, considérés surtout au point de vue de l'action du Moral sur le Physique*, by A. A. Liébault, *Nation* 7 (1868): 50–52, and of *Rapport sur le Progrès et la Marche de la Physiologie générale en France*, by Claude Bernard, *North American Review* 107 (1868): 322–328.

28. Perry, *Thought/Character*, I, 285.

29. Marcel Proust, *Jean Santeuil* (Paris: Éditions Gallimard [Bibliothèque de la Pléiade], 1971), 314.

30. William James, "What is an Emotion?" *Mind* XXXIV.9 (1884): 188–205.
31. William James, *The Principles of Psychology*, 2 vols. (New York: Holt, 1890).
32. William C. Carter, *Marcel Proust: A Life* (New Haven: Yale University Press, 2000), 283.
33. John Ruskin, *La Bible d'Amiens*, tras. M. Proust (Paris: Mercure de France, 1904).
34. William James, *The Varieties of Religious Experience* (New York: Longmans, Green and Co., 1902). Excerpted in *Annales de Philosophie Chrétienne*, 1903, *Revue de Philosophie*, 1905, trans. F. Abauzit, préface Émile Boutroux, as *L'Expérience religieuse: Essai de Psychologie descriptive* (Paris: Alcan, 1905). William James, *Pragmatism: A New Name for Some Old Ways of Thinking* (New York: Longmans, Green and Co., 1907). William James, *Psychology: Briefer Course* (New York: Holt, 1892; repr. Cambridge: Harvard University Press, 1984), trans. E. Baudin and G. Bertier (Paris: M. Rivière, 1909). All mentions of *Briefer Course* in the text refer to this 1984 edition.
35. While Proust jotted notes for his novel and wrote snatches of what would become the draft *Contre Sainte-Beuve* in 1907–1908, the conception and execution of the novel in the form it would take in *À la recherche du temps perdu* dates from 1909: "Mais comme Sainte-Beuve ne devait figurer que dans la conclusion, on comprend que, si Proust reprend son projet au printemps ou à l'été 1909 pour écrire de manière continue le début de ce qui sera *À la recherche du temps perdu*, l'essai aura le temps de se disperser, de se volatiliser. Sainte-Beuve aura servi de repoussoir, de ce médiateur momentané dont Proust a toujours eu besoin, quitte à le combattre, puis à l'effacer, comme Ruskin a été effacé. . . ." Jean-Yves Tadié, *Marcel Proust: Biographie* (Paris: Éditions Gallimard, 1996) 626. [This implies a substantive change.]
36. Perry, *Thought/Character*, II, 189.
37. Eliza Jane Reilly, "Concrete Possibilities: William James and the European Avant-Garde," *Streams of William James*, 2.3 (Fall 2000): 22. http://williamjamesstudies.org/newsletter/Streams_2.3.pdf.
38. Reilly, 23.
39. Certain of the *Mind* articles introducing James's thinking on art, his terminology for the stream of consciousness, his theory of emotion, and his philosophy of pragmatism invite comparison with *À la recherche du temps perdu*. See William James, "The Sentiment of Rationality," *Mind* 4 (1879): 317–346, trans. C. Renouvier, *Critique Philosophique* 8.2 (1879): 72–89, 113–118, 129–138, repr. *Essays in Philosophy* (Cambridge: Harvard University Press, 1978), 32–64. William James, "On Some Omissions of Introspective Psychology," *Mind* 9 (1884): 1– 26. William James, "On the Function of Cognition," *Mind* 10 (1885): 27–44, repr. *The Meaning of Truth* (New York: Longmans, Green & Co., 1909), repr. *Pragmatism and The Meaning of Truth* (Cambridge: Harvard University Press, 1978), [13]179–[32]198.
40. Ignas Skrupskelis, "William James," *American National Biography*, ed. John Garraty and Mark C. Carnes, vol. 11 (New York: Oxford University Press, 1999), 843.
41. Ralph Barton Perry, "William James," *Dictionary of American Biography*, ed. Dumas Malone, vol. IX (New York: Charles Scribner's Sons, 1932), 593.
42. Léon Marillier, *Revue Philosophique* XXXIV (1892): 449–470 and 603–627; XXXV (1893): 1–32 and 145–183. Cited in Théodore Flournoy, *The Philosophy of William James*, trans. Edwin B. Holt and William James Jr. (New York: Henry Holt & Co., 1917), 217.
43. Reilly, 24. See also Emile Durkheim, *Pragmatism and Sociology*, trans. J. C. Whitehouse, ed. John B. Allcock, preface by Armand Cuvillier (Cambridge: Cambridge University Press, 1983), cited by Reilly, 24, note 19.
44. Reilly, 23.
45. Théodore Flournoy, Letter to William James, 16 March 1907, William James and Théodore Flournoy, *The Letters of William James and Théodore Flournoy*, ed. Robert C. LeClair (Madison: The University of Wisconsin Press, 1966), 185.
46. William James, *A Pluralistic Universe* (New York: Longmans, Green & Co., 1909), trans. Le Brun and Paris, *La Philosophie de l'Expérience* (Paris: Flammarion, 1910).
47. George Santayana, *Character and Opinion in the United States* (New York: Scribner's, 1920), 94. Quoted in Reilly, 23.

48. William James, *Essais d'empirisme radical [1912]*, trans. et préface Mathias Girel et Guillaume Garreta (Marseille: Agone, 2005), 236 (Ouvrage traduit avec l'aide du C.N.L.), rééd. (Paris: Flammarion, Collection Champs, 2007). David Lapoujade, *William James: Empirisme et pragmatisme* (PUF, 1997; réed. Vrin, Les Empêcheurs de penser en rond, 2007).

49. Henri Bergson, *Correspondances*, éd. André Robinet (Paris: Presses Universitaires de France, 2002).

50. James, *Letters*, I, 138.

51. Perry, *Briefer Version*, 120.

52. Charles Renouvier, *Traité de psychologie rationelle*, 2nd essay of the *Essais de critique générale*, 1859. Cited in Perry, *Thought/Character*, I, 323.

53. James, *Letters*, I, 147, and Kallen, *Philosophy*, 28.

54. Ralph Barton Perry, *Annotated Bibliography of the Writings of William James* (New York: Longmans, Green and Co., 1920), 8.

55. John B. Allcock, notes in Durkheim, *Pragm. and Soc.*, 309, note 11. Citing Terry Clark's comments regarding "the general openness of French intellectual life to foreign ideas during this period," taken from *Gabriel Tarde on Communication and Social Influence* (Chicago: University of Chicago Press, 1969), 19ff.

56. Notable examples follow: "Quelques Considérations sur la méthode subjective" (William James, "Quelques Considérations sur la méthode subjective," *Critique Philosophique* 6.2 (1878): 407–413), the first of his articles to appear there. Others include "Brute and Human Intellect" (William James, "Brute and Human Intellect," *Journal of Speculative Philosophy* 12 (1878): 236–276; *Critique Philosophique* 8.1 (1879): 369–376, 394–397; *Critique Philosophique* 8.2 (1879): 17–26, 41–48). Repr. *Essays in Psychology* (Cambridge: Harvard University Press, 1983), "The Sentiment of Rationality," "Great Men, Great Thoughts and Their Environment" (William James, "Great Men, Great Thoughts and Their Environment," *Critique Philosophique* 9.2 (1881): 396–400, 407–415, *Critique Philosophique* 10.1 (1881): 1–14); "The Feeling of Effort" (William James, "The Feeling of Effort," *Anniversary Memoirs of the Boston Society of Natural History* (1880): 32pp, trans. *Critique Philosophique* 9.2 (1880): 123–128, 129– 135, 145–148, 200–208, 220–224, 225–231, 289–291); "Reflex Action and Theism" (William James, "Reflex Action and Theism," *Critique Philosophique* 10.2 (1882): 385–391, 401–410, *Critique Philosophique* 11.1 (1882): 5–13); "Rationality, Activity and Faith" (William James, "Rationality, Activity and Faith," *The Princeton Review* 2 (1882): 58– 86, trans. *Critique Philosophique* 11.2 (1882): 129–140, 161–166); "The Dilemma of Determinism" (William James, "The Dilemma of Determinism," *Critique Philosophique* 13.2 (1884): 273–280, 305–312; *Critique Philosophique* 13.2 (1885): 353–362); "What the Will Effects" (William James, "What the Will Effects," *Critique Philosophique* n.s. 4.1 (1888): 401–420); and "Réponse de M. W. James aux Remarques de M. Renouvier sur sa théorie de la volonté" (William James, "Réponse de M. W. James aux Remarques de M. Renouvier sur sa théorie de la volonté," *Critique Philosophique* n.s. 4.2 (1888): 401–404).

57. Allcock in Durkheim, xxvi.

58. William James, *Some Problems of Philosophy* (New York: Longmans, Green & Co., 1911). This work was published posthumously.

59. William James, "Remarks on Spencer's Definition of Mind as Correspondence," *Journal of Speculative Philosophy* 12.1 (1878): 1–18. "Are We Automata?" *Mind* 4.13 (January 1879): 1–22. "The Spatial Quale," *Journal of Speculative Philosophy* 13 (1879): 64–87; "On Some Omissions of Introspective Psychology" and "What is an Emotion?"

60. Perry, *Briefer Version*, 314, quoting W. J. to F. C. S Schiller, April 7, 1906.

61. "This morning I went to the meeting-place of the Congress to inscribe myself definitely, and when I gave my name, the lady who was taking them almost fainted, saying that all Italy loved me [. . .]. Strange to be told that *my* name was attracting many of the young professors to the Congress!" (William James, *Letters*, April 4, 1905, 225, 226).

62. John J. McDermott, introduction, *Essays in Radical Empiricism*, by William James, (Cambridge: Harvard University Press, 1976), xiii.

63. Robert D. Richardson, *William James: In the Maelstrom of American Modernism* (Boston: Houghton Mifflin Company, 2006), 348.
64. William James, *Memories and Studies* (New York: Longmans, Green & Co., 1911), cited in Perry, *Thought/Character*, II, 172.
65. A bibliographical summary of la Querelle de l'Hystérie is found at http://pierre-henri.castel.free.fr/QH18931914.htm.
66. Included among the members, according to the 1889–1890 issue of the *Revue de l'Hypnotisme expérimental et thérapeutique*, were MM. Franck, Paul Janet, Marion, Ribot, Sully-Prudhomme, Taine, Henri Joly, Rabier, Bertrand, and others.
67. "Bulletin: Les Congrès Scientifiques Internationaux," *Revue de l'Hypnotisme expérimental et thérapeutique* (1889–1890): 65.
68. Ian Hacking, *Mad Travelers: Reflections on the Reality of Transient Mental Illnesses* (Charlottesville: University Press of Virginia, 1998), 40.
69. Adrien Proust et G. Ballet, *L'Hygiène du neurasthénique*. (Bibliothèque d'hygiène thérapeutique Dirigé par le professeur Proust) (Paris: Éd. Masson et Cie. [Libraires de l'Académie de Médecine], 1897).
70. Henri F. Ellenberger, *The Discovery of the Unconscious: The History and Evolution of Dynamic Psychiatry* (New York: Basic Books, Inc., 1970), 242–243, 295, 301. (Ellenberger notes that toward the end of the nineteenth century, it was thought that masturbation would lead to neurasthenia and that this practice, as well as other sexual deviations, was responsible for the onset of asthma, perhaps accounting for Adrien Proust's interest in the subject.)
71. Premier Congrès International de Psychologie Physiologique, Premier Session, Paris, 1890. *Compte rendu présenté par la Société de psychologie physiologique de Paris.* (Paris: Bureau des Revues, 1890; repr. Nedeln/Liechtenstein: Kraus-Thomson Org. Ltd., 1974).
72. The Salpêtrière school viewed hypnotism as a pathological condition, while the Nancy adherents viewed hypnotism merely as suggestion and induced sleep.
73. *Revue de l'Hypnotisme expérimental et thérapeutique* (1889–1890): 66.
74. M. le Professeur [A.] Proust, Médecin de l'Hôtel-Dieu de Paris, "Automatisme ambulatoire chez un hystérique," *Revue de l'Hypnotisme expérimental et thérapeutique* (1889–1890): 267–269.
75. Adrien Proust, "Automatisme ambulatoire chez un hystérique," *Séances et travaux de l'Académie des sciences morales et politiques (France)* 133.2 (1890): 779–787.
76. Adrien Proust, "Automatisme ambulatoire chez un hystérique," *Bulletin Médical* IV (1890) I: 107–108.
77. Dr. Robert Le Masle, *Le Professeur Adrien Proust* (Paris: Lipschutz, 1935), 34.
78. William James, "The Congress of Physiological Psychology at Paris," *Mind* 14 (October 1889): 614–615.
79. George Beard, *A Practical Treatise on Nervous Exhaustion, Its Causes, Symptoms and Sequences* (New York, 1880), cited in A. Proust, *Neurasth*, Préface, vii. [See also Michael Murphy, *Proust and America* (Liverpool University Press, 2007), 14, citing George Beard, *Neurasthenia or Nervous Exhaustion*, 1869, and *Sexual Neurasthenia (Nervous Exhaustion,: Its Hygiene, Causes, Symptoms and Treatment*), 1895].
80. Weber, *Boston Medical Journal*, 1888. A. Proust, *L'hygiène du neurasthénique*, 122.
81. See a brief summary at http://expositions.bnf.fr/proust/grand/30.htm, which includes passages from Adrien Proust's book indicating that the neurasthenic is hypersensitive to his internal states and emotions, suffers vague and discomforting "impressions," poor memory, and attention. Hypnotism was sometimes employed as a cure, leaving the patient simultaneously awake and asleep.
82. See Edward Bizub, *Proust et le moi divisé: La Recherche: creuset de la psychologie expérimentale (1874–1914)* (Genève: Droz, 2006), 24.
83. Ellenberger cites *RTP* (Gallimard, 1961), III, 716. See Ellenberger, 167–168, notes 166 and 167, 180.
84. Ellenberger, 134.
85. Ellenberger, 262.

86. Perry, *Thought/Character*, II, 123, and note 19.
87. Perry, *Thought/Character*, II, 121.
88. Perry, *Thought/Character*, II, 361.
89. James, *Letters*, II, 314.
90. Henri Bonnet, *Alphonse Darlu* (Paris: A.G. Nizet, 1961), 77.
91. Émile Boutroux, " William James et l'éxpérience religieuse," *Revue de Métaphysique et de Morale* XVI (1908).
92. Émile Boutroux, *Science et religion dans la philosophie contemporaine* (Paris: Flammarion, 1908).
93. Daniel Penzac, *Le Docteur Proust: Père méconnu, précurseur oublié* (Paris: L'Harmattan, 2003), 202.
94. William James, "A Great French Philosopher at Harvard," *Nation* 90 (1910): 312–314.
95. Perry, *Thought/Character*, II, 568.
96. Émile Boutroux, "Les Conférences de M Émile Boutroux en Amérique," *Les Débats politiques et littéraires* (22 avril 1910). See James and Flournoy, *Letters of James and Flournoy*, 231.
97. Perry, *Thought/Character*, II, 569.
98. Émile Boutroux, *William James* trans. from the 2nd ed. by Archibald and Barbara Henderson (New York: Longmans, Green, & Co., 1912), 10–11, note 1.
99. *Corr.*, I, *21*, 137.
100. *Corr.*, 138 note 5. The editor of Proust's *Correspondance* has taken the quote from *Album Proust, Iconographie réunie et commentée par Pierre Clarac et André Ferré* (Paris: Gallimard, 1965), 121–122. See also, Jean-Yves Tadié, *Marcel Proust*, trans. Euan Cameron (New York: Viking, 2000), 205, and Proust, *CSB*, 337.
101. *Corr.*, I, *22*, 139; III, *221*, 384, 388; IV, *129*, 234; IV, *129*, 234; VIII, *2*, 26, *73*, 140, 215, 219; IX, *70*, 138; X, *86*, 183; XVII, *83*, 215, 219; XVIII, *100*, 229; XIX, xiii, 24, *105*, 239, *192*, 397; XX, 29; XXI, *145*, 207. *Index Général de la Correspondance de Marcel Proust*, éd. Kayuyoshí Yoshikawa (Presses de l'Université de Kyoto, 1998) 51.
102. *RTP*, III, 322.
103. William James, *Pragmatism; ett nytt namn för nagra gamla tankegangar. Allmänfattliga föreläsningar över filosofi av William James.* Till svenska av Algot Ruhe (Stockholm: A. Bonnier, 1916).
104. *RTP*, III, 1,557, note 1. Henri Bergson, *Le Rêve*, Conférence faite en 1901 à l'Institut général Psychologique, *Bulletin de l'Institut psycholog. intern.* 1.3 (May 1901): 103–122, reviewed by A. Binet, *L'année psychologique* 8.8 (1901): 518–519, later published in *L'énergie spirituelle* (Paris: Alcan, 1919).
105. *RTP*, III, 1,525, note 3. See also André Cresson, *Bergson: Sa vie, son oeuvre* (Paris: Presses Universitaires de France, 1961).
106. Allcock in Durkheim, xxvii, note 27. In support of this term, Allcock cites Terry Clark, *Gabriel Tarde*, and H. Stuart Hughes, *Consciousness and Society: The Reorientation of European Social Thought, 1890–1930* (London: McGibbon & Kee, 1967), 113ff.
107. *Corr.*, I, *65*, 190, note 2. See also Fernand Gregh, *L'Âge d'Or* (Paris: B. Grasset, 1948), 154–155 and 169–170.
108. *Corr.*, I, *280*, 431.
109. *Corr.*, II, *289*, 462, note 2.
110. *Corr.*, IV, *67*, 128–129, note 1.
111. *Corr.*, VIII, *51*, 106–107.
112. *Corr.*, VIII, *51*, 106.
113. *Corr.*, XIII, *8*, 39–41, and notes 16 and 17.
114. The interview is included in part in *Essais et articles*. Proust, *Essais et articles*, 557–559. Note 2 on page 557 describes the relation between the Bois article in *Le Temps* and Proust's authorship, while a further explanatory note (936 note 1) cites the letter to Bibesco written in November 1912 (published first in *Lettres à Bibesco*, préface Thierry Maulnier [Lausanne: La Guilde du Livre, 1949], 174 sq.) and also a refutation by Proust in a letter to René Blum written on November 16, 1913. A fuller version appears in

Philip Kolb's 1971 edition of Cahiers Marcel Proust 3, *Textes retrouvés*. Élie-Joseph Bois, "Variétés littéraires: *À la recherche du temps perdu* (1913)," *Le Temps* (novembre 1913). repr. Cahiers Marcel Proust 3: *Textes retrouvés*. éd. Philip Kolb (Paris: Éditions Gallimard, 1971), 285–291, 289.

115. "Swann expliqué par Proust," *Essais et articles*, 558.

116. Charles Blondel, *La Psychographie de Marcel Proust* (Paris: J. Vrin, 1932).

117. Joyce N. Megay, *Bergson and Proust: Essai de mise au point de la question de l'influence de Bergson sur Proust* (Paris: Librairie Philosophique J. Vrin, 1976).

118. In 1889 Bergson published what had originally been his doctoral dissertation as *Essai sur les données immédiates de la conscience* (Paris: F. Alcan, 1889).

119. Henri Bergson, *Matière et mémoire: Essai sur la relation du corps à l'esprit* (1896; Paris: Librairie Félix Alcan, 1913), 102, note 5. It is to be noted that all footnotes in the body of the text date from 1896. Footnotes in the avant-propos refer to the original publication in 1896 and include those written after that date and before 1913.

120. See also a letter from H. Bergson to Fl. Delattre, 24 août 1923, *Correspondances* (Année 1923), éd. André Robinet (Paris: Presses Universitaires de France, 2002), 1,052, in which Bergson stresses the possibility of confusing two very different conceptions.

121. Henri Bergson, "Réponse à M. Rageot," *Revue philosophique de la France et de l'Étranger* 60.2 (August 1905): 229–230. Criticism by Monsieur Rageot appears in G. Rageot, "5th International Congress of Psychology," *Revue Philosophique de la France et de l'Étranger* 60.1 (1905): 84–85. For a more complete discussion of the relations between James and Bergson and a close comparison of their philosophies, see Perry, *Thought/Character*, II, 599–636, and *Briefer Version*, and Horace M. Kallen, *William James and Henri Bergson* (Chicago: The University of Chicago Press, 1914), repr. Horace Kallen, *William James and Henri Bergson: A Study in Contrasting Theories of Life* (Chicago: The University of Chicago Press, 1980).

122. André Lalande, "Philosophy in France (1905)," *Philosophical Review* 15.3 (May 1906): 241–266, 241–242.

123. The complete letter appears in Perry, *Thought/Character*, II, 606–608. Extracts of this letter appear in Henri Bergson, *Correspondance*, 80.

124. Bergson, *Correspondance* 2 vols. 80. These included *The Principles of Psychology* (London: Macmillan, 1891), *The Will to Believe and Other Essays in Popular Philosophy* (New York: Longmans, 1897), *The Varieties of Religious Experience*. It is also likely that he had copies of "What is an Emotion?" *Mind* XXXIV.9 (1884): 188–205; "The Perception of Time," *The Journal of Speculative Philosophy* XX (1886): 374–407; *Human Immortality: Two Supposed Objections to the Doctrine* (Boston: Miffin [*sic*], 1898); "Personal Idealism," *Mind* 12 (1903): 93–97.

125. Perry, *Thought/Character*, II, 610.

126. Perry, *Thought/Character*, II, 614.

127. William James, "The Will to Believe," *New World* 5 (1896): 327–347, repr. *The Will to Believe and Other Essays in Popular Philosophy*.

128. William James, *Talks to Teachers on Psychology; and to Students on Some of Life's Ideals* (New York: Holt, 1899), trans. Pidoux (Paris: Alcan, 1900 and 1907).

129. William James, "Philosophical Conceptions and Practical Results," *University of California Chronicle* (1898): 24pp., trans. *Revue de Philosophie* 8 (1906): 463–484.

130. Henri Bergson, *L'Évolution créatrice* (Paris: F. Alcan, 1907).

131. Perry, *Thought/Character*, II, 618–621, repr. from *Letters*, II, 290–294.

132. Perry, *Thought/Character*, II, 621.

133. This was printed the following year in *Hibbert Journal* 7 (1909): 562–577, and appears abridged and altered as "Bergson and his Critique of Intellectualism," *A Pluralistic Universe: Hibbert Lectures to Manchester College on the Present Situation in Philosophy* (New York: Longmans, Green & Co., 1909), 223–273.

134. James, *Pluralistic*, 239.

135. Allcock in Durkheim, xxviii.

136. Bergson, *Corr.*, Année 1911, 416.

137. Floris Delattre et Maurice Le Breton, eds., *William James: extraits de sa correspondance* (Paris: Payot, 1924).
138. Bergson, *Corr.*, Année 1940, 1658–1659.
139. See Appendix for the full text of two letters referring to James found in Proust's published correspondence.
140. Allcock in Durkheim, xxix.
141. Allcock in Durkheim, xxviii.
142. Marcel Proust, *Le Carnet de 1908*, [Cahiers Marcel Proust 8], éd. Philip Kolb (Paris: Éditions Gallimard, 1976) 101.
143. William James, "A Suggestion about Mysticism," *Journal of Philosophy, Psychology, and Scientific Methods* 7 (1910): 85–92.
144. *Le Carnet de 1908*, 138, note 37.
145. Carter, 402–403.
146. Julien Bogousslavsky and Olivier Walusinski, "Marcel Proust and Paul Sollier: The Involuntary Memory Connection," *Schweizer Archiv für Neurologie und Psychiatrie* (submitted), http://www.baillement.com/lettres/sollier_english.pdf.
147. Dr. Paul Sollier, *Le Mécanisme des émotions* (Paris: Félix Alcan, 1905).
148. Dr. Paul Sollier, *Essai critique et théorique sur l'Association en psychologie* (Paris: Félix Alcan, 1907).
149. O. Walusinski and J. Bogousslavsky, "À la recherche du neuropsychiatre perdu: Paul Sollier (1861–1933)," *Revue Neurologique FMC.* (2008): F239–247. www.baillement.com/lettres/sollier.pdf.
150. Paul Sollier, *Les Troubles de la mémoire* (Paris: Rueff, 1892) and *Le Problème de la mémoire* (Paris: Alcan, 1900).
151. Edward Bizub, "Proust et le docteur Sollier: les 'molécules impressionnées,'" *Bulletin Marcel Proust* 56 (2006): 41–51, 48.
152. My own free translation.
153. J.-E. Blanche, *Mes modèles* (Paris: Stock, 1928), 80, cited in Lowery, 14, note 2.
154. J. -E. Blanche, "Quelques Instantanés de Marcel Proust," *Hommage à Marcel Proust (1871–1922), La Nouvelle Revue Française* XX, 10.112 (January 1923): 52–61, 52–53.
155. Lowery, 11.
156. André Ferré, *Les Années de collège de Marcel Proust*, 4e éd. (NRF: Librairie Gallimard, 1959), 43.
157. Ferré, 174.
158. The tantalizing possibility is that Proust's work is more than just a "parallel" with James's.
159. Robert de Billy, *Marcel Proust, lettres et conversations* (Paris: Éditions des Portiques, 1930) 181, cited in Lowery, 15.
160. P.-E. Robert, *Marcel Proust, Lecteur des Anglo-Saxons* (Paris: A.-G. Nizet, 1976).
161. Robert, 14.
162. Walter Berry, "Du côté de Guermantes," in *Hommage à Marcel Proust, La Nouvelle Revue Française* XX, 10.112 (January 1923): 77–80, 79–80, cited in P.-E. Robert, 184, note 47.
163. Daniel Karlin, *Proust's English* (Oxford: Oxford University Press, 2005).
164. Michael Murphy, *Proust and America.* (Liverpool University Press, 2007).
165. For bibliographical links, see www.pragmatism.org and for the history of pragmatism in France, see http://www.pragmatism.org/history/pragmatism_in_france.htm See also John R. Shook, *Pragmatism: An Annotated Bibliography 1898–1940* (Amsterdam: Editions Rodopi, 1998) and Emmanuel Leroux, *Bibliographie méthodique du Pragmatisme Américain, Anglais et Italien* (New York: Burt Franklin, 1968).
166. Cours inédit d'Émile Durkheim, *Pragmatisme et sociologie*, éd. Armand Cuvillier (Paris: Librairie philosophique J. Vrin, 1955).
167. Lalande, "Philosophy," 241–266. The article was mentioned above in connection with Bergson. This journal has published since 1892, including several articles by William James. It was edited until 2006 by the faculty at Cornell University, and has since been published by Duke University Press.

168. André Lalande, "Pragmatisme et pragmaticisme," *Revue Philosophique de la France et de l'étranger* 61.2 (February 1906): 121–146.
169. Lalande, "Philosophy," 248.
170. Lalande, "Pragmatisme," 131, 142.
171. *RTP*, I, 390.
172. *RTP*, I, 398–399.
173. *RTP*, I, 406. Marcel Proust, *In Search of Lost Time*, trans. C. K. Scott Moncrieff and Terence Kilmartin, rev. D. J. Enright (New York: The Modern Library, 2003), I, 587–588. [hereafter Enright].
174. *RTP*, I, 426–427.
175. *Le Journal des Débats Politiques et Littéraires*, 17e année (22 avril 1910): 170.
176. As stated above, James published his own account of what Ralph Barton Perry terms "Boutroux's professorial exchange" in Cambridge (see Perry, *Bibliography*, 58).
177. *Corr.*, VII, *137*, 239–242, and note 7.
178. Most were written between 1904 and 1908, with two exceptions: "Le Vrai Pascal" was written in 1900 and "Le Sentiment religieux en France" was written in 1903. The articles were also reprinted in the weekly *Revue hebdomadaire du Journal des Débats*. The notes to James's *The Meaning of Truth* suggest that James had seen what Bourdeau had written, most likely in the original newspaper articles sent to him by Thomas Sargeant Perry, an American critic. See note 113.37, 346 in William James, *Pragmatism* and *The Meaning of Truth*. (Cambridge: Harvard University Press, 1978).
179. J. Bourdeau, *Pragmatisme et modernisme* (Paris: Félix Alcan, éd. 1909), vi.
180. Bourdeau, *Pragmatisme*, vi. "La notion philosophique du pragmatisme a été vulgarisé en France surtout par M. J. Bourdeau, dans une série d'articles du *Journal des Débats* (24 février, 20 octobre et 9 novembre 1907, 12 janvier et 18 février 1908)." (Jean Bourdeau, *Pragmatisme*, 216 note 1) [The notion of pragmatism was popularized in France by M. J. Bourdeau in a series of articles in the *Journal des Débats*]. This quotation omits the article published in *Les Débats* on 21 January 1908, entitled "Le Pragmatisme contre le rationalisme." [Pragmatism vs. Rationalism] The article was included in *Pragmatisme and modernisme*.
181. Bourdeau, *Pragmatisme*, 40.
182. Bourdeau, *Pragmatisme*, vi.
183. Bourdeau, *Pragmatisme*, 42, 47.
184. John Elof Boodin, "William James as I Knew Him," *Personalist* 23 (1942), repr. *William James Remembered*, ed. Linda Simon (Lincoln: University of Nebraska Press, 1996), 206–232, 227.
185. His friend Richard Hodgson had done the same, and though James waited with pen at the ready, he never did receive any communication from Hodgson. Nor have we found any record of one from James. With his open mind, James was willing to pursue a multitude of psychological avenues in his research. Nevertheless, his obituary in *The New York Times* suggested that he had published over one hundred pages in the journal of the Society for Psychical Research on the topic of his "conversations" with Hodgson, indicating in summary that history would eventually prove or definitively dismiss the possibility of communication from beyond the grave.
186. *Le Journal des Débats Politiques et Littéraires*, Édition hebdomadaire, 17e année (2 septembre 1910): 440–441. This obituary is the source of the several quotes that follow.
187. James had been elected "Correspondent" member in 1898, and wrote to his friend François Pillon on June 15, 1898, to ask if he were responsible: "Have I *your* influence to thank for this?" and to tell him of the added honor of having been asked to deliver the Gifford Lectures in Edinburgh (James, *Letters*, II, 75). James was subsequently elected "Associé étranger" of the Académie des sciences morales et politiques in 1910; the news was reported in American newspapers "directly from Paris" in January 1910 (James, *Letters*, II, 328–329).
188. Émile Boutroux, funeral oration for William James, published as "Décès de M. William James: Paroles de M. Boutroux, Président," *Séances et travaux de l'Académie des sciences morales et politiques, compte rendu* (1910): 487–491.

189. On December 3, 1910, the *New York Times* noted that Boutroux must have also "delivered a memorial oration" for James at the Académie's annual public session.
190. É. Boutroux, "Décès," 489.
191. É. Boutroux, "Décès," 489.
192. É. Boutroux, "Décès," 489.
193. Michel Salomon, *Portraits et Paysages* (Paris: Perrin et Cie., 1920), 53. Articles by Salomon were collected after his death in 1912 and published in 1920 with a preface by Paul Bourget.
194. Salomon, *Portraits*, 65.
195. Salomon, *Portraits*, 73.
196. Salomon, *Portraits*, 75.
197. Bourdeau, *Pragmatisme*, 62–64.
198. Bourdeau, *Pragmatisme*, 77.
199. Proust, *Contre Sainte-Beuve*, 225.
200. Bourdeau, *Pragmatisme*, 68.
201. The French translation of James's *Pragmatism* with its preface by Bergson was reprinted in 1918, the year of Proust's first letter mentioning James.
202. Many of the essays gathered for publication by Ralph Barton Perry after James's death in *Essays in Radical Empiricism* (New York: Longmans, Green & Co., 1912) had been published originally in the *Journal of Philosophy, Psychology, and Scientific Methods* in 1904 and 1905.
203. These letters are included among James's papers, held at the Houghton Library, Harvard University, and are available for researchers' review (bMS Am 1092.9 (4293–4294). Both appear in Henri Bergson, *Correspondances*, 416–417, 461.
204. William James, *Le Pragmatisme*, trans. E. LeBrun, intro. Henri Bergson (Paris: Flammarion, 1911).
205. Henri Bergson's preface, "Sur le Pragmatisme de William James, Vérité et Réalité," (Ch. VIII) *La Pensée et le mouvant: essais et conférences* (Paris: Librairie Félix Alcan, 1934), 267.
206. Henri Bergson, "On the Pragmatism of William James: Truth and Reality," *The Creative Mind*, Ch. VIII, trans. Mabelle L. Andison (New York: Philosophical Library, 1946), 248.
207. Bergson, "On Pragmatism," 250; *Pensée*, 271.
208. Bergson, "On Pragmatism," 251.
209. Bergson, "On Pragmatism," 306, note 32.
210. Bergson, "Sur le Pragmatisme," 271–272.
211. James, preface to *The Meaning of Truth*, [3] 169. Pagination refers to the 1978 Harvard University Press edition, page 3 in *The Meaning of Truth* section of the book, page 169 of the volume.
212. Bergson, "On Pragmatism," 257–258.
213. Bergson, "On Pragmatism," 259.
214. René Gillouin, *Essais de critique littéraire et philosophique* (Paris: Bernard Grasset, 1913).
215. Marcel Proust, *Lettres à Mme. Scheikévitch* (Paris: Librairie des Champs-Élysées, 1928).

TWO

The Jamesian Stream and the Proustian Art of Consciousness

While Proust did not consider himself immune to the *philosophical* influences circulating in "l'air du temps," and attuned as he was to art, his literary patrimony, and the cultural moment (attested to by the myriad references in his correspondence and in the novel itself), he preferred that the inspiration for his creativity and for the surprising shape of his novel, whatever its origin, remain unmarked, unidentified, unsourced.[1]

What a writer's sources are and where they come from are open-ended questions, ripe for probing. How the novelist uses them is equally indeterminate and open to analysis. How closely and how successfully an author is able to guard his secrets—despite the most careful and extensive critical scrutiny—is one way of engaging future audiences in the determined pleasure of reading. But acknowledged or not, in matters of substance, structure, and style, evidence of William James's thought is present in Proust's unorthodox book.

Newspaper clippings found in Proust's room at the time of his death included one from *L'Intransigeant* dated December 28, 1913: "Ses descriptions de caractères participent des derniers progrès de la psychologie expérimentale"[2] [His descriptions of characters reflect the latest findings in experimental psychology]. This and a publicity "annonce" [announcement] that had appeared at the time *Du côté de chez Swann* was published calling Proust "le *réaliste de l'âme*"[3] [one who paints a realistic picture of the human spirit] emphasize Proust's finely tuned psychology.

Proust wrote to Paul Souday in 1920 that what he had wanted to do in his work was something that required great imaginative exertion; he wanted to inhabit the mind of a protagonist: "[J]'ai tâché de voir les choses par le dedans, d'étudier l'imagination"[4] [I tried to see things from the inside, to study the imagination]. His would be the story of a "moi spirituel,"[5] the biography of a mind, looking out from inside the Self through time.

How is the story of a life best told? Ever since its publication, there has been conjecture and controversy about *À la recherche du temps perdu*. Is it autobiography? Is it fiction? James's "stream of consciousness" supplied footing and framework for relaying the history of an individual's conscious experience, allowing Proust to develop his art.

CONSCIOUSNESS AND GENRE: AUTOBIOGRAPHY OR FICTION?

Although his tale of a consciousness in action may seem to conflate the author-narrator-hero, Proust was set upon denying that his book is a mere fact-intensive personal memoir directly recounting memories of the events of his own life and describing the individuals who peopled it. Rather than recounting a series of tangential anecdotes—"une suite de digressions"[6] —he wanted his story to expose human psychology over time. He tantalized his public and called attention to his work by emphasizing how his book differs tellingly from what readers might expect, emphasizing its architecture and its dynamic, its thick affective and imaginative fabric, the swirling historical and social context—and stressing while denying the close yet mystifying proximity the autobiography of a mind can have to fiction.

Writing in the first person, the author, narrator, and hero of true autobiography are one and the same. Genuine autobiography presents the reader an implied veracity, the history of a personality recounted with clarity and objectivity, with exacting adherence to the facts, an intersection of text and actual life.[7] Fiction, however, invents. It permits access in language to a character's "mental experiences,"[8] and utter intimacy with the narrator's innermost subjectivity—with all the inherent limitations—as if it were our own.

Strikingly, Proust briefly assigns his own name to the narrator as he develops his novel. Albertine addresses the hero as "Marcel,"[9] despite the author's initial disavowal of identification with the narrator in 1913.[10] By 1915 the distance between author and narrator seems to have narrowed when, in a letter recounting the Albertine story to Mme. Scheikévich, Proust writes entirely in first-person language as if he were the narrator. And in 1920, writing about memories recounted that belong specifically to the narrator, Proust flirts with a partial admission of authorial emotional involvement: the bits of madeleine dipped in tea "me rappellent (ou du moins rappellent au narrateur qui dit 'je' et qui n'est pas toujours moi) tout un temps de ma vie, oublié"[11] [remind me (or rather remind the narrator who says "I" and who is not always me) of a period of my life I had forgotten]. The sense of experiential participation in the Albertine story, often described as the most psychological of Proust's volumes, swells as the writer explores with close interest how the mind and emotions perform in a "moi spirituel."

William James's descriptions of consciousness offered an artist possibilities for an invented form with greater psychological density and distance from those more directly autobiographical experiences momentarily felt and gathered in Proust's early attempt at novel-writing in third-person voice in *Jean Santeuil*:

> Et pourtant notre vie n'est pas absolument séparée de nos oeuvres. Toutes les scènes que je vous raconte, je les ai vécues. . . . Et leur essence intime m'échappait[12]
>
> [Nonetheless, our life is not altogether separate from our writings. I have lived all the scenes I recount to you. . . . But their inner meaning escaped me].

The truths Proust intended to convey are psychological and philosophical truths that go much further in revealing the functioning human mind than the facts of events themselves. Looking at James's descriptions of the clumps and flow of attentive awareness, fitfully soaring and alighting on different objects in the human "stream of consciousness," the role of sensation and its surrounding vague aura of feeling that Proust as an artist could take from the inchoate and render exhaustively specific, the importance of desire as driver of interested attention, the dissociation of an "I" who perceives and a "Me" with a history over time, and truth as something that happens rather than as something singular or essential solidly buried in object, fact, or event, could furnish plot and technique for Proust's fiction. James's descriptions of the psychological mechanisms of consciousness resound in Proust's development from flailing novelist in *Jean Santeuil* to the more coherently fictionalized triumph of *À la recherche du temps perdu*.

"Chaque personne est bien seule" [Each of us is indeed alone], wrote Proust at the end of a description of his narrator's grandmother's visit to the distinguished "docteur E***." The diagnosis is tragic: "'Votre grand-mère est perdue.'" ["Your grandmother is doomed"]. The doctor seconds his own self-important superficialities and clichés by saying in way of farewell, "'Ah! la vie n'est pas que roses, comme on le croit à votre âge'" ["Ah! Life is not all a bed of roses, as one is apt to think at your age"].[13] The realization that each being lives alone in a world that is his apart implies the selfish and short-sighted nature of adolescence—the age of rosy vision—and also starkly presents the facts of life.

> Les liens entre un être et nous n'existent que dans notre pensée. [. . .] L'homme est l'être qui ne peut sortir de soi, qui ne connaît les autres qu'en soi, et en disant le contraire, ment.[14]

> [The bonds between ourselves and another person exist only in our minds. . . . Man is the creature who cannot escape from himself, who knows other people only in himself, and when he asserts the contrary, he is lying.[15]]

The perceptions and feelings belonging to each individual can be experienced, explored, and recounted by him alone, spoken authentically only in the first person.

In the end, Proust was determined to organize the many thoughts and notations jotted in his *carnets* and weave them successfully into a work that is more than merely the literary conjuring of an "autobiography," a fictional coming-of-age story, or a memoirist's tale of how a writer found his vocation. Something made it possible for him to hear a muse hidden in ordinary family conversation,[16] realizing that his individual interpretation of it, his feelings about it, and his conclusions from it, the unique unspoken associative patterning of his experience so intriguing to today's cognitive neuroscientists,[17] could develop into what Gérard Genette described as the "monstrous [. . .] expansion of a verb."[18] Looking at what changed and why Proust ultimately chose fictional form, however thinly disguised elements of its foundation matter may be, the conceit of looking at *À la recherche du temps perdu* as a "verb"—or as a term of action—places appropriate emphasis on the reproduction in the text of experience happening in a sort of fictionally foreshortened version of the real span of time, an idea suggested by Ribot and noted by James in his writing on memory and forgetting.[19] As Roger Shattuck remarks, fiction "accelerates" and renders visible the "opaque or imperceptible" aspects of everyday life.[20] The story of Proust's novel will be the story of the invisible experience of a Self, of "Je," set in motion and looking back upon itself to tell the tale of "Me."

Proust's interest in the close pursuit of the real, of a philosophical, artistic, psychological, and metaphysical form of "vérité" with visceral impact on the reader, is clearly seen in his letter to Jacques Rivière of February 6, 1914:

> Non, si je n'avais pas ces croyances intellectuelles, si je cherchais simplement à me souvenir et a faire double emploi par ces souvenirs avec les jours vécus, je ne prendrais pas, malade comme je suis, la peine d'écrire. Mais cette évolution d'une pensée, je n'ai pas voulu l'analyser abstraitement mais la recréer, la faire vivre.[21]

> [No, if I did not have these intellectual beliefs, if I simply sought to remember and have these memories duplicate the days I have lived, I would not, sick as I am, take the trouble to write. But this progression of thought, I did not want to analyze it abstractly but rather recreate it and give it life.]

The novel form, Vincent Descombes suggests, practically forced itself on the uncertain writer because it fleshed out and illuminated his work's theoretical basis in a manner only a mimetic work could do. It allowed the writer to make more sense of the halting truths, misperceptions, and possibilities inherent in the ordinary, impermanent, muddled daily facts of autobiography.[22]

Proust himself, seeing to the publicity of his book in an age before paid advertisements for literary works were common, wrote and paid for "écho[s]," or what might now be called publicity or product placements in editorial. To properly launch his book and ensure its success, these "échos" would be printed, Proust hoped, in an advantageous location more widely viewed by the public than the "chroniques sur 'Les Lettres'"[23] [literary review sections] generally relegated to the back of newspapers and revues at the time. He extracted portions of a flattering article written by his friend Jacques-Émile Blanche published in *l'Écho de* Paris, and sent this for placement by another friend, René Blum, in le *Gil Blas*. In the article, Blanche refers to almost magical qualities in Proust's *Du côté de chez Swann*, a book that casts a spell over its readers by weaving together a plastic uncertainty of genre he refers to as "la saveur d'une autobiographie et d'un essai" [the flavor of an autobiography and of an essay], with a recent and remembered historical moment and, most enticingly, teasing hints of contemporary models for its characters.[24] Proust continued to milk the Blanche article, sending a copy for *Le Miroir* to Louis Brun.

Élie-Joseph Bois began his 1913 interview with Proust about *À la recherche du temps perdu*, "Ce titre énigmatique est celui d'un roman dont le premier volume vient de paraître"[25] [This is the enigmatic title of a novel the first volume of which has just appeared]. In all of these early presentations, the word "roman" was emphasized, underscoring the work's fictional classification as an invented story. It was as a "novel" that Proust's unusual book was publicized by critics announcing it to potential readers and categorized in its initial literary reception. It was this fictional identity that Proust clearly wanted, and it was as such that he expected (and tried to ensure) the public's greeting.

Proust felt strongly that in its physical presentation in book form, *À la recherche du temps perdu* should most closely resemble the density of lived experience. This density as well as the ambiguous or "borderline" nature of the narrative, and the fact that Proust was not known as a novelist, made it difficult to find an editor sufficiently adventurous to tackle publication, as indicated by Léon Pierre-Quint:

> Le sujet du livre n'entre dans aucun genre déterminé et l'auteur lui-même n'ose l'appeler ni un roman ni des mémoires. Il tient à le publier non seulement sans chapitre, à peu près comme il a paru, mais encore

> sans alinéa, en pages serrées, compactes. "Cela fait entrer davantage les propos, dit-il, dans la continuité du texte".[26]
>
> [The subject of the book does not belong to any specific genre, and the author himself does not dare call it either a novel or a memoir. He intends to publish it not only without chapters, as it has appeared, but also without paragraphs, in tight compact pages. "That way the commentary is better incorporated into the continuity of the text."]

In a letter to René Blum, who helped arrange Proust's self-financed publication of *Du côté de chez Swann* by Grasset, the author admits the indeterminate and highly personal nature of his text that along with its form make it very different and new, difficult for the public as well as for the publishing establishment to accept, and calling it "un important ouvrage (disons roman, car c'est une espèce de roman)"[27] [an important work (let's call it a novel, because it is a sort of novel)]. In *À propos du "style" de Flaubert*, referring to his work as "mon roman" ["my novel"], Proust elaborates on certain constituent elements of its fictional composition. He indicates that readers—perhaps even well-read critics—have misunderstood *Du côté de chez Swann* when they assume "que mon roman était une sorte de receuil de souvenirs, s'enchaînant selon les lois fortuites de l'association des idées"[28] [that my novel is a sort of collection of memories, chained together according to the accidental laws of association theory]. There Proust was repeating the same sentiment (and some of the same words) of protestation he had included in a letter to Paul Souday the year before (November 10, 1919): "Je vois des lecteurs s'imaginer que j'écris, en me fiant à d'arbitraires et fortuites associations d'idées, l'histoire de ma vie"[29] [I foresee readers imagining that I am writing the my life story, leaning heavily on the arbitrary and accidental association of ideas].

The implications of Proust's statements are several, and they are significant. First, and most obviously, Proust does not deny that his work contains important elements of memory. Yet he is bent upon telling his readers that his work is not simply a collection of personal reminiscences—a sort of autobiographical scrapbook, the "récoltés" ["harvested bits"] of *Jean Santeuil*—with entries arranged one following the other as in a chain of associations *nor* according to rules of associationist theory. Proust wants to make it clear that his novel is composed, intricately woven, devised, and arranged according to a plan he terms "rigoureuse" [strictly observed], not simply aligned as a fact-intensive memoir: "Ma composition est voilée et d'autant moins rapidement perceptible qu'elle se développe sur une large échelle"[30] [My composition is hidden, and even less visible, because it develops on a wide scale].

The notion that his novel might be construed as a "chain" of ideas, or memories without structure or plan, refers to Hume's doctrine that human thought "is composed of separate independent parts and not a sensibly continuous stream."[31] According to William James, "the 'Associationist' manner of representing the life of the mind [would be] as an agglutination in various shapes of separate entities called ideas."[32] A closer description of the fabric created by Proust's novelistic practices and the physical form he wanted his work to take appears in language used by James when he states that a better theory of the nature of thought holds that

> consciousness, then, does not appear to itself chopped up in bits. Such words as a "chain" or "train" do not describe it fitly as it presents itself in the first instance. It is nothing jointed; it flows. A "river" or a "stream" are the metaphors by which it is most naturally described. *In talking of it hereafter, let us call it the stream of thought, of consciousness, or of subjective life.*[33]

From his study of philosophy, Proust is evidently familiar with theories of association. *Du côté de chez Swann* is not going to be structured as a chain-like series of associated ideas or memories connected randomly like box-cars, nor by Kantian "*acts of reason*" in which a "mind proceeds from one object to another by some rational path of connection."[34] Rather, it will be a relatively undelineated *flow* of succeeding states of mind, in which connections form and reflection is engaged in response to the nature of what James highlighted as the "*things thought of*"; instead of "ideas" abstracted from experience and conceptually formulated, "*it is things, not ideas, which are associated in the mind.*"[35] The fabric of Proust's text, suggests Bernard Brun, is memories remembered: "ce récit qui est toujours souvenir de souvenir."[36]

In his analysis of stream-of-consciousness writers, Melvin Friedman contends that William James had a significant impact on new developments in the craft of fiction. "James' [*sic*] work is a plea for man to live more imaginatively, more authentically, by a willful resignation to the superior creative powers of the sensibility."[37] With his "strong gift for metaphor," James could express in the very flow of his own writing the close relationship between thought, the sense data comprising perception and emotion, and imagination that he conceived as the "stream of consciousness." Citing elements from "The Stream of Thought" in James's *Principles of Psychology* and its forerunner article, "On Some Omissions of Introspective Psychology," which later appear as characteristics of the stream-of-consciousness school, Friedman suggests that James theorized the psychology of consciousness in a way that was far in advance of accepted literary technique of the 1880s, the time when he was composing the *The Principles of Psychology*. He understood that human language generally was limited in its abilities to represent the "intricacies" of the stream of consciousness and the fabric of "felt relations" it entails, which Maryanne Wolf characterizes as "the world of image and patterns inexpressible by speech."[38] "The *Principles of Psychology*," writes Friedman, "was probably a formidable weapon in the hands of the avant-garde of its time."[39]

James's version of thought is a perfect substratum for a novel like Proust's in which the text can at times lurch or flow and at others stop for reflection and analysis, feeling and fancy, "un roman plein de passion et de méditation et de paysages"[40] [a novel filled with passion and meditation and landscapes]:

> If pure thought runs all our trains, why should she run some so fast and some so slow, some through dull flats and some through gorgeous scenery, some to mountain-heights and jeweled mines, others through dismal swamps and darkness?—and run some off the track altogether, and into the wilderness of lunacy? [. . .] Reason is only one out of a thousand possibilities in the thinking of each of us.[41]

The affective basis of human consciousness was an early and intrinsic aspect of James's thinking. Emotion imbues every aspect of our experience, and the felt emotion is derived from the bodily state it accompanies according to the James-Lange Theory of Emotion: "We feel sad because we cry, angry because we strike, afraid because we tremble." "Without the bodily states following on the perception, the latter would be purely cognitive in form, pale, colorless, destitute of emotional warmth."[42] Much like James, Proust found the inspiration for his work in the keenness of his emotional sensitivity: "il n'y a pas un seul adjectif qui ne soit senti"[43] [there is not a single adjective that is not felt]:

> [C]'est qu'il n'est à aucun degré une oeuvre de raisonnement, c'est que ses moindres éléments m'ont été fournis par ma sensibilité, que je les ai d'abord aperçus au fond de moi-même, sans les comprendre.[44]
>
> [This is not in any way a work of reasoning; even its tiniest elements have been furnished by my sensibility, I first perceived them inside without understanding them.]

Proust's difficulty with his earlier attempt at fiction writing in *Jean Santeuil* did not stem from lack of subject matter. He seemed to know that the stuff of his own biography, or something similar, would be the material he would mould. What he lacked in *Jean Santeuil* was the structural means to arrange his "biographical" subject into a compelling story and the psychological tools enabling him to do so. These were ingrained in James's theories.

Often in his youth, Proust had felt himself functioning while at the same time observing—like a subject simultaneously acting and being examined by a psychologist or interpreter. William C. Carter notes, "the evening after his second day in class, he wrote to [his teacher] Darlu seeking a remedy to his intensive self-analysis that caused him to imagine his consciousness as containing multiple selves" and "the constant contemplation of his inner life."[45] How was Proust to reconcile the presence of that subjective, observing "I" with the objective experiences of "Me"?

> Je ne considère mon moi objectif (prenez ce mot dans le sens où l'entendent les philosophes) que comme un instrument d'expérimentation sans intérêt pour lui-même mais qui m'associe à mon esprit pour pénétrer dans certaines réalités et surtout dans les pénombres de la conscience, où je tâche de mettre de la lumière.[46]
>
> [I consider my objective self (as the word is understood by philosophers) merely as a tool of experimentation, without intrinsic interest for me but which connects me to my mind and allows me to penetrate certain realities, particularly the shadows of consciousness which I try to illuminate.]

The vantage point closest to experience is that of the participant, the focal lens through which all exterior and interior exchange takes place. Proust's narrator plays "psychologist" on himself by positioning himself in a manner James considers to be "reflective[ly]" as "a mind conscious of its own cognitive function."[47]

Yet, focusing on the action while simultaneously being on stage is an ambiguous position. The motives, interests, and emotions of the other actors remain opaque; between the perception and felt experience of one character and that of another there remains a gulf at which one can only guess or study for clues: "Each of these minds keeps its own thoughts to itself. There is no giving or bartering between them. No thought ever comes into direct *sight* of a thought in another personal consciousness than its own. Absolute insulation, irreducible pluralism, is the law."[48] Only a novelist can approach this opacity to render it "transparent":

> A real person [. . .] profoundly as we may sympathize with him, is in a great measure perceptible only through our senses, that is to say, he remains opaque, offers a dead weight which our sensibilities have no strength to lift [. . .]. The novelist's happy discovery was to think of substituting for those opaque sections, impenetrable by the human spirit, their equivalent in immaterial sections, things, that is, which the spirit can assimilate to itself.[49]

How was a writer to unlock the secret meaning from bits of the everyday world surrounding him and make sense of what he remembers of the past? An emotional and imaginative response ultimately blends associations with material sensations, "la réalité évoquée, songée, insaissable" ["evoked, dreamed, unseizable reality"[50]]. Like his readers, Proust's narrator, too, must strive to comprehend his experience by the effort of what Maryanne Wolf terms "contributing actively to the constructions."[51] Understanding or decoding it is something the author and the narrator are called upon to work at: "Ce plaisir, dont l'objet n'était que pressenti, que j'avais à créer moi-même" [That pleasure, the object of which I could only dimly feel, which I must create for myself].[52]

The narrator must access the multilayered emotive echo that will be key to his aesthetic as a writer, and stabilize the transitory in something permanent, capturing the savor and significance of streaming private individual experience, holding it fast with the weight of words. How could James's theories about the "self" and the "stream of consciousness" assist?

Roger Shattuck observes that for Proust 1909 was a turning point in his ability to conceive and create his novel: "For, during the first half of 1909, Proust resolved his personal and artistic crisis and redeemed much of the writing he thought he had been producing to no purpose." "He reached beyond autobiography toward the transformation of his life into the shape of a narrative that could convey his deepest sense of self." This narrative took the form of a novel in order to convey general aesthetic truths that daily life conceals in which the starring character is the Self, witnessing its own experience.[53]

In 1907 and 1908 when Proust jotted into notebooks ideas for what he hoped would be a substantial work, James's central ideas on the stream of consciousness and on emotion had been available in France for a long time. By 1909, when the *Précis de Psychologie* was first published in French translation, Proust had begun to write from the mixed vantage point of real writer/fictional writer in which he became both the subject and the observer, the character/narrator recounting a mixture of the real and the invented. In this guise he was enabled to portray experience as it feels when lived by the "je" or "I" experiencing it while simultaneously striving to glean the meaning of that experience, looking back retrospectively.

In *À la recherche du temps perdu*, recounting the past as present, Proust narrated experience as lived in a *Bildungsroman*, or what Genette calls "a novel of development."[54] Yet at the same time we join the narrator's experience in the novel after the fact, when he has already gleaned its meaning, felt its feelings, and sometimes already forgotten them. Genette remarks that although Proust spent over ten years writing *À la recherche du temps perdu*, it is narrated entirely without "mark of duration, or of division: it is instantaneous. The narrator's present, which on almost every page we find mingled with the hero's various pasts, is a single moment without progression."[55]

Proust decided to paint what William James called the "stubborn facts" of experience in its indecipherable opacity, but to do so with transparent colors, with the luminescence of emotional actuality, viewed through hindsight.

What was it that stimulated what Genette calls the "late, and deliberate, assumption of the *form* of direct autobiography" and provided Proust the narrative impetus that the third-person narrative of *Jean Santeuil* could not? Genette signals "the apparently contradictory fact that the narrative content of the *Recherche* is less directly autobiographical than the narrative content of *Santeuil*—as if Proust first had had to conquer a certain adhesion to himself, had to detach himself from himself, in order to win the right to say 'I,' or more precisely the right to have this hero who is neither completely himself nor completely someone else say 'I.'"[56] First-person narrative, minutely observed and described, permits use of sentient emotive coloration and the expression of hue, or "shading" of "relation" and "inward coloring," that William James ascribes to the stream of thought subjectively experienced.[57]

THE MENTAL ACTIVITY OF CONSCIOUSNESS

The mind was the scientific black box of William James's day, the "'dark chamber of the skull.'"[58] How we form and maintain an individual identity with knowledge of our own inner life were the questions that James considered in the context of the latest available theory and experimental data as he developed his view of the experiencing self and the structural nature of the stream of conscious awareness. According to Dorrit Cohn, James contrived the term "Stream of Consciousness" more for its metaphorical usefulness than as a description of what became its ultimate fictional realization: "consciousness metaphorically *labeled* a stream . . . but not *rendered* as a stream."[59]

William James took issue with Spencer's notion of mental life purely as cognition of fact, omitting "all sentiments, all aesthetic impulses, all religious emotions and personal affections." For James, cognitive "judgments of the actual" are merely one of the mind's functions. That mental life should omit the draw of our emotions, our "preferences or repugnances," is inconceivable; for then, how could one "laugh at a joke, [. . .] go to one theater rather than another, [. . .] long for a vacation"? In addition to "perception of fact," the mind's activities are governed by teleology: "subjective *interests* pure and simple," including intangibles like "logic," "fancy," "wit," "taste," "decorum, beauty, morals, and so forth."[60] These motivate our ends, succeeding or not in the outcomes,[61] and they constitute the stuff of Proust's fiction. Social life, art, mistakes, and silliness join the weightier "metaphysics and mythologies"[62] in feeding our curiosity, explaining the world around us, and adjusting our adaptive behavior.

James intended to study of the Stream of Thought analytically, introspectively, and not as a "synthetic" picture of the functioning mind erected from associated "ideas" of its activities. This was significant in his time, when the Associationist psychologists preferred to build theory about conscious experience upward from individual elements or entities, such as sensations, creating the wall from the stones, so to speak. Human experience, the inner life of the mind, suggested James, is not constructed that way. He used the process of introspection to evaluate a felt experience after the fact or "postmortem sentiri," retrospectively, the same way Proust depicted his narrator's experience, for it is the only way a psychologist or novelist can ever "grasp" felt experience for scientific study or extract from it any truth:

> In its bare immediacy it is of no use to him. For his purposes it must be more than experienced; it must be remembered, reflected on, named, classed, known, related to other facts of the same order. And as in the naming, classing, and knowing of things in general we are notoriously fallible, why not also here?[63]

To render his narrator's conscious experience into fiction, Proust used techniques surprisingly similar to those described by James: understanding an *individual*'s conscious, absorbing brain and how its activities enable speaking subjects like ourselves to think and to know the world around us; how when "struck" from without the brain processes and retains the impact; how inner feelings arise as personal emotions known only to ourselves; how subsequent thinking about our sensory experiences is a route to knowledge, becoming the "*conceptions* and *judgments*"[64] through which we acquire understanding; how attention and interest drive experience in fits and starts; how sensation, memory, habit, and the experiences of an adaptive pragmatic self allow us to observe, select, and create the reality around us; how special moments of disclosure that function nearly as religious revelations help to attain that other religious ideal, eternal meaning; how experience can be fixed and expressed in language, using the synthetic potential of metaphor to communicate what resonates around what is observed in a "fringe" of relational possibility, "le 'style'" that qualifies writing as literature.[65]

Featuring the self as actor, observer, and the subject, Proust's novel offers the reader a mélange of subjective immediacy and judgmental objectivity, composed neither in a fashion typical of autobiography nor usual in the seemingly unedited streams of interior musing captured in its most natural and spontaneous—even pre-verbal[66]—intimacy in texts such as those of Edouard Dujardin or later "stream of consciousness" writers James Joyce, Virginia Woolf, or Dorothy Richardson. Proust's narrator is an "I" who explores a "Me," measuring and describing every action, motivation, feeling, desire, reaction, mistake, and disappointment. Each changing vibration of the states of his consciousness is examined over the continuous course of a life cycle, beginning with the vivid novelty of the concrete and quotidian seen through the eyes of youth, and perceived throughout Proust's narrator's lifetime of cognitive adventure.

James notes the "wonder" perceived before systemic "assimilation" and valued freshly, even when recollected, by the experienced eye of a gifted reasoning adult.[67] Proust's novel is treated as experience happening, yet written retrospectively, truthful-seeming without necessarily being utterly actual or factually true. His arrogation of sentient experience and his interaction with it become the substance of the book.

The very length of Proust's novel, the separation of moments of experience one from another as recounted on widely separated pages of the book, form a very modern texture of vertical experience by the experiencing self embedded in the horizontal course of time. Like earthquakes, emotional upheavals expose past strata.[68] At every heave of a tectonic event, the narrator lingers to examine occurrence and aftermath, much as James did when he interviewed San Franciscans after the earthquake in 1906 to try to understand their experience of it and how it *felt* to have lived through such an event.

Certain elements of James's depiction of the structure of consciousness and his descriptions of how it functions, and even some of the metaphors that he uses to describe it, pervade and enrich *À la recherche du temps perdu.* Their echo enabled Proust's story-telling to mature into something radically new in fiction, something that has obsessed the generations of readers who followed.

As early in his career as 1879, when he published "Are We Automata?" in the British journal *Mind*,[69] James focused on the importance of human feeling and consciousness and attempted to distinguish his view from the prevalent materialist ideology. James's purpose was to demonstrate power of consciousness for dealing with those aspects of living that advantage a creature with adaptive capacity. In Proust's novel, desire is the ultimate driver of purposeful behavior and an example of James's cognitive teleology of self-interested attention, the "mystery of *interest* and *selective attention*."[70] James's painterly eye focused on both the bright light and the shade of human experience; for Proust as well, the bright light and shade both count. Events cast a subjective and affective shadow within the narrator that is critical to what he sees.

ME (MY SELF) AND I

Although hints of the importance that a memory's-eye viewpoint would have in Proust's fiction were already evident in passages of *Jean Santeuil*, and despite William C. Carter's assertion that Proust's "retrospective, organic unity" was due to a discovery made when translating Ruskin's *Sésame et les lys* in 1905,[71] James's description of the conscious Self proffers a convincing platform for Proust's creation of a fabricated retrospective work that feels autobiographical.

> The altogether unique kind of interest which each human mind feels in those parts of creation which it can call *me* or *mine* may be a moral riddle, but it is a fundamental psychological fact. No mind can take the same interest in his neighbor's *me* as in his own. The neighbor's me

> falls together with all the rest of things in one foreign mass against which his own *me* stands out in startling relief.[72]

For James, the first fact of consciousness is that consciousness is personal: "'I think' and 'I feel.'" Physical sensations and emotions come to us as embodied feelings that are applicable only to ourselves. We cannot feel the feelings of another person, experience how they become aware of sensations or know their inner life. The thread of continuous consciousness, the stream of thought that belongs to each individual separately and inaccessibly, is not shared. It is experienced by discreet individuals—"particular I's and you's."[73] "In this room—this lecture-room, say—there are a multitude of thoughts, yours and mine, some of which cohere mutually, and some not. [. . .] My thought belongs with *my* other thoughts, and your thought with *your* other thoughts."[74] My past history belongs to the body I inhabit and to the life I know I live; anyone else's is "cold and pale" and resides in a body I can only observe. "My present Me is felt with warmth and intimacy. The heavy warm mass of my body is there, and the nucleus of the 'spiritual me,' the sense of intimate activity [. . .] is there."[75]

> Other men's experiences, no matter how much I may know about them, never bear this vivid, this peculiar brand. [. . .] Each of us when he awakens says, Here's the same old Me again, just as he says Here's the same old bed, the same old room, the same old world.[76]

The contrast between this reassuring continuity of the Self in the "same old world" and the "startling relief" of the isolated Self surrounded by the foreignness of "the rest of things" is highlighted in Proust's description of his narrator's difficulty adjusting to the strangeness of new environments, new bedrooms. To the ultra-sensitive adolescent hero, the new surroundings in the Grand-Hotel in Balbec—the repulsive director, the small elevator and its operator, the bedroom, for example—all appear foreign and unsettling. He is the self-same man, an experiencing "je"; but his individuality is delineated most sharply from external realities by the newly reactive suffering of that aspect of himself, that singular "Me," so discomfited when faced with the solid actuality of what had formerly been only hypothetical:

> Il n'est peut-être rien qui donne plus l'impression de la réalité de ce qui nous est extérieur, que le changement de la position, par rapport à nous, d'une personne même insignifiante, avant que nous l'ayons connue, et après. J'étais le même homme qui avait pris à la fin de l'après-midi le petit chemin de fer de Balbec, je portais en moi la même âme. Mais dans cette âme, à l'endroit où, à six heures, il y avait, avec l'impossibilité d'imaginer le directeur, le Palace, son personnel, une attente vague et craintive du moment où j'arriverais, se trouvait maintenant [. . .] toute une frise de personnages de guignol sortis de cette boîte de Pandore qu'était le Grand-Hôtel.[77]

> [There is perhaps nothing that gives us so strong an impression of the reality of the external world as the difference in the position, relative to ourselves, of even a quite unimportant person before we have met him and after. I was the same man who had taken, that afternoon, the little train from Balbec to the coast; I carried in my body the same consciousness. But on that consciousness in the place where at six o'clock there had been, together with the impossibility of forming any idea of the manager, the Grand Hotel or its staff, a vague and timorous anticipation of the moment at which I should reach my destinations, were now . . . a whole frieze of puppet-show characters issuing from that Pandora's box which was the Grand Hotel.[78]]

In his intent to explore the "moi spirituel," Proust was drawn to a close internal examination of the Self. James defines this "spiritual me" as our inner "core," a dynamic composite totality of conscious awareness.[79] Its role is "*active-feeling*" and ongoing, gauging every action, motivation, feeling desire, reaction, mistake, and disappointment, each changing vibration of the state of conscious awareness, the perceptions, emotions, imaginings, fantasies, and memories that occur over the continuous course of a life.

> The consciousness of Self involves a stream of thought, each part of which as 'I' can remember those which went before, know the things they knew, and care paramountly for certain ones among them as *'Me,'* and *appropriate to these* the rest.[80]

In Proust's novel we find the narrative "I," "qui dit 'je'" [who says "I"], who consciously observes, feels, and recounts the story as well as the historical "Me" the book is about, who is observed and evolves over time. These are the two aspects—a curious doubling—of the narrator's conscious experiencing "Self," for James "the total self of me, being as it were duplex, partly known and partly knower, partly object and partly subject."[81]

In James's vision of the Self, continuity of identity of the "I" coexists with simultaneous, slow, successive changes in the "Me." The "I" is a "*functional* identity," actively feeling emotions and desires. Because states of consciousness succeed each other in the stream,[82] though past ones are "irrevocably dead and gone" their continuity is known as part of a unique individual history. The "I" is master of continuity between "the Me of now and the Me of then," able to recognize the contrasts and changes in the "Me," yet absorbing these as part of a same Self. "The ME, like every other aggregate, changes as it grows":[83] "if from one point of view I am one self, from another I am quite as truly many"[84] (an observation Proust will apply to Albertine). "As a concrete Me, I am somewhat different than I was [. . .] then poorer, now richer; then younger, now older, etc."

The "I" maintains the unbroken continuation of the stream of cumulative transient cognitive states that constitute experience for James at this time,[85] absorbing these states or "pulses" of activity in a unique individual brain, he hypothesizes, as the Stream of Consciousness.[86] The "moral" or emotive world described in *À la recherche du temps perdu* could not exist without the "conscious sensibility" of the "solitary thinker," who reveals to the reader his judgments of the private "moral" world he inhabits. In his vision and his art, "the facts of his own subjectivity" create his world.[87]

The "Me," according to James, has material, or physical, social, and spiritual aspects: "*In its widest possible sense, however, a man's ME is the sum total of all that he CAN call his,* not only his body and his psychic powers, but his clothes and his house, his wife and children, his ancestors and friends, his reputation and works" [emphasis original].[88] The "Me" has a history and readily serves as subject for Proust's "expérimentation."[89] The "Me's" material or corporeal aspects are the most obvious, and his social side the "most interesting,"[90] for it is many-faceted: "Properly speaking, *a man has as many social selves as there are individuals who recognize him* and carry an image of him in their mind [italics original]."[91] Different observers are likely to see the same individual differently from one another, and over time, a lone observer, such as an "I" recounting, will notice different aspects of any single individual—even of himself—detecting the variety in past vignettes and spotting specific alterations.

Like other writers before him, Proust made particular use of the multiformity of the human psyche examined in depth in James's theory. In his portrayal of the hero's experiences and relationships, he takes full advantage of the faceted notion of the multiplicity of a self over time: "Notre moi est fait de la superposition de nos états successifs" [Our ego is composed of the superimposition of our successive states];[92] and he readily exploits the potential for plot development inherent in the notion of the *social self* and the self in society.

Like the narrator, the social self craves approval.[93] The narrator is terribly shy but in Balbec wants to be noticed by Mlle. de Stermaria, accepted by and included among the vigorous young people he sees walking, riding horses, heading to the tennis court, or riding bicycles:

> À Combray, comme nous étions connus de tout le monde, je ne me souciais de personne. Dans la vie de bains de mer on ne connaît pas ses voisins. Je n'étais pas encore assez âgé et j'étais toujours resté trop sensible pour avoir renoncé au désir de plaire aux êtres et de les posséder.[94]
>
> [At Combray, since we were known to everyone, I took heed of no one. In seaside life one does not know one's neighbors. I was not yet old enough, and was still too sensitive to have outgrown the desire to find favour in the sight of other people and to possess their hearts.[95]]

Astonished surprise is the narrator's reaction to his own varying perceptions of members of "la petite bande" [the little band of girls]: "l'être que nous avons vu la dernière fois et celui qui nous apparaît aujourd'hui sous un autre angle, nous montrant un nouvel aspect [. . .] tout une grappe de visages justaposés dans des plans différents et qu'on ne voit pas à la fois" [the person whom we saw last time and the one who appears to us today from another angle and shows us a new aspect . . . a whole cluster of faces juxtaposed on different planes so that one does not see them all at once].[96] A function of memory, this idea has evident ramifications for the cubist kind of fractionalizing so important for the narrator's conception of Albertine. In "La Prisonnière" ["The Captive"] the narrator comments on her slippery identity: "Il me semblait posséder non pas une mais d'innombrables jeunes filles" [I seemed to possess not one but countless girls].[97] When he first encounters Albertine at Balbec, the narrator attempts to reconcile his several images—sightings, really—of an athletic brunette:

> [T]andis que les innombrables images que m'a présentées dans la suite la brune joueuse de golf, si différentes qu'elles soient les unes des autres, se superposent (parce que je sais qu'elles lui appartiennent toutes) et que si je remonte le fil de mes souvenirs, je peux, sous le couvert de cette identité et comme dans un chemin de communication intérieure, repasser par toutes ces images sans sortir d'une même personne.[98]

> [(W)hereas the countless images that have since been presented to me by the dark young golfer, however different they may be, are superimposed one upon the other (because I know that they all belong to her), and by retracing my memories I can, under cover of that identity and as if through an internal passageway, run through all those images in turn without losing my grasp of one and the same person.[99]]

She is at the same time opaque, hard, and impenetrable like metal, yet shifting, deep, and murky like the waters of the ever-changing unharnessable sea she would come to incarnate; like its mercurial surface, color, and horizon, she would be endlessly interesting, changing, unattainable, with myriad buried treasures and secrets:

> Si nous pensions que les yeux d'une telle fille ne sont qu'une brillante rondelle de mica, nous ne serions pas avides de connaître et d'unir à nous sa vie. Mais nous sentons que ce qui luit dans ce disque réflichissante n'est pas dû uniquement à sa composition matérielle; que ce sont, inconnues de nous, les noires ombres des idées que cet être se fait, relativement aux gens et aux lieux qu'il connaît [. . .] des projets qu'elle forme ou qu'on a formés pour elle; et surtout que c'est elle, avec ses désirs, ses sympathies, ses répulsions, son obscure et incessante volonté. Je savais que je ne posséderais pas cette jeune cycliste si je ne possédais aussi ce qu'il y avait dans ses yeux. Et c'était par conséquent toute

sa vie qui m'inspirait du désir; désir douloureux, parce que je le sentais irréalisable, mais enivrant.[100]

[If we thought that the eyes of such a girl were merely two glittering sequins of mica, we should not be athirst to know her and unite her life to ours. But we sense that what shines in those reflecting discs is not due solely to their material composition; that it is the dark shadows, unknown to us, of the ideas that that person cherishes about the people and places she knows . . . of the plans that she is forming or that others have formed for her; and above all that it is she, with her desires, her sympathies, her revulsions, her obscure and incessant will, I knew that I should never possess this young cyclist if I did not possess also what was in her eyes. And it was consequently her whole life that filled me with desire; a sorrowful desire because I felt that it was not to be fulfilled, but an exhilarating one.[101]]

François Mauriac, using Jamesian terminology, suggests that because of the streaming mobility of conscious experience and personality, ownership of another is unattainable: "Impossible, car l'être aimé n'est pas un mais multiple, comment posséder ce qui dure? Un moi, dans l'être aimé, succède indéfiniment à l'autre; autant vouloir immobiliser un fleuve, pour l'étreindre"[102] [Impossible, because the beloved is not singular but multiple, how can one possess something lasting? One self, in the beloved, follows another indefinitely; you might as well try to immobilize a river to embrace it.]

From the very first, knowing Albertine would be a voyage of discovery to rip the masks off her social self in order to penetrate and possess her in all senses of the verb "to know." Each experience with her will add dimensions through which the narrator can forage for tidbits of knowledge about who she really is, what her past experiences had really been, what she really thought. Her variability and her unknowability build the imaginative hold she retains in the narrator's mind. Thus, echoes of James's irreparable separation of individuals appear in Proust's novel. From the narrator's descriptions of watching Albertine sleep leaps the searing impossibility of ever fathoming her, knowing her past and her present, intimately and completely. The narrator can never completely vanquish Albertine's "Me." While she sleeps, she is entirely contained within herself and yet easiest to dominate; for then, her desires and her will, her half of any interaction, are completely eliminated; she does not change and is whatever his fancy dictates:

Son moi ne s'échappait pas à tous moments, comme quand nous causions, par les issues de la pensée inavouée et du regard. Elle avait rappelé à soi tout ce qui d'elle était en dehors, elle s'étai réfugiée, enclose, résumée, dans son corps. En la tenant sous mon regard, dans mes mains, j'avais cette impression de la posséder tout entière que je n'avais pas quand elle était réveillée.[103]

> [Her personality was not constantly escaping, as when we talked, by the outlets of her unacknowledged thought and of her eyes. She had called back into herself everything of her that lay outside, had withdrawn, enclosed, reabsorbed herself into her body. In keeping her in front of my eyes, in my hands, I had an impression of possessing her entirely which I never had when she was awake.[104]]

After her death, she will live on in recurrent flashes through the narrator's memory: "Mais ce fut surtout ce fractionnement d'Albertine, qui était son seul mode d'existence en moi" [But it was above all that fragmentation of Albertine into many parts, into many Albertines, that was her sole mode of existence in me].[105] Not quite faded to a ghostly spirit, she appears in a Picasso-like series of actual moments experienced over time and remembered in separate views. "Pour me consoler, ce n'est pas une, c'est d'innombrables Albertine que j'aurais dû oublier" [In order to be consoled I would have to forget, not one, but innumerable Albertines].[106]

For James, memory loss and misremembered facts help to account for changes in the "Me." "The passing states of consciousness, which should preserve in their succession an identical knowledge of its past, wander from their duty," and a goodly share is either not retained or is retained incorrectly.[107] The dreams, reveries, and occurrences that take place during hypnotic states are relatively brief, while more serious, lasting abnormal and pathological changes in the "Me" occurring in cases of mental disease (the delusions of insanity, multiple personality, and "possessions") represent significant aberrations affecting memory of the Self. But even in normal individuals, not all experience is retained whole cloth and with complete accuracy; those facts that are remembered can become embroidered, mixed with dreams, recounted more colorfully, or otherwise changed for effect, even inadvertently. Fiction is the only way to recount memory, because, in fact, it is the only way the past is retained. As James surmised without the same vocabulary, the "open architecture" of the brain allows for regrouping associative networks of nervous impulse that change or expand with experience and with reading, according to Maryanne Wolf, remodeling the facts in front of us into creative thought and adaptation,[108] and the fictionalizations of memory.

Memories fade and are forgotten, most typically with advancing age. But no matter how different the adult has become due to the "slow shifting" of conscious states that create a man's "Me" different from the child he once was, he still retains and recognizes a goodly portion of the memories of his childhood as his own. Proust will revisit the experience of his narrator's childhood "Me" in Combray and the sway of experience following it, replaying it in fiction as if the narrator were experiencing it in real time.

He is choosing an ambiguous position: to tell the tale of his narrator's experience, as the narrator lived it, as though it were happening in the present. Yet the tale is told from the perspective of someone looking back, reporting on events and the mechanisms of remembering them. Because Proust's work is not a memoir or direct report on the author's own life, since the speaker is "pas toujours moi," and because it is filtered through a distorting medium—memory—the story, even where there is a basis in fact, has of necessity become fiction; the author has become, necessarily, a "romancier."

This standpoint would certainly account for the view that biography and autobiography divorced totally from fictional embroidery or the interpretation and elaboration of hindsight is nigh impossible: "The most frequent source of false memory is the account we give to others of our experiences. Such accounts we almost always make both more simple [*sic*] and more interesting than the truth. [. . .] But ere long the fiction expels the reality from memory and reigns in its stead alone."[109] Oliver Sacks reiterates this notion today: "There is no way by which the events of the world can be directly transmitted or recorded in our brains; they are experienced and constructed in a highly subjective way [. . .] and differently reinterpreted or re-experienced whenever they are recollected. [. . .] [O]ur only truth is narrative truth."[110]

As the long, slowly moving history of the narrator unfurls, memory will hold his "Self" together: "Je suis le seul être que je/ ne puisse oublier" [I am the only being I cannot forget],[111] noted Proust. Childhood with its naïve anticipations, followed by initiation, experience, and error, a mix of "oubli" [forgetting] and "souvenirs" [memories] that transform him over time seem to furnish the author the scaffolding of a plot outline upon which to amplify a novel. This novel would contain all the substantive elements of a life lived in its fullness, as Proust listed in his carnets: family life, reading, art, music and travel, social, political, and sexual life, genealogy, and language, etc.; and it would have a potential author/hero like the normative person (whose psychological apparatus James analyzes), observing all but unready or unable to write: "Cette médiocrité du moi / l'empêche de se placer dans / l'état où était l'écrivain / donc de le comprendre,—elle / empêche aussi d'écrire"[112] [This mediocrity of self / prevents it from being placed in / the condition of a writer / or understanding that /—it also prevents writing].

In his carnet, Proust reflects on the difficulty of creation and the "warmth" of the self's memory that he—or his narrator—has carried within for a long time:

> Tout est fictif, laborieu / sement car je n'ai pas d'imagination / mais tout est rempli d'un sens / que j'ai longtemps porté en moi, / trop longtemps car ma pensée en a / oublié, mon coeur s'est refroidi, / et j'ai façonné

difficilement / pour lui ces gauches conduites / qui l'enferment mais d'où la / chaleur émane.[113]

[Everything is fictional but painstakingly, because I have no imagination; / but everything is filled with a sense that I have long carried within me, / too long, because my mind has / forgotten so much and my heart cooled, / and it is with difficulty that I have shaped the awkward conduct confining it but from which warmth still flows.]

Over time and with advancing age, the changes James calls "mutations" in the "Me," both as seen by others and as the "I" sees it,[114] may account for what seem like interruptions in consciousness. Like "lacunes" [gaps] for Proust, James acknowledges that the hiatus and spaces often hold just as much importance in the stream of consciousness as the elements they connect.

Some recent studies of nineteenth-century writings (especially work by Pierre Janet) on abnormal behavior, including multiple personality and wandering in the guise of an alternate identity or sleepwalking, attribute such periods of variant consciousness to Proust's notion of intermittence, as does Edward Bizub in *Proust et le moi divisé* [*Proust and the Divided Self*]. These James would consider highly aberrant variations of the normal disruptions in consciousness that occur during sleep or "breaks" in thought-content.[115] (James was certainly familiar with French research on personality disorders and the paranormal, especially the work of Janet and Binet, and in 1890 published "The Hidden Self" on that subject.[116])

But despite gaps in attention and memory, James felt that individual consciousness retained a sense of the continuity of the self. In the same way, a reader of Proust would never doubt—despite the changes in the narrator's interpretations of events, his mistakes and corrections, his reviving grief at his grandmother's death—that it is the self-same narrator we are reading about and not a schizophrenic suffering from multiple personality disorder. The narrator lives a continuous life; whatever intermittences do occur (in sleep, drunkenness, or forgetting), his remembered experience falls well within the range of psychological normalcy. "This community of self is what the time-gap cannot break in twain, and is why a present thought, although not ignorant of the time-gap, can still regard itself as continuous with certain chosen portions of the past."[117] The functional "I" continues, and memory serves as the glue holding personality together.

When Peter and Paul wake up in the same bed, and recognize they have been asleep, each one of them mentally reaches back and makes connection with but *one* of he two streams of thought which were broken by the sleeping hours. [. . .] so Peter's present instantly finds out Peter's past and never by mistake knits itself on to that of Paul. [. . .] He *remembers* his own states, whilst he only *conceives* Paul's.[118]

This statement is very nearly echoed by Proust. How is it that after a deep sleep, wonders the narrator, in which our dreams have taken us wandering, do we awaken to our same selves as before? Like James, Proust is examining consciousness from the point of view of the "normal" in psychology. Although dreams inhabit sleep, upon awakening memory reactivates personality:

> Comment, alors, cherchant sa pensée, sa personnalité comme on cherche un objet perdu, finit-on par retrouver son propre moi plutôt que tout autre? Pourquoi, quand on se remet à penser, n'est-ce pas alors une autre personnalité que l'antérieure, qui s'incarne en nous? On ne voit pas ce qui dicte le choix et pourquoi, entre les millions d'êtres humains qu'on pourrait être, c'est sur celui qu'on était la veille qu'on met juste la main.[119]
>
> [How then, searching for one's thoughts, one's personality, as one searches for a lost object, does one recover one's own self rather than any other? Why, when one begins again to think, is it not a personality other than the previous one that becomes incarnate in one? One fails to see what dictates the choice, or why, among the millions of human beings one might be, it is on the being one was the day before that unerringly one lays one's hand.[120]]

A basic tenet of human inner experience is an incessant shifting that accounts for the alterations and transformations that seem to take place over time. Changes that occur in the brain account for the dynamic flow of consciousness: because "*no* changes in the brain are physiologically ineffective, [. . .] presumably none are bare of psychological result."[121]

No experience is relived exactly as it was before, a completely identical duplicate of a previous state. "[A]n unmodified brain [. . .] is a physiological impossibility," wrote James, "so is an unmodified feeling an impossibility."[122] We can experience the "*same* object," the same concrete reality again, the same "perfume," color "green" or "pain,"[123] but it will always be experienced a little bit differently. "Often we are ourselves struck at the strange differences in our successive views of the same thing. [. . .] When the identical fact recurs, we *must* think of it in a fresh manner, see it under a somewhat different angle, apprehend it in different relations from those in which it last appeared."[124]

> From one year to another we see things in new lights [. . .] The friends we used to care the world for are shrunken to shadows; the women once so divine, the stars, the woods, and the waters, how now so dull and common!—the young girls that brought an aura of infinity, at present hardly distinguishable existences.[125]

Change over time, this dynamic multiplicity of view, is a psychological fact that became a critical theme in Proust's novel. The characters revisited at the "Bal de Têtes" in *Le Temps retrouvé* wear new guises, but in the narrator's mind they carry behind them, like the tail of Haley's Comet visible in 1910, the full trail of all the altering instants of their pasts. In his explanation of the physiology of sight, James describes the visual mechanism responsible for such a metaphor; the perception of a "trail of light" following an ascending rocket or "shooting stars" is caused by a delay in the eye's response to the alteration of the sensation.[126]

> Experience is remoulding us every moment, and our mental reaction on every given thing is really a resultant of our experience of the whole world up to that date. [. . .] [W]hilst we think, our brain changes, and that, like the aurora borealis, its whole internal equilibrium shifts with every pulse of change.[127]

Proust built his literary architecture around the framework of passing time and changing perception: the perpetual revisions of political and social opinion; questions of whether Albertine was offering true facts or outright lies that varied with the telling; places revisited that proved disappointing (the adult visit to the source of the Vivonne river reveals nothing more than a square pool filled by a bubbling spring used as a public wash basin, not a mysterious location "aussi extra-terrestre que l'entrée des Enfers" [as extraterrestrial as the Gates of Hell];[128] Gilberte's gesture considered "indécent" in *Du côté de chez Swann* explained later as "come-hither";[129] the disparate worlds of Guermantes and Méséglise in fact connected topographically and genetically in Mlle de Saint-Loup.[130] To offer cohesion to the many-sided Self, to aggregate the disparate social, material and spiritual aspects identified by James, Proust chose to portray recovery of the past.

The continuity of Self enables a person to recognize certain privileged "chosen portions" of his own past[131] through the gift of memory. But the past is not retained as lived it its entirety in a sort of Bergsonian durée. In fact, in a letter to H. Massis written at the end of 1937, Bergson makes it clear that does not think the Proust adopted his view of "la durée" any more than James had: "Sa pensée a bien pour essence de tourner le dos à la 'durée' et à l'élan vital'" [He basically turned his back to the "durée" and "l'élan vital"].[132]

Proust's narrator, at the very end of the book, digging deep into his personal history, remembers the tinkling bell on the gate at Combray when Swann came to visit. His knowing Self, the "I" that exists continuously with lasting presence, provides his salvation as a writer; he will be able to re-create the impressions of his past, because, functionally, his existence is unbroken:

> Quand elle avait tinté j'existais déjà et depuis pour que j'entendisse encore ce tintement, il fallait qu'il n'y eût pas eu discontinuité, que je n'eusse pas un instant cessé, pris le repos de ne pas exister, de ne pas penser, de ne pas avoir conscience de moi, puisque cet instant ancien

> tenait encore à moi, que je pouvais encore le retrouver, retourner jusqu'à lui, rien qu'en descendant plus profondément en moi.[133]
>
> [When the bell of the garden gate had pealed, I already existed and from that moment onwards, for me still to be able to hear that peal, there must have been no break in continuity, no single second at which I had ceased or rested from existing, from thinking, from being conscious of myself, since that moment from long ago still adhered to me and I could still find it again, could retrace my steps to it, merely by descending to a greater depth within myself.[134]]

Unlike characters viewed solely from the outside, the narrator carries his past selves with him continually, accessing his own private knowledge of them when memory revives an instant of that past. In time traveled ceaselessly his past will always accompany him:

> J'éprouvais un sentiment de fatigue et d'effroi à sentir que tout ce temps si long non seulement avait, sans une interruption, été vécu, pensé, sécrété par moi, qu'il était ma vie, qu'il était moi-même, mais encore que j'avais à toute minute à le maintenir attaché à moi, qu'il me supportait, moi, juché à son sommet vertigineux, que je ne pouvais me mouvoir sans le déplacer comme je le pouvais avec lui.[135]
>
> [And I felt, as I say, a sensation of weariness and almost of terror at the thought that all this length of Time had not only, without interruption, been lived, experienced, secreted by me, that it was my life, was in fact me, but also that I was compelled so long as I was alive to keep it attached to me, that it supported me and that, perched on its giddy summit, I could not myself make a movement without displacing it.[136]]

STRUCTURES OF CONSCIOUSNESS

Flights and Perchings

The varying states of mind that comprise a single individual's conscious thought, though unified in all belonging together to that one person, initially accounted for its description as a chain or train of separate entities. But we are not so restricted to experiencing the present moment that we cannot retain a memory or a *feeling* of what came just before: "[I]nto our awareness of the thunder the awareness of the previous silence creeps and continues; for what we hear when the thunder crashes is not thunder *pure*. But thunder-breaking-upon-silence-and-contrasting-with-it."[137] When Proust's narrator's consciousness is plunged into an environment marked by the unfamiliar, he is painfully sensitive to the newness, yet in his writing he embraces the contrast.

The narrator of the short introductory piece Proust wrote for his translation of Ruskin's *Sésame et les Lys*, originally entitled "Sur la lecture," describes the effects of such emotional "thunder." Just as James had emphasized the paramount interest of the Self in its own existence and the contrast between it and all that it is *not*, in "Sur la Lecture," Proust underscores the discrepancy between a comfortable and familiar sense of Self and the jarring yet stimulating dislocation of the new that will reappear later in *À la recherche du temps perdu*: "Pour moi, je ne me sens vivre et penser que dans une chambre où tout est la création et le langage opposé au mien, où je ne retrouve rien de ma pensée consciente, où mon imagination s'exalte en se sentant plongée au sein du non-moi" [As for me, I do not feel my self alive and thinking if not in a room where everything is organized and in language contrary to mine, where I find nothing of my conscious thought, where my imagination exults in finding itself plunged into the bosom of the not-me.]

The narrator's consciousness is not rent in two by the "thunder" of the unfamiliar but remains continuous. When released from the comfort of its regular nest, his sense of Self is sharpened to enhance its emotional excitability, sensitivity, and perceptiveness "où chaque bruit ne sert qu'à faire apparaître le silence en le déplaçant"[138] [where every noise only serve to highlight the silence it displaces]. Here Proust uses the *same kind of image* as James did to signal his magnified response to impinging sound creating awareness of previous silence. Ongoing consciousness in the face of contrasting stimuli results in imaginative provocation and arousal by the "other" (as in his pastiches, where contrast with the voices of other writers allowed him to find his own).

Reading in the Pré Catalan, the narrator of "Sur la lecture" can only sense the sound of church bells by the silence that follows them. While an unfamiliar room sparked his imaginative capacity, here, sitting among the plants and hearing the reverberations of the bells, feelings of past sensations resonate. They trigger a "flight": the narrator's fancy wanders, his mind's eye meanders, intermittently "perching" on various objects of attention.

Throughout his discussions of consciousness, James points to the intertwined relationship between streaming thought and language. Language itself affects our awareness, notes James, in a mode of thinking still current and crucial to Proust's imaginative interactions with words and names:

> Here again, language works against our perception of the truth. We name our thoughts simply, each after its thing, as if each knew its own thing and nothing else. What each really knows is clearly the thing it is named for, with dimly perhaps a thousand other things. [. . .] Some of them are always things known a moment ago more clearly; others are things to be known more clearly a moment hence.[139]

The fact that we are physical creatures experiencing through our physicality affects the subject matter of our thoughts and their pace, the speed of psychic adjustments among them. Though lacking twenty-first-century neuroscientific instrumentation, James theorized that physical alterations in the brain were analogous to kaleidoscopic changes in perception. Changes in the brain, variable in rate and lasting power, were thus responsible for the pace and "kind" of consciousness. Because of a lag in nervous activity accompanying thought, we experience feelings of relation in consciousness *between* the "substantive" or sensational end points of thought. These can extend from what James calls a "restful and stable" level of awareness to a condition of rapid transition[140]: "some forms of tension lingering relatively long, whilst others simply come and pass"[141]; "sensorial images are stable psychic facts [. . .] transitions, always on the wing, so to speak, and not to be glimpsed except in flight."[142]

James so well illustrated his concept of the structure of thought in the stream of human sentience that his description has become one of his most frequently quoted passages. He uses the avian metaphor "flights and perchings" to illustrate the sensory substantive and the resonant transitive aspects of thought inherent in the flow of the Stream of Consciousness.[143] In Proust's novel these are reconfigured into technique, texture, rhythm of writing. Thought that is long, complex, and filled with relational color, feeling, alternatives, etc., is reflected in the patterning of narrative language by the consciousness that produced it:

> When we take a general view of the wonderful stream of our consciousness, what strikes us first is the different pace of its parts. Like a bird's life, it seems to be an alternation of flights and perchings. The rhythm of language expresses this, where every thought is expressed in a sentence, and every sentence is closed by a period. The resting-places are usually occupied by sensorial imaginations of some sort, whose peculiarity is that they can be held before the mind for an indefinite time, and contemplated without changing; the places of flight are filled with thoughts of relations, static or dynamic, that for the most part obtain between the matters contemplated in the periods of comparative rest.
>
> *Let us call the resting-places the "substantive parts," and the places of flight the "transitive parts," of the stream of thought.*[144]

Bergson envisioned the "durée" as permanent flight along the trajectory of which we would find the more static points situated; for James, there is definite functional alternation, the "flights" or "transitive parts" leading from one "perching" or static point to the next accompanied by "a feeling of relation moving to its term."[145]

For James, the "transitive" or relational aspects of thought are fleeting. To represent their capture he uses images of a snowflake melting in the hand that seizes it, an attempt to discern the motion of a spinning top or moving arrow, or the effort to turn the gaslight up quickly enough to examine the dark. "Flights" are highly important affective bonds between the more stable "substantive" sensorial elements. They reveal tinges of impression or feeling, "the innumerable relations and forms of connection between the sensible things of the world"[146] and, although usually unarticulated, they are exactly what Proust's narrator searches to unveil in great detail.

> There is not a conjunction or a preposition, and hardly an adverbial phrase, syntactic form or inflection of voice, in human speech, that does not express some shading or other of relation which we at some moment actually feel to exist between the larger objects of our thought. [. . .] We ought to say a feeling of *and*, a feeling of *if*, a feeling of *but*, and a feeling of *by*, quite as readily as we say a feeling of *blue* or a feeling of *cold*.[147]

The evanescent, ephemeral connective halo often only momentarily felt, according to James, surrounds a clumping of mental fact or sensorial event in consciousness. Imagination infuses words.

For Proust, as for James, those objects we can sense and classify can be presented as nouns:

> Les mots nous présentent des chose une petite image claire et usuelle comme celles que l'on suspend aux murs des écoles pour donner aux enfants l'exemple de ce qu'est un établi, un oiseau, une fourmilière, choses conçues comme pareilles à toute celles de la même sorte.[148]
>
> [Words present to us a little picture of things, clear and familiar, like the pictures hung on the walls of schoolrooms to give children an illustration of what is meant by a carpenter's bench, a bird, an anthill, things chosen as typical of everything else of the same sort.[149]]

Like these representative nouns, sensations are hard data that can be grasped and examined, representative of others of the same sort. But it is James's descriptions of the more subjective "transitive" states of *feeling* between sense data, "the innumerable relations and forms of connection between the sensible things of the world,"[150] the surrounding "halo" or "fringe" of association, that are replicated in Proust's narrator's search to understand and elucidate his impressions, enhancing his natural style (his long, meandering, image-filled emotive prose), and fundamental to his theory of metaphor.

Similar to photography or cinema, the magic lantern confers meaning through an overlay of light; like legend or fancy or imagination, the meaning it carries is for the *viewer*. In Combray, the narrator's magic lantern has the effect of imposing the "transitive" in the Stream of Thought, the immaterial, magical color and story on the solid walls, window, curtains, lampshade, doorknob of his bedroom: "elle substituait à l'opacité des murs d'impalpables irisations, de surnaturelles apparitions multicolores, où des légendes étaient dépeintes comme dans un vitrail vacillant et momentané" [it substituted for the opaqueness of my walls an impalpable iridescence, supernatural phenomena of many colours, in which legends were depicted as on a shifting and transitory window].[151] This serves as symbol of the embroidery power the mind brings to the objective reality of things on which it focuses. Characters from the world of the magic lantern mix readily with fictional "real" people when "Golo s'arrêtait un instant pour écouter avec tristesse le boniment lu a haute voix par ma grand'tante, et qu'il avail l'air de comprendre parfaitement" [Golo stopped for a moment and listened sadly to the accompanying patter read aloud by my great-aunt, which he seemed perfectly to understand].[152] Why is this episode placed at the beginning of such a long book? The substantive elements of the room and its furnishings play into the images projected upon them in light, mingling stories.

> Le corps de Golo lui-même, d'une essence aussi surnaturelle que celui de sa monture, s'arrangeait de tout obstacle matériel, de tout objet gênant qu'il rencontrait en le prenant comme ossature et en se le rendant intérieur, fût-ce le bouton de la porte sur lequel s'adaptait aussitôt et surnageait invinciblement sa robe rouge ou sa figure pâle toujours aussi noble et aussi mélancolique, mais qui ne laissait paraître aucun trouble de cette transvertébration.[153]

> [The body of Golo himself, being of the same supernatural substance as his steed's, overcame every material obstacle—everything that seemed to bar his way—by taking it as an ossature and absorbing it into himself: even the doorknob—on which, adapting themselves at once, his red cloak or his pale face, still as noble and as melancholy, floated invincibly—would never betray the least concern or transvertebration.[154]]

The legends of Golo and of Geneviève de Brabant inhabit the room along with the narrator. They bring the strangeness of "un passé mérovingien" [a Merovingian past] and the "intrusion du mystère et de la beauté" [intrusion of mystery and beauty][155] to a room in which the narrator just barely feels comfortably at home, upsetting his very tentative emotional equilibrium. Fiction mixes with supposed "fact"; the truth of the experience is not solid like walls or a lamp; it is imparted by feelings and interpretation.

Proust describes how for some people interior decor and framed art is a pleasurable way to radiate around themselves a periphery reflective of their identity, tastes, and interests, their aesthetic preferences. The unknown or unfamiliar is more of a stimulant to the narrator's imaginative creativity: he favors milkmaids, chambermaids, shopgirls, and Albertine. Their attraction comes at least in part because they are so *different*. The feeling of "cette vie secrète" [the secret life] belonging the headboard, the carpeting, the fabric pattern of the drapes described in "Sur la Lecture," and the many strangers who have left the imprint of their heads on the pillow in an anonymous and mediocre "hôtel de province" [provincial hotel] is what the narrator will use to feel himself truly alive and sentient, free and stimulated to explore imagination and memory. He almost requires this reverberating sense of strangeness or blankness to elicit the transient halo of conscious resonance and romance, the enticing imaginative transitive space he will explore.

James depicts the transitive elements of thought as "but flights to a conclusion" that disperse before analysis can seize them in its grasp and that the harsh brightness of the conclusion obliterates.[156] So often left out of any analysis of mind,[157] according to James, these provide depth and seem so fresh and original in Proust's prose. Volatile, they must be expressed in the first person while they are happening. If a "biscotte" can become a more poetically named madeleine, it can also be imbued with the poetic power to evoke resurgent memory: "Mais l'imagination n'a pas d'expérience,"[158] [But imagination has no experience] complained Proust in *Jean Santeuil*. He had not yet discovered his ability to use this transitive surrounding aura of feeling, so fleeting mentally and emotionally, as focus for his plot. For in the broadest sense, the narrator's affective moments of resurgent memory, emanating in his mind from a variety of physical sensations, are Jamesian transitive experiences that bridge the distance between physical experiences now and physical experiences in his past, perfect fuel for his literary imagination.

In *À la recherche du temps perdu,* Proust attempts to articulate "sensibilité" and elucidate the "transitive" using metaphor. Ultimately, intellectual effort and analysis prove sterile. Truth is not handed to those who think hardest, who parse every fact using intellect and voluntary effort. Flight through emotion, impression, and memory yield a higher, aesthetic truth, one revealed by the narrator during the grand party at Mme. Verdurin's orchestrated to his detriment by M. de Charlus. In this passage, the narrator dwells on the coloration of feeling, the ramifications and associations hidden and overt, in pools of prose teeming with reflection. The shape of the text, the paragraph and sentence structure itself, relays meaning, with stopping points in the narrative for fantasy and commentary, forays of pensive attention, poetic musing, imaginative reverie alternating with explanation and lucid analysis characteristic of Proust's narrator.[159]

At the Verdurins', the narrator's body presumably sits and listens to Vinteuil's "rougeoyant septuor" [red septet], while his consciousness soars. Structured along the lines of James's analysis of the lurch and flow of thought (which he labeled "stream of thought" or "stream of consciousness"), there are multiple "flights" and "perchings" in which the narrator's attention wanders and alights, focuses on his surroundings and companions, on specific sounds, and then surges off into resonant associative thought, exploring the images or feelings the music arouses, beginning in confusion and ending with revelation.

Morel is playing music composed by Vinteuil but unexpected and unfamiliar to the narrator. At first, he describes it as virgin territory; he feels lost. Then, like a genie bounding out to help the hero at a confusing moment in the *Arabian Nights*, "la petite phrase" [the little phrase] decked out in new and tantalizing finery magically leads him to the thought that he is "en pleine sonate de Vinteuil" [right in the heart of Vinteuil's sonata].[160] But, like a genie, the presence of "la petite phrase" is gossamer and fleeting. The sense of familiarity is just a pointer to something truly new and surprising. Unlike the bucolic sonata, "l'oeuvre nouvelle" [this new work[161]] first resembles sunrise on a stormy sea. A displeasing sound recalling church bells distracts him from his solo "flight," and his attention perches on the substantive in the room around him: he views Mme. Verdurin's posture and expression, hears her dog snore, looks at the musicians. A phase in the music recaptures his regard; he sees it as a triumphant affirmation of a new direction only hinted at in Vinteuil's earlier works.

Correspondingly, he contemplates his previous loves as mere prelude to the complex relationship he now has with Albertine and muses on the breach in his heart made by what might jestingly be termed her "evil twin"—the painful and uncertain experience of her ultimate insuperable alterity. Like any real person, she is opaque and uncontrollable. He can absorb her image, he can imprison her body, but he cannot capture or even identify her feelings, her past, her individuality—her inescapable and impenetrable "otherness." She will always be a matter of experience, with a wide periphery of relations, and as fascinating, stimulating, yet difficult to grasp as the images projected by the translucent slides of the magic lantern or the bounding waves of the sea. Her opacity fascinates and frustrates.

Another flourish in the music refocuses him on the septuor, and his mind perches on the seeming resurrection of the composer through his opus and on the power of art to confer eternal life. How could the Vinteuil he knew in Combray produce so magnificent a work that through the prism of his individual talent turns a ray of ordinarily sunlight into dazzling treasure?[162]

Here is the discovery at the aesthetic heart of Proust's book: the artist's joy at recognizing his power to spark a creation with freshness of colors that are his alone.[163] This type of creation has little to do with intellectual analysis: it is "aussi débarassé des formes analytiques du raisonnement que si elle si elle s'était exercée dans le monde des anges" [as free from analytical forms of reasoning as if it were being carried out in the world of the angels], transcendent and as impossible to describe as "les secrets de la mort" [the secrets of death][164] arrayed by a medium summoning members of the spirit world. It cannot be related in conversation; it does not require an aerial view of great expanses to understand; it requires the unique view, the singular experience of an individual, a view that an artist attempting to express something new discovers and develops by examining the heart of his own perceptions, the diaphanous relational elements of his own consciousness. Proust wrote the feelings of "of" and "if" and "blue" that James had identified as the transitive aspects of thought, the endlessly varying shifts of the kaleidoscope of consciousness.

In *Albertine disparue* the hero examines writing on the envelope of Aimé's letter reporting on Albertine's licentious activities in Touraine. Where others would see the scrawls of an individual's handwriting, the narrator sees "ces petits êtres familiers, à la fois vivants et couchés dans une espèce d'engourdissement sur le papier, les caractères de son écriture que lui seul possède" [those little familiar creatures, at once alive and reclining in a sort of torpor upon the paper: the characters of his handwriting which he alone possesses].[165] *Everything* vibrates with life in the hypersensitivity of his consciousness, and in the novel form he can animate all the "relations" as he feels them.

Flights convey us between substantive focal points or "conclusions," according to James.[166] Held entranced by "la céleste phrase musicale avec laquelle je venais de m'entretenir" [the heavenly phrase of music with which I had just been communing],[167] while the ordinary mortals in the room were at best simply entertained, the narrative takes flight as the hero's attention turns from feeling to feeling, moment of experience to moment of experience, with minimal transition. Perching occurs between the periods of affective meandering through the fringes of sensation and memory, at junctures when the narrator focuses on "objects" drawn forth—music to names to love affairs. Would the transitive information discerned between sensory loci be what is communicated if, in the absence of language and logic, music sufficed to convey knowledge emotively from spirit to spirit?[168] Felt knowledge cannot be spoken, even between friends. Only art can reveal it.[169]

The intermission over, Vinteuil's septuor and the multiple flights and perchings it generates resume; the narrator tries once again to identify the particular "fairies" of phrasing dwelling in Vinteuil's works that appear in different guises.[170] He sees them dancing in a "brouillard violet" [a violet mist] or "captive dans une opale" [captive in the heart of an opal],[171] fearful and poised for flight. When his thought returns briefly to the audience around him, he imagines the "voile confus" [dim veil] blocking their view of what he sees in the music: the only mysterious and enticing "Inconnue" [Unknown Woman] ever encountered, one more appealing than any ordinary mortal lover. As it develops, he feels the music almost corporeally, unsure as to whether "ses reprises, si c'était celles d'un thème ou d'une névralgie" [at each of its re-entries whether it was a theme or an attack of neuralgia].[172]

His "spectateur intérieur" [inward spectator][173] senses the metaphysical—"une joie supraterrestre, [que] je n'oublierais jamais" [a supraterrestrial joy . . . I would never forget]. He asks, "Mais serait-elle jamais réalisable pour moi?" [But would it ever be attainable to me?] Will this intimate contact with Vinteuil's music enable him to condense and reproduce the several special "impressions" he has experienced, cutting them out of the ordinary fabric of his own life[174] to reproduce the way they felt in his own work of art, in a book?

And how could it be, he wonders once again, that this glimpse of the eternal emanated from the ordinary little man he knew in Combray? How did this work come to light, since it was unknown at the time of Vinteuil's death? Here, beauty had to pass through a circle of "fire"—or vice—a meaningful parable for Proust's narrator. Homosexuality—with its sadistic side—surfaces, and the narrator considers this in yet another flight, finally to perch on the thought that the lesbian lover of Vinteuil's daughter must have painstakingly transcribed his notes, bequeathing to the public the lasting legacy of his genius despite the ugly cloak of depravity encircling it.[175] As he listened to this "red septuor," the narrator's observations, like shoreline rocks, were bathed by waves of the invisible affective "transitive."

The Fringe of Relations

"Feelings of contact reproduce [. . .] sights, sounds, and tastes with which experience has associated them," wrote William James. "In fact, the 'objects' of our perception, as trees, men, houses, microscopes, of which the real world seems composed, are nothing but clusters of qualities which through simultaneous stimulation have so coalesced that the moment one is excited actually it serves as a sign or cue for the idea of the others to arise."[176] The qualitative information about objects of our awareness, the descriptive, adjectival, expressive, evocative "knowledge about" the things that we encounter, is difficult to communicate directly. But these are just as significant as the transitive portions of the stream of thought, and just as laden with cognitive consequence.

For James the transitional and the apparently barren spots in mental function are as important as concrete sensational objects: "It is [. . .] the reinstatement of the vague and inarticulate to its proper place in our mental life which I am so anxious to press on the attention."[177] Thought is not a blank slate even when it is not sensibly specific. It contains directional information, the forward leaning of intent. It may consist of something forgotten that we try to remember or the hints of meaning we draw from language. In normal directed thinking just such a void "swims in a felt fringe of relations." They cloak the impression as a "mood" or mimetic state.[178] The fringe enhances what we know about a topic and may consist of verbal or other sensory input, including that generated by memory, fantasy, or dream. Its critical feature is its contribution to a "feeling of harmony or discord, of a right or wrong direction in the thought."[179]

James knows the color "blue" when he sees it and the way a "pear" tastes, but what is it that actually constitutes and transmits that knowledge he cannot say.[180] Proust understood how to use style and the comparative terms of metaphor to supply the indirect expressive and evocative information surrounding the terms in James's fringe. The fringe accounts for the recognition that accompanies a privileged moment of resurgent memory; it is the associative ability of the brain at work:

> Again, what is the strange difference between an experience tasted for the first time and the same experience recognized as familiar, as having been enjoyed before, though we cannot name it or say where or when? A tune, an odor, a flavor sometimes carry this inarticulate feeling of their familiarity so deep into our consciousness that we are fairly shaken by its mysterious emotional power. But strong and characteristic as this psychosis is—it probably is due to the submaximal excitement of wide-spreading associational brain-tracts—the only name we have for all its shadings is "sense of familiarity."[181]

An inarticulable impression registers in Proust's narrator when he sees the three trees at Hudimesnil from Mme. de Villeparisis's moving carriage. He interprets these trees as a harbinger of meaning, a déjà vu or inchoate and undefined memory, a vague wafting back and forth in time that he cannot place in his experience: "[J]e sentais qu'il m'avait été familier autrefois; de sorte que mon esprit ayant trébuché entre quelque année lointaine et le moment présent" [I felt that it had been familiar to me once; so that, my mind having wavered between some distant year and the present moment].[182] Perhaps it is something he dreamed or generalized from what he was reading in a book.[183] There is a margin of associative feeling that he wants to decode and describe but cannot, so it remains unverbalized; he simply feels it, "un sens aussi obscur, aussi difficile à saisir qu'un passé lointain de sorte que, sollicité par eux d'approfondir une pensée, je croyais avoir à reconnaître un souvenir" [a meaning as obscure, as hard to grasp, as is a distant past, so that, whereas they were inviting me to probe a new thought, I imagined that I had to identify an old memory].[184] Only later, when the circular construction of the story becomes evident, will the narrator (and the reader) understand the idea of double vision in time that, at the moment, the narrator thinks might simply have been caused by fatigue.[185] Not surprisingly, fatigue, according to James, limits associative ability.[186]

The fringe and transitive flow are essential for developing novelty in consciousness. To illustrate this, James uses imagery very similar to language Proust will use later to sketch crystalline beakers in the Vivonne River. First, James:

> The traditional psychology talks like one who should say a river consists of nothing but pailsful, spoonsful, quartpotsful, barrelsful, and other moulded forms of water. Even were the pails and the pots all actually standing in the stream, still between them the free water would continue to flow. It is just this free water of consciousness that

psychologists resolutely overlook. Every definite image in the mind is steeped and dyed in the free water that flows round it. With it goes the sense of its relations, near and remote, the dying echo of whence it came to us, the dawning sense of whither it is to lead. The significance, the value, of the image is all in this halo or penumbra that surrounds and escorts it [. . .] leaving it, it is true, an image of the same *thing* it was before, but making it an image of that thing newly taken and freshly understood.[187]

Proust exploits the perceptive novelty of the fringe when he writes about the "carafes" children were using to try to catch minnows in the Vivonne on his family's riverside stroll "du côté de Guermantes." Like James, the narrator notices the contrast between the uncapturable fluidity of the river and the solidity of the clear enclosures. The free-streaming water, like the vague halo in James's description, cannot be seized for refreshment, while the crystal of the beaker is as clear but also solid and hard (like James's "definite" psychological objects) and cannot quench:

> Je m'amusais à regarder les carafes que les gamins mettaient dans la Vivonne pour prendre les petits poissons, et qui, remplies par la rivière où elles sont à leur tour encloses, à la fois "contenant" aux flancs transparents comme une eau durcie et "contenu" plongé dans un plus grand contenant de cristal liquide et courant, évoquaient l'image de la fraîcheur d'une façon plus délicieuse et plus irritante qu'elles n'eussent fait sur une table servie, en ne la montrant qu'en fuite dans cette allitération perpétuelle entre l'eau sans consistance où les mains ne pouvaient la capter et le verre sans fluidité où le palais ne pourrait en jouir.[188]
>
> [I enjoyed watching the glass jars which the village boys used to lower into the Vivonne to catch minnows, and which, filled by the stream, in which they in their turn were enclosed, at once "containers" whose transparent sides were like solidified water and "contents" plunged into a still larger container of liquid, flowing crystal, conjured up an image of coolness more delicious and more provoking than they would have done standing upon a table laid for dinner, by showing it as perpetually in flight between the impalpable water in which my hands could not grasp it and the insoluble glass in which my palate could not enjoy it.[189]]

Words, the medium of Proust's narrator's intended art, are in James's view laden with fringes of association: "The words in every language have contracted by long association fringes of mutual repugnance or affinity with each other and with the conclusion, which run exactly parallel with like fringes in the visual, tactile and other ideas."[190] They retain associative echoes that are essentially "the unpredictable indirections of [. . .] inference" brought to situations, paintings, text,[191] the mimetic ability to conjure for a reader pointed out by Michael Riffaterre, and the metonymic "irradiation" or "contagion" noted by Gérard Genette in *Fig-*

ures III. "[W]ords, uttered or unexpressed, are the handiest mental elements we have. Not only are they very *rapidly* revivable, but they are revivable as actual sensations more easily than any other items of our experience."[192] The *"halo of relations around the image"* theorized by James is due, as demonstrated by today's neuro-cognitive scientists, to spreading neuronal activity in the brain:[193]

> It is just like "overtones" in music: they are not separately heard by the ear; they blend with the fundamental note, and suffuse it, and alter it; and even so do the waxing and waning brain-processes at every moment blend with and suffuse and alter the psychic effect of the processes which are their culminating point.[194]

These indirect referential inclusions of image that are inherent in words are the basis of Proust's narrator's vocation and the essence of his style. The image he uses to depict a simple prosaic childhood experience—chunks of bread pilfered from the family's packed "goûter" [snack] and launched into the water in lieu of pebbles—offers these imaginative nuances. The bread becomes supersaturated and "crystallize[s]" the water's flow around it, shaping fringes or coalescing out of nowhere clutches of previously immaterial tadpoles.[195]

When Odette distances herself from Swann, his jealous pain, his overweening curiosity and anxiety about her actions constitute an *emotional* fringe: "cette formidable terreur qui le prolongeait comme un trouble halo, cette immense angoisse de ne pas savoir" [the fearsome terror which extended like a cloudy halo all around her, the immense anguish of not knowing].[196]

Proust used exploration of the fringe and of knowledge—or lack thereof—of relations in a tantalizing way to add depth to fictional depiction of the rift between what is obvious and what is significant in everyday experience. Echoed later in the white space of the narrator's relationship with Albertine is Swann's familiarity with the "bare bones" absence of Odette, while missing from his understanding is the mysterious truth of her comportment.

For James, feelings elicited in the fringe may be comparable even though their descriptions differ. "These feelings of relation, these psychic overtones, halos, suffusions, or fringes about the terms may be the same in very different systems of imagery."[197] And different thinkers may process the same fact in radically different ways though they arrive at similar conclusions. Thus, the fringe can be rendered nearly tangible by the doubling analogy of metaphor, the stereoscopic process Proust used to suggest the overlapping of different images, the intersection of different loops of association.[198] This is the Proustian art of consciousness.

As Swann listens to a violin and piano duet at the Verdurins', the pleasure of the instruments' blended sound is enhanced as images of color and motion, moonlight on waves:

> Et ç'avait été déjà un grand plaisir quand, au-dessous de la petite ligne du violon, mince, résistante, dense et directrice, il avait vu tout d'un coup chercher à s'élever en un clapotement liquide, la masse de la partie de piano, multiforme, indivise, plane et entrechoquée comme la mauve agitation des flots que charme et bémolise la clair de lune.[199]
>
> [And it had been a source of keen pleasure when, below the delicate line of the violin-part, slender but robust, compact and commanding, he had suddenly become aware of the mass of the piano-part beginning to emerge in a sort of liquid rippling of sound, multiform but indivisible, smooth yet restless, like the deep blue tumult of the sea, silvered and charmed into a minor key by the moonlight.[200]]

Swann searches to identify his pleasure and realizes that the melody and harmony have opened a doorway to diffuse and normally silent impalpable and sensual delight, passing and gone like a beautiful moist floral scent before he can capture and analyze it.

For James the "shadowy scheme of the 'form' of an opera, play, or book, which remains in our mind and on which we pass judgment when the actual thing is done"[201] is also an expression of the fringe of relations. Each time Proust's narrator goes to see la Berma play Phèdre, he looks for what makes the play great, what distinguishes the actress and accounts for her fine reputation, for the unique magic (between and) in the lines he knows so well but that he feels can only be evident on stage. He looks so hard that the secrets of this allure were not accessible to him the first time he saw her play the part. The second time, with greater maturity, he realizes that the way la Berma incarnated the character brings these words to life in a way no other actress could duplicate.

Why does the child hero of *Du côté de chez Swann* respond so strongly to the pink hawthorn flower? Unlike the usual white ones, it has a unique and different "psychic overtone."[202] It stands out, and the child narrator's attention selects it. According to James, "We notice only those sensations which are signs to us of *things* which happen practically or aesthetically to interest us."[203] They interest us, because they are permeated with *special* connotations that have particular meaning—perhaps because they arouse desire.

> Alors, me donnant cette joie que nous éprouvons quand nous voyons de notre peintre préféré une oeuvre qui diffère de celles que nous connaissions, ou bien si l'on nous mène devant un tableau dont nous n'avions vu jusqu-là qu'une esquisse au crayon, si un morceau entendu seulement au piano nous apparaît ensuite revêtu des couleurs de l'orchestre, mon grand-père, m'appelant et me désignant la haie de Tansonville, me dit: "Toi qui aimes les aubépines, regarde un peu cette épine rose; est-elle jolie!" En effet c'était une épine, mais rose, plus belle encore que les blanches.[204]

> [And then, inspiring me with that rapture which we feel on seeing a work by our favourite painter quite different from those we already know, or, better still, when we are shown a painting of which we have hitherto seen no more than a pencilled sketch, or when a piece of music which we have heard only on the piano appears to us later clothed in all the colours of the of the orchestra, my grandfather called me to him, and, pointing to the Tansonville hedge, said to me: "You're fond of hawthorns just look at this pink one—isn't it lovely?" And it was indeed a hawthorn, but one whose blossom was pink, ad lovelier even than the white.[205]]

Not only does the pink flower express these metaphorical analogies, it also has the holiday overtones of a religious festival and connotes small-town values where pink cookies are more costly than plain ones. The color has the gustatory associations of a delicious privilege, "le fromage à la crème rose, celui où l'on m'avait permis d'écraser des fraises" [cream cheese when it was pink, when I had been allowed to tinge it with crushed strawberries].[206] And the color looks dressed up, like the "tendre embellissement à une toilette pour une grande fête" [some fond embellishment of a costume for a major feast].[207] Why such a profound reaction to a pink flower?[208] The emotional resonance of the hawthorn hedge is the setting and frame for the first experience of desire—the first sighting of Gilberte:

> Je la regardais, d'abord de ce regard qui n'est pas que le porte-parole des yeux, mais à la fenêtre duquel se penchent tous les sens, anxieux et pétrifiés, le regard qui voudrait toucher, capturer, emmener le corps qu'il regarde et l'âme avec lui.[209]

> [I gazed at her, at first with that gaze which is not merely the messenger of the eyes, but at whose window all the senses assemble and lean out, petrified and anxious, a gaze eager to reach, touch, capture, bear off in triumph the body at which it is aimed, and the soul with the body.[210]]

The brain activity of an energetic mind has wide powers of association to give flavor or cast to a word, idea, or concept, and Proust took the time to observe and analyze this "halo of felt relations";[211] he exerted great effort to express it lucidly and to milk its imaginative potential.

Desire in *À la recherche du temps perdu* is as tyrannical as it is obsessive. The desperate neediness of the child, who manipulates circumstances to obtain the calming effect of his mother's goodnight kiss in Combray, unleashes the emotional overtones that will color every amorous relationship.[212]

Desire goes from initial pink to very dark, and it is accompanied by intensive reflection and questioning to elucidate its fringe of unknown gray area. Gilberte resents the narrator's subtle but overweening demands; Mme. de Guermantes refuses to acknowledge his stalking; he can never completely imprison and control Albertine, the most beguiling object of desire because she inspires the strongest emotional and imaginative responses: "C'est qu'en effet sa personne même y est pour peu de chose; pour presque tout, le processus d'émotions, d'angoisses que tels hasards nous ont fait jadis éprouver à propos d'elle et que l'habitude a attaché à elle" [The fact is that her person itself counts for little or nothing; what is almost everything is the series of emotions and anxieties which chance occurrences have made us feel in the past in connexion with her and which habit has asssociated with her].[213]

The narrator's description of an evening spent in a restaurant in the company of Robert de Saint-Loup also illustrates the powerful elevation of Proust's art when incorporating James's notion of the fringe of relations. It is essentially a reprise of an incident originally recounted in *Jean Santeuil.* The retelling differs from the original because of the extensive and *fertile* fringe, the amplitude of associated feeling and imagery in the newer version.

Robert de Saint-Loup has inherited, among other personal qualities, a perfect face and charmingly open mind and heart, qualities exemplifying the best of his glorious aristocratic French heritage. His robust physique, exquisite manners, genial concern, and respect for the intellect of the hero mingle in the narrator's mind with memories of pleasant evenings spent dining with fellow officers in Doncières. Robert thus incarnates the pleasurable companionship of the present, fond memories of the recent past (Doncìeres), and the noble legacy of the distant past (his genealogical Guermantes inheritance).

Bertrand de Réveillon "courant sur les tables pour me rejoindre" [running on the tables to join me] is a section of *Jean Santeuil,* a set of observations in which the author tries to express how he felt in response to what he saw. The supple calf and effortlessly athletic performance of his friend walking on tables to reach his seat in the restaurant stimulated the following comment about artistic duty:

> [L]es impressions un peu profondes, qui ont frappé plus avant que son moi phénoménal et y ont apporté plus qu'une vérité phénoménale, l'artiste a le devoir de les exprimer en les laissant à leur profondeur.[214]
>
> [I]mpressions which are a bit profound and have impacted him with more than an obvious objective truth, that is what the artist is called upon to express, leaving them in their original profound state.]

The series of references to Réveillon's vigorous childhood and the education particular to his class, his noble spirit, "tout son passé rassemblé" [his entire past], try as he might, do not give the narrator what he needs to flesh out the "vérité [. . .] cachée" [hidden truth] he senses and that he will succeed in describing with greater imaginative latitude in the later version.[215] In the earlier text, the narrator is intent upon recording what he observes and feels, but he has not yet arrived at a coherent structure or the right colorations for presenting them as experienced. In *À la recherche du temps perdu* there is a more developed and more nuanced story line; it begins with a halo of disquietude. In fog so thick no one can see, the trip to the restaurant is marked by an uneasy sense of danger and fear of being "dépaysé" [lost]. On Saint-Loup's face briefly appears something unexpected: the narrator does not know how to understand the fleeting, unsavory, almost treacherous glimpse he catches of his friend, "une expression hideuse de bassesse, presque de bestialité toute passagère et sans doute ancestrale" [a hideous expression of baseness, almost of bestiality, quite transitory and no doubt inherited].[216] Hinted at here is the fact that Robert's character has facets usually masked. This transient emergence of a disturbing, normally hidden, perhaps ancestral trait dissipates as soon as the carriage arrives in front of the brightly lighted restaurant filled with disparate social groups engaged in noisy, animated conversation. The hero enters alone first and in confusion struggles with the revolving door; he is awkward, inept, and inadvertently chooses to sit in the side of the restaurant reserved for the nobility. Rudely, he is ushered to a drafty seat on a banquette facing the "Jewish" door.

When Saint-Loup enters and finds his friend, he demonstrates all the self-confidence and congenital physical and social skills of his class—those that belonged initially to Bertrand de Réveillon in *Jean Santeuil.* The aura of his aristocratic background surrounds and guides his every thought and move. Added to the benefits of this background and education is a breadth of character all his own. Indicating to his noble peers that he prefers to sit with his friend, he borrows a vicuna coat from the Prince de Foix, climbs on the red velvet banquette, and, to applause of diners and wait-staff alike, scales the distance to their table with the "sûreté" of an aristocratic "cheval de course" [nimbly . . . like a steeplechaser][217] jumping fences. What ensues is a meditation on what makes the aristocracy different from the rest. Looking at Robert this way is a matter of apprehending and scrutinizing an impression akin to appreciating a painting or sculpture intellectually and aesthetically. The "rêverie" meanders through the lens of the narrator's appreciative response to his friend's surface and his depths.

The events in the restaurant are the rapidly occurring seeds of the narrator's meditative flight, an extensive thought process to which the reader is privy. Events are refracted as through a mental prism to reveal their artistic value for the narrator. The episode serves a double function: telling us what the narrator supposedly could not write because he went out for the evening with his friend instead of staying home with his thoughts, while providing the very material for the work in question. The original story has undergone a Jamesian transformation in which past experience is seen anew, in a process and using language that illustrates the relational fringe:

When the identical fact recurs, we *must* think of it in a fresh manner, see it under a somewhat different angle, apprehend it in different relations from those in which it last appeared. And the thought by which we cognize it is the thought of it-in-those-relations, a thought suffused with the consciousness of all that dim context.[218]

For Proust, the fringe is an indispensable vehicle for seeing the historical import of the present moment, for bringing into view what is objectively absent but relationally present, for resuscitating the Guermantes family as far back as Geneviève de Brabant in the genes of Saint-Loup and Mme. de Guermantes, or for feeling Balbec in the arms of Albertine:

Sans doute, c'est seulement par la pensée qu'on possède des choses et on ne possède pas un tableau parce qu'on l'a dans sa salle à manger si on ne sait pas le comprendre, ni un pays parce qu'on y réside sans même le regarder. Mais enfin j'avais autrefois l'illusion de ressaisir Balbec, quand, à Paris, Albertine venait me voir et que je la tenais dans mes bras.[219]

[No doubt it is only in one's mind that one possesses things, and one does not possess a picture because it hangs in one's dining-room if one is incapable of understanding it, or a landscape because one lives in it without even looking at it. But still, I had had in the past the illusion of recapturing Balbec, when in Paris Albertine came to see me and I held her in my arms.[220]]

The "teinte maîtresse" [dominant colour][221] of an individual's emotive response permeates all it touches, just as a primary experience of desire colors all desire. Even when events or love affairs are widely separated in time, they fall into the same sweep of personal disposition or reaction, a personal zone of the fringe of relations.

In "Phases of Fiction," Virginia Woolf explains Proust's very modern attempt to seize and render in words those felt relations best expressed indirectly: "It is as though there were two faces to every situation; one full in the light so that it can be described as accurately and examined as minutely as possible; the other half in shadow so that it can be described only in a moment of faith and vision by the use of metaphor."[222] It was Proust's exploitation of the *artistic potential* inherent in the Jamesian "fringe" of relations that allowed him to develop his mature style.[223]

CONSCIOUSNESS AND ART: A WAY OF SEEING

Like the narrator's objects of affection, all subject to his selfsame neediness, consciousness presents to each of us a world of our own interpretation, a world of our own construction, a world, wrote James, that is "individualized by our mind's selective industry [. . .] by our habits of attention."[224] This is particularly true of the realm of the artist. Each artist inhabits an identifiable world of his own formulation, be he Vinteuil, Vermeer, or Proust, as *"elimination"* of what is merely "accidental" and explicit expression of the fringe, the unique tenor of his impressions, give his works a distinct identity, or style, as if all his works were one.

> Vous m'avez dit que vous aviez vu certains tableaux de Ver Meer, vous vous rendez bien compte que ce sont les fragments d'un même monde, que c'est toujours, quelque génie avec lequel elle soit recréée, la même table, le même tapis, la même femme, la même nouvelle et unique beauté, énigme à cette époque où rien ne lui ressemble ni ne l'explique, si on ne cherche pas à l'apparenter par les sujets, mais à dégager l'impression particulière que la couleur produit.[225]

> [You told me you had seen some of Vermeer's pictures: you must have realised that they're fragments of an identical world, that it's always, however great the genius with which they have been re-created, the same table, the same carpet, the same woman, the same novel and unique beauty, an enigma at that period in which nothing resembles or explains it, if one doesn't try to relate it all through subject matter but to isolate the distinctive impression produced by the colour.[226]]

For James, a particular "dustwreath" blown about by a breeze may be worthy of note, just as a ray of light stealing through the curtains might be for Proust's narrator. Four travelers visiting the same cities would report four different visions; in a world surrounded by insect life, only the entomologist would note the bugs' particulars. "Out of what is in itself an undistinguishable, swarming *continuum*, devoid of distinction or emphasis, our senses make for us, by attending to this motion and ignoring that, a world full of contrasts, of sharp accents, of abrupt changes, of picturesque light and shade."[227] It is the particular tint of the fringe of relations as the artist alone sees it, the colors of his imagination's overlay, like magic lantern light, that infuses with romance and mystery the sound of names, obsolete dialects or customs, the particular "velours" of color or scent, the glow selective memory adds to experience.

> À l'âge où les Noms, nous offrant l'image de l'inconnaissable que nous avons versé en eux, dans le même moment où ils désignent aussi pour nous un lieu réel, nous forcent par là à identifier l'un à l'autre au point que nous partons chercher dans une cité une âme qu'elle ne peut contenir mais que nous n'avons plus le pouvoir d'expulser de son nom [. . .], ce n'est pas seulement l'univers physique qu'ils diaprent de différences, qu'ils peuplent de merveilleux, c'est aussi l'univers social: alors chaque château, chaque hôtel ou palais fameux a sa dame ou sa fée comme les forêts leurs génies et leurs divinités les eaux. Parfois, cachée au fond de son nom, la fée se transforme au gré de la vie de notre imagination qui la nourrit.[228]

[At the age when Names, offering us an image of the unknowable which we have poured into their mould, while at the same moment connoting for us also a real place, force us accordingly to identify one with the other to such a point that we set out to seek in a city for a soul which it cannot enshrine but which we have no longer the power to expel from its name, it is not only to towns and rivers that they give an individuality, as do allegorical paintings, it is not only the physical universe which they speckle with differences, people with marvels, it is the social universe also; and so every historic house, in town or country, has its lady or its fairy, as every forest has its genie, every stream its deity. Sometimes, hidden in the heart of its name, the fairy is transformed to suit the life of our imagination, by which she lives.[229]]

As a result the narrator suffers "déception" or disappointment when these are encountered as they really are without their imaginatively tinted fringe. Under certain propitious circumstances, the magic of resurgent memory is that it is able to reconstitute the fringe and add it to a sensibly experienced actuality:

Pour un instant, du ramage réentendu qu'il avait en tel printemps ancien, nous pouvons tirer, comme des petits tubes dont on se sert pour peindre, la nuance juste, oubliée, mystérieuse et fraîche des jours que nous avions cru nous rappeler quand, comme les mauvais peintres, nous donnions à tout notre passé étendu sur une même toile les tons conventionnels et tous pareils de la mémoire volontaire.[230]

[For a moment, from the clear echo of its warbling in some distant springtime, we can extract, as from the little tubes used in painting, the exact, forgotten, mysterious, fresh tint of the days which we had believed ourselves to be recalling, when, like a bad painter, we were giving to the whole of our past, spread out on the same canvas, the conventional and undifferentiated tones of voluntary memory.[231]]

The challenging prose and form of Proust's "roman" would be best suited to reflect the pregnancy of thought and feeling, the richness of Jamesian conscious experience, and to deliver it in its entirety as directly as possible to the reader. Art alone, in music, in painting, or in the painterly written metaphorical language of literature, could bridge the ineffable gap between even the best of friends or most intimate of lovers and render visible the private, normally imperceptible transitive fringe of experience in a Jamesian mimetic conversion of the dynamic of individual sensory life:

[T]out ce résidu réel que nous sommes obligés de garder pour nous-mêmes, que la causerie ne peut transmettre même de l'ami à l'ami, du maître au disciple, de l'amant à la maîtresse, cet ineffable qui différencie qualitativement ce que chacun a senti et qu'il est obligé de laisser au seuil des phrases où il ne peut communiquer avec autrui qu'en se limitant à des points extérieurs communs à tous et sans intérêt, l'art,

> l'art d'un Vinteuil comme celui d'un Elstir, le fait apparaître, extériorisant dans les couleurs du spectre la composition intime de ces mondes que nous appelons les individus, et que sans l'art nous ne connaîtrions jamais?[232]

> [A]ll the residuum of reality which we are obliged to keep to ourselves, which cannot be transmitted in talk, even from friend to friend, from master to disciple, from lover to mistress, that ineffable something which differentiates qualitatively what each of us has felt and what he is obliged to leave behind at the threshold of the phrases which he can communicate with others only by limiting himself to externals, common to all and of no interest—are brought to the art of a Vinteuil like that of an Elstir, which exteriorizes in the colours of the spectrum the intimate composition of those worlds which we call individuals and which, but for art, we should never know?[233]]

This private "stream of sentiency"[234] is continuous but continually changing, neither enduring, in a Bergsonian sense, nor duplicable. The meaning develops for us as we interpret events and impressions, investing in them our varying associations at different times in our lives. We may read the same book, smell the same rose again and again, or hear the same sonata, but each turn yields new and fresh responses that are affected by the surroundings and by our history.

What Elstir paints as water and sky may intermingle; his view is based on his impression of light and dark at the specific moment he chooses to depict it. No other viewer may see it exactly the same way, and a week later even he may not see the harbor at Carquethuit exactly as he painted it the week before. "The entire history of what is called Sensation," explained James, "is a commentary on our inability to tell whether two sensible qualities received apart are exactly alike. What appeals to our attention far more than the absolute quality of an impression is its *ratio* to whatever other impressions we may have at the same time."[235] "The grass out of the window now looks to me of the same green in the sun as in the shade, and yet a painter would have to paint one part of it dark brown, another part bright yellow, to give its real sensational effect," wrote James. "We take no heed, as a rule, of the different way in which the same things look and sound and smell at different distances and under different circumstances."[236] But Proust did.

He attributes to Elstir Turner's phrase about painting what is "seen" rather than what is "known": in reply to a naval officer commenting on a drawing Turner had done of Plymouth Harbor in which the ships had no visible port-holes, the painter answered, "'I know that [the port-holes are there] well enough; but my business is to draw what I see, and not what I know is there.'"[237]

Dying, Bergotte went to see a Vermeer exhibit, because he had read a critical article describing la *Vue de Delft,* a painting he knew and loved.

The critic had written that "un petit pan de mur jaune" [a little patch of yellow wall], which Bergotte was unable to call to mind, "était si bien peint qu'il était, si on le regardait seul, comme une précieuse oeuvre d'art chinoise, d'une beauté qui se suffirait à elle-même" [was so well painted that it was, if one looked at it by itself, like some priceless specimen of Chinese art, of a beauty that was sufficient in itself].[238] This little patch of sunshine had the complexity and stand-alone beauty of a work of art, the painterly effects that render sensational impact palpable. Seeing the painting this time with the eyes of a dying man, Bergotte had a whole new view of it; for the first time he noticed little figures painted in blue, sand painted pink and he saw the yellow patch of sunshine on the wall. He had not actually sensed its importance until he saw it in the context of the dull color of the surrounding wall. Focusing on it with his diminishing strength, but intently like a child staring at a yellow butterfly he wants to catch ("il attachait son regard, comme un enfant à un papillon jaune qu'il veut saisir"), he lamented that his recent books needed the same degree of complexity ("il aurait fallu passer plusieurs couches de couleur") ["I ought to have gone over them with a few layers of colour"] and linguistic beauty ("rendre ma phrase en elle-même précieuse") ["made my language precious in itself"],[239] sensitivity to emotion and to the ramifications of sensation and color, greater emphasis on the sparkle and highlight of intense feeling beautifully rendered in order to convey reality more directly.

A corresponding patch of golden sunshine lights the wall outside the narrator's room when, each morning in Balbec, Françoise opens the drapes. Gone is his anticipation of a foggy, stormy coast, and in its place a harsh glare as timeless and enduring as the gilt case of a mummy enclosing the games, walks, social interactions, and desires awakened at the seaside.

Seen from a train window by a tipsy teenage narrator, village and bay intermingle, valley and seaside appear layered, darkness and dawn seem simultaneous depending on the angle of view, and a blue window-shade is magnificent for the unique beauty in the sheer intensity of its color. "The mind," wrote James, "chooses certain of the sensations to represent the thing most *truly*, and considers the rest as its appearances, modified by the conditions of the moment."[240] In this way, style is a value judgment, dependent upon personal impression, a unique field of association, and selection.

We are surrounded by things we hardly ever notice, but "a thing met only once in a lifetime may leave an indelible experience in the memory."[241] We note what is significant but may be absent,[242] and we forget much more than we remember: "[M]emory can seldom accurately reproduce such an object, when once it has passed from before the mind. It either makes too little or too much of it [. . .] the mass of our thinking vanishes for ever, beyond hope of recovery."[243] In other words, forgetting is the normal state. Unanticipated remembering is special. It adds depth to our present.

Turning around and around what is felt amidst the stream of conscious experience, leaping from sensory perch through affective fringe, picking apart and exploring the prismatic colors emitted by the beam of attention, gave Proust and his narrator a structure within which to work plot, social commentary, generalized maxims. It enabled both to become a new kind of novelist in whose work the ricochet of metaphor would reflect the density of Jamesian "full sensible-image-value," rather than a dry, conceptual "thought [. . .] left unrealized and pale."[244]

Henri Ghéon wrote in the January 1, 1914, issue of *La Nouvelle Revue Française,* as quoted in Pierre-Quint: "La phrase de Proust 'épouse le tout d'un moment'; elle tend une sorte de filet indéfiniment extensible qui traîne sur le fond océanique du passé et en ramasse toute la flore et la faune à la fois" [Proust's sentence "milks everything from a moment"; it extends a sort of infinitely stretchable net that drags the ocean floor of the past, gathering all the flora and fauna at once]. Ghéon sensed that Proust had created "un vrai trésor de documents sur l'hypersensibilité moderne"[245] [a true treasure documenting modern hypersensitivity]. Ghéon has used an image very similar to one used in the philosophy text James was preparing at the time of his death, published from notes by his student H. M. Kallen under the title *Some Problems of Philosophy*. Here James strives to explain conceptual thought as the thinker's retrospective use of a string net to be filled with the captive butterflies of real experiences.[246] But in his day, Proust's readers did not recognize his ties to James.

NOTES

1. Denying, for example, that he had fictionalized Bergson.
2. See *Corr.*, XIII, *8*, 37–41, note 16, 40.
3. *Corr.*, XIII, *8*, 37–41, note 18, 41.
4. *Corr.*, XIX, *312*, 573–577, 574.
5. Marcel Proust, interview with André Arnyvelde, "À propos d'un livre récent: L'Oeuvre écrite dans la chambre close. Chez M. Marcel Proust (1913)," [Cahiers Marcel Proust 3]: *Textes retrouvés*, éd. Philip Kolb (Paris: Éditions Gallimard, 1971): 294–295.
6. Léon Pierre-Quint, *Proust et la stratégie littéraire* (Paris: Corréa, 1954), 3.
7. See Philippe Lejeune, *Le Pacte autobiographique* (Paris: Éditions du Seuil, 1975).
8. Dorrit Cohn, *The Distinction of Fiction* (Baltimore: The Johns Hopkins University Press, 1999), 7.
9. *RTP*, III, 583, 663.
10. Élie-Joseph Bois, "Swann Expliqué par Proust," *Le Temps*, 13 novembre 1913, repr. *Essais et articles*, 557–559.
11. Marcel Proust, "À propos du 'style' de Flaubert," *Essais et articles, Contre Sainte-Beuve* (Paris: Éditions Gallimard [Bibliothèque de la Pléiade], 1971), 586–600, 599.
12. *Jean Santeuil*, 490.
13. *RTP*, II, 614. Enright, III, 431, 432.
14. *RTP*, IV, 34.

15. Enright, V, 607.
16. See *RTP*, IV, 253. Enright, V, 918.
17. And to those who study reading, including Maryanne Wolf, *Proust and the Squid: The Story and Science of the Reading Brain* (New York: HarperCollins, 2007), 17.
18. Gérard Genette, *Narrative Discourse: An Essay in Method*, trans. Jane E. Lewin (Ithaca, NY: Cornell University Press, 1980), 30.
19. James, *Briefer Course*, 262.
20. Roger Shattuck, *Proust's Way: A Field Guide to "In Search of Lost Time"* (New York: W.W. Norton, 2000), 146.
21. *Corr.*, XIII, *43*, 98–101, 99. Also quoted in Vincent Descombes, *Proust: Philosophie du roman* (Paris: Les Éditions de Minuit, 1987), 13, 185.
22. Descombes, *Philosophie*, 30.
23. Pierre-Quint, *Stratégie*, 90.
24. Pierre-Quint, *Stratégie*, 93.
25. Bois, *Variétés*, 285.
26. Pierre-Quint, *Stratégie*, 24.
27. Pierre-Quint, *Stratégie*, 30.
28. Proust, "Flaubert," 598–599.
29. *Corr.*, XVIII, *266*, 462–465, 464.
30. *Corr.*, XVIII, *266*, 462–465, 464.
31. James, *Principles*, I, 232.
32. James, "Omissions," 6.
33. James, *Principles*, I, 233; *Briefer Course*, 145.
34. James, *Principles*, I, 520.
35. James, *Principles*, I, 522.
36. Bernard Brun, "Narrateur (*CSB*)," *Dictionnaire Marcel Proust* (Paris: Honoré Champion, 2004) 675.
37. Melvin Friedman, *Stream of Consciousness: A Study in Literary Method* (New Haven: Yale University Press, 1955), 74–75.
38. Wolf, 162.
39. Friedman, *Stream*, 80.
40. Proust, *Corr.*, XII, *135*, 299.
41. James, *Principles*, I, 520–521.
42. James, *Briefer Course*, 326.
43. Pierre-Quint, *Stratégie*, cited without source in Bois, "*À la recherche*," 287.
44. Bois, "*À la recherche*," 287, 290.
45. Carter, *Proust: A Life*, 81.
46. Proust, quoted by André Arnyvelde, "À propos d'un livre récent," 295.
47. James, *Principles*, I, 263.
48. James, *Principles*, I, 221.
49. Cohn, *Transparent Minds*, 4.
50. *RTP*, II, 80. Enright, II, 409.
51. Wolf, 16.
52. *RTP*, II, 77. Enright, II, 405.
53. Shattuck, *Proust's Way*, 139–141.
54. Genette, *Narrative Discourse*, 227.
55. Genette, *Narrative Discourse*, 223.
56. Genette, *Narrative Discourse*, 249.
57. James, *Principles*, I, 238.
58. James, *Principles*, I, 215–216. James is quoting B. P. Bowne, 403–410. James provides no publication information, but reference is likely to Borden Parker Bowne, *Metaphysics: A Study in First Principles* (New York: Harper & Brothers, 1882).
59. Cohn, *Transparent Minds*, 55.
60. James, "Spencer," 2–3.
61. James, "Spencer," 16.
62. James, "Spencer," 10.

63. James, "Omissions," 1–2.
64. James, *Principles*, I, 218.
65. *RTP*, IV, 468. Enright, VI, 290.
66. Robert Humphrey, *Stream of Consciousness in the Modern Novel* (Berkeley and Los Angeles: University of California Press, 1954), 3–4.
67. James, *Briefer Course*, 306–307.
68. *RTP*, IV, 125. Enright, V, 733.
69. James, "Are We Automata?" *Mind* 4.13 (January 1879): 1–22.
70. James, "Automata," 8.
71. William C. Carter, "'Am I a Novelist?' Proust's Search for a Genre," *Proust in Perspective*, ed. Armine Kotin Mortimer and Katherine Kolb (Chicago: University of Chicago Press, 2002), 35.
72. James, *Briefer Course*, 158.
73. James, *Briefer Course*, 141.
74. James, *Principles*, I, 220–221; *Briefer Course*, 140–141.
75. James, *Briefer Course*, 181.
76. James, *Briefer Course*, 182.
77. *RTP*, II, 26.
78. Enright, II, 332.
79. James, *Briefer Course*, 163.
80. James, *Briefer Course*, 190–191.
81. James, *Briefer Course*, 159.
82. James, *Briefer Course*, 181.
83. James, *Briefer Course*, 183.
84. James, *Briefer Course*, 180.
85. James, *Briefer Course*, 180–181.
86. James, *Briefer Course*, 178.
87. William James, "The Moral Philosopher and the Moral Life, " *International Journal of Ethics* 1 (1891): 330–354, repr. *The Will to Believe, and Other Essays in Popular Philosophy* (New York: Longmans, Green & Co., 1897); *The Writings of William James*, ed. John J. McDermott (Chicago: University of Chicago Press, 1977), 610–629, 614–615. repr. *The Will to Believe and Other Essays in Popular Philosophy* (Cambridge: Harvard University Press, 1979), 141–162, 146.
88. James, *Briefer Course*, 160.
89. Arnyvelde, 295.
90. James, *Briefer Course*, 172.
91. James, *Briefer Course*, 162.
92. *RTP*, IV, 125. Enright, V, 733.
93. James, *Briefer Course*, 161.
94. *RTP*, II, 35.
95. Enright, II, 334.
96. *RTP*, II, 269–270. Enright, II, 677–678
97. *RTP*, III, 580. Enright, V, 87.
98. *RTP*, II, 201.
99. Enright, II, 580.
100. *RTP*, II, 152.
101. Enright, II, 510–511.
102. François Mauriac, *Du côté de chez Proust* (Paris: La Table Ronde, 1947), 81, 82.
103. *RTP*, III, 578.
104. Enright, V, 84–85.
105. *RTP*, IV, 110. Enright, V, 713.
106. *RTP*, IV, 60. Enright, V, 645.
107. James, *Briefer Course*, 183.
108. See Wolf, 17.
109. James, *Briefer Course*, 184.

110. Oliver Sacks, "Speak, Memory," *New York Review of Books* LX.3 (February 21, 2013): 19–21. See also Donald P. Spence, *Narrative Truth and Historical Truth: Meaning and Interpretation in Psychoanalysis* (New York: W.W. Norton, 1982).
111. *Le Carnet de 1908*, 54.
112. *Le Carnet de 1908*, 77.
113. *Le Carnet de 1908*, 69.
114. James, *Briefer Course*, 183.
115. See James, *Briefer Course*, 144.
116. William James, "The Hidden Self," *Scribner's Magazine* 7 (1890): 361–373.
117. James, *Principles*, I, 232–233; *Briefer Course*, 145.
118. James, *Psychology*, 158; 1984, 145.
119. *RTP*, II, 387.
120. Enright, III, 110.
121. James, *Principles*, I, 229.
122. James, *Briefer Course*, 143.
123. James, *Briefer Course*, 142.
124. James, *Briefer Course*, 143.
125. James, *Principles*, I, 227; *Briefer Course*, 144.
126. James, *Briefer Course*, 45. James cites as source H. Newell Martin, *The Human Body* (New York: Holt, 1881), 517.
127. James, *Principles*, I, 228.
128. *RTP*, IV, 268. Enright, VI, 3.
129. *RTP*, IV, 269.
130. *RTP*, IV, 268.
131. James, *Briefer Course*, 145.
132. Henri Bergson, Letter to H. Massis [fin décembre 1937], *Correspondances*, 1585. Bergson compares his view of the "durée" to the "flights" and "perchings" in James's conception of the stream of consciousness in a letter to Floris Delattre (24 août 1923), *Correspondances*, 1053–1054. Bergson wrote regarding Delattre's book, *William James, bergsonien* (Paris: Presses Universitaires de France). The only information available regarding date of publication indicates that it was sometime in the 1920s.
133. *RTP*, IV, 624.
134. Enright, VI, 530.
135. *RTP*, IV, 624.
136. Enright, VI, 530–531.
137. James, *Briefer Course*, 146.
138. Marcel Proust, "Sur la lecture," *La Renaissance latine* (15 juin 1905), repr. as "Journées de lecture," *Pastiches et mélanges* in *Contre Sainte-Beuve* (Paris Éditions Gallimard [Bibliothèque de la Pléiade], 1971), 167.
139. James, *Principles*, I, 234–235. For this explanation, James credits the Rev. James Wills's "buried and forgotten paper" entitled "Accidental Association," *Transactions of the Royal Irish Academy* XXI (1848).
140. James, *Principles*, I, 236.
141. James, *Briefer Course*, 148–149.
142. James, *Principles*, I, 244.
143. James's image is sustained by the very similar pattern by which our eyes gather information: "small movements called saccades, [are] followed by very brief moments when the eyes are almost stopped, called fixations," notes Maryanne Wolf, "while we gather information from our central [...] vision" (Wolf, 148).
144. James, *Briefer Course*, 146.
145. James, *Briefer Course*, 147.
146. James, *Briefer Course*, 147.
147. James, *Briefer Course*, 148.
148. *RTP*, I, 380–381. James makes specific reference to the way children learn to associate letters and objects in *Principles*, I, 525.
149. Enright, I, 551.

150. James, *Briefer Course*, 147.
151. *RTP*, I, 9. Enright, I, 10.
152. *RTP*, I, 9–10. Enright, I, 10.
153. *RTP*, I, 10.
154. Enright, I, 11.
155. *RTP*, I, 10. Enright, I, 11.
156. James, *Principles*, I, 236.
157. James, *Briefer Course*, 148.
158. Proust, *Jean Santeuil*, 255.
159. Roger Shattuck employs the word "flight" in connection with the narrator's meditation on the alternative views of the universe revealed by art as he listens to the Vinteuil septuor. Music allowed Proust greater latitude for expansive commentary. Shattuck, *Proust's Way*, 148.
160. *RTP*, III, 753. Enright, V, 332.
161. Enright, V, 333.
162. *RTP*, III, 758.
163. *RTP*, III, 758–759.
164. *RTP*, III, 760. Enright, V, 341.
165. *RTP*, IV, 105. Enright V, 707.
166. James, *Briefer Course*, 146.
167. *RTP*, III, 762. Enright, V, 344.
168. *RTP*, III, 763.
169. *RTP*, III, 762. Enright, V, 343.
170. *RTP*, III, 763. Enright, V, 345.
171. *RTP*, III, 763–764. Enright, V, 345–346.
172. *RTP*, III, 764. Enright, V, 346.
173. *RTP*, III, 764. Enright, V, 347.
174. *RTP*, III, 764–765. Enright, V, 347.
175. *RTP*, III, 765–766.
176. James, *Principles*, I, 524.
177. James, *Briefer Course*, 150.
178. James, *Principles*, I, 250.
179. James, *Briefer Course*, 153.
180. James, *Principles*, I, 216–217.
181. James, *Principles*, I, 244.
182. *RTP*, II, 77. Enright, II, 404.
183. Or perhaps a vague recollection of Rembrandt's print *The Three Trees* (1648).
184. *RTP*, II, 78. Enright, II, 406–407.
185. *RTP*, II, 78.
186. James, *Principles*, I, 247.
187. James, *Principles*, I, 246.
188. *RTP*, I, 166.
189. Enright, I, 237.
190. James, *Briefer Course*, 153.
191. Wolf, 16.
192. James, *Principles*, I, 256.
193. James, *Briefer Course*, 151.
194. James, *Briefer Course*, 152.
195. *RTP*, I, 166.
196. *RTP*, I, 340. Enright, I, 491–492.
197. James, *Briefer Course*, 154.
198. See "Proust's Binoculars" in Shattuck, *Proust's Way*, 117.
199. *RTP*, I, 205.
200. Enright, I, 294.
201. James, *Principles*, I, 246–247.
202. James, *Briefer Course*, 151.

203. James, *Briefer Course*, 155.
204. *RTP*, I, 137.
205. Enright, I, 195–196.
206. *RTP*, I, 138. Enright, I, 196.
207. *RTP*, I, 138. Enright, I, 196.
208. Also associated medically with the heart. See http://www.umm.edu/altmed/articles/hawthorn-000256.htm.
209. *RTP*, I, 138–139.
210. Enright, I, 198.
211. James, *Principles*, I, 247.
212. For a discussion of the significant role of separation anxiety, see Inge Crosman Wimmers, *Proust and Emotion: The Importance of Affect in "À la recherche du temps perdu"* (Toronto: University of Toronto Press, 2003).
213. *RTP*, IV, 16. Enright, V, 582.
214. Proust, *Jean Santeuil*, 452.
215. See Proust, *Jean Santeuil*, 452–454.
216. *RTP*, II, 693. Enright, III, 547.
217. *RTP*, II, 705. Enright, III, 563.
218. James, *Briefer Course*, 143.
219. *RTP*, IV, 132.
220. Enright, V. 744.
221. *RTP*, IV, 133. Enright, V, 745.
222. Virginia Woolf, "Phases of Fiction," *The Bookman* (April, May, and June 1929), repr. *Granite and Rainbow* (New York: Harcourt Brace, 1958), 139. Cited in Nicola Luckhurst, *Science and Structure in Proust's "À la recherche du temps perdu"* (Oxford: Clarendon Press, 2000), 2.
223. In his art, Proust utilized the potential of the "fringes" of association inherent in language and image that James had theorized.
224. James, *Briefer Course*, 156.
225. *RTP*, III, 878–879.
226. Enright, V, 308.
227. James, *Briefer Course*, 155.
228. *RTP*, II, 310–311.
229. Enright, III, 3.
230. *RTP*, II, 311–312.
231. Enright, III, 4.
232. *RTP*, III, 762.
233. Enright, III, 343.
234. James, "Omissions," 4.
235. James, *Briefer Course*, 142.
236. James, *Principles*, I, 225–226.
237. Robert de la Sizeranne, *Ruskin and the Religion of Beauty*, trans. Countess of Galloway (London: George Allen, 1899), 195. According to Robert de la Sizeranne in *The Genius of J.M.W. Turner, R.A.*, "Turner was the first of the Impressionists." See Robert de la Sizeranne, *The Genius of J.M.W. Turner, R.A.* (New York: John Lane, Offices of the International Studio, 1903), XIV.
238. *RTP*, III, 692. Enright, III, 244.
239. *RTP*, III, 692. Enright, V, 244.
240. James, *Briefer Course*, 156.
241. James, *Briefer Course*, 156.
242. James, *Principles*, I, 275.
243. James, *Principles*, I, 266.
244. James, *Principles*, I, 262.
245. Cited in Pierre-Quint, *Stratégie*, 85.
246. James, *Problems* 65, 99.

THREE

Parallels in the Penumbra

Tracking James's Psychology in Proust's Novel

In the dim light of a darkened room, we first encounter the hero of *À la recherche du temps perdu* nestled in bed, on the verge of sleep, hero of his own dream, or, presciently, of a book: "il me semblait que j'étais moi-même ce dont parlait l'ouvrage"[1] [it seemed to me that I myself was the immediate subject of my book[2]]. Sleep here is more than a gap in consciousness. Out of the half-shadows, and the obscure realm of private memory, will emerge the analysis of mind and experience that is the subject of the author's search.

This state of diffused awareness focused on nothing in particular lies on the margin of concentration: "The eyes are fixed on vacancy, the sounds of the world met into confused unity, the attention is dispersed so that the whole body is felt, as it were, at once, and the foreground of consciousness is filled, if by anything, by a sort of solemn sense of surrender to the empty passing of time,"[3] wrote James.

The narrator seems to float in the penumbral, shadowy room, taking pleasure in the dark, sweet void: "[J]'étais bien étonné de trouver autour de moi une obscurité, douce et reposante pour mes yeux, mais peut-être plus encore pour mon esprit, à qui elle apparaissait comme une chose sans cause, incompréhensible, comme une chose vraiment obscure"[4] [I would be astonished to find myself in a state of darkness, pleasant and restful enough for my eyes, but even more, perhaps, for my mind, to which it appeared incomprehensible, without a cause, something dark indeed[5]]. Such moments unleash the dormant imagination: "Trains of faces, landscapes, etc., pass before the mental eye, first as fancies, then as pseudo-hallucinations, finally as full-fledged hallucinations forming dreams."[6] For the narrator, a train whistle is like a far-off birdcall. Space and time are elongated as in a voyage for a traveler in search of adventure or a lover whose desire propels him to search for the woman of his dreams.

Due to the general "torpor" of the sleeping brain, what would ordinarily be experienced as a minor thought during the waking state seems very intense during sleep: "A slight peripheral irritation, then, if it reaches the centres of consciousness at all during sleep, will give rise to the dream of a violent sensation."[7] Sleep revives the dismay of "telle de mes terreurs enfantines comme celle que mon grand-oncle me tirât par mes boucles"[8] [one of my childhood terrors, such as that old terror of my great-uncle's pulling my curls[9]], an incident of childhood fright long lost to recollection that feels real enough to induce the adult narrator to wrap his head in the pillow.

James's description of the margin between the waking life and sleep is highly coincidental with Proust's portrayal of such moments: at the point of falling asleep, there is "a curious exaggeration of time-perspective" that contributes to a feeling that events close together in actual occurrence are separated by a much longer period of time. When interrupted by sleep, awareness requires memory to reconstruct events that took place on the borderline, giving them an accompanying sense of pastness.[10]

When the narrator is slightly roused from a heavy sleep, place and time are dissolved into pure physical existence. His body acts as a projector of reality, identifying the surroundings and the palpable isolation of his individual consciousness moving through time at the pace of memory. "Toujours est-il que, quand je me réveillais ainsi, mon esprit s'agitant pour chercher, sans y réussir, à savoir où j'étais, tout tournait autour de moi dans l'obscurité, les choses, les pays, les années"[11] [For it always happened that when I awoke like this, and my mind struggled in an unsuccessful attempt to discover where I was, everything revolved around me through the darkness: things, places, years[12]].

Proust begins his book with the sensations and tenses of habit and duration: "Longtemps, je me suis couché de bonne heure"[13] [For a long time I would go to bed early[14]]. He offers the reader an uncertain mix of real present moment in continuity with the span of an indeterminate past, a "pénombre" [penumbra], where memory and present sensations and thoughts mingle undelineated.

The term "pénombre" poetically suggests the shadowy sensuality of Odette's living room where Swann is surrounded by exotic chrysanthemums and oriental porcelains; it evokes the sparkling half-light of Elstir's studio; and paints a dream-like, glassy, almost marine background to showcase the limpid aquatic splendor of the Princesse de Guermantes swathed in pearls in her box at the Opera. It marks the intense emotional intimacy of shadows conjoined at dusk, when the narator strolls in the Bois with his "prisonnière" and recalls dimmed restaurants and shadowy by-ways in a city darkened during wartime, where perhaps vice lurks. Contrasting the pleasure of social interaction with the even greater pleasure of solitary introspection, the narrator reveals that friendship with Robert de Saint-Loup distracts him from exploring the most important "pénombre" of all—his inner world: "je me disais que j'avais un bon ami, qu'un bon ami est une chose rare, et je goûtais, à me sentir entouré de biens difficiles à acquérir, ce qui était justement l'opposé du plaisir d'avoir extrait de moi-même et amené à la lumière quelque chose qui y était caché dans la pénombre"[15] [I told myself that I had a good friend, that a good friend was a rare thing, and I savoured, when I felt myself surrounded by assets that were difficult to acquire, what was precisely the opposite of the pleasure that was natural to me, the opposite of the pleasure of having extracted from myself and brought to light something that was hidden in my inner darkness[16]]. The narrator's crucial discoveries lay buried in the riches of his obscure memories: the beam of his attention will disclose those he must transcribe.

Like sleep, the particulars of attention, habit, association, memory, time, sensation, imagination, perception, reasoning, effort, will, and desire found in James's psychology texts were current during Proust's lifetime and are inscribed in his work. These parallels deepen our understanding of the novel in the context of its moment and the role James played in disseminating the ideas it chronicled.

In the opening penumbra of *À la recherche du temps perdu*, a sort of anxiety pervades. The security of stability hardly exists; intermittences and lacunae abound in incoherent views. Proust's preference for a series of "takes" or unconnected moments,[17] as suggested by Georges Poulet, and the instability and "erosion"[18] observed by Gérard Genette expose the fragmented and disjointed views and difficulty of sustained attention inherent in consciousness as described by James. "The palimpsest of time and space, these discordant views, ceaselessly contradicted and ceaselessly brought together by an untiring movement of painful dissociation and impossible synthesis—this, no doubt, is the Proustian vision."[19] Names, as vehicles of the imagination, "disintegrate," according to Genette, when compared to the actuality they represent,[20] exposing the contradiction between expectation and informed actuality. But the solidity of place is not *destroyed* by refocus in a second or subsequent experience, as Genette suggests; it is volatilized into experience. Another layer of the palimpsest is laid down every time the self is reintegrated in the material world and its experience enclosed in language. Echoing James without naming him, Genette agrees that language incorporates a "fringe" or "density," an indiscernible yet redolent layering of experiential color and shading, "suggesting something other than what it is, or of being both what it is and something other."[21]

How will the sleepy narrator reconstruct his personal identity? In the dim room, hints of focused attention in wakeful moments combine with physical sensations of the cool, soft pillow, the wall alongside the bed, stability in placement of furniture. As the comfort of habit resurrects the present, identity resurfaces as memories of the past recast him in his own image.

Other luxuriant moments of solitude release the narrator's unfocused attention from the strictures of habit, and his thought becomes intensely creative: "*[. . .] the substantive strength of a state of consciousness bears an inverse proportion to its suggestiveness*"[22] (emphasis in original). When unexpected sounds from the street and even slight alterations of temperature and sunshine are mirrored internally, they stimulate creative attention: "Mais c'était surtout en moi que j'entendais avec ivresse un son nouveau rendu par le violon intérieur [. . .] En notre être, instrument que l'uniformité de l'habitude a rendu silencieux, le chant naît de ces écarts, de ces variations, source de toute musique"[23] [But it was above all in myself that I heard, with rapture, a new sound emitted by the violin within. . . . Within our being, an instrument which the uniformity of habit has rendered mute, song is born of these divergences, these variations, the source of all music[24]]. Sensations and associations invade the heedless automatic. This mental ambiance is exhilarating.

James's *Psychology* was a toolbox of theory Proust could use to plumb the mechanics operative in the penumbra of awareness and impression. His narrator's goal is to capture in permanent form the way an individual mind experiences—"Ne vient de nous-même que ce que nous tirons de l'obscurité qui est en nous et que ne connaissent pas les autres"[25] [From ourselves comes only that which we drag forth from the obscurity which lies within us, what which to others is unknown[26]]. This pseudo-autobiography will be his psychological experiment and his ineluctable work of art.

ATTENTION AND DISCRIMINATION

First to penetrate the shadows of Proust's narrator's drowsy "torpor" is a memory, one of a childhood nightlight or "veilleuse de nuit" in Combray. His mind then wanders through the firelight and moonlight of all the rooms he has inhabited. Blended with them are the red rays of a sunset he sees when he awakens from a nap at the home of Gilberte de Saint-Loup in the present—the end of his story. Time ricochets, framing the novel in snapshots of memory captured in light and easily accessed through voluntary attention. The limited focus of such a "pan lumineux" [luminous panel] lights up only a constricted section of space—the ziggurat or fan-like "pyramide irrégulière" [irregular pyramid] projection from an electric light—a narrow memory of life in Combray, "le petit salon" [the little parlour], etc.[27]

Attention, voluntary and involuntary, sustained or easily interrupted, is basic to noticing the metamorphoses that define the Self over time and in space. Described by James, explored by Proust, the various aspects of the beam of attention lead us through the novel.

It excavates a "tiny rill through a broad flowery mead" in James's metaphor for the "Narrowness of Consciousness." Despite the teeming stimuli all around, we actually pay attention to only a very limited number. "The sum total of our impressions never enters into our *experience*."[28] We focus on the ones that *interest* us. Amused by Françoise's errors and unusual expressions, the "bit[s] of bad grammar" that draw his attention, Proust's hero observes regional and class distinctions in speech; they jar the hearing and "wound the ear of the purist."[29] Stimuli not actively attended to, however, do penetrate awareness in a shadowy way, one that is "involuntary, effortless."[30] Affecting the "'fringe' and margin of our thought,"[31] these have important parallels in Proust's work: Combray is resurrected with a fullness that the narrator's voluntary attention could never summon.

"Involuntary attention" is common in children whose attention easily wanders from the task or lesson at hand because they are particularly prone to the unfocused excitability of sensory stimulation.[32] In childhood Proust's narrator is portrayed as hypersensitive. According to James, "childhood is characterized by great active energy, and has few organized interests by which to meet new impressions and decide whether they are worthy of notice or not, and the consequence is that extreme mobility of the attention with which we are all familiar in children."[33] The literary potential inherent in this observation, as much as any autobiographical explanation, may have contributed to Proust's portrayal of his high-strung young narrator, who does not yet know how to interpret what he encounters and what he feels. To create, the mature narrator must work to focus and sustain effort.

"Sensitiveness to immediately exciting sensorial stimuli," according to James, "characterizes the attention of childhood and youth. In mature age we have generally selected those stimuli which are connected with one or more so-called permanent interests, and our attention has grown irresponsive to the rest."[34] The adult narrator retains only the most intense emotional moments of childhood experience. Still highly attentive to the fearsome pain of separation anxiety, the stairway is "cruel" and the room at the top "isolé" [isolated]. The rest of his early experience of Combray is hidden away for the moment. He is oblivious to it until later released by happenstance; for now, the "tiny rill" is all that he consciously retains.

A sensory stimulant experienced as "very intense, voluminous, or sudden"[35] can provoke involuntary attention. In *Jean Santeuil*, Proust had already utilized the device of involuntary attention to a memory awakened by sensation. A certain musical phrase causes Jean to shudder. He struggles to identify it, to reawaken the photographic "archives" of a time in childhood when he heard his grandfather Sandré's piano.[36] The forceful and unanticipated response to the normally benign taste of tea and a sweet provokes intense attention to thoughts of Combray, complying with James's observation that "an imagined visual object may, if attention be concentrated on it long enough, acquire before the mind's eye almost the brilliancy of reality."[37] Through the agency of memory, something present only to the mind can seem as real to conscious attention as the surroundings at hand.

Music and reading, according to James, similarly focus the listener's attention or the reader's eyes inward. Despite its seeming distracted vacancy, this type of "dispersed attention," occurring involuntarily, visible "quand on regarde les yeux 'lointains' de ceux qui pensent 'à autre chose'"[38] [when one looks with the "distant" eyes of someone thinking about something else], is an intensely dynamic hub of feeling and mind activity not evident on the exterior. Both James and Proust's narrator prescribe energetic activity to disperse the psychic excitement, and James urges us "never to have an emotion at a concert, without expressing it afterwards in *some* active way, including "speaking genially with one's grandmother."[39]

A weak impression or sensation may draw our attention because of its associates: "A faint tap *per se* is not an interesting sound; it may well escape from the general rumor of the world. But when it is a signal, as that of a lover on a window-pane, hardly will it go unperceived."[40] A sound with little meaning in itself, like the bell on the gate in Combray, signals Swann's arrival and ominously portends the absence of a maternal goodnight kiss. A faint rapping is the mode of communication between the narrator and his grandmother in the next room in the hotel in Balbec; the reassuring echo of his taps alleviates his anxiety; her response signifies her presence and love. When the narrator hears what sounds like a window opening in Albertine's room down the hall in his apartment, he becomes apprehensive and worries that this sound portends something significant: Albertine is refusing to obey his rule against drafts. The implications of her rebellion are borne out the next morning: she is gone. Like auditory bookends to the narrator's emotional life, minor sounds are attended to with significant emotional response, reverberating with anxiety or devastating loss.

Attention can be inspired, as good teachers know, by building on existing interest and by directing its focus. In highly involved moments of concentration or problem-solving, attention can be so intent on a particular focus that it distracts from physical discomfort: for "brain-currents," according to James, the "absorption in their object [may] be so deep, as to banish not only ordinary sensations, but even the severest pain."[41] The pain may be physical, or it may be emotional. The narrator obsessively researches Albertine's past, her habits, her acquaintances and appetites, even well after her death when the answers will provide little succor.

When Bergotte decides to see the exhibition of Vermeer's *View of Delft*, he almost forgets the attack of "urémie" [kidney failure] for which bed rest has been prescribed. He is strongly motivated to see the painting because it provokes his "involuntary intellectual attention" consisting of "a train of images exciting or interesting *per se*; [. . .] [or] because they are associated with something which makes them dear."[42] Bergotte is willing to endure physical malaise in order to admire this *particular* painting, qualitatively different and more stimulating to him than any of the others in the gallery. What drew his attention was the critical article he had read reflecting a process James had described as aesthetic direction in perception:

> It is for this reason that men have no eyes but for those aspects of things which they have already been taught to discern. Any one of us can notice a phenomenon after it has once been pointed out [. . .]. Even in poetry and the arts, someone has to come and tell us what aspects we may single out, and what effects we may admire, before our aesthetic nature can "dilate" to its full extent.[43]

The narrator in turn is guided by Elstir to interpret what he senses and to focus in a new and voluntary way. When he visits Elstir's studio at the seashore, the narrator is escorted through this aesthetic lesson in visual attention by the master himself: "par toutes les études qui étaient autour de moi, je sentais la possibilité de m'élever à une connaissance poétique, fécondes en joies, de maintes formes que je n'avais pas isolées jusque-là du spectacle total de la réalité"[44] [with the help of all the sketches and studies that surrounded me, I foresaw the possibility of raising myself to a poetical understanding, rich in delights, of manifold forms which I had not hitherto isolated from the total spectacle of reality[45]]. His ability to discern the "rill" is being honed.

The aesthetic lesson of the objective gaze is generalized by the narrator to the mimetic possibilities of language and the power of metaphor in particular. "L'effort qu'Elstir faisait pour se dépouiller en présence de la réalité de toutes les notions de son intelligence"[46] [The effort made by Elstir to strip himself, when face to face with reality, of every intellectual notion[47]] affords the narrator a new perspective on his own experience. Intellectual preconceptions summarize and restrict the imaginative or poetic resonance that the artist restores:

> Mais j'y pouvais discerner que le charme de chacune [des peintures] consistait en une sorte de métamorphose des choses représentées, analogue à celle qu'en poésie on nomme métaphore et que si Dieu le Père avait créé les choses en les nommant, c'est en leur ôtant leur nom, ou en leur en donnant un autre qu'Elstir les recréait. Les noms qui désignent les choses répondent toujours à une notion de l'intelligence, étrangère à

nos impressions véritables et qui nous force à éliminer d'elles tout ce qui ne se rapporte pas à cette notion.[48]

[But I was able to discern from these that the charm of each of them lay in a sort of metamorphosis of the objects represented, analogous to what in poetry we call metaphor, and that, if God the Father had created things by naming them, it was by taking away their names or giving them other names that Elstir created them anew. The names which designate things correspond invariably to an intellectual notion, alien to our true impressions, and compelling us to eliminate from them everything that is not in keeping with that notion.[49]]

Visual attention, in James's view, involved brain response to an outside stimulus, "a brain-cell played upon from two directions." There is outward stimulus plus inward brain-cell activation, both required to create "an object fully attended to and perceived."[50] Certain "ambiguous" figures illustrated in James's chapter on attention feature combinations of patterns that differ based on what we expect to see. "Let us show how universally present in our acts of attention this reinforcing imagination, this inward reproduction, this anticipatory thinking of the thing we attend to is. [. . .] When [. . .] sensorial attention is at its height, it is impossible to tell how much of the percept comes from without and how much from within."[51]

James describes experiments demonstrating how the mind normalizes, interprets, or compensates for what the eye actually measurably sees.[52] Similarly, Proust's narrator describes "un effet de soleil" [some effect of sunlight] that confuses the horizon line between sky and sea or between sea and a distant shore. Because the visual stimulus confuses what the brain knows in memory, normalization has to occur in interpretation, as James had theorized: "Bien vite, mon intelligence rétablissait entre les éléments la séparation que mon impression avait abolie"[53] [But presently my reason would reestablish between the elements the distinction which my first impression had abolished[54]]. Elstir is a master at capturing this visual ambiguity and confusion:

Mais les rares moments où l'on voit la nature telle qu'elle est, poétiquement, c'était de ceux-là qu'était faite l'oeuvre d'Elstir. Une de ses métaphores les plus fréquentes dans les marines qu'il avait près de lui en ce moment était justement celle qui comparant la terre à la mer, supprimait entre elles toute démarcation.[55]

[But the rare moments in which we see nature as she is, poetically, were those from which Elstir's work was created. One of the metaphors that occurred most frequently in the seascapes which surrounded him here was precisely that which, comparing land with sea, suppressed all demarcation between them.[56]]

Elstir's paintings describe the visual stimulus or impression before the mental reconciliation is added in. An impression is thus liable to illusion. Art, according to Proust's narrator, based on his lesson from Elstir and gleaned perhaps from Turner, has the responsibility of capturing the freshness of the initial unadulterated view: "Les surfaces et les volumes sont en réalité indépendants des noms d'objets que notre mémoire leur impose quand nous les avons reconnus. Elstir tâchait d'arracher à ce qu'il venait de sentir ce qu'il savait; son effort avait souvent été de dissoudre cet agrégat de raisonnements que nous appelons vision"[57] [Surfaces and volumes are in reality independent of the names of objects which our memory imposes on them after we have recognised them. Elstir sought to wrest from what he had just felt what he already knew; he had often been at pains to break up that medley of impressions which we call vision[58]].

Voluntary attention, according to James, attempts to obtain a particular result and can only be sustained for very brief periods. The "intellectual" version of voluntary attention is at work when we pursue a faint idea, parse a slight distinction of "meaning," or remain focused on an idea even when others more raucously beckon.[59] When the hero of *À la recherche du temps perdu* tries to decipher his impressions, he can only glimpse their significance and hold his attention to any particular aspect for a very short interval. Too much daily life and too many social interactions prevent him from spending the time necessary to parse their hidden meaning.

Emotional excitement and sensory overload reduce the narrator's ability to concentrate and remember "avec exactitude" anything beyond the most trivial and circumstantial details of a love interest. He only retains "des photographes manquées" [unsuccessful photographs] of Gilberte to replay over and over in his mind on the days when she does not come to the Champs-Élysées to play. The emotional involvement that makes the lover so attentive to every little detail of his love object prohibits a static image; he cannot sustain any one thought about her for long as he tries to project beyond the evident:

> La manière chercheuse, anxieuse, exigeante que nous avons de regarder la personne que nous aimons, notre attente de la parole qui nous donnera ou nous ôtera l'espoir d'un rendez-vous pour le lendemain, et, jusqu'à ce que cette parole soit dite, notre imagination alternative, si non simultanée, de la joie et du désespoir, tout cela rend notre attention en face de l'être aimé, trop tremblante pour qu'elle puisse obtenir de lui une image bien nette. Peut-être aussi cette activité de tous les sens à la fois et qui essaye de connaître avec les regards seuls ce qui est au delà d'eux, est-elle trop indulgente, aux mille formes, à toutes les saveurs, aux mouvements de la personne vivante que d'habitude, quand nous n'aimons pas, nous immobilisons. Le modèle chéri, au contraire, bouge.[60]

> [The questing, anxious, exacting way that we have of looking at the person we love, our eagerness for the word which will give us or take from us the hope of an appointment for the morrow, and, until that word is uttered, our alternate if not simultaneous imaginings of joy and despair, all this makes our attention in the presence of the beloved too tremulous to be able to carry away a very clear impression of her. Perhaps, also, that activity of all the senses at once which yet endeavours to discover with the eyes alone what lies beyond them is over-indulgent to the myriad forms, to the different savours, to the movements of the living person whom as a rule, when we are not in love, we immobilise. Whereas the beloved model does not stay still.[61]]

The series of interrupted views of Gilberte (or la petite bande or Albertine) also illustrate James's notion that "sustained voluntary attention requires "successive efforts":[62] "The condition *sine quâ non* of sustained attention to a given topic of thought is that we should roll it over and over incessantly and consider different aspects and relations of it in turn."[63] James's theory anticipates the way the hero of Proust's novel analyzes every facet of his relationships, facts as well as speculations. The narrator is preoccupied with questions about each one of his emotional entanglements; that is the symptom of his interest. Exhaustive attention is applied to exploring the details of past and present, to examine every element of his feelings for each woman, ending with a detailed and exhaustive psychological exhumation.

Voluntary attention provides the "drama," "the sting and excitement of voluntary life,"[64] just as the narrator's romantic curiosity drives much of his action. The arena in which Proust's hero strikingly demonstrates his will to alter events is that of desire; voluntary attention keeps him teetering on an emotional ledge as he pursues and then breaks off with Gilberte, lurks in wait for Mme. de Guermantes, captures and confines Albertine, loves her, is bored with her, toys with her, playing "à mon insu cette partie de cache-cache où Albertine m'échapperait toujours"[65] [I had arranged unawares this game of hide and seek in which Albertine would always elude me[66]], exorcized only as attention fades and she is forgotten.

The narrator is able to scrutinize his feelings and thoughts about what he encounters because his "genius" gives him greater ability here than the average man to sustain attention, examine detail, speculate. Using an image he will elaborate in later philosophical writing, James described the "genius": "In such minds, subjects bud and sprout and grow. At every moment they please by a new consequence and rivet the attention afresh. [. . .] Their ideas coruscate, every subject branches infinitely before their fertile mind, and so for hours they may be rapt."[67]

Why would an irresolute "genius" like the narrator or a successful society gallant like Swann choose to maintain feelings for mediocre women who probably do not love them in return? Such women allow for emotional creativity. And Swann and the narrator are riding the waves of obsession, the outer limit of attention. According to James, "to every man actuated by passion the thought of interests which negate the passion can hardly for more than a fleeting instant stay before the mind."[68] Nothing else is quite that interesting, and denying a compulsive passion hurts more than anything else: "un être très sensible et très intellectuel aura généralement peu de volonté, sera le jouet de l'habitude et de cette peur de souffrir dans la minute qui vient, qui voue aux souffrances perpétuelles—et que dans ces conditions il ne voudra jamais répudier la femme qui ne l'aime pas"[69] [a man who is highly sensitive and highly intellectual will generally have little will-power, will be the plaything of habit and of that fear of suffering in the immediate present which condemns to perpetual suffering—and that in these conditions he will never be prepared to repudiate the woman who does not love him[70]]. In addition to the latitude and fertile field someone entirely different from one's self presents to the explorations of an active mind, the prospect of taking deliberate and decisive action to break an amorous fixation is more painful than the pain of living with it. Although his impassioned obsessive dependency—the ultimate emotional habit—powerfully focuses his attention, Proust's weak-willed narrator is all too easily swayed from the sustained attention and purposeful steadfast endeavor required to become a writer. He is too distractible.

Just as we associate, connect, combine, and correlate, from the soup of sensations and impressions that enter our awareness, we discriminate, differentiate, divide, and categorize. We appraise distinctions between sensations, "different, either in time, place or quality"[71]—and consider a present felt sensation in the light of one remembered.[72] Discrimination differentiates between layers of experience over time. It enables Swann to identify "la petite phrase" [the little phrase] in a piece of music and experience it in different emotional contexts; it permits the narrator to recognize the individuality of a particular artist or novelist, to recognize the style of Vinteuil in the red "septuor" [septet] to feel the privilege in certain moments.

"It often happens, when the interval is long between two experiences, that our judgments are guided, not so much by a positive image or copy of the earlier one as by our recollection of certain facts about it."[73] Because of what he remembers, discrimination allows the narrator to distinguish the changes in individuals as they age and to observe his fellow characters in novel roles (Morel, Charlus, Saint-Loup in unsavory ones). It allows him to witness the disjointed incoherence of a single individual. "Indeed, many of the characters assume the most contradictory roles *simultaneously*."[74] The constant revision of palimpsest Genette discerns in Proust's novel results from the ability to discriminate.

James uses the example of looking for a book in a library. We may know the title, but additional detailed knowledge of how it looks, or how it feels, attributes of our original acquaintance with it, will help us locate it. Similarly, Proust's hero prefers by far the particular copy of a book first encountered. He has a visceral relationship with that book. His reaction to a subsequent edition would miss much of the first copy's particularity.

Hypersensitive discrimination places the narrator on a perceptive threshold and contributes to emotional intensity and descriptive plenitude. "Any personal or practical interest in the results to be obtained by distinguishing, makes one's wits amazingly sharp to detect differences,"[75] wrote James. Albertine is singled out from among "la petite bande" [the little band] by certain sensual aspects. Her careless physicality and irreverent attitude, her thick, curling black, hair and her utility as stimulus to reverie set her apart.

On his second visit to Balbec, Proust's hero reacts differently than on his first; he recognizes places and people and feels a greater degree of familiarity and comfort in the surroundings. A soothing security replaces the anguish of hypersensitive discrimination.

Unlike the fine-tuning of Discrimination, Habit diminishes the amount of attention we must devote to a particular action. Habit is physically derived because of the malleable nature of nerves and brain tissue. "[P]aths" of "discharge" are created in physiological response to experience, and thereafter these govern certain acts.[76] For Proust, Habit has double meaning.

THE DOUBLE-EDGED COMFORT OF HABIT

William James used a mélange of contemporary concepts in physics and mechanics to account for his hypothesis of how habits are formed and retained in the mutable matter of the brain, including "inertia," "friction,"[77] electric current, and "drainage-channels."[78]

Exterior events bear effect on the brain, entering through sensory nerves that transmit "currents." Just as a river's channel is the conduit for the flow of water draining land, a *routine* trajectory of electrical "discharge"—or habit—is the physical "trace," or "pathway," in the brain created by the route of outflow of nerve currents in response to incoming stimuli.[79] The brain forms habits because the living "nervous tissue" composing it is "plastic"; it develops pathways with use that are retained but can change albeit "slowly" and with a "certain resistance."[80] The acquisition of habit is a process of physical and psychological patterning; instinctive as well as intentional clusters of behavior fall into its realm.

Habit allows us to ignore much of the plethora of sensation to which we are exposed. "Habits depend on sensations not attended to"; they are "felt" but relegated to the background of conscious experience.[81] Once formed, a habit facilitates response to repeated stimuli, relieving conscious attention of the permanent unflinching duty. In fact, full attention may be otherwise engaged. Habit thus puts an end to hyperdiscrimination. Once the physical or "sensation[al]" prompt to begin occurs, habit facilitates action, expediting a cascade of familiar behaviors.[82]

> [J]e songeais combien la conscience cesse vite de collaborer à nos habitudes, qu'elle laisse à leur développement sans plus s'occuper d'elles et combien dès lors nous pourrions être étonnés si nous constations simplement du dehors, et en supposant qu'elles engagent tout l'individu, les actions d'hommes dont la valeur morale ou intellectuelle peut se développer indépendamment dans un sens tout différent.[83]
>
> [I reflected upon the speed with which conscience ceases to be a partner in our habits, which she allows to develop freely without bothering herself about them, and upon the astonishing picture which may consequently present itself to us if we observe simply from without, and in the belief that they engage the whole of the individual, the actions of men whose moral or intellectual virtues may at the same time be developing independently in an entirely different direction.[84]]

Habit has extraordinary power to shape behavior, to make a retired soldier drop his dinner in the street if he hears someone shout "Attention!"[85] or return a "riderless" horse to the stable. Its power for Proust's narrator includes "l'insoupçonnable puissance défensive de l'habitude invétérée" [the unsuspected defensive power of inveterate habit] responsible for "réserves cachées" [hidden reserves] of energy as mysterious as that driving the return of a comet in orbit[86] or propelling the narrator to the train station in Venice to meet his mother for the trip home.

Many of Proust's characters, the narrator among them, clearly and sometimes comically demonstrate the "bundles of habits" James attributes to all of us.[87] Proust's narrator takes evident pleasure depicting his Aunt Léonie's religio-medicinal habits and the fun she repeatedly enjoys verbally jousting with Françoise, tormenting Eulalie, and (snobbishly) commenting from the elevated viewpoint of her bedroom window on the events and local folk (including canines) passing by on the street outside.[88] The narrator's parents and grandparents display individual habits as well as group routines. Swann and Odette, the "petit clan" of the Verdurin salon, the girls at play on the Champs-Élysées and those roving the beach in Balbec, the soldiers billeted at Doncières, the lackeys and servants, homosexuals of both sexes, and the aristocrats of Guermantes society all exhibit, even flaunt, habitual traits and group customs with strict rules and rituals to which the reader, sharing the experience of the narrator, is initiated. The narrator himself is a "bundle of habits," whose love affairs gradually lose the spontaneity of youth and accumulate habitual behaviors:

> D'autant plus que les situations tout en se répétant, changent, et qu'il y a chance pour qu'au milieu ou à la fin de la vie on ait eu pour soi-même la funeste complaisance de compliquer l'amour d'une part d'habitude que l'adolescence, retenue par d'autres devoirs, moins libre de soi-même, ne connaît pas.[89]
>
> [All the more because situations, while repeating themselves, tend to alter, and there is every likelihood that, in middle life or in old age, we shall have had the fatal self-indulgence of complicating our love by an intrusion of habit which adolescence, detained by too many other duties, less free to choose, knows nothing of.[90]]

Habit increases the narrator's rapport with new surroundings and helps to wear off the sharp edges of their novelty, allowing his hypersensitive attention to relax: "C'est notre attention qui met des objets dans une chambre, et l'habitude qui les en retire et nous y fait de la place" [It is our noticing them that puts things in a room, our growing used to them that takes them away again and clears a space for us].[91]

> L'habitude! aménageuse habile mais bien lente et qui commence par laisser souffrir notre esprit pendant des semaines dane une installation provisoire; mais que malgré tout il est bien heureux de trouver, car sans l'habitude et réduit à ses seuls moyens il serait impuissant à nous rendre un logis habitable.[92]
>
> [Habit! that skilful but slow-moving arranger who begins by letting our minds suffer for weeks on end in temporary quarters, but whom our minds are none the less only too happy to discover at last, for without it, reduced to their own devices, they would be powerless to make any room seem habitable.[93]]

In James's day, it was thought that inorganic or inanimate matter was subject to "habituation" to explain acquired changes (as when your shoes mold to your feet or your sleeve to the bend in your arm). For Proust, too, habit has this inanimate side: as an effect of human territoriality, habit forces the surrounding environment to conform to the inhabitant's personality by virtue, not of folds and creases, but of acquired familiarity "qui consiste à poser sur les choses l'âme qui nous est familière au lieu de la leur qui nous effrayait" [the imposition of our own familiar soul on the terrifying soul of our surroundings]. Ironically, once he has adjusted, a little too comfortable in his Balbec hotel room on the second visit, the narrator wonders if in order to find the brio of novelty, he would have to stay elsewhere, "où l'habitude n'aurait pas encore tué à chaque étage, devant chaque porte, le dragon terrifiant qui semblait veiller sur une existence enchantée" [where Habit will not yet have killed upon each landing, outside each door, the terrible dragon that seemed to be watching over an enchanted existence].[94]

The familiar landscape of the narrator's chldhood bedroom in Combray is refashioned by the magic lantern's light images, disrupting the comfort of habit. What had been familiar—his knowing where everything was located—becomes newly stimulating, disconcerting, with added "mystery,"[95] veiled and exotic with its gossamer overlay of historical myth. Plaintively, Proust's narrator complains that the magic lantern robs him of the comfort of automatic behavior, echoing James's "opening and shutting of familiar cupboards, and the like" with little thought to the routine act involved:[96] "L'influence anesthésiante de l'habitude ayant cessé, je me mettais à penser, à sentir, choses si tristes" [The anaesthetic effect of habit being destroyed, I would begin to think—and to feel—such melancholy things]. No longer is the doorknob a part of his comfort zone of habit that "semblait ouvrir tout seul, sans que j'eusse besoin de le tourner, tant le maniement m'en était devenu inconscient" [seemed to move of its own accord and without my having to turn it, so unconscious had its manipulation become].[97] Habit is a learning tool, a "short cut" to action,[98] permitting automatic, unconsidered routine behavior and curtailing the need for perpetually purposeful voluntary performance. But by disconnecting will and action, habit has a destructive effect on the narrator's ability to exercise volition. Habit's "analgésique" capacity provides a relaxing and secure contentment in the soothing calm of a goodnight kiss or the comfort of spatial familiarity, but like heavy narcotizing, it can lead to "l'assoupissement de l'habitude" [the torpor of habit[99]] that robs life of its "zing":

> [Le] voile lourd de l'habitude (habitude abêtissante qui pendant tout le cours de notre vie nous cache à peu près tout l'univers et dans une nuit profonde, sous leur étiquette inchangée, substitue aux poisons les plus dangereux ou les plus enivrants de la vie quelque chose d'anodin qui ne procure pas de délices).[100]
>
> [T]he heavy curtain of habit (stupefying habit, which during the whole course of our life conceals from us almost the whole universe, and in the dead of night, without changing the label, substitutes for the most dangerous or intoxicating poisons of life something anodyne that procures no delights).[101]]

Habit has the same effect for people; we get used to them: "l'habitude [. . .] se charge aussi bien de nous rendre chers les compagnons qui nous avaient déplu d'abord, de donner une autre forme aux visages, de rendre sympathique le son d'une voix, de modifier l'inclination des coeurs" [Habit . . . undertakes as well to make dear to us the companions whom at first we disliked, to give another appearance to their faces, to make the sound of their voices attractive, to modify the inclinations of their hearts].[102]

By rounding the corners, blurring sharp demarcations, making things comfortable, habit also makes them boring. Because comfort takes you off the edge of stimulation and novelty, the narrator grows tired of Albertine's constant presence. She is exasperatingly uncontrollable yet stale; she prevents him from prowling for others. Habit once acquired can have great force in altering behavior in a relatively stable if not permanent way. "And not only is it the right thing at the right time that we thus involuntarily do," writes James, "but the wrong thing also, if it be an habitual thing."[103] Proust's narrator likens habit's persistent strength to an emotional atomic "force immense" to Tristan and Isolde's magic philter: "l'habitude physique de la femme" [the physical presence of the woman][104] that develops with living together even when love no longer dazzles.

If a habitual emotional need is thwarted and the narrator is deprived of the maternal goodnight kiss (the hardest habit to alter) or the routine of living with Albertine is contravened by her sudden departure, the resulting disorientation creates an imperious sense of displacement, anguish, and insurmountable frustration, and all past occasions of emotional habit interrupted crowd together to create an overwhelming feeling of strangulation. For Proust's narrator, as for Swann when in love with Odette, the line between habit and the domineering physical need characteristic of a craving or addiction ("un si invincible et si douloureux besoin" [so irresistible and painful a need][105]) is a very fine knife-edge:

> J'avais une telle habitude d'avoir Albertine auprès de moi, et je voyais soudain un nouveau visage de l'Habitude. Jusqu'ici je l'avais considérée surtout comme un pouvoir annihilateur qui supprime l'originalité et jusqu'à la conscience des perceptions, maintenant je la voyais comme une divinité redoutable, si rivée à nous, son visage insignifiant si incrusté dans notre coeur que si elle se détache, si elle se détourne de nous, cette déité que nous ne distinguions presque pas, nous inflige des souffrances plus terribles qu'aucune et qu'alors elle est aussi cruelle que la mort.[106]
>
> [I was so much in the habit of having Albertine with me, and now I suddenly saw a new aspect of Habit. Hitherto I had regarded it chiefly as an annihilating force which suppresses the originality and even the awareness of one's perception; now I saw it as a dread deity, so riveted to one's being, its insignificant face so incrusted in one's heart, that if it detaches itself, if it turns away from one, this deity that one had barely distinguished inflicts on one sufferings more terrible than any other and is then as cruel as death itself.[107]]

Only in alliance with forgetting will habit help soften the desperate pangs of separation at the end of a failed love affair or when a loved one dies. This form of habit is in some ways as terrifying for the narrator as the original suffering because it represents a final, an eternal form of separation, a death of that aspect of the self, the part that loved.

Certain social customs or biases typical of their time appear in James's psychological writing and in Proust's novel. "Habit is thus the enormous fly-wheel of society, its most precious conservative agent," wrote James.[108] "You see little lines of cleavage running through the character, the tricks of thought, the prejudices [. . .] from which the man can by-and-by no more escape than his coat-sleeve can suddenly fall into a new set of folds."[109] The seemingly rigid and elaborate social configurations were held together by group habit; delineated expectations dominated interaction. Proust depicted in detail certain of the contemporary social structures and strictures, the tics and snobberies of the various classes in their voluntary isolation and the way they rubbed against each other in new ways during his lifetime. He witnessed class and racial frictions, the dissolution of the aristocracy, the remnants of crowned royalty coming to France to display what remained of their status as they retreated from new political entities in their home countries.

Genette remarks upon the fact that time does not pass at the same rate for all.[110] In the first decade of the twentieth century Einstein and Poincaré worked on the difficult problem of synchronizing time and longitude, reconciling clocks and train timetables. "Change is not what you measure with time; time is what you measure with changes," wrote William R. Everdell.[111] In 1890, James's psychology had highlighted the idea of different successive views. Proust incorporated this instability and the struggle between habit and change, and he rendered it artistically.

The word "habit" appears over four hundred times in *À la recherche du temps perdu*. For individuals, small groups such as the narrator's family, and large swaths of society, habit was an organizing principle, as it was for James, highlighting by contrast the kaleidoscope of seemingly abrupt social and political upheavals characteristic of the period and reflected in the novel. Just as individual character is rewritten over time, group behavior evolves, following social and historical events and trends.

Group habits are reflected in social codes and in language. Proust tackled both. Dialects and code words characteristic of the various groups are articulated to reflect the cultural disparities. To capture the witticisms, exclusionary gossip, aristocratic mannerisms of *Le Côté de Guermantes,* Norpois's formulaic diplomaticisms and the frozen demeanor characteristic of his profession, Bloch's quasi-literary and pseudo-philosophical jargon, the hidden body language of glances and nods among male and female homosexuals, the bourgeois concerns for propriety, solid professional career, and advantageous marriage, Proust depicted his hero moving from one group to another. The narrator is initiated to the "habitudes" of them all. Proust's hero is interested in the words, in their spheres of meaning, and prefers the authentic patina of an obsolete expression or one a bit démodé but of long use. He is enthralled by the imaginative potential of terms from "la vieille [or vraie] France" [old (or real) France], just as his grandmother preferred an item of furniture bearing the aura of "une belle imagination du passé" [a brave conceit of the past], even if it can no longer bear the weight of someone sitting on it.[112]

Life in Combray is highly routinized, and Aunt Léonie has her sacred rituals. Among them is the extraordinary change that occurs on Saturdays, when the lunch hour is advanced so Françoise can go to the market at Roussainville-le-Pin: "Et ma tante avait si bien pris l'habitude de cette dérogation hebdomadaire à ses habitudes, qu'elle tenait à cette habitude-là autant qu'aux autres" [And my aunt had so thoroughly acquired the habit of this weekly exception to her general habits, that she clung to it as much as to the rest]. For the rest of the family, too, Saturdays have special significance with "une figure particulière, indulgente, et assez sympathique" [an individual character, kindly and rather attractive][113] that allows for adventures that structure the narrative. (There is a lingering mist of religious significance in the fact that Saturday should be considered the special day, reminiscent of the Jewish Sabbath. This would suggest an ever-so-subtle alteration in the dominant Catholic way of looking at life.) When lunchtime is advanced by an hour, habit is breached and the drama of discovery on each of the two "côtés" ensues. By habit, however, the two "côtés" are never visited on the same day—they represent two different, closed off, ostensibly unconnected worlds in the narrator's imagination.

> Et cette démarcation était rendue plus absolue encore parce que cette habitude que nous avions de n'aller jamais vers les deux côtés un même jour, dans une seule promenade, mais une fois du côté de Méséglise, une fois du côté de Guermantes, les enfermait pour ainsi dire loin l'un de l'autre, inconnaissables l'un à l'autre, dans les vases clos et sans communication entre eux, d'après-midi différents.[114]

> [And this distinction was rendered still more absolute because the habit we had of never going both ways on the same day, or in the course of the same walk, but the "Méséglise way" one time and the "Guermantes way" another, shut them off, so to speak, far apart from one another and unaware of each other's existence, in the airtight compartments of separate afternoons.[115]]

Only time and experience will be able to open the "vases clos" of these spaces, creating from them the "vase rempli" of *Le Temps retrouvé* as memories are revisited and the two "côtés" are interconnected to reflect the adult discovery of alterations in the habitual social structure.

Habit is a blunt instrument for the artist and for the lover. Habit masks the underlying reality. Proust's narrator, on his second visit to Balbec, wants to discover what is essential and real before it has been clouded by habit. He wants to see like an artist who is not confined by expectation. The change of context from Paris to Balbec eliminates the daily routine of home. The prospect of meeting "la femme de chambre de Mme Putbus" [Mme. Putbus's chambermaid] (although she is not authentically local, having been imported from Paris like the narrator) would take place somewhere not dulled by quotidian familiarity. It would retain all the freshness of "l'illusion [. . .] qu'il m'ouvrait accès à une nouvelle vie. (Car si l'habitude est une seconde nature, elle nous empêche de connaître la première dont elle n'a ni les cruautés, ni les enchantements)" [the illusion that it was opening the door for me to a new life. (For if habit is a second nature, it prevents us from knowing our first, whose cruelties it lacks as well as its enchantments)].[116]

This notion of escaping habit to attain novelty recurs when Proust's hero returns to the hotel from dinner at La Raspelière with Albertine. He sees himself as having more than a double life. In multiplicity he finds a form of excitement that is addictive:

> J'étais heureux de cette multiplicité que je voyais ainsi à ma vie déployée sur trois plans; et puis, quand on redevient pour un instant un homme ancien, c'est-à-dire différent de celui qu'on est depuis longtemps, la sensibilité n'étant plus amortie par l'habitude reçoit des moindres chocs des impressions si vives qui font pâlir tout ce qui les a précédées et auxquelles, à cause de leur intensité, nous nous attachons avec l'exaltation passagère d'un ivrogne.[117]
>
> [I was delighted by the multiplicity in which I saw my life thus spread over three planes; and besides, when one becomes for an instant one's former self, that is to say different from what one has been for some time past, one's sensibility, being no longer dulled by habit, receives from the slightest stimulus vivid impressions which make everything that has preceded them fade into insignificance, impressions to which, because of their intensity, we attach ourselves with the momentary enthusiasm of a drunkard.[118]]

This kind of "choc" will fill the narrator with overwhelming surprise when a sensation not normally attended to, a taste mundane but inhabitual, has the unusual impact of releasing his story from storage and reviving a Self he no longer "inhabits."

Habit acts like a "gomme à effacer" [eraser], rubbing out the sharper edges of sensibility and homogenizing experience; it silences the simple joy of living, the "violon intérieur" [interior violin] that makes beautiful music only in solitude. It blunts the authentic form of personal response the narrator relishes when variations in light and sound from the city outside enter his silent apartment on a day when his prisoner is out.[119]

When life with Albertine has become reduced to a noxious mix of boredom and jealous mistrust, in order to win her devotion and submission, to spice things up imaginatively and emotionally, the narrator stages an artificial break-up ostensibly intended to dispel the low-level warfare between them. He hopes to relieve the suffering that has become the norm of his life, to alter the habit of having her near him without possessing her fully. Habit is a crutch, a pernicious potion. But how could he survive without it?

> On vivait au jour le jour, qui, même pénible, restait supportable, retenu dans le terre à terre par le lest de l'habitude et par cette certitude que le lendemain, dût-il être cruel, contiendrait la présence de l'être auquel on tient.[120]
>
> [We lived a day-to-day life which, however tedious, was still endurable, held down to earth by the ballast of habit and by the certainty that the next day, even if it should prove painful, would contain the presence of the other.[121]]

He lacks the strength of will to adopt the Jamesian formula for eliminating bad habits: "attention" plus "effort"[122] with the constant reinforcement of James's mantra: practice, practice, practice. "So with the man who has daily inured himself to habits of concentrated attention, energetic volition, and self-denial in unnecessary things. He will stand like a tower when everything rocks around him."[123] Proust's hero's manner of dealing with his habit is a game; it is fake, inauthentic, and fraught with insecurity, a moment of theater without footing in reality that "flotte sans racines comme une journee de départ" [floats without roots like a day of departure] and provides only additional ineffectual "rêveries sentimentales" [sentimental dreams].[124]

"Could the young but realize how soon they will become mere walking bundles of habits, they would give more heed to their conduct while in the plastic state."[125] The narrator missed his chance to develop strength of character when Swann came to dinner and his mother did not come upstairs to kiss him goodnight. Instead, the need to indulge emotional habit became imperious. For James, education should "*make our nervous system our ally instead of our enemy.*" It should reinforce "useful action" and "guard against the growing into ways that are likely to be disadvantageous to us, as we should guard against the plague."[126] Proust discerned the disadvantages of habit and noted in one of his maxim-like statements that the staying power of a habit is often in proportion to how ridiculous the habit is. He used as an example the repetitive behaviors of the mentally ill, and echoes James in saying, "Il suffirait d'un petit mouvement d'énergie, un seul jour, pour changer cela une fois pour toutes. Mais justement ces vies sont habituellement l'apanage d'êtres incapables d'énergie" [A slight burst of energy, for a single day, would be sufficient to change these habits for good and all. But the fact is that lives of this sort are on the whole peculiar to people who are incapable of energy],[127] much like his own.

Professional habits are formed before the age of thirty, wrote James,[128] and bad habits that whet the imagination without concomitant effort to hone the will are detrimental. As early as the Combray years, Proust's narrator knew he wanted to be a writer. His vocational *interests* are set, but doubt about his talent, confusion about his subject, and a general habit of daydreaming more than doing impede definitive progress. He demonstrates the worst of James's "contemptible type of human character [. . .] the nerveless sentimentalist and dreamer, who spends his life in a weltering sea of sensibility and emotion, but who never does a manly concrete deed."[129] Maxims quoted may reflect good intentions, but it is action that counts in forming the will and willful action that life requires to handle its exigencies, wrote James.[130] "The habit of excessive novel-reading and theatre-going" or "excessive indulgence in music" are deleterious: "One becomes filled with emotions which habitually pass without prompting any deed, and so the inertly sentimental condition is kept up"[131] without concomitant action. Here we see clear parallels to the plot of *À la recherche du temps perdu* so often attributed solely to the author's biography.

On an outing along the Vivonne, the young narrator fantasizes meeting Mme. de Guermantes; she would show interest in his writing career and ask him to share with her his literary efforts and "le sujet des poèmes que j'avais l'intention de composer" [all about the poems I intended to compose].[132]

> Et ces rêves m'avertissaient que puisque je voulais un jour être un écrivain, il était temps de savoir ce que je comptais écrire. Mais dès que je me le demandais, tâchant de trouver un sujet où je pusse faire tenir une signification philosophique infinie, mon esprit s'arrîetait de fonctionner, je ne voyais plus que le vide en face de mon attention, je sentais que je n'avais pas de génie ou peut-être une maladie cérébrale l'empêchait de naître.[133]
>
> [And these dreams reminded me that, since I wished some day to become a writer, it was high time to decide what sort of books I was going to write. But as soon as I asked myself the question, and tried to discover some subject to which I could impart a philosophical significance of infinite value, my mind would stop like a clock, my consciousness would be faced with a blank, I would feel either that I was wholly devoid of talent or that perhaps some malady of the brain was hindering its development.[134]]

He finds daunting the task of recovering some all-embracing meaning from the experience he has had thus far and is paralyzed with writer's block. Here, the amiable side of habit as defined by James might be of help—it would free him from the anxious indecision that immobilizes his creative impulse.

> The more of the details of our daily life we can hand over to the effortless custody of automatism, the more our higher powers of mind will be set free for their own proper work. There is no more miserable

> human being than one in whom nothing is habitual but indecision, and for whom the lighting of every cigar, the drinking of every cup, the time of rising and going to bed every day, and the beginning of every bit of work, are subjects of express volitional deliberation.[135]

Only when he realizes, riding in Dr. Percepied's carriage and seeing the shifting placement of church towers, that by capturing just what is ephemeral and personal in the permanent form of language will he know what muse his "genius" will serve. The "dreamer" with weakness of will becomes the central character in Proust's novel; his examination of Jamesian topics—his consciousness, his awareness of his world, emotional and cultural, his feelings and dreams—becomes the subject of the novel that is the subject of Proust's novel. Although the deck was stacked against our Proustian hero, according to Jamesian criteria for success—"habits of highly concentrated attention, energetic volition, and self-denial in unnecessary things"[136]—the evolution from poetic response to responsible poetics structures the story, as the narrator develops his will to create an overarching aesthetic philosophy upon which to build.

Breaking a habit requires active effort. New behavior must substitute for old: "It is not in the moment of their forming, but in the moment of their producing *motor effects*, that resolves and aspirations communicate the new 'set' to the brain."[137] A visit to Balbec with its new bed and new breakfast interrupt the habit of love for Gilberte: "It is surprising how soon a desire will die of inanition if it never be fed."[138] Imperious automatic Habit is capitalized in the following passage, while the acts employed to alter it, the changes of habit, are not:

> Mais cette souffrance et ce regain de l'amour pour Gilberte ne furent pas plus longs que ceux qu'on a en rêve, et cette fois au contraire parce qu'à Balbec, l'Habitude ancienne n'était plus là pour les faire durer. Et si ces effets de l'Habitude semblent contradictoires, c'est qu'elle obéit à des lois multiples. À Paris, jétais devenu de plus en plus indifférent à Gilberte, grâce à l'Habitude. Le changement d'habitude, c'est-à-dire la cessation momentanée de l'Habitude, paracheva l'oeuvre de l'Habitude, quand je partis pour Balbec. Elle affaiblit mais stabilise, elle amène la désagrégation mais la fait durer indéfiniment. Chaque jour depuis des années je calquais tant bien que mal mon état d'âme sur celui de la veille. À Balbec, un lit nouveau, à côté duquel on m'apportait le matin un petit déjeuner différent de celui de Paris, ne devait plus soutenir les pensées dont s'était nourri mon amour pour Gilberte.[139]

> [But this pain and this recrudescence of my love for Gilberte lasted no longer than such things last in a dream, and this time, on the contrary, because at Balbec the old Habit was no longer there to them alive. And if these effects of Habit appear to be incompatible, that is because Habit is bound by a diversity of laws. In Paris I had grown more and more indifferent to Gilberte, thanks to Habit. The change of habit, that is to

say the temporary cessation of Habit, completed Habit's work when I set out for Balbec. It weakens, but it stabilises; it leads to disintegration but it makes the scattered elements last indefinitely. Day after day, for years past, I had modelled my state of mind as best I could upon that of the day before. At Balbec a strange bed, to the side of which a tray was brought in the morning that differed from my Paris breakfast tray, could no longer sustain the thoughts upon which my love for Gilberte had fed.[140]]

In James's view, physical traces are "grooved out by habit in the brain": "Nothing we ever do is, in strict scientific literalness, wiped out." Similar language appears in *Albertine disparue*: emotional events mark us. "Mais la sensibilité même la plus physique, reçoit comme le sillon de la foudre, la signature originale et longtemps indélébile de l'événement nouveau" [But the sensibility, even in the most physical form, receives, like the wake of a thunderbolt, the original and for long indelible imprint of the novel event].[141] That our experience creates us is evident for both James and Proust. "The physiological study of mental conditions is thus the most powerful ally of hortatory ethics. The hell to be endured hereafter [. . .] is no worse than the hell we make for ourselves [. . .] by habitually fashioning our characters in the wrong way."[142] After Albertine and the concomitant suffering that cleaved his experience and altered the balance of habits from "pales fac-similés" [colourless facsimiles][143] to suffering that was life-altering, Proust's narrator could not evade "les chaînes que j'avais forgées moi-même" [the chains which I myself had forged].[144] He is haunted. Nothing in his privileged background could protect him from his habit of her: "notre passé et les lésions physiques où il s'est inscrit, déterminent notre avenir" [our past, and the physical lesions in which it is recorded, determine out future].[145]

Only forgetting, the converse of memory and companion to intermittence will assist. "The life of the *individual* consciousness in time," wrote James, is found to be "an interrupted one."[146] Intermittence thus permeates attentive consciousness, memory and feelings, as they exist in time. "Our possessions notoriously," James wrote, "are perishable facts."[147]

In the end, the discoveries of art will return the complexity to experience and eliminate the shortcut of habit. Removing the quotidian and contingent from experience does not delete the emotional tenor of the content, it just pulls "les mauvaises herbes de l'habitude" [the weeds of habit]:[148]

> Il me fallait rendre aux moindres signes qui m'entouraient (Guermantes, Albertine, Gilberte, Saint-Loup, Balbec, etc.) leur sens que l'habitude leur avait fait perdre pour moi. Et quand nous aurons atteint la réalité, pour l'exprimer, pour la conserver nous écarterons ce qui est différent d'elle et que ne cesse de nous apporter la vitesse acquise de

> l'habitude. Plus que tout j'écarterais ces paroles que les lèvres plutôt que l'esprit choisissent.[149]
>
> [I was surrounded by symbols (Guermantes, Albertine, Gilberte, Saint-Loup, Balbec, etc.) and to the least of these I had to restore the meaning which habit had caused them to lose for me. Nor was that all. When we have arrived at reality, we must, to express it and preserve it, present the intrusion of all those extraneous elements which at every moment the gathered speed of habit lays at our feet. Above all I should have to be on my guard against those phrases which are chosen rather by the lips than by the mind.[150]]

How can the operations of an individual's mind, the activities taking place in this murky "pénombre," be transposed into a conception of art and inspire a novel?

ASSOCIATION AND METAPHOR

"Who can count all the silly fancies, the grotesque suppositions, the utterly irrelevant reflections he makes in the course of a day? Who can swear that his prejudices and irrational opinions constitute a less bulky part of his mental furniture than his clarified beliefs?"[151] In Proust's novel, the "palimpsest" of superimposed associations is not simply the result of shadowy manifestations of alternating imaginations, dreams, or fantasies, nor is it solely the result of the author's varying ideas over the course of a lengthy period of composition, reflecting many successive revisions of what was essentially a single story written out over the length of a whole career.[152] Genette's insightful observations help to confirm the opinion that Proust's composition is an illustration of how the actual processes of association operate in the brain and how memory functions. They are the actions, in James's terms, of the physiological "law of neural habit."[153]

The brain's "habits," in James's view, are "due to the way in which one elementary process of the cerebral hemispheres tends to excite whatever other elementary process it may have excited at any former time."[154] Genette has astutely observed the theoretical underpinnings of association theory in Proust's artistic rendering of metaphor, which he terms a "figuratics centered [. . .] (as in Proust) on a poetics of discourse."[155] Principles of association, such as contiguity, similarity, and contrast, arise in Genette's discussion of Proustian metaphor as analog or comparison. These demonstrate "the relation of the part to the whole or that of the part to the remainder."[156] James had described the principles of association from a psychological point of view, explaining how the mind employs them in patterning.

Genette is sensitive to the fact that Proustian metaphor attempts to reconcile feelings or reactions, the Jamesian "fringe," and clarify just what those very personal responses are by using a comparison. When Genette describes Proust's depiction of Venice as recalling and supplanting Combray, it is not the concrete bricks and mortar depictions, the actual place views, the maps or photos that count in the comparison; it is a Rembrandt-like vaporous quality of reaction[157] occurring in the narrator's mind to the light bouncing simultaneously off the village roof tiles and the golden domes that Proust is accentuating. As Genette rightly notes, Proust employs a technique of "abandoning the direct use of our senses and of borrowing the link provided by imagination."[158] The resonant "superimposition" or "palimpsest" of Combray churchbells with Doncières heating noises[159] occurs in the mind of the narrator. It is not merely a personality trait that determines the narrator's approach, his X-ray-like technique of probing beyond surface "appearances" that drives his effort to attain something deeper, to ascertain some ultimate knowledge or "essence."[160] In always going beyond the obvious, he is attempting to incorporate his own intimate reactions to what he experiences because that is the only "essence" he *can* attain. The narrator discovers the layers of experience deposited by time, all the changes that resonate through his memory, and relates them to the currently evident. Proust's "mirages"[161] are James's "fringes." The disconnected views that conscious experience retains of an existence that is lived sequentially and remembered are Genette's "superimpositions."[162]

The "places that are active" and attached to particular characters[163] are the associations carried in the narrator's memory. If he has interacted with them in more than one context, the contexts come to resound additively, as do Méséglise and Guermantes incarnated in the person of Mlle. de Saint-Loup; or Balbec, Paris and Albertine; Combray, Venice, Paris, and family. Was the narrator's reaction to the physical sensation of the particular taste of tea and madeleine only possible in his mother's home? What would have resulted if that had been what was served at Odette's teatime, Mme. de Villeparisis's gathering, or Oriane de Guermante's table?

> But in every one of us there are moments when this complete reproduction of all the items of a past experience occurs. What are those moments? They are moments of emotional recall of the past as something which once was, but is gone for ever—moments, the interest of which consists in the feeling that our self was once other than it now is. When this is the case, any detail, however minute, which will make the past picture more complete, will also have its effect in swelling that total contrast between *now* and *then* which forms the central interest of our contemplation.[164]

Were we to change the last word of this passage from "contemplation" to composition, what would ensue for a writer gifted with the talent of Proust would surely be something akin to *À la recherche du temps perdu*.

We find the slumbering narrator at the beginning of *À la recherche du temps perdu*, his "moi" resurging slowly out of dream-like confusion, the nebulous mix of space and time as it might have existed before Creation—or the creation of this story. Various moments from his past his life, locations in which they occurred, rooms he slept in, reconstitute him as a specific individual, ending the amorphous uncertainty of the "pénombre" in which he finds himself.

> All this happens with no voluntary effort [. . .]. Rooms, landscapes, buildings, pictures, or persons with whose look we are very familiar, surge up before the mind's eye with all the details of their appearance complete, so soon as we think of any one of their component parts.[165]

With the stimulus of one of these visual "component parts," the complete picture will resurge through memories; "le branle était donné à ma mémoire" [my memory had been set in motion][166] by images of oil lamps or the style of shirt collars ("col rabattu" [turned-down collars][167]), the affective associations of a life lived in sequential detail, like "les positions successives que nous montre le kinétoscope" [the successive positions . . . as they appear upon a bioscope];[168] "à Combray chez ma grand-tante, à Balbec, à Paris, à Doncières, à Venise, ailleurs encore, [. . .] les lieux, les personnes que j'y avais connues" [at Combray with my great-aunt, at Balbec, Paris, Doncières, Venice, and the rest; . . . all the places and people I had known].[169]

Lasting patterns remain as residue of the sensory inputs from which they derive and can be recalled even at great interval due to the power of association:

> Seen things and heard things cohere with each other, and with odors and tastes, in representation, in the same order in which they cohered as impressions in the outer world. [. . .] Smells notoriously have the power of recalling the other experiences in whose company they were wont to be felt, perhaps long years ago; and the voluminous emotional character assumed by the images which suddenly pour into the mind at such a time forms one of the staple topics of popular psychologic wonder.[170]

The child's tortured climb up the stairway in Combray is impregnated with a scent of sadness; his initial experience and its lasting memory inundate him with a rapid and "toxic" rush of emotion.[171] Association by contiguity determines that "*objects once experienced together tend to become associated in the imagination, so that when any one of them is thought of, the others are likely to be thought of also, in the same order of sequence or coexistence as before*" (emphasis in original). Because of the associative powers of language ("the most notorious and important case of the mental combination of auditory with optical impressions originally experienced together"[172]) and its ability to conjure mental images redolent with emotion, reading compacts the extensiveness and condenses the intensity of experiences that otherwise could only have been lived over long periods of time. Interpreted by Proust, reading takes on the ancillary associations of his hero's search for meaning: "vers la découverte de la vérité" [toward the discovery of truth]. It concentrates more than a lifetime's worth of action: "les emotions que me donnait l'action à laquelle je prenais part [. . .] étaient plus remplis d'événements dramatiques que ne l'est souvent toute une vie" [the emotions aroused in me by the action in which I was taking part . . . were crammed with more dramatic events than occur, often, in a whole lifetime].[173]

Proust's novel spreads the action of a lifetime over many pages, simulating the slow passage of time and an illusion of the autobiographical. Past selves are resurrected like the souls in Celtic lore locked away and lost to the living until released from their imprisonment, in a manner analogous to resurgent memories, to live among us once again when we accidentally encounter and repossess them.[174]

Contiguity between things thought of—on the basis of their "objective properties"[175]—has a physiological basis in neural patterning because "*nerve-currents [in the brain] propagate themselves easiest through those tracts of conduction which have been already most in use*" (emphasis in original).[176] A place is thus associated with a certain feeling, the sound of a spoon tapping a plate with the sound of clattering train wheels, the roughness of one napkin with another touched previously that had a similar feel, an uneven paving stone with a comparable one in a completely different city, the savor of a bit of cake dipped in tea with the entire context—lost past world of family and childhood—in which it was first tasted.

If the law of association by contiguity can thus account for connections between the physical and emotional, according to James, it can also connect thoughts, or the "coupling paths" of "ideational centres"[177] that explain their flights and perchings. Here, what James calls "trains of imagery and consideration [that] follow each other through our thinking" emerge with abrupt alterations or leaps over lacunae as they meander or race from thought to thought.[178]

Association by contiguity characterizes the kind of thinking that occurs in storytelling. Such thinking, rooted in "actual experience," is characteristically "narrative," guided by goal-directed attention, some common thread: "in the main it consists of a procession through the mind of groups of images of concrete things, persons, places, and events, together with the feelings which they awaken, and in an order which, if our attention is guided by some dominant interest, such as recollecting an actual set of facts, or inventing a coherent story."[179]

Proust used the principle of association to describe the force of his feelings for Albertine: "Ma tendresse pour Albertine," states Proust's narrator, "ma jalousie tenaient on l'a vu à l'irradiation par association d'idées de certains noyaux d'impressions douces ou douloureuses" [My feeling for Albertine, my jealousy, stemmed, as we have seen, from the irradiation, by the association of ideas, of certain pleasant or painful impressions].[180] Associations lead in many possible directions as new compounds form, creating new suffering as memories bubble to the surface: "de chaque idée comme d'un carrefour dans une forêt, partent tant de routes différentes, qu'au moment où je m'y attendais le moins, je me trouvais devant un nouveau souvenir" [from each of our ideas, as from a crossroads in a forest, so many paths brand off in different directions that at the moment when I least expected it I found myself faced by a fresh memory].[181]

In "association by similarity,"[182] like the flares from core emotions about Albertine, we find a "partial identity"[183] or overlap, "[w]hen the *same* attribute appears in two phenomena, though it be their only common property."[184] According to James, association by similarity is characteristic of "compounds" where "the *same* attribute appears in two phenomena" that are otherwise unrelated.[185] This type of association is not driven by a dominant focal "interest." It allows thoughts to burgeon one from the previous "according to the caprice of our revery [*sic*]" and is characteristic of minds that tend toward the poetic.[186] In this form of association, there are startlingly "abrupt transitions between two dissimilar elements,"[187] and the connector can be emotional.[188] The thinker enjoys a great breadth of source material.[189] He has a less "dry, prosaic, literal sort of mind" and is more "fanciful, poetic, or witty,"[190] traits appropriately applicable to Proust. In *The Principles of Psychology,* James uses a striking image to illustrate association by similarity, one that we find later reprised in Proust's description of how truth in art is transmitted through style. James's image looks like a daisy or flower with elongated petals or oval rings overlapping in a center circle; it illustrates clearly the way Proust employed metaphor to capture the essential similarities that exist between disparate elements of felt experience (in James's terms, the mysterious "links"[191]).

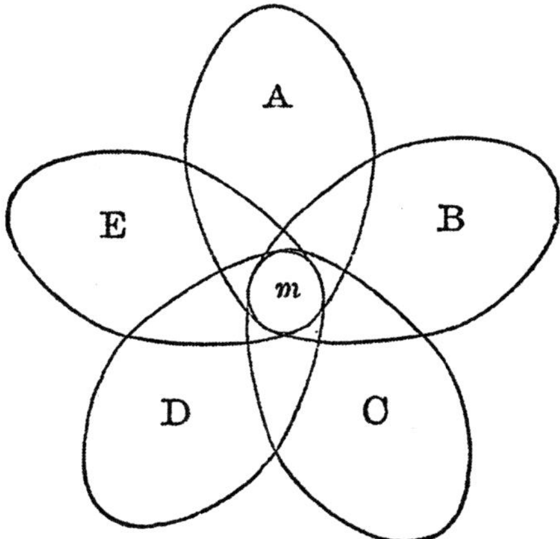

Figure 1. Reprinted by permission of the publisher from *The Works Of William James—The Principles Of Psychology: Volume II*, p. 972, Frederick Burkhardt, General Editor, Fredson Bowers, Textual Editor, Ignas K. Skrupskelis, Associate Editor, Cambridge, Mass.: Harvard University Press, Copyright (c) 1981 by the President and Fellows of Harvard College.

Proust's narrator considers the process by which Elstir creates art, the mixing and re-fashioning the elements of a scene, analogous to Creation: "une sorte de metamorphose des choses representées, analogue à celle qu'en poésie on nomme métaphore" [a sort of metamorphosis of the objects represented, analogous to what in poetry we call metaphor].[192] Such removal of the existing "name" or the givens of realistic observation, supplying instead a new view more closely related to "impressions véritables," is one of the functions of metaphor for Proust.

In the chapter of *The Principles of Psychology* on "Reasoning," James describes the process of association by similarity. The concept he depicts and the language he uses resemble Proust's later description of metaphor. James asks how one observes the similarities or distinctions that exist between things.

> He transfers his attention as rapidly as possible, backwards and forwards, from one to the other. The rapid alteration in consciousness shakes out, as it were, the points of difference or agreement, which would have slumbered forever unnoticed if the consciousness of the objects compared had occurred at widely distant periods of time. [. . .] [W]e need that the varying concomitants should in all their variety be brought into consciousness *at once*. Not till then will the character in question escape from its adhesion to each and all of them and stand alone.[193]

This is the method that, according to James, a scientist would use to conduct a "search" for "the reason or law embedded in a phenomenon."[194] Proust conducted a similar "search" for the "essence" of meaning in his experience and used metaphor as the means to express that essence, in the way James had described.

Resurgent memory brings disparate moments of experience together at the same time, so that Proust's narrator can distill the crucial common aspects not otherwise evident, a process typical of scientific research, he notes (as had James), and express them in permanent form. The new certainties engendered are the central core of overlap of the Jamesian petals or rings of association by similarity in the "fringe." They contain a common thread of emotional truth and connect disparate observations, entities, sensations, feelings. The process "operates of itself in highly gifted minds without any deliberation, spontaneously collecting analogous instances, uniting in a moment what in nature the whole breadth of space and time keeps separate, and so permitting a perception of identical points in the midst of different circumstances."[195] For Proust, the central commonalities are enclosed in the overlapping "anneaux necessaries":

> Une image offerte par la vie nous apportait en réalité, à ce moment-là, des sensations multiples et différentes. [. . .] Ce que nous appelons la réalité est un certain rapport entre ces sensations et ces souvenirs qui nous entourent simultanément [. . .] rapport unique que l'écrivain doit retrouver pour en enchaîner à jamais dans sa phrase les deux termes différents. [. . .] [L]a vérité ne commencera qu'au moment où l'écrivain prendra deux objets différents, posera leur rapport, analogue dans le monde de l'art à celui qu'est le rapport unique de la loi causale dans le monde de la science, et les enfermera dans les anneaux nécessaires d'un beau style; même, ainsi que la vie, quand, en rapprochant une qualité commune à deux sensations, il dégagera leur essence commune en les réunissant l'une et l'autre pour les soustraire aux contingences du temps, dans une métaphore.[196]

> [An image presented to us by life brings with it, in a single moment, sensations which are in fact multiple and heterogeneous. . . . [W]hat we call reality is a certain connexion between these immediate sensations and the memories which envelop us simultaneously with them . . . a unique connexion which the writer has to rediscover in order to link for ever in his phrase the two sets of phenomena which reality joins together. [T]ruth will be attained by him only when he takes two different objects, states the connexion between them—a connexion analogous in the world of art to the unique connexion which in the world of science is provided by the law of causality—and encloses them in the necessary links of a well-wrought style; truth—and life, too,—can be attained by us only when, by comparing a quality common to two sensations, we succeed in extracting their common essence and in reuniting them to each other, liberated from the contingencies of time, within a metaphor.[197]]

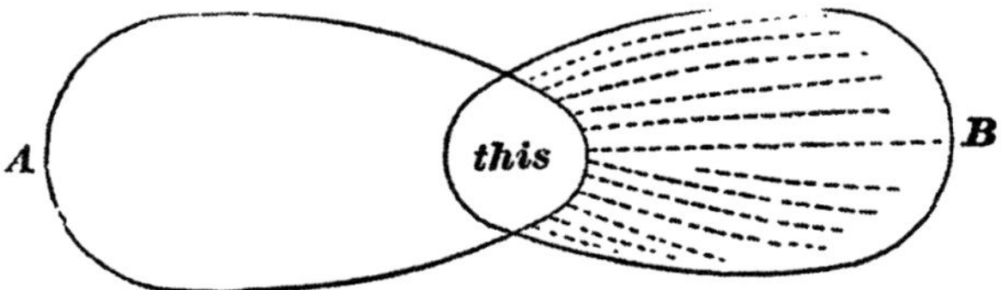

Figure 2. Reprinted by permission of the publisher from *The Works Of William James—The Principles Of Psychology: Volume II*, p. 729, Frederick Burkhardt, General Editor, Fredson Bowers, Textual Editor, Ignas K. Skrupskelis, Associate Editor, Cambridge, Mass.: Harvard University Press, Copyright (c) 1981 by the President and Fellows of Harvard College.

The writer who seizes and depicts the kernel of overlap reveals added depth. The point of intersection in a comparison reveals and clarifies the truth. For the poetic artist, metaphor is the appropriate means of disclosing and expressing the conjunction. Proust's "beau style"[198] illustrates in theory and in practice what James had described.

Recall, however it is attained, is unlikely to be "total," for that would condemn us to rewinding experience on an endless "treadmill of concrete reminiscences from which no detail could be omitted."[199] Resurgent memories so vivid that they seem almost real allow Proust's narrator to reexperience the feelings of a bygone moment. But they are generally, in James's view, only certain hot spots of past experience, a "partial recall" corresponding most closely to what is meaningful to us.[200] Revived by their emotional draw, based on *"habit, recency, vividness, and emotional congruity"*[201] of the past event to the present situation, the elements of James's "partial recall" are made "prepotent" in his terms and "privileged" in Proust's. While some of their material detail has been lost, association by similarity enriches those that remain and makes them more meaningful than when they were originally lived and experienced first-hand, as they are enhanced by their "own associates."[202] Contemporary neuroscientists continue to explain this process, confirming a connection between James's description of the process and Proust's recognition and literary use of it.

Factors that are lost when recall is only "partial" mysteriously become "inert" or "decay," a word James takes from Hodgson's *Time and Space*.[203] For Proust's narrator, what "decay[s]" is forgotten, truly "mort à jamais" [permanently dead].[204] What is recalled is, according to James, "largely a matter of accident—accident that is, for our intelligence,"[205] because they recur not by voluntary selection but by involuntary and inadvertent resuscitation.

Dull and prosaic minds characterized by "general flatness and poverty of their aesthetic nature" are more likely to retain "the literal sequences of their local and personal history." In more educated, cultured, gifted individuals, James feels, "musings pursue an erratic course, swerving continually into some new direction traced by the shifting play of interest."[206]

> The train of imagery wanders at its own sweet will, now trudging in sober grooves of habit, now with a hop, skip and jump, darting across the whole field of time and space. This is revery, or musing.[207]

Proust's narrator seems to wallow in deep puddles of thought, jumping from present to past, from object in front of him to distant fringe of emotional or historical detail. The mechanism of association James describes allows Proust to go beyond simple description, to use his "telescope" to chronicle the distant orbs—people and places—that once surrounded his narrator, in a process of "meta-metaphor." He records sounds, scents, colors, and happiness, the transparent bubbles of sensation and feeling of a springtime long past.

> Aussi le côté de Méséglise et le côté de Guermantes restent-ils pour moi liés à bien des petits événements de celle de toutes les diverses vies que nous menons parallèlement, qui est la plus pleine de péripéties, la plus riche en épisodes, je veux dire la vie intellectuelle. Sans doute elle progresse en nous insensiblement et les vérités qui en ont changé pour nous le sens et l'aspect, qui nous ont ouvert de nouveaux chemins, nous en préparions depuis longtemps la découverte; mais c'était sans le savoir; et elles ne datent pour nous que du jour, de la minute où elles nous sont devenues visibles. [. . .] Parfois ce morceau de paysage amené ainsi jusqu'à aujourd'hui se détache si isolé de tout, qu'il flotte incertain dans ma pensée comme une Délos fleurie, sans que je puisse dire de quel pays, de quel temps—peut-étre tout simplement de quel rêve—il vient. Mais c'est surtout comme à des gisements profonds de mon sol mental, comme aux terrains résistants sur lesquels je m'appuie encore, que je dois penser au côté de Méséglise et au côté de Guermantes.[208]
>
> [So the Méséglise way and the Guermantes way remain for me linked with many of the little incidents of the life which, of all the various lives we lead concurrently, is the most episodic, the most full of vicissitudes; I mean the life of the mind. Doubtless it progresses within us so imperceptibly, and we had for a long time been preparing for the discovery of the truths which have changed its meaning and its aspect, have opened new paths for us; but that preparation was unconscious; and for us those truths date only from the day, from the minute when they became apparent. [. . .] Sometimes the fragment of landscape thus transported into the present will detach itself in such isolation from all associations that it floats uncertainly in my mind like a flowering Delos, and I am unable to say from what place, from what time—perhaps, quite simply, from what dream—it comes. But it is preeminently as the deepest layer of my mental soil, as the firm ground on which I still stand, that I regard the Méséglise and Guermantes ways.[209]]

Voluntary thought, on the other hand, in James's view, is "guided by a distinct purpose or conscious interest"[210] in scientific inquiry or when we try to remember something we have forgotten or fill what we sense as a "gap."

> The inquirer starts with a fact of which he seeks the reason, or with an hypothesis of which he seeks the proof. In either case he keeps turning the matter incessantly in his mind until, by arousal of associate upon associate, some habitual, some familiar, some similar, one arises which he recognizes to suit his need.[211]

Proust uses such voluntary "research" as the modus operandi of the jealous lover. Like Swann before him with Odette, Proust's narrator torments himself by reexamining every memory he has of Albertine, reviewing everything she has said to him, comparing, evaluating. He interviews Andrée and the chauffeur in an effort to capture all the details of Albertine's contacts and movements: "Même les premiers temps de notre arrivée à Paris, insatisfait des renseignements qu'Andrée et le chauffeur m'avaient donnés sur les promenades qu'ils faisaient avec mon amie, j'avais senti les environs de Paris aussi cruels que ceux de Balbec" [Even in the first days after our return to Paris, not satisfied by the information that Andrée and the chauffeur had given me as to their expeditions with my mistress, I had felt the environs of Paris to be as baleful as those of Balbec].[212] But her experience is not within his ken. James had described such a search for understanding or for information, for finding a forgotten fact, in this way: "But all these details refuse to shoot together into a solid whole, for the lack of the missing thing, so we keep running over them in our mind, dissatisfied, craving something more."[213] Proust's narrator's need to know, his imaginative access to "le monde des possibles," [the world of potentiality]; is a torment not appeased or satisfied by anything he can discover from the outside world, the missing answers remain elusive.

> Ma jalousie naissait par des images, pour une souffrance, non d'après une probablilté. [. . .] La réalité n'est jamais qu'une amorce à un inconnu sur la voie duquel nous ne pouvons aller bien loin. Il vaut mieux ne pas savoir, penser le moins possible, ne pas fournir à la jalousie le moindre détail concret. Malheureusement à défaut de la vie extérieure, des incidents aussi sont amenés par la vie intérieure; à défaut des promenades d'Albertine, les hasards rencontrés dans les réflexions que je faisais seul me fournissaient parfois de ces petits fragments de réel qui attirent à eux, à la façon d'un aimant, un peu d'inconnu qui, dès lors, devient douloureux. On a beau vivre sous l'équivalent d'une cloche pneumatique, les associations d'idées, les souvenirs continuent à jouer.[214]
>
> [Productive of suffering, my jealousy was born of mental images, not based on probability. [. . .] Reality is never more than a first step to-

wards an unknown on the road to which one can never progress very far. It is better not to know, to think as little as possible, not to feel one's jealousy with the slightest concrete detail. Unfortunately, in the absence of an outer life, incidents are created by the inner life, too; in the absence of expeditions with Albertine, the random course of my solitary reflexions furnished me a times with some of those tiny fragments of the truth which attract to themselves, like a magnet, and inkling of the unknown, which from that moment becomes painful. Even if one lives under the equivalent of a bell jar, associations of ideas, memories, continue to act upon us.[215]]

For James as well as for Proust, voluntary remembrance includes an involuntary component. While we are working at remembering, we surround the thought we are seeking with a series of associative partners: "From each detail there radiate lines of association forming so many tentative guesses."[216]

> Now all these added associates *arise independently of the will,* by the spontaneous processes we know so well. *All that the will does is to emphasize and linger over those which seem pertinent, and ignore the rest.* Through this hovering of the attention in the neighborhood of the desired object, the accumulation of associates become so great that the combined tensions of their neural processes break through the bar, and the nervous wave pours into the tract which has so long been awaiting its advent. And as the expectant, sub-conscious itching, so to speak, bursts into the fullness of vivid feeling, the mind finds inexpressible relief.[217]

The brain, or mind, finds the solution without the assistance of conscious voluntary intent: "But the final stroke of discovery is only prepared, not effected, by them [our voluntary efforts]. The brain-tracts must, of their own accord, shoot the right way at last, or we shall still grope in darkness."[218]

Proust's narrator is equally unsuccessful when he tries to use the techniques of voluntary association to comprehend the elation he feels during moments of involuntary reminiscence:

> D'où avait pu me venir cette puissante joie? Je sentais qu'elle était liée au goût du thé et du gâteau, mais qu'elle le dépassait infiniment, ne devait pas être de même nature. D'où venait-elle? Que signifiait-elle? Où l'appréhender? Je bois une seconde gorgée où je ne trouve rien de plus que dans la première, une troisième qui m'apporte un peu moins que la seconde. [. . .] Il est clair que la vérité que je cherche n'est pas en lui, mais en moi. Il l'y a éveillée, mais ne la connaît pas [. . .]. Je pose la tasse et me tourne vers mon esprit. C'est à lui de trouver la vérité. Mais comment?[219]
>
> [Whence could it have come to me, this all-powerful joy? I sensed that it was connected with the taste of the tea and the cake, but that it

infinitely transcended those savours, could not, indeed, be of the same nature. Where did it come from? What did it mean? How could I seize and apprehend it? I drink a second mouthful, in which I find nothing more than in the first, then a third, which gives me rather less than the second [. . .]. It is plain that the truth I am seeking lies not in the cup but in myself. The drink has called it into being, but does not know it [. . .]. I put down the cup and examine my own mind. It alone can discover the truth. But how?[220]]

Proust used James's "stroke of discovery"[221] and his explanation of the functioning of involuntary memory as major creative and asthetic keys to his work. Memories unlocked in an involuntary manner solved his hero's epistemological urges to discover through his "biography" the meaning of his life's experience and to unleash his artistic methodology, sparking his will to create and prompting him to exert the effort required.

Involuntary association is like a deus ex machina: it is dramatic, mysterious, unexpected. In a fertile mind, involuntary association and metaphorical creation just happen, a result of their individual physiology. In some minds, along with an increased capacity for focusing attention voluntarily comes a high ability to associate in this creative involuntary manner. The physiology of their brains permits greater latitude of associative imagery.

> The direction of its course and the form of its transitions are due to the unknown conditions by which in some brains action tends to focalize itself in small spots, while in others it fills patiently its broad bed. What these differing conditions are, it seems impossible to guess. Whatever they are, they are what separate the man of genius from the prosaic creature of habit and routine thinking.[222]

Proust's prose flames with dazzling fireworks of metaphorical association, flights based on the smell his narrator remembers of the first fire of a distantly past fall season in Combray or Doncières or the sounds of a streetcar outside his apartment. To feel the music of the spheres takes little more than a bit of solitude:

> Mais c'était surtout en moi que j'entendais avec ivresse un son nouveau rendu par le violon intérieur. Ses cordes sont serrées ou détendues par de simples différences de la temperature, de la lumière extérieures. [. . .] Des portes de communication depuis longtemps condamnés se rouvraient dans mon cerveau. [. . .] Frémissant tout entière autour de la corde vibrante, j'aurais sacrifié ma terne vie d'autrefois et ma vie à venir, passées à la gomme à effacer de l'habitude, pour cet état si particulier.[223]

> [But it was above all in myself that I heard, with rapture, a new sound emitted by the violin within. Its strings are tautened or relaxed by mere differences in the temperature or the light outside [. . .]. Communicating doors, long barred, reopened in my brain. [. . .] With my whole

> being quivering around the vibrating string, I would have sacrificed my dim former existence and my life to come, erased by the india-rubber of habit, for a state so unique.[224]]

A scientific or reasoned approach has limitations and is not necessarily of greater assistance in understanding human relations than it is in generating metaphor: "l'intelligence n'est pas l'instrument le plus subtil, le plus puissant, le plus approprié pour saisir le vrai" [our intelligence is not the subtlest, most powerful, most appropriate instrument for grasping the truth]. But that does not mean that one should entirely avoid the benefits of a reasoned examination or the application of voluntary attention to the problem. One cannot simply rely, according to the narrator, on "un intuitisme de l'inconscient, par une foi aux pressentiments toute faite" [an unconscious intuition, a ready-made faith in presentiments].[225] Like James, Proust is willing to allow for forces beyond logic in order to enrich the range of possibilities while retaining a narrowed use of voluntary attention. Unwilling to abandon its benefits completely, they are subsidiary to something "other" that has to be taken on faith:

> C'est la vie qui, peu à peu, cas par cas, nous permet de remarquer que ce qui est le plus important pour notre coeur, ou pour notre esprit, ne nous est pas appris par le raisonnement mais par des puissances autres. Et alors, c'est l'intelligence elle-même qui se rendant compte de leur supériorité, abdique par raisonnement devant elles, et accepte de devenir leur collaboratrice et leur servante. Foi expérimentale.[226]
>
> [It is life that, little by little, case by case, enables us to observe that what is most important to our hearts or to our minds is taught us not by reasoning but by other powers. And then it is the intelligence itself which, acknowledging their superiority, abdicates to them through reasoning and consents to become their collaborator and their servant. Experimental faith.[227]]

EXPERIENCING TIME THROUGH MEMORY

In *À la recherche du temps perdu,* Proust recognizes the stream of consciousness as the flow of his narrator's experience over time, filled with places, people, and events that are past and remembered. "Pastness" is a concept James placed in a category he called "conceived time,"[228] while the "sensible present"[229] is a shard, a short moment in the constant stream of conscious awareness, a time of attention and response in the "now." In James's view, there is a flow of such individual moments of brief "duration" during which we "sit perched"[230] looking simultaneously backward and forward into time past and time future, time recent and time distant. Some elements of the past are always intermingled with the present.[231] The "specious present has [. . .] a vaguely vanishing backward and forward fringe; [. . .] but itself has at most a length of perhaps twelve seconds, as demonstrated by experimentation."[232] In James's view, any unit of time extending into the past beyond this short interval would belong to the realm of memory. Proust situates his narrator in a Jamesian "specious present."

While some critics locate Proust's hero sliding forward and backward in an endless Bergsonian subjective duration, Proust himself frequently used the term "durée" to indicate a particularly short period of time: "la durée d'un éclair" is a momentary fragment of pure time [a moment as brief as a flash of lightning][233] when an insight occurs revealing a connection between present sensation and past experience.

When the narrator goes to the theater for the first time to see La Berma play Phèdre, his attempts to seize "la divine Beauté que devait me révéler le jeu de la Berma" [the goddess of beauty whom Berma's acting was to reveal to me][234] as he studies her gestures and soliloquies are met with frustration because everything she says flies by before he can grasp it. "Mais que cette durée était brève! À peine un son était-il reçu dans mon oreille qu'il était remplacé par un autre" [But how short their duration was! Scarcely had a sound been received by my ear than it was displaced there by another].[235] "Mais en même temps tout mon plaisir avait cessé; j'avais beau tendre vers la Berma mes yeux, mes oreilles, mon esprit, pour ne pas laisser échapper une miette des raisons qu'elle me donnerait de l'admirer, je ne parvenais pas à en recueillir une seule." [But at the same time all my pleasure had ceased; in vain did I strain towards Berma eyes, ears, mind, so as not to let one morsel escape me of the reasons which she would give me for admiring her, I did not succeed in gleaning a single one].[236] The "specious present" speeds by too quickly for the leisurely contemplation the narrator needs in order to appreciate what the actress brings to the words, the depths of individuality her particular talent adds to the part. While she is on stage the entire experience blurs together, too muddled for serious analysis and real comprehension.

> Mon intérêt pour le jeu de la Berma n'avait cessé de grandir depuis que la représentation était finie parce qu'il ne subissait plus la compression et les limites de la réalité; mais j'éprouvais le besoin de lui trouver des explications, de plus il s'était porté avec une intensité égale, pendant que la Berma jouait, sur tout ce qu'elle offrait, dans l'indivisibilité de la vie, à mes yeux, à mes oreilles; il n'avait rien séparé et distingué.[237]
>
> [My interest in Berma's acting had continued to grow ever since the fall of the curtain because it was no longer compressed within the limits of reality; but I felt the need to find explanations for it; moreover it had been concentrated with equal intensity, while Berma was on the stage, upon everything that she offered, in the indivisibility of a living whole, to my eyes and ears; it had made no attempt to separate or discriminate.[238]]

To fully comprehend, he requires a long and leisurely period of contemplation to consider the performance in depth and appreciate what others in the audience were applauding. The "specious present" does not allow for this type of reflection. The operation must be accomplished, like the composition of the novel as a whole, over time and retrospectively, examined in its full length in the past.

As a family with a long history, the Guermantes name has a greater "durée" than any of its individual members. It is an ensemble of diversity and succession[239] and in that way corresponds to a Jamesian single self composed of "moi successifs" [successive aspects of a single person][240] in "la durée de la vie, comme une suite de moi juxtaposés mais distincts qui mourraient les uns après les autres" [duration through life, . . . a sequence of juxtaposed but distinct "I's" which would die one after the other].[241] Like La Berma's performance, it is only through historical memory that the assemblage can be explored and understood.

Looking back is the only way we can tell where an experience begins and where it ends, what its outlines are. "[W]e see that in the time-world and the space-world alike the first known things are not elements, but combinations, not separate units, but wholes already formed."[242] It is our mental reconstruction of a particular moment in the stream of consciousness with all its contiguous impressions that permits us to recognize the fringes of experience in moments and places that slip by through the specious present. Retrospection permits us to see all four dimensions of each particular experience; it is appropriated into Proust's technique as a novelist, furnishing the surprise ending when the reader discovers that the novel he has just read is about to be written. If Proust's intention were to distill eternal verities from the jumble of daily contingency, the only valid analysis would be by looking back. Creating a fictional framework in which his narrator looks backward at his own experience while progressing forward in time permits ongoing adventure coupled with analysis appropriate to the hero's advances in insight. It allows for the construction of a fictional consciousness filled to the brim rather than the flat silhouette of events witnessed only at a distance and reported rather than lived.

When "reproduced with the duration and neighbors which it originally had,"[243] through the agency of memory, space is linked with time, according to James, in exactly the manner described by Proust at the end of *Du côté de chez Swann*: "We construct the miles just as we construct the years."[244]

> Les lieux que nous avons connus n'appartiennent pas qu'au monde de l'espace où nous les situons pour plus de facilité. Ils n'étaient qu'une mince tranche au milieu d'impressions contigües qui formaient notre vie d'alors; le souvenir d'une certaine image n'est que le regret d'un certain instant; et les maisons, les routes, les avenues, sont fugitives, hélas, comme les années.[245]

[The places we have known do not belong only to the world of space on which we map them for our own convenience. They were only a thin slice, held between the contiguous impressions that composed our life at that time; the memory of a particlar image is but regret for a particular moment; and houses, roads, avenues are as fugitive, alas, as the years.[246]]

According to James, time is never "empty"; we are unable to conceptualize the blossoming of duration without the "sensible" (as in sensory or sentient) content of experience. As a result, "our perception of time's flight, [. . .] is due to the *filling* of the time, and to our *memory* of a content which it had a moment previous, and which we feel to agree or disagree with its content now."[247] Consciousness at its most basic is a "dim habitat" filled with a perceptible blooming or "*changing process*" on which our notion of the passage of time is based. The "heart-beats, "breathing," "pulses of attention," "fragments of words or sentences that pass through our imagination"[248] constitute the sensations upon which our awareness of this flow is founded. Only very short periods of time are experienced as concrete. Longer periods are conceived symbolically: "It is but dates and events representing time [. . .] with no pretence of imagining the full durations that lie between them."[249] Before the revelations of the madeleine, the narrator's past is drawn as dry and flat.

> *In general, a time filled with varied and interesting experiences seems short in passing, but long as we look back.* [. . .] The length in retrospect depends obviously on the multitudinousness of the memories which the time affords. Many objects, events, changes, [. . .] immediately widen the view as we look back.[250]

For Proust, retrospective time after the madeleine has the enormity James describes, and so we have a long, dense book, filled with the narrator's unfurling memories, far exceeding any spot in space taken up by the lifetime of a man:

> Aussi, si elle m'était laissée assez longtemps pour accomplir mon oeuvre, ne manquerais-je pas d'abord d'y décrire les hommes, cela dût-il les faire ressembler à des êtres monstrueux, comme occupant une place si considérable, à côté de celle si restreinte qui leur est réservée dans l'espace, une place au contraire prolongée sans mesure puisqu'ils touchent simultanément, comme des géants plongés dans les années à des époques, vécues par eux si distantes, entre lesquelles tant de jours sont venus se placer—dans le Temps.[251]

> [So, if I were given long enough to accomplish my work, I should not fail, even if the effect were to make them resemble monsters, to describe men as occupying so considerable a place, compared with the restricted place which is reserved for them in space, a place on the contrary prolonged past measure, for simultaneously, like giants

plunged into the years, they touch the distant epochs through which they have lived, between which so many days have come to range themselves—in Time.[252]]

According to James, lengthy periods in a sickbed alter perception such that memories replace experience in a manner "analogous to the enlargement of space by a microscope; fewer real things at once in the immediate field of view, but each of them taking up more than its normal room."[253] While Proust utilyzes a telescopic imagination so his narrator can peer at distant "others," the microscopic view allows extensive description and appraisal with little action but with a great deal of cogitation and assay.

"The feeling of past time is a present feeling."[254] It occurs as brain processes permit reproductive memory to replicate an event as it originally was for us. Revisiting Combray in memory, Proust's narrator re-experiences it and presents it to the reader as if it were present.

James defines memory as "*the knowledge of an event or fact,* of which meantime we have not been thinking, *with the additional consciousness that we have thought or experienced it before*" (emphasis in original).[255] It is familiar but not identical: "The successive editions of a feeling are so many independent events, each snug in its own skin."[256] Proust's narrator discovers that his involuntary memories are free of the fortuity attached to the original experience. There is an eternal quality associated with the memory because it is a "copy" or "image"[257] of the original experience now unshackled from its exact material conditions: "Certes, ce qui palpite ainsi au fond de moi, ce doit être l'image, le souvenir visuel, qui, lié à cette saveur, tente de la suivre jusqu'à moi" [Undoubtedly what is thus palpitating in the depths of my being must be the image, the visual memory which, being linked to that taste, is trying to follow it into my conscious mind].[258]

James compares the sense of pastness of an event in memory to the effect of a painted set at the back of a stage. The set gives the impression of a scene "in a continuous perspective," when in fact what we see is the empty space in front of us with a decorated panel at the rear. Our imagination takes over and supplies the detail not actually present. Similarly, "we paint the remote past, as it were, upon a canvas in our memory, and yet often imagine we have direct vision of its depths."[259] Memory thus described is directly allied with fiction: "the object of memory is only an object imagined in the past (usually very completely imagined there) to which the emotion of belief adheres."[260] Proust himself uses the image of a theater set when he describes the effect of the taste of madeleine and tea reviving Aunt Léonie's room compared to what he is voluntarily able to remember of Combray: "Et dès que j'eus reconnu le goût du morceau de madeleine trempé dans le tilleul qui me donnait ma tante [. . .], aussitôt la vieille maison grise sur la rue, où était sa chambre, vint comme un décor de théâtre" [And as soon as I had recognised the taste of the piece of madeleine soaked in her decoction of lime-blossom which my aunt used to give me . . . immediately the old gray house upon the street, where her little room was, rose up like a stage set]. Out of the tea unfold memories heretofore lost and "indistincts." They recur with the illusory "forme et solidité" [shape and solidity] of an imaginary set painted in words.[261]

What we retain, James notes, is only a portion of what we have experienced; most is forgotten, but some things remain with us forever.[262] Like James, Proust explores the psychological mechanisms of how we remember. James quotes James Mill to illustrate how the search for a forgotten name uses what he calls "*recollection* by association" (emphasis in original):

> I meet an old acquaintance, whose name I do not remember, and wish to recollect. I run over a number of names, in hopes that some of them may be associated with the idea of the individual. I think of all the circumstances in which I have seeen him engaged; the time when I knew him, the persons along with whom I knew him, the things he did, or the things he suffered; and, if I chance upon any idea with which the name is associated, then immediately I have the recollection; if not, my pursuit of it is in vain.[263]

Very similarly, Proust's hero tries to remember the name of a woman who has greeted him warmly by name. He is certain he knows her, but her name escapes him. The passage that follows closely echoes James (although no reference to James Mill is found in indices to Proust's works). He appears to have ruminated and elaborated on the subject, and similarly tries to determine the name by a mental review of the facts, interests, friendships of this woman. He accepts the fact that association helped the name bubble to the surface of his mind, though it seemed to appear all by itself.

> Je cherchais à retrouver le sien tout en lui parlant; je me rappelais très bien avoir dîné avec elle, je me rappelais des mots qu'elle avait dits. Mais mon attention, tendue vers la région intérieure où il y avait ces souvenirs d'elle, ne pouvait y découvrir ce nom. [. . .] Ma pensée avait engagé comme une espèce de jeu avec lui pour saisir ses contours, la lettre par laquelle il commençait, et l'éclairer enfin tout entier. C'était peine perdue [. . .] Enfin d'un coup le nom vint tout entier: "Madame d'Arpajon." J'ai tort de dire qu'il vint, car il ne m'apparut pas, je crois, dans une propulsion de lui-même. Je ne pense pas non plus que les légers et nombreux souvenirs qui se rapportaient à cette dame, et auxquels je ne cessais de demander de m'aider (par des exhortations comme celle-ci: "Voyons, c'est cette dame qui est amie de Mme de Souvré, qui éprouve à l'endroit de Victor Hugo une admiration si naïve, mêlée de tant d'effroi et d'horreur"), je ne crois pas que tous ces souvenirs, voletant entre moi et son nom, aient servi en quoi que ce soit à le renflouer. Dans ce grand "cache-cache" qui se joue dans la mémoire quand on veut retrouver un nom, il n'y a pas une série

> d'approximations graduées. On ne voit rien, puis tout d'un coup apparaît le nom exact et fort différent de ce qu'on croyait deviner.[264]
>
> [I tried to recall hers as I talked to her; I remembered quite well having met her at dinner, and could remember things that she had said. By my attention, concentrated upon the inward region in which these memories of her lingered, was unable to discover her name. [. . .] My thoughts began playing a sort of game with it to grasp its outlines, its initial letter, and finally to bring the whole name to light. It was labour in vain. [. . .] Finally, in a flash, the name came back to me in its entirety: "Madame d'Arpajon." I am wrong in saying that it came, for it did not, I think, appear to me by a spontaneous propulsion. Nor do I think that the many faint memories associated with the lady, to which I did not cease to appeal for help (by such exertions as "Come now, it's the lady who is a friend of Mme de Souvré, who feels for Victor Hugo so artless an admiration mingled with so much alarm and horror")—nor do I think that all these memories, hovering between me and her name, served in any way to bring it to light. That great game of hide and seek which is played in our memory when we seek to recapture a name does not entail a series of gradual approximations. We see nothing, then suddenly the correct name appears and is very different from what we thought we were guessing.[265]]

In the dark and shadowy place that is the mind, things are easily lost as time passes: "pendant longtemps, quand, réveillé la nuit, je me ressouvenais de Combray, je n'en revis jamais que cette sorte de pan lumineux découpé au milieu d'indistinctes ténèbres, pareil à ceux que l'embrasement d'un feu de Bengale ou quelque projection éléctrique éclairent et sectionnent dans un édifice dont les autres parties restent plongées dans la nuit" [And so it was that, for a long time afterwards, when I lay awake at night and revived old memories of Combray, I saw no more of it than this sort of luminous panel sharply defined against a vague and shadowy background, like the panels which the glow of a Bengal light or a searchlight beam will cut out and illuminate in a building the other parts of which remain plunged in darkness].[266]

Memories retrievable intentionally are restricted to the "drame du coucher"; everything else about Combray has been exiled to the penumbra of consciousness. According to James, "in general a few parts are strongly emphasized to consciousness and the rest sink out of notice."[267] Intentional recall dredges up a "buried" object we can revive using rational thought typical of a researcher using voluntary attention; for Proust, such intentional digging, "les efforts de notre intelligence" [the efforts of our intellect], are inadequate to resuscitate the full flavor of experience: "Il est ainsi de notre passé. C'est peine perdu que nous cherchions de l'évoquer, tous les efforts de notre intelligence sont inutiles" [And so it is with our own past. It is labour in vain to attempt to recapture it: all the efforts of our intellect must prove futile].[268]

"The machinery of recall is [. . .] the same as the machinery of association, [. . .] the elementary law of habit in the nerve-centres."[269] What our brain has retained allows for the possibility of recall when properly coaxed. "Whatever accidental cue may turn this tendency into an actuality, the permanent *ground* of the tendency itself lies in the organized neural paths by which the cue calls up the memoriable experience, the past associates, the sense that the self was there, the belief that it all really happened, etc."[270] We hunt for a memory "just as we rummage our house for a lost object," by hunting through "its *associates*." James theorized that in memory, the brain's action diverged in part from the original experience: "*the brain tracts excited by the event proper, and those excited in its recall, are in part DIFFERENT from each other*" (emphasis in original).[271] While some aspects of the memory are lost, the addition of associated aspects enhances the memory recalled, altering or expanding the recollection.

For the narrator, "accidental" cues bring memories to life with this affective resonance, triggering them unexpectedly and seemingly whole, fuller than the original experience felt. "[S]oudain ils refaisaient en moi, de moi tout entier, par la vertu d'une sensation identique, l'enfant, l'adolescent qui les avait vus. Il n'y avait pas eu seulement changement de temps dehors, ou dans la chambre modification d'odeurs, mais en moi différence d'âge, substitution de personne. L'odeur dans l'air glacé des brindilles de bois, c'était comme un morceau du passé" [suddenly recreated out of my present self, the whole of that self, by virtue of an identical sensation, the child or the youth who had first seen them. There had been not merely a change in the weather outside, or, inside the room, a change of smells; there had been in myself an alteration in age, the substitution of another person. The scent, in the frosty air, of the twigs of brushwood was like a fragment of the past].[272]

James recognizes a special quality of memory in people gifted with the type of "brain-tissue" that leads to an uncommon degree of retentiveness. These individuals who "retain names, dates and addresses, anecdotes, gossip, poetry, quotations, and all sorts of miscellaneous facts, without an effort [. . .] owe it to the unusual tenacity of their brain-substance for any path once formed therein."[273] The capacity of Proust's memory appears to have been enormous for two aspects of retention highlighted by James: "*the more other facts a fact is associated with in the mind, the better possession of it our memory retains*" and "*the one who THINKS over his experiences most, and weaves them into systematic relations with each other, will be the one with the best memory*" (emphasis in original).[274] The author and hero of *À la recherche du temps perdu* enjoy both talents; the richness of the fabric of the book authenticates such a fecund mind.

James's description of the process of identifying a painting by Fra Angelico from the Florentine Academy aligns well with Proust's description of the experience first of partial and then increasing recall:

> I enter a friend's room and see on the wall a painting. At first I have the strange, wondering consciousness, "Surely I have seen that before," but when or how does not become clear. There only clings to the picture a sort of penumbra of familiarity,—when suddenly I exclaim: I have it! It is a copy of part of one of the Fra Angelicos in the Florentine Academy—I recollect it there.[275]

A similar sense of confused familiarity and sudden recognition occurs in the Guermantes courtyard:

> Un azur profond enivrait mes yeux, des impressions de fraîcheur, d'éblouissante lumière tournoyaient près de moi et dans mon désir de les saisir, sans oser [. . .] bouger [. . .] je restais [. . .] un pied sur le pavé plus élevé, l'autre pied sur le pavé le plus bas. Chaque fois que je refaisais rien que matériellement ce même pas, il me restait inutile [. . .]. Et presque tout de suite je le reconnus, c'était Venise.[276]
>
> [(A) profound azure intoxicated my eyes, impressions of coolness, of dazzling light, swirled around me and in my desire to seize them, [. . .] afraid to move [. . .] I continued, [. . .] with one foot on the higher paving-stone and the other on the lower. Every time that I merely repeated this physical movement, I achieved nothing [. . .] And almost at once I recognised the vision: it was Venice.[277]]

The same process had preceded the narrator's recollection of the madeleine: "Mais il se débat trop loin, trop confusément; [. . .] Et tout d'un coup le souvenir m'est apparu" [But its struggles are too far off, too confused [. . .]. And suddenly the memory revealed itself].[278] Why was it that just seeing the madeleine did not awaken memories of Combray? Something experienced, according to James, loses specificity when observed in different ways.

> If [. . .] a phenomenon be met with too often, and with too great a variety of contexts, although its image is retained and reproduced with correspondingly great facility, it fails to come up with any one setting, and the projection of it backwards to a particular past date consequently does not come about. We *recognize* but do not *remember* it—its associates form too confused a cloud.[279]

Proust's account emphasizes a similar array of clashing links distancing the original experience from the present. Observing rows of little shell-shaped cakes in bakers' windows, he passes by without tasting them. They are detached from memories of Combray and have no special significance:

> La vue de la petite madeleine ne m'avait rien rappelé avant que je n'y eusse goûté, peut- être parce que, en ayant souvent aperçu depuis, sans en manger, sur les tablettes des pâtissiers, leur image avait quitté ces jours de Combray pour se lier à d'autres plus récents, peut-être parce que de ces souvenirs abandonnés, si longtemps hors de la mémoire rien ne survivait, tout s'était désagrégé, les formes [. . .] s'étaient abolies, ou, ensommeillées, avaient perdu la force d'expansion qui leur eût permis de rejoindre la conscience.[280]
>
> [The sight of the little madeleine had recalled nothing to my mind before I tasted it; perhaps because I had so often seen such things in the meantime, without tasting them, on the trays in pastry-cooks' wondows, that their image had dissociated itself from those Combray days to take its place among others more recent; perhaps because, of those memories so long abandoned and put out of mind, nothing now survived, everything was scattered; the shapes of things [. . .] were either obliterated or had been so long dormant as to have lost the power of expansion which would have allowed them to resume their place in my consciousness.[281]]

For James, as for Proust, forgetting plays a substantial role: "In the practical use of our intellect, forgetting is as important a function as remembering."[282] James quotes Ribot on the advantages of eliminating the intellectual clutter that total recall would entail. Forgetting emphasizes the salience of what we do remember and allows for the "foreshortening" of experience in memory's fictional recounting. Forgetting is a normal and critical part of the cycle of memory in *À la recherche du temps perdu*.

First impressions yield to successive experiences. Swann's feelings for Odette gradually evolve away from his initial negative view that she is not his type; she appeals to his fantasy as a Botticelli figure and then captures him in a more durable, though painful and obsessive relationship followed by a relatively placid marriage. The tangled emotions of Swann's amorous obsession are mirrored in the narrator's at first curious and playful infatuation with Albertine's sportive nonchalance, full cheeks, and raven ringlets. Fearful of losing her to deviant sexual attractions elsewhere, he takes her prisoner. Sequestered, she becomes pale and fat. Certain physical details and the response she elicits in him draw him to her, but he can never totally possess anything more than the *idea* of her. After her death, he is utterly unable to abandon this ideational object until the gradual natural process of forgetting permits it.

Whereas Swann forgot Odette's initial image but retained the woman, the narrator lost the woman but retained the "mind stuff," her multiple immaterial images and their accompanying emotional turmoil, until natural psychological processes allowed him the peace of forgetting: "[L]a permanence et la durée ne sont promises à rien, pas même à la douleur" [permanence and stability being assured to nothing in this world, not even to grief].[283]

Without forgetting, there would be no sudden resurgent memory. For his fiction Proust highlighted the play between memory and forgetting:

> Or, les souvenirs d'amour ne font pas exception aux lois générales de la mémoire, elles-mêmes régies par les lois plus générales de l'habitude. Comme celle-ci affaiblit tout, ce qui nous rappelle le mieux un être, c'est justement ce que nous avons oublié (parce que c'était insignifiant, et que nous lui avions ainsi laissé toute sa force). C'est pourquoi la meilleure part de notre mémoire est hors de nous, dans un souffle pluvieux, dans l'odeur de renfermé d'une chambre ou dans l'odeur d'une première flambée.[284]
>
> [Now the memories of love are no exception to the general laws of memory, which in turn are governed by the still more general laws of Habit. And as Habit weakens everything, what best reminds us of a person is precisely what we had forgotten (becase it was of no importance, and we therefore left it in full possession of its strength). That is why the better part of our memories exists outside us, in a blatter of rain, in the smell of an unaired room or of the first crackling brushwood fire in a cold grate.[285]]

Memories preserved in art, the narrator will discover, have true power of duration: poetry lasts longer than love.[286] The waft of the past felt in the present, the trigger for the intermittent memory his book will preserve, is sensation.

SENSATION AND IMAGINATION, PERCEPTION, AND MISPERCEPTION

A thinking mind is never completely divorced from its physical environs. James noted the importance for the psychologist of the connection of thoughts with the "physical environment of which they take cognizance."[287] The first envoy from world to brain is sensation, an adaptive learning tool. Sensation provides first-hand direct knowledge of our surroundings and leaves indelible traces on our brain. Sensations possess the "pungency, or tang" of actual existence[288] and "*bring* space and all its places to our intellect."[289] First conscious objectively of the outside world, human beings subsequently develop a sense of the subjective "inner world,"[290] a pale reflection in thought, memory, or imagination.[291]

James describes a child's view of his room at first only dimly illuminated by candlelight, then followed by descrimination of the space and the objects that fill it:

> For the places thus first sensibly known are elements of the child's space-world which remain with him all his life; and by memory and later experience he learns a vast number of things *about* those places which at first he did not know. But to the end of time certain places of

> the world remain defined for him as the places *where those sensations were.*[292]

The intellect of the child emerging from this cocoon-like environment of sensation and emotional reaction has much in common with how Proust draws a hero venturing to decipher the Jamesian "big blooming buzzing Confusion" of his experience.[293] Sensations of place are initially felt by the narrator in his bed: darkness, since the candle is extinguished (sight), train whistle (sound), pillow (tactile), etc. These are followed by Jamesian "subjective notions,"[294] the emotions he feels with regard to the place he is in, and include separation anxiety and the need for comfort. In James's view, we develop further knowledge *"about"* our sensory world (emphasis original) through intellectual understanding or perception: "[W]e name it, class it, compare it, utter propositions concerning it," successive experiences arousing and associating with our previous experience.[295] In retrospect, experience and association augment knowledge: "For as the currents vary, and the brain-paths are moulded by them, other thoughts with other 'objects' come, and the 'same thing' which was apprehended as a present *this* soon figures as a past *that*, about which many unsuspected things have come to light."[296] The problem for Proust's narrator, as for James, is to identify which of the myriad possibilities is "the thing's truest representative"[297] or "essence."

James uses an example with conspicuous structural relevance to *À la recherche du temps perdu*:

> If, wandering through the woods to-day by a new path, I find myself suddenly in a glade which affects my senses exactly as did another I reached last week at the end of a different walk, I believe the two identical affections to present the same persisting glade, and infer that I have attained it by two differing roads. The spaces walked over grow congruent by their extremities; though apart from the common sensation which those extremities give me, I should be under no necessity of connecting one walk, with another at all.[298]

The young narrator begins his story with a very clear idea of the distinct and total separation of the two spaces or "côtés," a separation as much social as topographical. Family walks toward Tansonville or toward the Guermantes estate pass through distinctly different types of terrain, one a plain and one a river valley. Different classes of people inhabit the two locations: Swann and the bourgeoisie at Tansonville and the ancient and highly placed aristocratic Guermantes at their family estate. Sealing the separation completely in the young hero's mind is the fact that separate exits from the house are used when heading in one direction or the other. Only at the very end of the book when all those childhood experiences have receded to memory will the paths conjoin and bridge the mental divide.

Sensory input that becomes highly subjective is also evident when the narrator asks Robert de Saint-Loup to bring back Albertine. To be sure to find the right person, Saint-Loup looks at her photograph. He is disconcerted by the image: the girl in the photo is not sufficiently attractive in his estimation to stimulate the degree of suffering she is causing. For the narrator, however, such sensations and other more subjective emotions are additive, like layers of sediment or palimpsest:

> Le temps était loin où j'avais bien petitement commencé à Balbec par ajouter aux sensations visuelles quand je regardais Albertine, des sensations de saveur, d'odeur, de toucher. Depuis, des sensations plus profondes, plus douces, plus indéfinissables s'y étaient ajoutées, puis des sensations douloureuses.[299]
>
> [The time was long past when I had all too tentatively begun at Balbec by adding to my visual sensations when I gazed at Albertine sensations of taste, of smell, of touch. Since then, other more profound, more tender, more indefinable sensations had been added to them, and afterwards painful sensations.[300]]

The narrator's imagination plays a starring role here; he has constructed a personal aureole of feeling around Albertine that is distanced from any objective view. For both James and Proust, imagination is an offshoot of sensation, sensation a springboard for imagination. "*Sensations, once experienced, modify the nervous organism, so that copies of them arise again in the mind after the original outward stimulation is gone,*" wrote James (emphasis original). "Fantasy or Imagination are the names given to the faculty of reproducing copies of originals once felt."[301] In this way, Proust's narrator is able to imagine sensations as well as feel them, finding the combination revelatory: "réels sans être actuels, idéaux sans être abstraits" [real without being actual, ideal without being abstract].[302]

The narrator examines these subjective feelings so he can re-create them in his work. Yet he requires the simultaneous integration of present sensation and subjective imagination, sensation and fringe of emotive response, sensation and memory, to be able to visualize, understand, and objectify that which is no longer objective, by feeling it as real once again in order to reproduce its most profound and essential reality in his art: "miroiter une sensation [. . .] à la fois dans le passé, ce qui permettait à mon imagination de la goûter, et dans le présent où l'ébranlement effectif de mes sens [. . .] avait ajouté aux rêves de l'imagination ce dont ils sont habituellement dépourvus, l'idée d'existence" [to be mirrored at one and the same time in the past, so that my imagination was permitted to savour it, and in the present, where the actual shock to my senses . . . had added to the dreams of the imagination the concept of "existence"].[303]

In writing fiction, "data freely combined" into new entities constitutes creative imaginative engineering.[304] Certain individuals, according to

James, are particularly talented at retaining and reproducing highly detailed "images of past sensible experiences." Proust chose to make his narrator one of them.

> Anything which affects our sense-organs does also more than that: it arouses processes in the hemispheres which are partly due to the organization of that organ by past experiences, and the results of which in consciousness are described as ideas which the sensation suggests.[305]

The idea that sensory experience shapes the brain and that the prejudices and opinions one holds affect future interpretive activity are modern, compelling, and permeate not only Proust's text but also those of many twentieth-century scientists, writers, and critics. James offered a physiological explanation of the "neural" underpinnnings of imagination and the brain's networking: "the same nerve-tracts are concerned in the two processes. [. . .] Association is surely due to currents from one cortical centre to another."[306]

Normally, actual sensations would cause "strong explosions" with greater intensity than the brain activity associated with the "fainter" ones likely for imagination: "the process which gives the sense that the object is really there ought normally to be arousable only by currents entering from the periphery and not by currents from the neighboring cortical parts."[307] This enables us to tell the difference between them, distinguishing between the physical external reality and the internal operations of thought, experience and memory, fact and fantasy.

However, there are exceptions in which what is imagined seems real: "Sometimes, by exception, the deeper sort of explosion may take place from intra-cortical excitement alone." These supply the enhanced "'vividness' or sensible presence" that is normally associated with sensations actually happening.[308]

Proust utilized this notion and even used similar terminology, employing the word "décharge" corresponding to James's "explosions" of nerve current. Memory stimulated by an analogous sensation would essentially electrify brain-paths previously carved by antecedent experience in the enhanced and "vivid" manner.

Albertine is dead. But every act of his daily life ripples with waves of memory. At every sensation, every turn he takes in his room, every noise that comes through the window, every ray of sunshine, he feels "la décharge douloureuse d'un des mille souvenirs invisibles qui a tout moment éclataient autour de moi dans l'ombre" [the painful discharge of one of the thousand invisible memories which incessantly exploded around me in the darkness].[309]

"Privileged moments" of involuntary memory are entirely Jamesian in nature. They are supremely happy moments when the narrator's imagination is gifted with the sparkling "décharge" [discharge] of a combination of present sensation and past experience with all the beauty of its dazzling fringes. Unlike the flatness of a dull prosaic present, or the dryness of intentionally dredged-up snapshot memories, or a future narrowly formulated to attain specific ends, "l'attente d'un avenir que la volonté construit avec des fragments du présent et du passé auxquels elle retire encore de leur réalité en ne conservant d'eux que ce qui convient a la fin utilitaire, étroitement humaine, qu'elle leur assigne" [in the anticipation of a future which the will constructs with fragments of the present and the past, fragments whose reality it still further reduces by preserving of them only what is suitable for the utilitarian, narrowly human purpose for which it intends them], privileged moments are enhanced beyond ordinary experience; they incarnate an awareness of time sublimated into something timeless,[310] something unique and evanescent that can be forged into permanent form in language. This is the supreme function of the imagination.

> Mais qu'un bruit, qu'une odeur, déja entendu ou respirée jadis, le soient de nouveau, à la fois dans le présent et dans le passé, [. . .] aussitôt l'essence permanente et habituellement cachée des choses se trouve libérée, et notre vrai moi qui, parfois depuis longtemps, semblait mort, mais ne l'était pas entièrement, s'éveille, s'anime en recevant la céleste nourriture qui lui est apportée.[311]
>
> [But let a noise or a scent, once heard or once smelt, be heard or smelt again in the present and at the same time in the past [. . .], and immediately the permanent and habitually concealed essence of things is liberated and our true self, which seemed—had perhaps for long years seemed—to be dead but was not altogether dead, is awakened and reanimated as it receives the celestial nourishment that is brought to it.[312]]

Pure sensation bare of a halo of associations is normally not possible in adult life, according to James. Perception integrates sensation with all the "attributes" present and remembered that we link with it, combining them through learning into a single entity that we identify by naming it.[313]

Unusual instances occur, however, when normal perception is altered, "divested" of its "cloud of associates" and drawn down to "its sensational nudity" or when it stimulates an incorrect aura and is experienced as an "illusion."[314] Perception can be altered by expectation. Misperception can occur when we have incorrect or only limited information upon which to build.

Often, Proust's narrator is led by desire, anxiety, or other strong emotion to read events incorrectly or misinterpret them. Waiting for the carriage he hired to fetch Mme. de Stermaria for an evening in the Bois de Boulogne he hopes to be as pleasurable as a warm summer night in Combray or as merry as one at Rivebelle, stirrings of restless unease, hints of desire disappointed, and thoughts that perhaps he would have been better off in solitude or free to trawl for unknown company are disclosed in misperceptions. He walks through his apartment's dark and empty dining room wiping his hands on a towel and approaches what he mistakes for the entryway:

> Elle me parut ouverte sur l'antichambre éclairée, mais ce que j'avais pris pour la fente illuminée de la porte, qui au contraire était fermée, n'était que le reflet blanc de ma serviette dans une glace posée le long du mur en attendant qu'on la plaçât pour le retour de maman. Je repensai à tous les mirages que j'avais ainsi découverts dans notre appartement et qui n'étaient pas qu'optiques, car les premiers jours j'avais cru que la voisine avait un chien, à cause du jappement prolongé, presque humain, qu'avait pris un certain tuyau de cuisine chaque fois qu'on ouvrait le robinet. Et la porte du palier ne se refermait d'elle-même très lentement, sur les courants d'air de l'escalier, qu'en exécutant les hachures de phrases voluptueuses et gémissantes qui se superposent au choeur des Pèlerins, vers la fin de l'ouverture de *Tannheuser*.[315]
>
> [It appeared to be open on to the lighted hall, but what I had taken for the bright crevice of the door, which in fact was closed, was only the gleaming reflexion of my towel in a mirror that had been laid against the wall in readiness to be fixed in its pace before Mamma's return. I thought again of all the other illusions of the sort which I had discovered in different parts of the house, and which were not optical only, for when we first came there I had thought that our nextdoor neighbour kept a dog on account of the prolonged, almost human, yapping which came from a kitchen pipe whenever the tap was turned on. And the door on to the outer landing never closed by itself, very gently, against the draughts of the staircase, without rendering those broken, voluptuous, plaintive phrases that overlap the chant of the pilgrims towards the end of the Overture to *Tannhäuser*.[316]]

Auditory illusions of this sort occur, according to James, when "sounds have altered their character as soon as the intellect referred them to a different [incorrect] source."[317] He posits examples such as a clock chime misinterpreted as a "hand-organ in the garden" or "a most formidable noise" perceived as "low, mighty, alarming, like a rising flood or the *avant-coureur* of an awful gale," which turns out to be "nothing but the breathing of a little Scotch terrier which lay asleep on the floor."[318]

Proust transposes Jamesian auditory illusion using an inverse instance of "dog" misperception. Where James heard a noise and found it to be a dog, Proust's narrator thought he had heard a dog that turned out to be just a noise. He also used a dog image with closer similarity to James's example in the passage on the red septuor, when his narrator's attention alights on Mme. Verdurin's little dog snoring at her feet.

For Proust's narrator, the most significant and painful result of inadequate or false perception is the disappointment of deception. The fluid and opaque nature of tales and imaginings about the doings of his love objects leads to jealous agony. Confrontations with reality driven by reading or daydreaming are engendered by expectations without adequate experience. Playing imaginatively with ordinary street sounds outside his window, on the other hand, can lead to a joyous riot of misperception.

When, as a small boy, he meets "la dame en rose," he experiences a small disappointment, "une petite déception," because she appears neither highly dramatic nor wicked as he had expected based on hearsay; she simply resembles other pretty women.[319] Seeing Mme. de Guermantes in the church at Combray during the marriage of Dr. Percepied's daughter provides the first instance of more serious deception: "Ma déception était grande" [My disappointment was immense],[320] he says. She does not look so different from bourgeois women he knows, so how can this be the aristocratic descendant he had anticipated would step off a tapestry or out of the magic lantern's projections on his wall? There is a significant discrepancy between terre-à-terre reality and the gauzy web of fringe-like relation he had mentally spun around her name and family history.

Mysteries of emotional response do not always correspond closely to "normal" expectations either. Passion and fixation do not depend on a particular type of beauty, as Proust reflected on in *Les Plaisirs et les Jours*. Swann spent a number of years flirting with women he found physically attractive and charming; yet, the one great love and obsession of his life involves Odette de Crécy, a woman of questionable background, behaviour, and looks who does not even appeal to him physically. The story of Swann and Odette serves as meditation on the role of deception in amorous relations. Facts are not what they seem; mystery, frustration, pain prepare the reader for the narrator's amorous itinerary. Love is found to be a relation where the self is always an outsider, the love object always incomprehensible and untrustworthy.

The misty mix of facts real and imagined about women and places is the source of stimulation, desire, misperception, and disappointment for Proust's narrator. Train schedules and meteorological reports stimulate the narrator's desire to travel. But names of villages or churches dazzle him with desire—perhaps better left unfulfilled in order to avoid the disappointments of reality compared to imagined stormy seas and Tuscan sunshine and flowers that have for effect, "en accroissant les joies arbitraries de mon imagination, d'aggraver la déception future de mes voyages" [by increasing the arbitrary delights of my imagination, aggravated the disenchantment that was in store for me when I set out upon my travels].[321]

Judged from the perspective of their extraordinary creations, Bergotte, Vinteuil, and Elstir, presumed übermenschen in their arts, turn out to be disappointingly ordinary fellows. The talent of La Berma and the vaunted Romanesque church in Balbec disappoint the narrator because he has not yet learned to see them properly; he is still using his intellect to examine rather than letting himself be inspired by the poetry they incarnate and enjoying the private interior response their beauty engenders. Asthetic evaluations cannot be done on the same rational basis as intellectual or conceptual analysis. Tools of scientific examination do not suffice. Artistic works attain a transparent level of communicative immateriality in the mimetic value of the language, the quality of the color, the construction and juxtaposition of the sound, in addition to emotional effect, that surpasses love by enabling communication and understanding of the thoughts and feelings of another person in a way that love cannot.[322]

For Proust's narrator, relationships always seem to incorporate a disparity between appearance and actuality, leading to deception. Had Gilberte deceived him when he loved her? Did Albertine's postcards from Versailles legitimate her actions? Deciding he is bored with her and just as happy she is going to the Trocadéro with Andrée for a matinée is nearly the biggest self-deception of all. How can he know?

A long elegy of happy associative misperception evokes the narrator's delight at the sounds and sights of the "petits métiers" in the streets of his neighborhood, construed as a vast urban orchestra. The tramway's horn and the whistle of a tripe-seller are heard at an interval that sounds like the work of "un accordeur de piano aveugle" [a blind piano-tuner]. Another peddler makes a sound that the narrator compares to a stationary tram "ou en panne, immobilisé, criant à petits intervalles comme un animal qui meurt" [broken down, immobilised, screeching at brief intervals like a dying animal].[323] Here, the narrator is finding sheer fun in letting his imagination wander through the fringes of his reactions and misinterpretations of what he sees and hears. A "woman" appears on the pavement. She is "une femme peu élégante (ou obéissant à une mode laide) [. . .] trop claire dans un paletot sac en poil de chèvre; mais non, ce n'était pas une femme, c'était un chauffeur [!!] qui, enveloppé dans sa peau de bique, gagnait à pied son garage" [a woman with no pretence to fashion (or else obedient to an ugly fashion) . . . too brightly dressed in a sack overcoat of goatskin; but no, it was not a woman, it was a chauffeur who, enveloped in his goatskin, was proceeding on foot to his garage].[324] The music of misperception is in the air all around: "Le ronflement d'un violon était dû au passage d'une automobile, parfois à ce que je n'avais pas mis assez d'eau dans ma bouillote éléctrique" [The whirring of a violin was due at one time to the passing of a car, at another to my not having put enough water in my electric hot-water bottle].[325] The neighborhood is teeming with life, a veritable cornucopia of genus and species. In misperceiving metaphor our naturalist-narrator relishes the entire spectrum of the animal world and would not mind tying a naturalist's identification tag to a young girl he notices in his doorway, so he could follow her movements and find her again one day.

James had written that "in every illusion what is false is what is inferred, not what is immediately given."[326] Misperception applies what Proust's narrator calls a "retouche" [touch-up] to reality. Normally we see only one aspect of another person at a time. What we noticed yesterday will be superseded by what we we experience today. Our memory of them could therefore lead us to a misperception: "Nous nous souvenions [. . .] d'un paon et nous trouvons une pivoine" [We remembered . . . a peacock, and we find a peony].[327] Memory is not the only purveyor of misperception with regard to others. By virtue of their being "other" and showing different sides of themselves at different times, and because we forget, the multiple and changing slivers of the kaleidoscope of character are only visible as a series, disappointing expectation. "Le visage humain est vraiment comme celui du Dieu d'une théogonie orientale, toute une grappe de visages juxtaposes dans des plans différents et qu'on ne voit pas à la fois" [The human face is indeed, like the face of the God of some oriental theogony, a whole cluster of faces juxtaposed on different planes so that one does not see them all at once].[328]

Perception is so closely aligned with memory, with associations in the brain, that we cannot retain the original sensation, just what James had thought of as the "faint" version. Proust says similarly that we cannot retain an active impression of "le goût d'un fruit" (James's taste of the pear) and "qu'à peine l'impression reçue, nous descendons insensiblement la pente du souvenir et sans nous en rendre compte, en très peu de temps, nous sommes très loin de ce que nous avions senti" [no sooner is the impression received than we begin imperceptibly to descend the slope of memory and, without realising it, in a very short time we have come a long way from what we actually felt].[329]

What defines misperception—or deception—is the fact that memory accompanies each new experience, with some aspects retained and some forgotten. "Dans la confrontation de notre souvenir à la réalité nouvelle, c'est cela qui marquera notre déception ou notre surprise, nous apparaîtra comme la retouche de la réalité en nous avertissant que nous nous étions mal rappelé" [In confronting our memory with the new reality it is this that will mark the extent of our disappointment or surprise, will appear to us like a revised version of the reality by notifying us that we had not remembered correctly].[330] Proustian misperception is a close relation of Jamesian variable, "fictional" memory.

And yet, the mystery and changeability of others, provoking the author to write his book about time, is also what holds the narrator's interest, keeping his imagination stimulated. Unlike mathematical, scientific, or logical ideas that we strive to shape such that they are "so adequate and exact that we shall never need to change them," our experience, in James's terms, "'our conceptions of things' alter by being used."[331] Proust's narrator derives pleasure from his observations of character, relishing the instability and evolution of thought that James had identified as "the everlasting struggle in every mind between the tendency to keep unchanged, and the tendency to renovate, its ideas."[332]

Proust's narrator revels in escaping what James calls "Old-fogyism." Because he is an artist, the narrator is enticed more by "fresh experiences," not "less and less capable of assimilating impressions in any but the old ways." "Genius, in truth," wrote James, "means little more than the faculty of perceiving in an unhabitual [i.e., Proustian] way."[333] It means enjoying the depths of the imagination:

> Pourtant, quelques déceptions inévitables qu'elle doive apporter, cette démarche vers ce qu'on n'a qu'entrevu, ce qu'on a eu le loisir d'imaginer, cette démarche est la seule qui soit saine pour les sens, qui y entretienne l'appétit. De quel morne ennui est empreinte la vie des gens qui par paresse ou timidité, se rendent directement en voiture chez des amis qu'ils ont connus sans avoir d'abord rêvé d'eux, sans jamais oser sur le parcours s'arrêter auprès de ce qu'ils désirent![334]
>
> [And yet, whatever the inevitable disappointments that it must bring in its train, this movement towards what we have only glimpsed, what we have been free to dwell upon and imagine at our leisure, this movement is the only one that is wholesome for the senses, that whets their appetite. How drearily monotonous must be the lives of people who, from indolence or timidity, drive in their carriages straight to the doors of friends whom they have got to know without having first dreamed of knowing them, without ever daring, on the way, to stop and examine what arouses their desire![335]]

The antidote to misperception realigns desire and daydreaming with actuality and determines the narrator's course. For James this incorporation of experience allows us

> [T]o assimilate the new to the old, to meet each threatening violator or burster of our well-known series of concepts, as it comes in, see through its unwontedness, and ticket it off as an old friend in disguise. This victorious assimilation of the new is in fact the type of all intellectual pleasure. The lust for it is scientific curiosity. The relation of the new to the old, before the assimilation is performed, is wonder.[336]

While Edward Bizub explains Proustian multiplicity as stemming from the multiple visions of split personality and hysteria, James describes the more *acute* instances of "false perceptions"[337] appearing in abnormal hallucinations and illusions as "the *extremes* of the perceptive process in which the secondary cerebral reaction is out of all normal proportion to the peripheral stimulus which occasions the activity." It approaches the outer limit of overreaction, something that may seem objective to the individual involved but is outwardly absent,[338] invisible to the observer, and certainly not typical of more routine misperception.

REASONING AND MULTIPLE INTERPRETATIONS

James saw reasoning as a "productive" activity useful for isolating the implications of interest to us from among the multiple possible interpretations embedded in a given set of facts. "To reason, then we must be able to extract characters,—not *any* characters, but the right characters for our conclusion."[339] Certain gifted individuals, Proust's narrator among them, demonstrate the capacity for the sophisticated analysis and logical thinking, the talent to draw particularly interesting conclusions from the information or situation at hand that James described as the talent to "seize fresh aspects in concrete things."[340] "Reasoning is always to attain some particular conclusion or to gratify some special curiosity."[341]

Reasoning can be used to select from frequent or extensive experience certain meaningful and universal inferences, to generalize. These would constitute the maxims, or pithy tenets of reassuringly generalized principles and truths, distilled in *À la recherche du temps perdu*.

In his introduction to *The Maxims of Marcel Proust*, Justin O'Brien calls Proust's maxims his "two-dimensional" and "purely intellectual discoveries," "the fruit of an observant and reflective life."[342] Without indicating exactly where he found it, O'Brien puts between quotation marks a statement made purportedly by Proust that says: "'I felt the presence within me, all ready for this purpose, of a swarm of truths relating to passions, to characters, and to manners.'"[343] O'Brien distinguishes this "fruit" of reasoning from the more multidimensional truth of resuscitated memory. He briefly recounts Proust's connections to the French tradition of didactic epigram and posits a connection between Proust and La Rochefoucauld. He notes, and we underscore, that if indeed La Rochefoucauld served as a model for Proust's maxim-generating writing, he was (like William James) an unacknowledged source: "[I]t is noteworthy that the only La Rochefoucauld he mentions in his work is a friend and contemporary, a remote descendant of the famous cynic."[344]

O'Brien selects one particular maxim from "Du côté de chez Swann" (#71 in his book): "On cherche à retrouver dans les choses, devenues par là précieuses, le reflet que notre âme a projeté sur elles; on est deçu en constatant qu'elles semblent dépourvues dans la nature du charme qu'elles devaient, dans notre pensée, au voisinage de certaines idées"[345] [One searches to recognize in things something that makes them precious to us, the gleam that our spirit has projected onto them; one is disappointed in noting that in nature they seem devoid of the charm that, in our thoughts, they owed to their proximity to certain ideas]. In this particular maxim we find the enchanting illumination of the inclined beam of light projected by the imagination, the disappointment of how things really are compared to how they appeared to the mind with its enhancing power of our particular fringe of associations. Proust's reasoned insights, intellectualized in this manner, are no less lustrous than truths revealed by means of the literary expedient of a "privileged" moment. As author, he made an aesthetic choice to build his plot around the more dramatic and unusual device.

Reason can only go so far to reveal the truths that interest Proust's narrator. An X-ray is only one diagnostic tool among others for the talented reasoning of a good physician; documents disclose only certain elements of a political strategy. Often, multiple conclusions may be drawn from a given set of facts. The hero's agonizing conjectures about unknowable actions and motives expose the shortcomings inherent in the use of reasoning. Life exceeds it.

Like Swann before him with Odette, the narrator tries to use his reasoning powers to untangle what he suspects to be Albertine's web of lies. But the intellectual endeavor does not lead to truth. There are too many possible options and too few reliable indicators. Albertine is at the hub of a very full circle of potentiality that the narrator tries to master. The truths of her life are surmised rather than witnessed, derived more "par le raisonnement, qu'à observer, qu'à surprendre dans la réalité" [by a process of reasoning than to detect and observe in reality], and though we can guess at them or theorize about them (in Proust's day), they, "comme les lois astronomiques" [like astronomical laws], would never be explicable.[346] This accounts for Proust's reaction to readers who suggested that his view was as if through a microscope. He assured them that his viewpoint was definitely telescopic: like that of James the psychologist, his effort was to bring the mysteries of the distant "other" into clearer and closer focus.

When it comes to experience, reason falters; the calm reassurance of the distilled truth of maxim is vaporized in an anxious grasp. Reason attempts to investigate what can only really be expressed aesthetically and known through the participation of interpretation.

EFFORT, WILL, AND DESIRE

James labels as "will" the desire that we determine it is possible to accomplish.[347] Unless blocked by a competing interest or emotion, action naturally follows such feelings of interest. However, James concedes, deciding to act is a complicated business: "The process of deliberation contains endless degrees of complication. At every moment of it, our consciousness is of an extremely complex thing, namely the whole set of motives and their conflict. [. . .] The deliberation may last for weeks or months, occupying at intervals the mind."[348] So, too, for Proust's narrator—it takes years before he can translate the decision-making process into the act of writing the story we are reading.

Vacillating and distractible, the narrator of *À la recherche du temps perdu* plans to begin his great work "tomorrow": "Si j'avais été moins décidé à me mettre définitivement au travail j'aurais peut-être fait un effort pour commencer tout de suite" [Had I been less firmly resolved upon settling down definitely to work, I should perhaps have made an effort to begin at once].[349] There is always some excuse for putting off serious effort: "Quand je ne connaissais pas les Swann je croyais que j'étais empêché de travailler par l'état d'agitation où je me mettait l'impossibilité de voir librement Gilberte. Mais quand leur demeure me fut ouverte, à peine je m'étais assis à mon bureau de travail que je me levais et courais chez eux" [When I still did not know the Swanns I thought that I was prevented from working by the state of agitation into which I was thrown by the impossibility of seeing Gilberte when I chose. But now that their door stood open to me, scarcely had I sat down at my desk than I would get up and hurry round to them].[350] Upon returning home, instead of settling down to work writing, the narrator daydreamed and rehashed their conversations in "une vie de salon mentale" [a mental social round].[351] Social and emotional teleology trumps intention.

Spending time with Robert de Saint-Loup is a social pleasure, too. It takes the narrator's attention away from his work by shifting it outward toward the warmth of companionship and away from the difficult task of deciphering the murky interior "pénombre" he feels it his task to explore. However, as in all his social adventures, the narrator will gain certain experience in return. He realizes this when he tries to express his impression of Saint-Loup in words, generalizing from one individual aristocrat to "un être plus général que lui-même, le 'noble', et qui comme un esprit intérieur mouvait ses membres, ordonnait ses gestes et ses actions" [a personality more generalised than his own, that of the"'nobleman," which like an indwelling spirit moved his limbs, ordered his gestures and his actions].[352]

A tipsy night out with Robert, a risky ride along the coast to a restaurant and casino at Rivebelle, literally throw reason, caution, and ambition to the wind and sea in favor of living in the moment. James classifies this as the "unhealthiness of will" in which inhibitions are relaxed: "the normal actions are impossible, and [. . .] the abnormal ones are irrepressible."[353]

The narrator's is an ambiguous relationship with the solitude needed to write. The hard work that lies ahead of him—to mine his past for art—fades into a haze of alcoholic frolic: "C'est que pas plus que ce n'est le désir de devenir célèbre, mais l'habitude d'être laborieux qui nous permet de produire une oeuvre, ce n'est l'allégresse du moment présent, mais les sages réflexions du passé, qui nous aident à préserver le futur" [For just as it is not the desire to become famous but the habit of being industrious that enables us to produce a finished work, so it is not the activity of the present moment but wise reflexions from the past that help us to safeguard the future].[354] Too much pleasure in the present prevents the hero from even thinking about the grand work he dreamed of writing:

> Or, si déjà, en arrivant à Rivebelle, j'avais jeté loin de moi ces béquilles du raisonnement, du contrôle de soi-même qui aident notre infirmité à suivre le droit chemin, et me trouvais en proie à une sorte d'ataxie morale, l'alcool, en tendant exceptionnellement mes nerfs, avait donné aux minutes actuelles une qualité, un charme qui n'avaient pas eu pour effet de me rendre plus apte ni même plus résolu à les défendre; car en me les faisant préférer mille fois au reste de ma vie, mon exaltation les en isolait; j'étais enfermé dans le présent, comme les héros, comme les ivrognes; momentanément éclipsé, mon passé ne projetait plus devant moi cette ombre de lui-même que nous appelons notre avenir; plaçant le but de ma vie, non plus dans la réalisation des rêves de ce passé, mais dans la félicité de la minute présente, je ne voyais pas plus loin qu'elle.[355]
>
> [But if already, before this point, on my arrival at Rivebelle, I had flung irretrievably away from me those crutches of reason and self-control which help our infirmity to follow the right road, if I now found myself the victim of a sort of moral ataxia, the alcohol that I had drunk, in stretching my nerves exceptionally, had given to the present moment a quality, a charm, which did not have the effect of making me more competent or indeed more resolute to defend it; for in making me prefer it a thousand times to the rest of my life, my exaltation isolated it therefrom; I was enclosed in the present, like heroes and drunkards; momentarily eclipsed, my past no longer projected before me that shadow of itself which we call our future; placing the goal of my life no longer in the realisation of the dreams of the past but in the felicity of the present moment, I could see no further than it.[356]]

We know that a young man's desire for a little boozy fun is not the only side to the narrator's "unhealthiness of will." From the very start of his story, he has suffered from bedtime separation trauma and dire need for the calming reassurance of his mother's kiss. A visit to Saint-Loup's military post in Doncières creates the opportunity for description of an exceedingly nervous and fearful temperament unable to summon the will to control the anxiety of facing a new situation and trepidation at bedtime: "Je pensais que Saint-Loup viendrait coucher cette nuit-là à l'hôtel où je descendrais afin de me rendre moins angoissant le premier contact avec cette ville inconnue" [I thought that Saint-Loup might come and sleep that night in the hotel at which I should be staying, in order to make the first shock of contact with this strange town less painful for me].[357]

Much later, growing tired of the restrictions of his life with Albertine, the narrator imagines a time when he can enjoy the pleasures of solitude. Sunshine and confidence that she will return at the end of the day make it possible for him to convince himself that she and her bad behavior are no more important than if they were only imaginary. This act of free will is like a pulse of new energy: "faisant jouer les gonds assouplis de ma pensée, j'avais, avec une énergie que je sentais, dans ma tête, à la fois physique et mentale comme un mouvement musculaire et une initiative spirituelle, dépassé l'état de préoccupation habituelle où j'avais été confiné jusqu'ici et commençais à me mouvoir à l'air libre" [manipulating the supple hinges of my thought, with an energy which I felt, in my head, at once physical and mental, as it were a muscular movement and a spiritual impulse, I had broken away from the state of perpetual preoccupation in which I had hitherto been confined, and was beginning to move in a free atmosphere].[358]

The few decisions that actually are motivated by what James termed "[t]he slow dead heave of the will" are decisions that require what he called a "creative contribution" and a "feeling of effort," in which "we ourselves by our own willful act inclined the beam."[359] This is the quandary in which Proust chose to place his narrator throughout the story. Until, as a result of a series of transcendent and illuminating experiences, he became aware that time had passed but could be captured for all eternity in an aesthetic production, the narrator was unable to act. James describes the process as follows: "When I said [. . .] that *consciousness* (or the neural process which goes with it) *is in its very nature impulsive,* I should have added the proviso that *it must be sufficiently intense.* Now there are remarkable differences in the power of different sorts of consciousness to excite movement."[360]

In order to write, Proust's narrator has to trounce the lazy glide of what James calls "the *dolce far niente,*" the "habitual inhibitions" that hinder his ability to take control and act. It is only by the time in *Le Temps retrouvé* that illness forces him to withdraw from social life that he has accumulated sufficient aesthetic and life lessons—following a series of unexpected revelations that spur his will to act and prepare him to write. At that point he is able to overcome the roadblocks preventing him from composing his novel.[361] No longer is he a figure "whose life is one long contradiction between knowledge and action, and who with full command of theory, never get to holding their limp characters erect."[362] What moves Proust's narrator to action is his own affective history and the discoveries that can serve him as fictional scaffolding for plot, a focus on the mind's experience we can trace to James.

With the tools of James's psychology available—at hand or "in the wind"—to assist his understanding of experience, the associative echoes of sensation in his individual impressions, an analysis of habit, memory, and imagination, the narrator is able to summon the will to create a work of literary art revealing a "moi" [self] at the same time unique and universal. Recalling the past, "le secret éternel de chacun" [the eternal secret within each of us], becomes the motivator and plot of his story. His goal will be to expose the alterations that take place in time, like the history of the Guermantes family's "origins presque fabuleuses, charmante mythologie de relations devenues si banales ensuite, mais qu'elles prolongeaient dans le passé comme en plein ciel, avec un éclat pareil à celui que projette la queue étincelante d'une comète" [origin almost in legend, in a delightful mythology which still at a later date prolonged them into the past as into some Olympian heaven where they shone with the luminous brilliance of a comet's tail].[363] He knows now that he is an artist. The "urgency"[364] and final impetus to action that impels him to sit down to create the story we have just read is the fear that his time will be cut short by death.

In order to write, says James, "I will to write, and the act follows." Although this is not true for the will to sneeze or to have the table cross the room of its own volition or under its own steam, the inspiration was clear for a fellow writer. Stimulating his narrator's will was Proust's literary task. "[A]ttention with effort is all that any case of volition implies," wrote James.[365] "The difficulty lies in the gaining possession of that field."[366] The series of experiences that take place for Proust's narrator when he goes to the matinée at the hôtel de Guermantes focus his attention and, so, as James so well reminds us, "[t]he idea to be consented to must be kept from flickering and going out. It must be held steadily before the mind until it *fills* the mind."[367]

Proust's narrator adopts a tone of self-assurance once he realizes what he, as an artist, must do. He exhibits what James calls "the heroic mind" that is able to confront difficulties and by determination transcend them.[368]

NOTES

1. *RTP*, I, 3.
2. Enright, I, 1.
3. James, *Briefer Course*, 193.
4. *RTP*, I, 3.
5. Enright, I, 1.
6. James, *Principles*, II, 768.
7. James, *Principles*, II, 770.
8. *RTP*, I, 4.
9. Enright, I, 3.
10. James, *Principles*, I, 602–603, note 53.
11. *RTP*, I, 6.
12. Enright, I, 5.
13. *RTP*, I, 3.
14. Enright, I, 1.
15. *RTP*, II, 95.
16. Enright, II, 431.
17. G. Poulet, *Études sur le temps humain* (Paris: Plon, 1950), 396–397; *Studies in Human Time*, trans. Elliott Coleman (Baltimore: Johns Hopkins University Press, 1959), 293.
18. Gérard Genette, "Proust Palimpseste," *Figures of Literary Discourse*, trans. Alan Sheridan (New York: Columbia University Press, 1982), 203–228, 214.
19. Genette, "Pr. Pal.," 213.

20. Genette, "Pr. Pal.," 205.
21. Genette, "Pr. Pal.," 207.
22. James, *Principles*, II, 767.
23. *RTP*, III, 535.
24. Enright, V, 23.
25. *RTP*, IV, 459.
26. Enright, VI, 276.
27. *RTP*, I, 43. Enright, I, 58.
28. James, *Briefer Course*, 192.
29. James, *Briefer Course*, 196.
30. James, *Briefer Course*, 195.
31. James, *Briefer Course*, 193.
32. James, *Briefer Course*, 195.
33. James, *Briefer Course*, 196.
34. James, *Briefer Course*, 196.
35. James, *Briefer Course*, 195.
36. Proust, *Jean Santeuil*, 897–898.
37. James, *Principles*, I, 402.
38. Proust, "Journées de Lecture," *Pastiches et mélanges*, 170.
39. James, *Principles*, I, 129–130, and *Briefer Course*, 137.
40. James, *Briefer Course*, 196.
41. James, *Briefer Course*, 197.
42. James, *Briefer Course*, 197.
43. James, *Principles*, I, 420.
44. *RTP*, II, 190.
45. Enright, II, 564.
46. *RTP*, II, 196.
47. Enright, II, 572.
48. *RTP*, II, 191.
49. Enright, II, 566.
50. James, *Briefer Course*, 206.
51. James, *Principles*, I, 415.
52. James, *Principles*, I, 418.
53. *RTP*, II, 191.
54. Enright, II, 566.
55. *RTP*, II, 192.
56. Enright, II, 566–567.
57. *RTP*, II, 712–713.
58. Enright, III, 574.
59. James, *Briefer Course*, 198.
60. *RTP*, I, 480– 481.
61. Enright, II, 84.
62. James, *Briefer Course*, 198–199.
63. James, *Briefer Course*, 200.
64. James, *Briefer Course*, 208–209.
65. *RTP*, III, 533.
66. Enright, V, 20.
67. James, *Briefer Course*, 200.
68. James, *Briefer Course*, 199.
69. *RTP*, IV, 195.
70. Enright, V, 835.
71. James, *Briefer Course*, 216.
72. James, *Briefer Course*, 217.
73. James, *Briefer Course*, 218.
74. Genette, "Pr. Pal.," 216.
75. James, *Briefer Course*, 221.

76. James, *Briefer Course*, 128.
77. James, *Principles*, I, 110.
78. James, *Principles*, I, 113.
79. James, *Briefer Course*, 125, 127–128.
80. James, *Briefer Course*, 126.
81. James, *Briefer Course*, 131–132.
82. James, *Briefer Course*, 129–130.
83. *RTP*, IV, 415.
84. Enright, VI, 212–213.
85. James, *Briefer Course*, 132.
86. *RTP*, IV, 233. Enright, V, 888.
87. James, *Briefer Course*, 138.
88. Léonie was the name of one of Pierre Janet's patients treated for dissociative personality using hypnotism (James, *Principles*, I, 364–367).
89. *RTP*, I, 575–576.
90. Enright, II, 219.
91. *RTP*, II, 27. Enright, II, 333.
92. *RTP*, I, 8.
93. Enright, I, 8–9.
94. *RTP*, III, 161. Enright, IV, 221.
95. See Genette, "Pr. Pal.," 208.
96. James, *Briefer Course*, 130.
97. *RTP*, I, 10 Enright, I, 11.
98. James, *Briefer Course*, 129.
99. *RTP*, IV, 72. Enright V, 662.
100. *RTP*, IV, 124.
101. Enright, V, 732–733.
102. *RTP*, II, 31. Enright, II, 339.
103. James, *Briefer Course*, 129.
104. *RTP*, I, 599. Enright, II, 254.
105. *RTP*, I, 340. Enright, I, 492.
106. *RTP*, IV, 4.
107. Enright, V, 564–565.
108. James, *Briefer Course*, 132.
109. James, *Principles*, I, 126.
110. Genette, "Pr. Pal.," 219.
111. William R. Everdell, rev. of *Einstein's Clocks, Poincaré's Maps*, by Peter Galison (New York: W. W. Norton, 2003), "Books," *New York Times*, August 17, 2003.
112. *RTP*, I, 40. Enright I, 55.
113. *RTP*, I, 109. Enright, I, 153.
114. *RTP*, I, 133.
115. Enright, I, 189–190.
116. *RTP*, III, 151. Enright, IV, 208.
117. *RTP*, III, 423.
118. Enright, IV, 490–491.
119. *RTP*, III, 535.
120. *RTP*, III, 856.
121. Enright, V, 476.
122. James, *Principles*, I, 130, and *Briefer Course*, 137.
123. James, *Briefer Course*, 137–138.
124. *RTP*, III, 857. Enright, V, 477.
125. James, *Briefer Course*, 138.
126. James, *Principles*, I, 126.
127. *RTP*, III, 553. Enright, V, 49.
128. James, *Briefer Course*, 133.
129. James, *Principles*, I, 129, and *Briefer Course*, 136.

130. James, *Briefer Course*, 136.
131. James, *Briefer Course*, 137.
132. *RTP*, I, 170. Enright, I, 243.
133. *RTP*, I, 170.
134. Enright, I, 243–244.
135. James, *Briefer Course*, 134.
136. James, *Principles*, I, 130.
137. James, *Briefer Course*, 135–136.
138. James, *Briefer Course*, 135.
139. *RTP*, II, 4–5.
140. Enright, II, 301.
141. *RTP*, IV, 8. Enright, V. 570.
142. James, *Principles*, I, 130.
143. *RTP*, IV, 110. Enright, V, 713.
144. *RTP*, IV, 85. Enright, V, 679.
145. *RTP*, IV, 86. Enright, V, 681.
146. James, *Principles*, I, 197.
147. James, *Principles*, I, 351.
148. *RTP*, IV, 485. Enright, VI, 314.
149. *RTP*, IV, 476.
150. Enright, VI, 302.
151. James, *Briefer Course*, 224.
152. See Genette, "Pr. Pal.," 224.
153. James, *Briefer Course*, 226.
154. James, *Briefer Course*, 225.
155. Gérard Genette, "Rhetoric Restrained," *Figures of Literary Discourse*, trans. Alan Sheridan (New York: Columbia University Press, 1982), 103–126, 110.
156. Genette, "Rhetoric," 108–110.
157. Genette, "Pr. Pal.," 207.
158. Genette, "Pr. Pal.," 207.
159. Genette, "Pr. Pal.," 211–212.
160. Genette, "Pr. Pal.," 212, 203.
161. Genette, "Pr. Pal.," 214.
162. Genette, "Pr. Pal.," 214.
163. Genette, "Pr. Pal.," 220.
164. James, *Principles*, I, 538.
165. James, *Principles*, I, 523.
166. *RTP*, I, 9. Enright, I, 9.
167. *RTP*, I, 6. Enright, I, 5.
168. *RTP*, I, 7. Enright, I, 7.
169. *RTP*, I, 9. Enright, I, 9.
170. James, *Principles*, I, 524.
171. *RTP*, I, 27–28.
172. James, *Principles*, I, 525.
173. *RTP*, I, 83. Enright, I, 116.
174. *RTP*, I, 43–44.
175. James, *Principles*, I, 529, note 9.
176. James, *Principles*, I, 531.
177. James, *Principles*, I, 530.
178. James, *Briefer Course*, 223.
179. James, "Brute and Human Intellect," 2.
180. *RTP*, IV, 221. Enright, V, 871.
181. *RTP*, IV, 123. Enright, V, 731.
182. James, "Brute and Human Intellect," 2–3.
183. James, *Briefer Course*, 236.
184. James, *Briefer Course*, 236.

185. James, *Principles*, I, 545.
186. James, "Brute and Human Intellect," 3.
187. James, "Brute and Human Intellect," 5.
188. James, *Principles*, I, 535.
189. James, "Brute and Human Intellect," 22.
190. James, "Brute and Human Intellect," 3.
191. James, *Briefer Course*, 223.
192. *RTP*, II, 191. Enright, II, 566.
193. James, *Principles*, II, 971.
194. James, *Principles*, II, 971.
195. James, *Principles*, II, 972.
196. *RTP*, IV, 467–468.
197. Enright, VI, 289–290.
198. *RTP*, II, 180.
199. James, *Briefer Course*, 228.
200. James, *Principles*, I, 538–539.
201. James, *Briefer Course*, 234.
202. James, *Briefer Course*, 235.
203. James, *Principles*, I, 539. See Shadworth H. Hodgson, *Time and Space: A Metaphysical Essay* (London: Longmans, Green, Roberts, 1865), 266.
204. *RTP*, I, 43. Enright, I, 59.
205. James, *Principles*, I, 544.
206. James, *Principles*, I, 539–540.
207. James, *Briefer Course*, 238.
208. *RTP*, I, 181–182.
209. Enright, I, 259–260.
210. James, *Briefer Course*, 238.
211. James, *Principles*, I, 555.
212. *RTP*, III, 532. Enright, V, 20.
213. James, *Briefer Course*, 239.
214. *RTP*, III, 533–534.
215. Enright, V, 21–22.
216. James, *Briefer Course*, 239.
217. James, *Briefer Course*, 240.
218. James, *Principles*, I, 555.
219. *RTP*, I, 44–45.
220. Enright, I, 60–61.
221. James, *Briefer Course*, 242.
222. James, *Briefer Course*, 243.
223. *RTP*, III, 535– 536.
224. Enright, V, 23.
225. *RTP*, IV, 7. Enright, V, 569.
226. *RTP*, IV, 7.
227. Enright, V, 569.
228. James, *Principles*, I, 605.
229. James, *Briefer Course*, 245.
230. James, *Briefer Course*, 245.
231. James, *Principles*, I, 571.
232. James, *Principles*, I, 578.
233. *RTP*, IV, 451. Enright, VI, 264.
234. *RTP*, I, 435. Enright, II, 18.
235. *RTP*, I, 441. Enright, II, 26–27.
236. *RTP*, I, 440. Enright, II, 26.
237. *RTP*, I, 449.
238. Enright, II, 38–39.
239. *RTP*, IV, 548.

240. See *RTP*, IV, 549. Enright, VI, 360.
241. *RTP*, IV, 516. Enright, VI, 352.
242. James, *Principles*, I, 585.
243. James, *Principles*, I, 593.
244. James, *Principles*, I, 594, n. 44.
245. *RTP*, I, 419–420.
246. Enright, I, 606.
247. James, *Briefer Course*, 246, and *Principles*, I, 583.
248. James, *Briefer Course*, 246–247.
249. James, *Briefer Course*, 247–248.
250. James, *Briefer Course*, 248.
251. *RTP*, IV, 625.
252. Enright, VI, 531–532.
253. James, *Principles*, I, 602.
254. James, *Briefer Course*, 249.
255. James, *Briefer Course*, 251.
256. James, *Briefer Course*, 252.
257. James, *Principles*, I, 610.
258. *RTP*, I, 45. Enright, I, 62.
259. James, *Principles*, I, 605.
260. James, *Principles*, I, 614.
261. *RTP*, I, 47. Enright, 64.
262. James, *Principles*, I, 605.
263. James, *Briefer Course*, 253. James cites as source of this passage James Mill's *Analysis of the Phenomena of the Human Mind*, ed. John Stuart Mill, 2 vols. (London: Longmans, Green, Reader, and Dyer, 1869), chapter x.
264. *RTP*, III, 50–51.
265. Enright, IV, 67–68.
266. *RTP*, I, 43. Enright, I, 58.
267. James, *Principles*, II, 788.
268. *RTP*, I, 44. Enright, I, 59.
269. James, *Briefer Course*, 254.
270. James, *Briefer Course*, 254.
271. James, *Briefer Course*, 255.
272. *RTP*, III, 536. Enright, V, 25.
273. James, *Briefer Course*, 256.
274. James, *Briefer Course*, 257.
275. James, *Briefer Course*, 255. Several references to Fra Angelico appear in Proust's correspondence and in *À la recherche du temps perdu*.
276. *RTP*, IV, 445–446.
277. Enright, VI, 256.
278. *RTP*, I, 45–46. Enright, I, 62–63.
279. James, *Briefer Course*, 261.
280. *RTP*, I, 46.
281. Enright, I, 63.
282. James, *Principles*, I, 639, and *Briefer Course*, 262.
283. *RTP*, I, 620. Enright, II, 283.
284. *RTP*, II, 4.
285. Enright, II, 300.
286. See *RTP*, I, 629.
287. James, *Briefer Course*, 11.
288. James, *Briefer Course*, 19.
289. James, *Principles*, II, 682.
290. James, *Principles*, II, 679.
291. James, *Briefer Course*, 19.
292. James, *Principles*, II, 682.

293. James, *Briefer Course*, 21, and *RTP*, I, 3.
294. James, *Principles*, II, 682–683.
295. James, *Briefer Course*, 18.
296. James, *Principles*, II, 658.
297. James, *Principles*, II, 675.
298. James, *Principles*, II, 825.
299. *RTP*, IV, 22.
300. Enright, V, 590.
301. James, *Briefer Course*, 264.
302. *RTP*, IV, 451. Enright, VI, 264.
303. *RTP*, IV, 451. Enright, VI, 263–264.
304. See James, *Briefer Course*, 264.
305. James, *Briefer Course*, 273.
306. James, *Briefer Course*, 271.
307. James, *Briefer Course*, 271.
308. James, *Briefer Course*, 271.
309. *RTP*, IV, 61. Enright, V, 646.
310. *RTP*, IV, 451. Enright, VI, 264.
311. *RTP*, IV, 451.
312. Enright, VI, 264.
313. James, *Briefer Course*, 273–274.
314. James, *Briefer Course*, 275, 277.
315. *RTP*, II, 685–686.
316. Enright, III, 535–536.
317. James, *Briefer Course*, 283.
318. James, *Briefer Course*, 283.
319. See Proust, *RTP*, I, 76.
320. *RTP*, I, 172. Enright, I, 246.
321. *RTP*, I, 380. Enright, I, 551.
322. *RTP*, III, 665. By forcing us to participate as interpreters—and thus identify with the feelings of others—reading and the arts stimulate "empathy" of appreciation (see Wolf, 86).
323. *RTP*, III, 643. Enright, V, 174–175.
324. *RTP*, III, 643–644. Enright, V, 175.
325. *RTP*, III, 644. Enright, V, 175.
326. James, *Briefer Course*, 278.
327. *RTP*, II, 269. Enright, II, 677.
328. *RTP*, II, 269–270. Enright, II, 677–678.
329. *RTP*, II, 270. Enright, II, 678.
330. *RTP*, II, 270–271. Enright, II, 679.
331. James, *Briefer Course*, 285.
332. James, *Briefer Course*, 286.
333. James, *Briefer Course*, 286.
334. *RTP*, II, 229.
335. Enright, II, 620.
336. James, *Briefer Course*, 286.
337. James, *Briefer Course*, 287.
338. James, *Briefer Course*, 288.
339. James, *Briefer Course*, 314.
340. James, *Briefer Course*, 307.
341. James, *Briefer Course*, 310.
342. Justin, O'Brien, ed., *The Maxims of Marcel Proust* (New York: Columbia University Press, 1948), xiii.
343. O'Brien, *Maxims*, xii.
344. O'Brien, *Maxims*, xvi.
345. O'Brien, *Maxims*, 36.

346. *RTP*, III, 652. Enright V, 187.
347. James, *Briefer Course*, 358.
348. James, *Briefer Course*, 369.
349. *RTP*, I, 569. Enright, II, 210.
350. *RTP*, I, 569. Enright, II, 210–211.
351. *RTP*, I, 569. Enright, II, 210.
352. *RTP*, II, 96. Enright, II, 432.
353. James, *Briefer Course*, 375.
354. *RTP*, II, 172. Enright, II, 538.
355. *RTP*, II, 172.
356. Enright, II, 538–539.
357. *RTP*, II, 370. Enright, III, 86.
358. *RTP*, III, 538–539. Enright, V, 28.
359. James, *Briefer Course*, 372–373.
360. James, *Briefer Course*, 373.
361. James, *Briefer Course*, 380.
362. James, *Briefer Course*, 379.
363. *RTP*, IV, 552. Enright, VI, 418.
364. James, *Briefer Course*, 384.
365. James, *Briefer Course*, 386.
366. James, *Briefer Course*, 388.
367. James, *Briefer Course*, 388.
368. James, *Briefer Course*, 393.

FOUR

From Jean to Je

Experience in the First-Person Singular

"J'ai trouvé plus probe et plus délicat comme artiste de ne pas laisser voir, de ne pas annoncer que c'était justement à la recherche de la Vérité que je partais, ni en quoi elle consistait pour moi," wrote Proust to Jacques Rivière on February 6, 1914[1] [I found it more honest and more discreet as an artist to conceal and not announce that it was precisely in search of the Truth that I started, nor to disclose what that consisted of for me]. As late as November 1921, Proust lamented the constant need to justify himself as a writer against the critical charge that he wrote self-indulgently, disorderedly, without the appeal of a universal message. Because it was written in the first person and not published in full until 1927, the extended architecture of his composition was not yet evident, leaving readers and critics confused. Proust's intent to pursue and illuminate the essential and universal truth in his narrator's individual experience was misunderstood.

For William James, the outsider, the third person, can never truly catch and appreciate the truth that the experiencing subject discerns: "The spectator's judgment is sure to miss the root of the matter, and to possess no truth. The subject judged knows a part of the world of reality which the judging spectator fails to see."[2] Proust disclaimed and attempted to dissociate the simple *facts* of biography from the artist's creative endeavor; so what is it that the perspective of first-person experience could provide his fiction?

In 1909, as the drafts of Proust's novel veer toward the psychological, perceptive sensitivity becomes increasingly essential to knowledge and is portrayed in the narrator's encounters with novelty, in moments of daze or reverie, in the opening "obscurité" [murky uncertainty] on the borderline of sleep. Moments like these are described by James in his psychology and characterized in *A Pluralistic Universe* as instances of "pure experience," another name for the unnamed and unanalyzed flow of "feeling or sensation" evident to "new-born babes, or men in semi-coma from sleep, drugs, illnesses or blows."[3] Proust's novel of introspection, like James's texts, will incline a beam ("projeter de la lumiere") on unseen general principles of human behavior portrayed with the vitality of an individual life as lived[4] with all its emotional immediacy and epistemological limitations, giving readers a glimpse of what is most authentic to the self.

The realization that experience (as James described it) would be the force propelling his narrator altered Proust's course from Jean, hero of *Jean Santeuil* (Proust's early attempt to write a novel, which he composed in third person), to "je"—and emboldened the design of his book.

James had enthusiastically embraced the "untamed, unrefined, and unselected" aspects of human experience outside facile conceptual norms.[5] As the narrator examines and recounts experience in first-person voice, he depicts the limitations and the singularities, the blindness and understanding, the penetrating substratum of memory and the elation of mystical-like impressions impossible to fathom so intimately from the outside looking on. Like James's, his is a world of "moral" intangibles in which the thinking witness is enveloped by the "sensibly present"[6] and the open-ended "vague" beyond unclothed fact, by the unresolved and unclarified "thickness" of individual experience as lived,[7] a world fabricated by temperament, attitude, and language, marked by multiplicity, error, and the continuing attempt to verify. This becomes the writer's aesthetic and structures his novel.

James saw philosophizing as supremely personal, an expression of the individual "I" in theoretical interaction with existence and knowledge. The "je" is the locus of conscious awareness, the experiencing self with its individual temperament situated within a body and set into a pluralistic field, and through which all interested interaction with the roiling waves of chaotic experience of the universe takes place.[8]

In a piece written for the *Revue Lilas* when he was a student, Proust expresses his own preference for explaining psychic life directly and in the first-person singular: "Je vis dans un sanctuaire, au milieu d'un spectacle. Je suis le centre des choses et chacune me procure des sensations et des sentiments magnifiques ou mélancoliques, dont je jouis"[9] [I live in a sanctum in the midst of a spectacle. I am the center of things, and each one procures me magnificent and melancholy sensations and feelings that I enjoy]. This sentience of being at the center of the universe is reiterated by the narrator lying in his bed: "c'était laisser tourner les ombres autour de moi comme d'un tronc d'arbre" [it was like letting the lights and shadows spin around me as round a tree-trunk].[10]

"Personal histories are processes of change in time, and *the change itself is one of the things immediately experienced,*" wrote James in "A World of

Pure Experience": "like the thin line of flame advancing across the dry autumnal field which the farmer proceeds to burn. In this line we live prospectively as well as retrospectively."[11] This is the confusing cognitive paradox of the Proustian tale: the story being lived by the narrator going forward is only known and understood cumulatively, told retrospectively as a dynamic reality of the experiencing self—forever fixed. The narrator lives on the cusp of past and present, the one permeating the other in an intertwining of prospective and retrospective. Proust wanted his work to demonstrate a living experience and the development of a means of interpreting that experience.[12]

FIRST-PERSON EXPERIENCE OR A POOR PARTIAL SNAPSHOT?

On May 25, 1903, the centennial of Ralph Waldo Emerson's birth, William James delivered a commemorative address in Concord reflecting on memory and the meager legacy a man leaves behind compared to the amplitude and intricacy of experience that constitutes a life. Once gone, a man's actions, efforts and choices, his attitudes and interpretations, his passions, his reveries, his recollections are dissipated and evaporate, leaving behind at best a trace:

> The pathos of death is this, that when the days of one's life are ended, those days that were so crowded with business and felt so heavy in their passing, what remains of one in memory should usually be so slight a thing. The phantom of an attitude, the echo of a certain mode of thought, a few pages of print [. . .] are all that can survive the best of us. [. . .] [H]appy are those whose singularity gives a note so clear as to be victorious over the inevitable pity of such diminution and abridgment.[13]

This third-person memory is just a poor partial snapshot and, like a photograph, it does not begin to reveal the depths of perception and relation embedded in a life—or in art.

Surveying the aftermath of the San Francisco earthquake in 1906, James was curious to observe and record the "'subjective' phenomena"[14] of his own reactions to the traumatic event: "I discerned retrospectively certain peculiar ways in which my consciousness had taken in the phenomenon." Scientific analysis could summarize the physical events, the intensity of the rumblings and the resulting cracking of the earth, but for James the quake took on agency. It had a "moral" side for him as first-person eyewitness; it had "animus and intent."[15] A natural event became a *personal* experience in writing.

In Proust's hands, the "few pages of print" James alluded to at Concord turned into a multivolume work projecting to a long posterity of readers the fullness and emotional tenor of that "moral" side of a "singular" life.

James saw the events in a life as "facts" that do not change with time. "They simply *are*." They constitute the "muddy particulars,"[16] the events of Proust's "passé perdu." The vibrato, the or surrounding affective content, could be explored later and subjected to constantly revised interpretation in light of what happens over *time*. Truth, according to James, is a process of "mutation"[17] and is dependent only in part upon its snapshot value, our momentary and perhaps temporary confidence in its accuracy: "Truth is the function of the beliefs that start and terminate among them [the facts of experience]."[18] This would be the subject of Proust's "search."

James, like Proust, uses optical terms common in the technology of the time. Telescope and microscope are important for the perspective they proffer. To paraphrase a comment James reportedly made about his brother, Henry, and that could equally well have been said of Proust: his characters, like the people we encounter, seem to arise from nowhere, living lives that briefly coincide with our own, and then disappear, leaving us with just a taste of their presence and the desire to understand their origins and their ends, to penetrate the enigmas of the little of them we have seen.[19] The description of other people in the writer's universe, like planets circling in their own orbits, is analogous to the voyeuristic view Proust's narrator sees through his "téléscope" and from other more secret vantage points.

Just as a single static and objective snapshot was of value in Proust's work (despite its third-person limitations) because it could reveal telling details overlooked by a casual glance, if taken in series over time it would disclose changes that would otherwise be missed. The telescope, and not the microscope as mistaken readers had assumed, could be trained on and peer into the intimacy of the distant worlds of others and expose them as they move in and out of view, be they artists of genius, provincial neighbors, the bourgeoisie or demi-monde, foreign service functionaries, professors, doctors, homosexuals in hiding, or high society. For similar reasons, the notion had been applied to James himself: "'[H]e had a profound admiration for other types of mind,' one of James's students recalled, 'just because they seemed like other universes.'"[20]

In James's view, experience in the first-person singular—"direct acquaintance"—is paramount, "the only way to apprehend reality's thickness" and understand "what really makes it go."[21] The world's actuality can at the same time take the form of an external, objective entity and as individual, thence collective, experience: "This very desk which I strike with my hand strikes in turn your eyes. It functions at once as a physical object in the outer world and as a mental object in our sundry mental worlds,"[22] wrote James. Proust and his narrator employ art to reassemble the world according to notations that lie beyond merely describing a desk—those of an individual observing mind's experience of it. According to the narrator, that task is not an easy one; it requires effort.

Reasoning alone is insufficient to ascertain truth. The critical opinions Proust expressed in "La Méthode de Sainte-Beuve" parallel, among others, James's criticisms of materialist and intellectualist philosophers for whom conceptual permanence and theoretical purity outweigh the varying and sometimes contradictory nature of experience. The senses, which deliver fact supposedly more accurate (apprehended in the first person), are fallible because they colored by attitudes and prejudices, by what we choose to attend to. The "fluctuations of attention" affect even our awareness of sensation; it is a "mental" act[23] and subject to the influence of belief. "Le témoignage des sens est lui aussi une operation de l'esprit où la conviction crée l'évidence" [The evidence of the senses is also an operation of the mind in which conviction creates the facts],[24] corroborates Proust's narrator.

And in a notion strongly anticipating how Proust's narrator will experience Albertine, with her manifold and mysterious involvements: "The very girl you love," wrote James, "is simultaneously entangled elsewhere."[25] Proust's narrator presents *his* world—one of the sundry many—to his readers in a very Jamesian way: "L'univers est vrai pour nous tous et dissemblable pour chacun" [The universe is real for us all and dissimilar to each one of us].[26] What interests him is the experiential truth beyond the physical desk, the observations that only a single individual can draw of the "lois psychologiques" [psychological laws][27] lying below the surface dress and banter of a dinner party or "au delà de l'apparence elle-même dans une zone un peu plus en retrait" [behind actual appearances, in a zone that was rather more withdrawn].[28]

James's discussion of the task facing the philosopher included snaring the "glimmers and twinkles" so difficult to capture in language or system. He contrasts the three-dimensional views possible using "stereoscope or kinetoscope" with the flatness seen when the slides are viewed separately without the technical aid of the apparatus; "they lack the depth, the motion, the vitality."[29]

> As in stereoscopic or kinetoscopic pictures seen outside the instrument, the third dimension, the movement, the vital element, are not there. We get a beautiful picture of an express train supposed to be moving, but where in the picture, as I have heard a friend say, is the energy or the fifty miles an hour?[30]

The episodes of the "three trees" and the "aubépines" [hawthorn flowers] involve considerable perceptive (sensational and emotive) reaction to a factual experience in three dimensions. The first experience Proust's narrator can successfully bring to paper and to publication, however, is his view of church towers "moving" relative to one another as he passes in a carriage. The piece he writes, like his major work yet to be, involves description of four dimensions and includes the immaterial dynamic element of change through time in the way a scene appears to an individual witness. It is Proust's narrator's first literary foray into "fifty miles an hour."

James's concern for such intangible aspects of experience as speeding change or the "vague" in which imagination and memory exert their force on the mind is echoed in Proust's narrator's fervent exploration of uncertainty. A plenitude of possibility exists as events occur independent of the observer. Actualities can be indeterminate and misperception or loss through forgetting is always imminent. A margin of potential lies beyond the evident: the feelings it arouses, the memories it evokes, the relations between the conscious and the subliminal, the light shed on daily life by purported mystical encounter, or the fraying of old assumptions in the progress of cultural alteration over time. Life is change, a flow of experience in an intangible "moral" atmosphere; the only way really to *know* it is to be *in* it in the first-person singular, and the best way to retrieve it is through the inward focus of memory where it retains its dynamic and bloom. Truth is not found to be a single static essence; it is an unfolding dynamic.

To counter the difficulties of translating experience into communicative language, James used the example of reading. He finds that a book is more than its contents. It is a sensorial experience with a brown leather cover experienced in a particular place, the Museum of Zoology near his home in Cambridge, Massachusetts, and bringing to mind the particular time when its author wrote it and people wore curled wigs. "To find such sensational *termini* should be our aim with all our higher thought. They end discussion; they destroy the false conceit of knowledge; and without them we are all at sea with each other's meaning."[31] The senses here have the power to transmit meaning beyond the book's subject matter. What Proust could have learned from James about reading would have taken him beyond Jean to "je" and from description of event to distillation of the truth behind it.

Re-created in *Jean Santeuil* is a lesson Proust's philosophy teacher Darlu had taught. In an exchange of New Year's gifts, Jean presented his teacher Beulier with a "petit buste," and received in turn a copy of a book by Joubert, which they read together. Jean describes his pleasure in reading the book. At the end of the lession, Beulier takes the book home. The gift had served its purpose: reading the content, not the book itself, was the true gift. Its substance imparted, nothing remained to be gained: "En ayant donné tout le sens, l'âme, le secours moral à Jean, il lui en avait tout donné"[32] [Having given all the meaning, the essence, the ethical uplift, he had imparted everything].

But in the preface that Proust prepared for his translation of Ruskin's *Sésame et les lys*, it is the associative connections surrounding the act of reading that are paramount.[33] As is true for James, the physical experience, stimulant to memories of the most personal aspects of an individual's history, transcends the story: "ce qu'elles [les lectures d'enfance] laissent surtout en nous, c'est l'image des lieux et des jours où nous les avons faites"[34] [what they (childhood readings) chiefly leave in us is the image of the places and the days we did them].

In 1907, Proust explored the artifice of historical memory expressed in memoir in a brief meditation on social history:[35] how does a generation or an individual memorialize itself in what it leaves behind intentionally? And how it is remembered as a matter of happenstance and interpretation created by the historians and archeologists who come later? Proust wonders about the facts of past generations. How did they look to their contemporaries? How are they viewed later? How would his own generation choose to memorialize itself? How are the historical linkages between past and present incarnated in what we would call genetic variation, the living descendants of old families (genetics as representation)?

The memoirs of Mme. de Boigne were being published at the time, and Proust considers whether her portrayal of a brilliant social life was the one she actually lived or an artifice of writing. What control does a writer exert over the "poor partial snapshot" left behind? Proust is probing James's idea of individual experience, comparing the richness of daily existence as lived with the meagerness of a snapshot view, the proximity of fictional to actual in an autobiographical-style first-person portrayal. How truthful can first-person narration be within the limitations of a written work compared to the vast and vigorous constant change and development in daily life? Anything written simultaneously filters and magnifies, arrests and immobilizes.

In a long section of Proust's article that *Le Figaro* chose not to print, Proust refers to the "immenses catacombes du passé" [the immense catacombs of the past] that bear the "sillon"—or imprint—of even the tiniest or most frivolous events, "les plus oiseux détails" [the most useless details]. This is the Jamesian "richness" of detail in daily life's experiences. The next year Proust jotted down the importance of the arresting physical detail: "Culte pour la chose / physique qui est une / trace vivante sous laquelle / il y a l'haleine du passé, / vieux récits, vieux mots, vieux objets, vieux métiers /—et aussi la trace physiologique"[36] [Cult for the physical object which is a living trace within which there is the breath of the past, old narratives, obsolete terms, ancient objects, outdated trades—and also bodily markers].

Proust's evolving Jamesian-style meditation on a book culminates a passage in *Le Temps retrouvé* in which the narrator describes the *experience* of a book read by associating it with the reader's fringe of impressions, sensory and other, that existed at the moment of reading it.[37] Just like James's experience in the Museum of Zoology, a volume by Bergotte that Proust's narrator discovers in the Duc de Guermantes's library evokes the snow that covered the Champs-Élysées the day he read it. For Maryanne Wolf, "[T]his associative dimension is part of the generative quality at the heart of reading."[38] It engages the reader within and outside the text. Proust associates, as did James, in Wolf's terms, "beyond" the content of the text, beyond the book, to the entire sensory experience.

The material experience of George Sand's novel *François le champi* with its "couverture rougeâtre" [red binding][39] is felt with the same familiar complexities we attribute to our acquaintances. Communicated through the material object "book" are the sensorial yet profoundly immaterial experiences surrounding the reading of it, recalling for the narrator the moment when, his mind wandering, he hears his mother's voice reading words aloud and revealing to him their magic fringe. A book is so much more than content to be processed by the intellect; reading allows us to enter the experience the writer portrays and to surpass his terms of discourse. The gray areas less well understood rationally are (for Proust's narrator as they were for James) the more significant avenues to truth:

> Car les vérités que l'intelligence saisit directement à claire-voie dans le monde de la pleine lumière ont quelque chose de moins profond, de moins nécessaire que celles que la vie nous a malgré nous communiquées en une impression, matérielle parce qu'elle est entrée par nos sens, mais dont nous pouvons dégager l'esprit.[40]
>
> [For the truths which the intellect apprehends directly in the world of full and unimpeded light have something less profound, less necessary than those which life communicates to us against our will in an impression which is material because it enters us through the senses but yet has a spiritual meaning which it is possible for us to extract.[41]]

To the mind of the narrator's grandmother, a photograph, like James's poor partial snapshot, is a limited, vulgar, utilitarian object with narrow educational value compared to an artist's interpretation or an antique engraving that encompasses and mirrors abundant layered personal experience embellished by historical reference to something that may no longer exist—"comme plusieurs 'épaisseurs' d'art" [several "thicknesses" of art].[42] At the Verdurins' home on le quai de Conti, the baron de Charlus invites the narrator to inspect some fantastically valuable pieces of silver. But like his grandmother, the narrator would rather see "une belle gravure, de ceux de Mme du Barry" [a fine engraving, of Mme du Barry's],[43] because it would be richer in historical provenance and interpretive value than bourgeois silver collectibles. It reflects experience that resonates: "our own things are *fuller* for us than those of others because of the memories they awaken and the practical hopes and expectations they arouse."[44] Moving from room to room with the narrator and Charlus, Brichot espies furniture he had seen at the Verdurins' previous home, rue Montalivet, twenty-five years earlier:

> [D]ans un salon comme en toutes choses, la partie extérieure, actuelle, contrôlable pour tout le monde, n'est que le prolongement, c'était cette partie devenue purement morale, d'une couleur qui n'existait plus que

pour mon vieil interlocuteur qu'il ne pouvait pas me faire voir, cette partie qui s'est détachée du monde extérieur pour se réfugier dans notre âme, à qui elle donne une plus-value,[45] où elle s'est assimilée à sa substance habituelle, s'y muant [. . .] en cet albâtre translucide de nos souvenirs [. . .] que nous ne pouvons considérer en nous-mêmes sans une certain émotion, en songeant que c'est de l'existence de notre pensée que dépend pour quelque temps encore leur survie, le reflet des lampes qui sont éteintes et l'odeur des charmilles qui ne fleuriront plus.[46]

[I]n a drawing-room as in everything else, the actual, external aspect, verifiable by everyone, is but the prolongation, the aspect which has detached itself from the outer world to take refuge in our soul, to which it gives as it were a surplus-value, in which it is absorbed into its habitual substance, transforming itself . . . into that translucent alabaster of our memories of which we are incapable of conveying the colour which we alone can see, . . . and that we ourselves cannot inwardly contemplate without a certain emotion, reflecting that it is on the existence of our thoughts that their survival for a little longer depends, the gleam of lamps that have been extinguished and the fragrance of arbours that will never bloom again.[47]]

The richness and "moral" value that exists *only* because we *remember* is reflected in the pastel drawing of a bouquet of pansies and violets given to Mme. Verdurin by an artist now deceased: "[S]eul fragment vivant d'une vie disparue sans laisser de traces, résumant un grand talent et une longue amitié, rappelant son regard attentif et doux, sa belle main grasse et triste pendant qu'il peignait" [the sole surviving fragment of a life that had vanished without leaving any trace, epitomising a great talent and a long friendship, recalling his gentle, searching eyes, his shapely, plump and melancholy hand as he painted it].[48] This sense of the artist James calls "presence in absence."[49] It is available to us as "representative" or "symbolic" knowledge, a connection we try to draw to elucidate the passage of time between experiences current or "remote" and imprinted in our memory. "[H]owever absent in body, [these] become in some way present to our thought." An active imagination ("mon seul organe pour jouir de la beauté") [my imagination, which was the only organ that I possessed for the enjoyment of beauty[50]] *can* elucidate the meaning of experience because it can embrace presence in absence, "ce qui est absent" [what is absent] when past sensation is mirrored in the present:

Or la recréation par la mémoire d'impressions qu'il fallait ensuite approfondir, éclairer, transformer en équivalents d'intelligence, n'était-elle pas une des conditions, presque l'essence même de l'oeuvre d'art telle que je l'avais conçue tout à l'heure dans la bibliothèque?[51]

[But was not the re-creation by the memory of impressions which had then to be deepened, illuminated, transformed into equivalents of

> understanding, was not this process one of the conditions, almost the very essence of the work of art as I had just now in the library conceived it?[52]]

The interior of the Verdurins' salons overflows with the gifts and bits and pieces of all the rendezvous of the "petit clan," items that recall the history of all that has taken place there. Unlike the "fat hand" of the artist friend, the material things remain; and they, too, have attained a "moral" quality. They stimulate historical memory. They have retained "l'empreinte et la fixité d'un trait de caractère" [the fixity of a trait of character].[53]

The experience of Combray is permanently distant and solely representative. It cannot be reproduced in the present as it was, and it is enduringly absent save for the memory. The human mind can retain such a memory for the brief period of a lifetime; but art—with all the resonant connections it evokes—can vouchsafe memory to posterity repeatedly and forever. This is the practical magic of art, of language.

Even in memory, the "cash-value of matter is our physical sensations [. . .] all that we can concretely verify of its conception." Individual and private—but real and substantive—they connect our experience and the truth of our interpretations to the world around us.[54] Brichot's "plus-value" is the clustering of his memories with physical sensations current and past in the presence of the Verdurins' furniture.

This philosophical discovery so important for Proust's narrator reflects James's notion that, taken cumulatively, the Self is a matter of memory.[55] Memories are all anyone has that is irrefutable. Proust's narrator realizes that, like Brichot's, his exist outside time and the vagaries of events. Given form, they confer eternal life. His book will *reconstitute* them as his narrator's experience rather than simply *recounting* them, as the author's denials underscore. For James and for Proust, experience ultimately includes all the relations that give it flavor and depth, like the "fat hand" of the artist: "The organization of the Self as a system of memories, purposes, strivings, fulfillments or disappointments, is incidental to this most intimate of all relations, the terms of which seem in many cases actually to compenetrate and suffuse each other's being."[56]

For both James and Proust, the point of view is through the eyes and experience of the individual, the first-person singular: "Each, from his particular angle of observation, takes in a certain sphere of fact and trouble, which each must deal with in a unique manner."[57] Laying out sentient personal experience as the benchmark for weighing truth, James's writings could act as exemplar—if not catalyst—for *À la recherche du temps perdu*, where an individual's actual sensory impressions are essential and are sifted for what they can reveal as personal truth despite errors that may occur in their interpretation.

After earliest childhood, our perception, according to James—our reactions to incoming sensations—is affected by memories and associations.[58] These are the "erreurs de nos sens . . . qui faussent pour nous l'aspect réel de ce monde" and "que le raisonnement déplacera ensuite de distances quelquefois énormes"[59] [errors . . . by which our senses falsify for us the real nature of the world . . . which the reasoning mind subsequently corrects by, sometimes, a very large displacement[60]]—the occasions when our personal moods and desires alter how we see, and our intellect struggles to reconcile what is true.

Yet, the single static objective frame of the snapshot or "instantané," a fix of light in a snippet of time, can be revealing by its very limitations: details of the sculpted capitals of the church in Balbec had escaped the narrator's notice until he saw them in a photograph.[61] Or they can be candid, revealing, unflattering: Saint-Loup refuses to show the narrator the snapshots of his mistress Rachel that he took himself with his Kodak.[62] They can be contrived: the narrator's grandmother dresses up artificially for her photo in Balbec and incurs his unsympathetic disapproval. Or they can be stimulating to the imagination and emotions: Odette's actual looks are enhanced in Swann's mind by ripples of resemblance to a photograph of Botticelli's painting *Jethro's Daughter.*[63]

Even when the photo captures an objective and undistinguished actuality, for James and for Proust's narrator the eye of the beholder interprets imparting the beauty to the girl: "Whatever of value, interest, or meaning our respective worlds may appear endued with [*sic*] are thus pure gifts of the spectator's mind. The passion of love [. . .] transforms the value of the creature loved as utterly as the sunrise transforms Mont Blanc from a corpse-like gray to a rosy enchantment."[64] Proust's narrator uses a tiny but wonderful example of the objective depth of field captured as in a photographic series that might not have been visible to the usual scanning and generalizing of an observer's casual glance: the picture graphically catches details that the mind would have glossed over:

> Mais qu'au lieu de notre œil, ce soit un objectif purement matériel, une plaque photographique, qui ait regardé, alors ce que nous verrons, par exemple dans la cour de l'Institut, au lieu de la sortie d'un académicien qui veut appeler un fiacre, ce sera sa titubation, ses précautions pour ne pas tomber en arrière, la parabole de sa chute, comme s'il était ivre ou que le sol fût couvert de verglas.[65]

> [But if, instead of our eyes, it should happen to be a purely physical object, a photographic plate, that has watched the action, then what we see, in the courtyard of the Institute, for example, instead of the dignified emergence of an Academician who is trying to hail a cab, will be his tottering steps, his precautions to avoid falling on his back, the parabola of his fall, as though he were drunk or the ground covered in ice.[66]]

The filtering and highlighting power of the narrowed impression conveyed in a static photo is evident the moment Proust's narrator reenters his home and finds his grandmother reading. She is in a private state or space, not expecting his return. His regard is that of a stranger, an objective view severed from the normal dynamic ("le mouvement perpétuel") affective fringe layer ("notre incesssante tendresse") [the perpetual motion of our incessent love for them[67]] that usually surrounds close relationships. Relinquishing the baggage of the past and the dynamic of the present, he sees her objectively, that she has aged, suffered: "[J]'aperçus sur le canapé, sous la lampe, rouge, lourde et vulgaire, malade, rêvassant, promenant au-dessus d'un livre des yeux un peu fous, une vieille femme accablée que je ne connaissais pas" [I saw, sitting on the sofa beneath the lamp, red-faced, heavy and vulgar, sick, day-dreaming, letting her slightly crazed eyes wander over a book, an overburdened old woman whom I did not know].[68]

As James intimates, and Proust's novel corroborates, the flattened, inflexible photographic view can be also be as faulty as any other form of misperception when we construe it as literal or when it arouses expectations that result in disappointment. Our perceptions are almost never frozen and unwavering or devoid of affective fringe, as a name, photo, or psychologist's notation would have us believe. We *always* incorporate an element of meaning or signal in what we observe, deducing as we distinguish. We surround everything with a fringe, halo, or cloud of interpretation, and we are often wrong: "Nous voyons, nous entendons, nous concevons le monde tout de travers" [We see, we hear, we conceive the world in a lopsided fashion].[69]

Snapshots *mechanically* capture an instant of time in detail. They stimulate but do not represent the right or wrong assumptions, expectations, fears, pains, and desires that constitute interpretation, the cross-wise or transverse multidimensional view, the "thickness" of the "moral" component. In them, the dynamic fluidity of life comes to a rigid halt.

A cinematic view, or novel as a series of "moving pictures," suffers similarly from inadequate expressiveness. A succession of visual snapshots or written vignettes, however realistic, does not reconstitute reality, only its carapace. It is their almost tangible rigidity that causes "snapshot" memories, however revealing, to remain unsatisfying. They are phenomena made for third-person view. They are flat and two-dimensional, devoid of life's vivacity and randomness. They include the detail but lack the flavor, the joyful experience of the experience, "l'ébranlement effectif de mes sens par le bruit, le contact du linge, etc. avait ajouté aux rêves de l'imagination ce dont ils sont habituellement dépourvus, l'idée d'existence" [the actual shock to my senses of the noise, the touch of the linen napkin, or whatever it might be had added to the dreams of the imagination the concept of "existence" which they usually lack].[70]

For James, certain "hallowed moments" when an individual, especially someone young, has the sense that there is a hidden meaning, mysterious "essence," or truth in his impressions if only he could decode and understand it[71] are probed compulsively in Proust's book. The "essence" of any particular moment is that it is *felt* to be "unique."

James acknowledged, however, the role language plays in organizing perception: "Every reality has an infinity of aspects or properties."[72] Usually, we normalize our sensory input to accommodate the unexpected. The mind chooses what it deems real for its own "aesthetic" reasons.[73] "*There is no property* ABSOLUTELY *essential to any one thing.* The same property which figures as the essence of a thing on one occasion becomes a very inessential feature upon another."[74] For James, the "sign" or *name* functions to bring to mind the reality for which it stands, to capture all the moving parts, the color, flow, and flutter of its multiple aspects. We use "our sensible impressions as stepping-stones to pass over to the recognition of the realities whose presence they reveal."[75] Because we think "in words," we normalize the cacophony of impression, and "we substitute terms few and fixed for terms manifold and vague."[76] (Later, in *Pragmatism*, James revisits this view: the names we assign come to represent a summarization, a coalescing in language that must be verified against experience for "fit," a practice central to Proust's fiction.)

For Proust's narrator, young and visiting Combray, "quelque image qui m'avait forcée à la regarder, un nuage, un triangle, un clocher, une fleur, un caillou" [some image which had compelled me to look at it, a cloud, a triangle, a church spire, a flower, a stone],[77] promised to reveal more than appeared on their material surface. The decoding demanded adult effort and forced a search for a hidden truth, a task complex and problematical: "Sans doute ce déchiffrage était difficile mais seul il donnait quelque vérité à lire" [No doubt the process of decipherment was difficult, but only by accomplishing it could one arrive at whatever truth there was to read].[78] This search for "essence" or meaning, "the sense of ideal presence of what is absent in fact, of an absent, in a word, which the only function of the present is to *mean*,"[79] becomes for Proust's narrator a mission to obtain transparency for the "lois et idées, en essayant de faire sortir de la pénombre de ce que j'avais senti, de le convertir en un équivalent spirituel" [laws and ideas, by trying to think—that is to say, to draw forth from the shadow—what I had merely felt, by trying to convert it into its spiritual equivalent] and into "une oeuvre d'art" [a work of art].[80] The young narrator needs an aesthetic frame to infuse the snapshot with life. Literature's task is to reconstitute "the manifold and vague," to regenerate the noisy and bustling welter of sensation in time, the "days that were crowded with business and felt so heavy in their passing."[81]

Using an image of "the skull" at "the banquet," James touches on the notion of life's brevity: "Old age has the last word."[82] We are struck by the similarity with Proust's narrator's thoughts at the "Bal de Têtes" [the "costume" ball where guests are disguised by old age]. Fixed expressions once thought flattering in photo portraits have now become ridiculous still caricatures devoid of affect and dynamic as the individuals who adopted them have aged and turned into "d'immutables instantanés d'eux-mêmes" [snapshots of themselves insusceptible of change].[83] At first, the narrator does not recognize the actors in the slow artifice of this drama, but quickly he realizes that he, like them, is older now and must make sense of his life's experiences and promptly fix their meaning in a creative monument or else suffer "the curdling cold and gloom and absence of all permanent meaning."[84] He must take advantage of his acute sensitivities and plunge beneath the superficialities of conventional socializing, "below the smooth and lying official conversational surface,"[85] to unleash the creative self. He needs a method.

MAKING ART FROM EXPERIENCE

James wrote "The Sentiment of Rationality" near the beginning of his career and referred to it as his first published paper. It was "his virgin effort."[86] Published in the British Journal *Mind* in 1879, it was immediately translated into French for publication in Charles Renouvier's *Critique philosophique*. Sections were subsequently included in James's essay *Rationality, Activity and Faith* in 1882, in the *Principles of Psychology* in 1890, in *The Will to Believe* in 1897, and then republished in 1905 for private use in his classroom. Clearly, James persisted in the conviction that what he had written in the original article held true. His former student John Elof Boodin praised it as the original statement of James's pragmatism, its roots in James's own autobiography.[87]

The ostensible subject of this article is the psychology of philosophizing. In it James describes the human creative proclivity to process the disorderly information of experience into some organized comprehensible form, be it theoretical (i.e., philosophical) or aesthetic. It is the "desire to attain a conception of the frame of things which shall on the whole be more rational than the rather fragmentary and chaotic one which everyone by gift of nature carries about with him under his hat."[88] The aesthetic conveys a theoretic frame. But in so doing, the involved encounter with the actual world that it represents loses none of its impromptu flavor and diversity. It attains form.

Proust as author needed a conceptual format to buttress the experiences worth fictionalizing relayed in *Jean Santeuil*. Vincent Descombes suggests that in his novel's creative portrayal of experience Proust discloses his theoretical suppositions more clearly than in his actual statements of theory in *Le Temps retrouvé*:

> By this I mean that the novel is philosophically bolder; that it pursues further the task Proust identifies as the writer's work: the elucidation of

life, the elucidation of what was experienced in obscurity and confusion.[89]

Writing or painting with utmost brilliance, the creative endeavor is an internal *necessity* for the artist and not a matter of choice, remarks Proust's narrator.[90] Following James's "proclivity," he *must* rationalize his experience. Reworking the little patch of yellow is an internalized moral obligation for a painter like Vermeer regardless of reward, as it is for other artists, Bergotte, the narrator—and the author.

In "The Sentiment of Rationality" James proposes what we might see as a curious and perhaps far-fetched coincidence, something likely to have caught Proust's attention. Citing unspecified "psychological speculations" of his time, James argues that feeling impeded is feeling felt. He characterizes the free and easy flow of unimpeded breathing—something so challenging for Proust—as something barely felt by a healthy person, hardly noticed or appreciated. Obstructed respiration, such as plagues Proust and his sickly narrator, when relieved is comparable to the pleasure attained when confusion is resolved or explained, like "the transition from a state of puzzle and perplexity to rational comprehension."[91] The specific solution James suggests here is the formulation of some rationalizing system.

Proust's narrator's frantic attempts to unravel the strands of Albertine's behavior and motivations, to untangle the mysteries of her past and her inclinations, keep him on a pinnacle of anxiety. This he paints as feeling definitely felt and unrelieved. Wrestling with facts and with suppositions, what he relates reflects James's example of grappling with "men's mental worry about things incongruous with personal desire."[92] His restless efforts to settle the contradictions recall the "pent-up irritated mind recoiling on its present consciousness [that] will criticize it, worry over it, and never cease in its attempts to discover some new mode of formulation which may give it escape from the irrationality of its actual ideas."[93] The narrator ultimately learns more from the depths of his anguished waffling and his "illusion d'optique" [optical illusion][94] from the "minceur menteuse" [mendacious flimsiness][95] of his incessantly wrong-minded interpretations than he might have from a simpler and more satisfying relationship, because, as James puts it, "there is no 'problem of happiness'"[96] requiring comparable digging. "Comme la souffrance va plus loin en psychologie que la psychologie!" [how much further does anguish penetrate in psychology than psychology itself!][97] observes the narrator, underscoring for his readers the depth of his suffering and the potential psychological intertext of his work.

What James calls "mental peace" arrives for Proust's narrator only when the mental and emotional fireworks cease and forgetting lessens the pain: "J'avais définitivement cessé d'aimer Albertine. De sorte que cet amour [. . .] après m'avoir fait faire un détour si long et si douloureux, finissait [. . .] par rentrer, tout comme mon amour pour Gilberte, dans la loi générale de l'oubli" [I had finally ceased to love Albertine. So that this love, . . . after obliging me to make so long and painful a detour, had ended, too . . . by succumbing, like my love for Gilberte, to the general law of oblivion].[98] The display, however, made great art. That became its rationalized form.

While their apologies for aesthetic creation are strikingly similar, James's article sheds added light on other of Proust's concerns about certain "philosophical" problems: how to make use of the knowledge we accumulate through our experience. How to find the basic meaning of things. How to arrive at resolution through artistic creation. Proust portrays the narrator's need to theorize or conceptualize in *Le Temps retrouvé* as part of his hero's quest to become a writer, but he wanted artistic impression to live in its expression rather than in an intellectual or conceptual presentation. The aesthetic solution answers the dilemma he had so earnestly posed for himself: "suis-je romancier?"[99] Perhaps his ultimate willingness to adopt an artistic resolution to fundamental philosophical questions may be placed at least in part on the shoulders of James's article. Proust's narrator can get to work once he discovers a structural "frame"—one that deploys the benefits of episodic memory—over which to drape the fabric of his narrator's emotional experience and to resolve the chaos of diverse events into an aesthetic order. Only then can he proceed.

How does an individual know when this task has been accomplished, asks James. He knows because it feels good, by the "recognition" of a certain state of happiness when, in the struggle to make sense of our shreds of experience, those disconcertingly inexplicable and disconnected events are ordered by effort into something that can be processed and apprehended. "[W]e strive to formulate rationally a tangled mass of fact by a propensity as natural and invincible as that which makes us exchange a hard high stool for an arm-chair."[100] It is much more comfortable.

This accounts in part for the incomprehensible happiness Proust's narrator will feel when he first tastes a madeleine and that he will feel again later when he arrives at an understanding of his task as a writer, when his subject matter takes form in his mind. It is a kind of broadening joy that encloses his past in form as a comprehensive but ever-so-brief glimpse of eternal life, a literary fortune like Bergotte's that he can bequeath to posterity.

A philosophy equates to a utilitarian[101] or "*teleological instrument*" that, using James's word here, employs the "essence" to stand for the whole.[102] "Essence" here is the one important aspect relative to the goal in mind, central but *variable* depending upon the interests of the individual involved, the use to which it is put. By putting a rationalizing aesthetic philosophy in place, Proust allows his narrator to enjoy the pleasure of discovery and the understanding of "essences"; obstacles are eliminated and the mystery of experience is decoded:

> L'être qui était rené en moi quand, avec un tel frémissement de bonheur, j'avais entendu le bruit commun à la fois à la cuiller qui touche l'assiette et au marteau qui frappe sur la roue, à l'inégalité pour les pas des pavés de la cour des Guermantes et du baptistère de Saint-Marc, etc., cet être-là ne se nourrit que de l'essence des choses, en elle seulement il trouve sa substance, ses délices.[103]
>
> [The being which had been reborn in me when with a sudden shudder of happiness I had heard the noise that was common to the spoon touching the plate and the hammer striking the wheel, or had felt, beneath my feet, the unevenness that was common to the paving-stones of the Guermantes courtyard and to those of the baptistery of St Mark's, this being is nourished only by the essences of things, in these alone does it find its sustenance and delight.[104]]

James stresses the parallel and competing needs to simplify or narrow as well as "to recognize the particulars in their full completeness."[105] His description of the artist's need to forge the work to put order to his experience is particularly compelling in the light of Proust's narrator's determined awareness that out of the confused and disparate elements of his experiential "biography," the work of art *needs* to be isolated, revealed, created. The notion that the artist gives form to his experience and creates his own personal expression is neither revolutionary nor new. What is striking is that Proust chooses to make the creation of the work out of the confusion of experience the very subject of the work—the *process* of discovering the *process* of expressing it is his subject, just as James's theory had explained it.

Proust's narrator's preoccupation with discovering the "essence" or vital nugget of his experience turns out to be a distraction from the realization that it is in the *vitality* of an individual's own experience, the way he alone sees it as it happens, in his discovery of the *common qualities of his responses* that its meaning is best disclosed: "Ainsi, j'étais déjà arrivé à cette conclusion que nous ne sommes nullement libres devant l'œuvre d'art, que nous ne la faisons pas à notre gré, mais que préexistant à nous, nous devons, à la fois parce qu'elle est nécessaire et cachée, et comme nous ferions pour une loi de la nature, la découvrir" [I had arrived then at the conclusion that in fashioning a work of art we are by no means free, that we do not choose how we shall make it but that it pre-exists us and therefore we are obliged, since it is both necessary and hidden, to do what we should have to do if it were a law of nature—to discover it].[106]

James calls this creative type of rationalizing the formulation of "passions" according to the "aesthetic Principle of Ease" by which composers—from sounds—create a work of music; philosophers—from thoughts—a philosophic system; painters—from colors—a picture; and writers—from words and impressions—a poetic or novelistic piece. It is the "unify[ing]" implementation of artistic vision into some concrete work.[107] The impressions are there, the sounds hover in the mind; the task, the ineluctable obligation, is to attend to them, plumb their depths, and give them form. James calls this a form of "labor-saving contrivance" setting out the author's vision in a personal form of shorthand: "any character or aspect of the world's phenomena which gathers up their diversity into simplicity will gratify that passion, and in the philosopher's mind [as in the composer's, the painter's, the sculptor's, or the writer's] stand for that essence of things."[108] This would include the transcription of the "livre intérieur" [the inner book].[109]

James recognizes, however, that such unification can be simplistic. A single essence, as Proust's narrator discovers with such frustration, is not the entire picture. The intellectual construct added later to explain the initial impression is not all there is to express.[110] Nor is a mere train of atomistic ideas or a simplistic "chain" of memories better.

> Phenomena are analyzable into feelings and relations. [. . .] To abstract the relation from the feelings, to unify all things by referring them to a first cause, and to leave this latter relation with no term of feeling before it, is to violate the fundamental habits of our thinking, to baffle the imagination, and to exasperate the minds of certain people.[111]

While "essence" for Proust is the basic underlying and constitutive nature of something, in the end and in his art, it must be dynamic rather than static, expressing simultaneously impression and association, present and past,[112] the subjective resonance emanating from sensation[113] that James described as the backward glance that accompanies all forward-facing acts. For Gilles Deleuze essence is this "unity" of "Immaterial Sign" and "Spiritual Meaning" communicated through art.[114]

As Vincent Descombes points out, Proustian theory is only comprehensible as a result of close reading of the novel. It does not appear as an a priori coherently formulated abstract system; like all first-person experience of life, it must be gleaned from the flood of events, sensations, emotions and memories that his narrator enjoys and endures.[115] No single subject meriting development in a unified philosophy presented itself to the narrator as fit subject for a written work. Any totally unifying system that omits the heterogeneity of events and all-important feeling in favor of abstraction would be frustratingly unrepresentative, for him as for James: "much as everyone's eye is exasperated by a magic lantern picture or microscope object out of focus."[116] To create the novel, Proust the author and his narrator must each develop a central conception to order but not to replace their multitude of experiences, the ostensible form of an autobiographical tale of "muddy particulars" that in the end turns out to be unified retrospective fiction.

In "The Sentiment of Rationality," key for James is the relation that connects the "essence" and its associations. It is the common ground between different vertebrates in the Darwinian interpretation of the zoological world that James uses to illustrate how two things with broad fields of association can have meaningful overlap from which much can be learned.[117] Proust will exploit this concept of overlap in metaphor and extend James's notion that "a common essence may make the sensible heterogeneity of things inwardly rational";[118] he will use it to demonstrate the harmonic accord that James calls the "one thing in two aspects brought prominently forward":[119]

> To stand before a phenomenon and say *what* it is; [. . .] to pick out from it the embedded character (or characters) also embedded in the maximum number of *other* phenomena, and so identify it with them—here lie the stress and strain, here the test of the philosopher.[120]

James's philosopher's "test" becomes Proust's artist's style. Further parallels include mention of the properties of a "name" that James says here as well as in his *Psychology* are "never the same when used twice."[121] For example, the Balbec of the narrator's imagination was a church, a beach, a shortcut vision of a town he knew nothing about. Between the station at Balbec-le-Vieux, Balbec-en-Terre where the Paris train disembarked and the hotel at Balbec-Plage, the name is reframed and reused. The "petit chemin de fer d'intérêt local" connects the entire trajectory of little towns and villages—their names echoing prefixes and suffixes, ringing of sand and salt air—that must be traversed between them. The Balbec church, five leagues from the sea, looks toward the prosaic—a square where two tramways branch off opposite a café featuring "Billiards" on a sign. It does not have at its base foaming waves or even a sandy beach. So often imagined, the church and its sculptures are much more—and less—than the fantasy built on photos or the reproductions in the Trocadero museum. Instead of the glorious "essential" view of a larger-than-life entity, the Virgin on the portal turns out to be a more ordinary statue in an ordinary setting: "l'oeuvre d'art immortelle et si longtemps désirée que je trouvais métamorphosée, ainsi que l'église elle-même, en une petite vieille de pierre dont je pouvais mesurer la hauteur et compter les rides" [the immortal work of art so long desired, whom I found transformed, as was the church itself, into a little old woman in stone whose height I could measure and whose wrinkles I could count],[122] small in stature and worn with age like ordinary mortals.

Thus, a major inheritance incorporated into Proust's literary structure that may have been acquired from James's "Sentiment of Rationality" is the identification of similarity of feeling caused by two disparate sensations:

> [T]he sensation I got from a cloud yesterday and from the snow today. The white of the snow and that of the cloud differ in place, time and

> associates; they agree in the quality, and we may say in origin, being in all probability both produced by the activity of the same brain tract.[123]

This idea, so presciently suggested by James, will continue to be of interest to cognitive neuroscientists. The process of identification James uses here is the exact one Proust will reproduce as his narrator's defining moments of aesthetic discovery and as frame for his novel: the clink of a spoon brings to mind the clank of a hammer against railroad wheels, the quality of light bouncing off he dome of St. Mark's in Venice and roof tiles in Combray.

As Proust will after him, when his narrator attempts to deduce the hidden motives that influence the behavior of another being, James highlights the way optical tools such as "prisms, bowls of water, and strata of air as distorting media"[124] redirect the passage of light and necessitate investigation and interpretation in order to deduce the laws governing their action and affecting our view. Just because we observe something and choose to interpret it a certain way does not make it so. We may "see" it askew—as if bent through a refracting medium. "[N]ous croyons percevoir directement et [. . .] nous composons à l'aide d'idées qui ne se montrent pas mais sont agissantes" [we believe ourselves to be directly perceiving and . . . we compose with the aid of ideas that do not reveal themselves but are non the less efficacious].[125] And different eyes, Proust's narrator surmises, constructed differently than our own, might observe and explain otherwise.

Although we may think we understand the motives and feelings of another person, in fact, they remain truly obscure, a matter almost solely of interpretation. We may try to correct our notions about them but may end up merely substituting one error for another. Françoise is deceptive and opaque. She was first to teach the narrator just how impenetrable the character of another person can truly be. Although we may think we know someone, guess at their plans, acknowledge their faults, understand their motivations in our regard, we are only deceiving ourselves.

The primary characteristic of a system reliant only upon "essences," James concludes, is its limitation, because they are "a most miserable and inadequate substitute for the fullness of the truth."[126] In the end, philosopher, novelist, and narrator all arrive at the same understanding. Essential meaning is gathered from the individual's full experience of the "teeming and dramatic richness of the concrete world."[127] When lived, then remembered, expressed, and preserved in literature, it is externalized from "under our hat," where it lay as "le secret éternel de chacun" [for ever the secret of every individual];[128] it is dematerialized and thus freed from the constraints of passing time, no longer subject to decay or alteration. But such refinement and disclosure are impossible without the coherent personal vision to structure it and the talent in a chosen medium to express it.

In 1882, James revisited some of these issues in a sequel article,[129] and here James stresses the importance of freely flowing thought, more organized than "a maze of hapless wonder," yet ungirdled by conceptual inhibitions. Certain elements of this article, too, resonate in Proust's text,[130] and among them, notably, is a reference to a Beethoven string quartet. James describes the range of possible reactions to music, noting the response in human consciousness to the "irritant" of what is novel,[131] a continuing preoccupation for Proust's narrator—particularly evident in his reactions to Vinteuil's "red septuor." The anxiety of stimulation that accompanies what is new is eased, James notes, because "custom *per se* is a mental sedative" acting very much like the process of "habit" that eases the narrator's transition to new spaces in Balbec and Doncières:

> What is meant by coming "to feel at home" in a new place, or with new people? it is simply that, at first, when we take up our quarters in a new room, we do not know what draughts may blow in upon our back, what doors may open, what forms may enter, what interesting objects may be found in cupboards and corners. When after a few days we have learned the range of all these possibilities, the feeling of strangeness disappears. And so it does with people when we have got past the point of expecting an essentially new manifestation from their character.[132]

James touches here on what will become several very central elements of Proust's novel, the notion of movement or change over time, adaptation to new surroundings, or, even more central to Proust's plot, the appearance of hidden aspects of character that surface in people we think we know, and the way we may become bored once their characters have become familiar. James also notes the relationship of desire and "déception" or disappointment that is so significant a part of Proust's narrator's experience: "incompatibility of the future with their desires and active tendencies is, in fact, to most men a source of more fixed disquietude than uncertainty itself."[133] How to manage and control his emotional future is a constant worry: such a significant proportion of the narrator's thinking and activity is devoted to minute examination of desire anticipated, disappointed, and in a life relatively indolent and contemplative, so much effort is devoted to and expended in playing cat and mouse with the objects of his amorous obsessions.

Central to the development of his story is the tenor of his temperament: sensitive, anxious, needy. It impacts his actions and propels the plot, and as James had stated, "personal temperament will [. . .] make itself felt" in "[m]en's active impulses."[134]

Philosophically, James set great store by the creative potential of the personal and the benefits of novelty, and possibility for an individual life, according to John J. McDermott. James helped to alter perspective, to "restructure our very context of apprehension." And much like Proust's narrator, whose story is often driven by the unexpected twists and turns of his unique experience, James valued these new directions, "the complications and surprises which invariably attend even the most ordinary aspect of our lives."[135]

An omniscient narrator writing in the third person, even when using free indirect discourse to get as close as possible to his character's thoughts, lends less credibility to the complexities, errors, and ignorance that comprise real life. He can know too much. Real life meanders along random paths, heads in false directions. Its approach to resolution does not wrap itself neatly around a prefabricated or conceptualized plot but rather may be totally accidental, like stepping on an uneven paving stone.

If "risk lends a zest to worldly activity,"[136] Proust's narrator will make the leap of courage over the emotional chasm of self-doubt lying between him and his serial desires and put his genius and observations to work in the creation of an aesthetic philosophy and a very long novel. He must believe he can surmount his weak will and fulfill his vocational aspirations by telling his own "history." "But what is the use of being a genius," wrote James, "unless *with the same scientific evidence* as other men, one can reach more truth than they?"[137] But how can he seize and write anything permanent, if experience changes one's view of things, if social opinion, politics, and fashion metamorphosize?

Making a novel of the *process* of deploying an individual's unique talents (with as little distance as possible between witness and reporter), and using that individual's unchanging episodic memory as "rationalized" structural support, allows Proust's narrator to emerge from his bed-chrysalis as a writer, saying very much as James had: "Il semble que l'originalité d'un homme de génie ne soit que comme une fleur, une cime superposée au même moi que celui des gens de talent médiocres de sa génération"[138] [It seems that the originality of a man of genius is only like a flower, a crown superimposed over the same sort of self of the mediocre talents of his generation].

When rational explanation fails to reconcile the drive for essential truth with the facts, James turns to the religious experience of epiphany: "The peace of rationality may be sought through ecstasy when logic fails."[139] This last echo from "The Sentiment of Rationality" that we identify in *À la recherche du temps perdu* leads to a faith-based interpretation of the madeleine and other moments of resurgent memory. These "privileged moments" are instances of literary epiphany expressed in language resonant of James's *Varieties of Religious Experience*. They are occasions conveying the same great and tumultuous joy that James describes as associated with enhanced understanding and commitment to action. In *Pragmatism*, he characterized them as "turning-places, where we seem to ourselves to make ourselves and grow."[140] They are powerful moments of insight and catalysts for action that fall outside the realm of logic. The "madeleine"[141] is religious as an experience because it helps the narrator over his crisis of confidence, returning his emotional sanguinity, his ability to make sense of the world around him, and his willingness to produce. In this way it is very Jamesian in spirit.

THE MYSTICAL MADELEINE: PROUST'S AESTHETIC VARIATIONS ON A RELIGIOUS THEME BY JAMES

Although Proust was not a "religious" writer, an apologist for dogma, or enthusiast for piety any more than he was a practitioner, his narrator wonders aloud about Bergotte: "Mort à jamais? Qui peut le dire?" [Dead forever? Who can say?][142] Standing open in a bookstore window like the outspread wings of angels, Bergotte's books serve as "le symbole de sa résurrection" [the symbol of his resurrection].[143] Similarly, the narrator's novel re-creates and presents to a posterity of readers his first-person experience, monument to an experiencing mind and actor whose lightning-like insights originate in sensation and culminate in enduring form.

At a moment when institutional religion no longer enjoyed absolute revealed authority, it seemed to Proust's narrator that human beings were nonetheless hard-wired (psychologically or spiritually) to live according to rules of an order beyond the conscious quotidian: "sous l'empire de ces lois inconnues [. . .], ces lois dont tout travail profond de l'intelligence nous rapproche" [beneath the sway of those unknown laws . . . those laws to which every profound work of the intellect brings us nearer].[144] Even for "l'artiste athée" [an atheist artist][145] there is a feeling of faith and religious idiom associated with the obligations and privileges of his craft.

As absolutes and received certainties fractured under scrutiny in Proust's day, truth was subjected to social pressure, cultural contingency, and the persuasive ability of language. The narrator's search for essential meaning contrasts sharply with the multiplicity of potential interpretive truths and the continual pragmatic need to verify to which he is subject. He floats through a stream of significations and identities dependent upon who is looking: "un milieu dont la perméabilité varie à l'infini et nous reste inconnue" [a medium the permeability of which is infinitely variable and remains unknown to ourselves].[146] The locus of meaning would be personal, forged as it is "lived" or as woven into the fabric of a work of art.

Such intimate personal expression using language with numinous overtones is evident in a letter Proust wrote to Lionel Hauser on May 2, 1918, that specifically mentions William James and Pragmatism. It is one of two letters providing direct evidence that Proust knew of William James and was familiar with Pragmatism and the debate surrounding it. A functional philosophy centered on the individual thinker testing alternatives and revising interpretation in order to determine truth ultimately validated not by conventional assumptions but by experience alone, Pragmatism was integral to James's *Varieties of Religious Experience* and was incorporated into Proust's novel.

"Comme ta théosophie," wrote Proust to Hauser in the first of the letters, "le Pragmatisme est à la fois pratique et transcendant et va de William James à Eusapina Paladino."[147] Describing it this way, Proust suggests that Pragmatism might extend from a serious attempt to research religious experience and understand the metaphysical possibilities beyond material events to the flamboyant and perhaps fraudulent wild psychical yonder of séance. The subtext in his letter to Hauser reveals to today's reader something that would have been fairly common knowledge in Proust's time and milieu: while he was writing *À la recherche du temps perdu,* James was viewed as a cultural benchmark associated with a certain contemporary notion of religion. Eight years after James's death, Hauser's book of Theosophy brought James and his Pragmatism and spiritual writings to Proust's mind,[148] proving his awareness of them. In this letter, Proust affirms his own "sympathie" for a more genuine form of religious experience, one not founded on adherence to liturgical dogma, scientific principle, or the completely irrational, but a simpler affective spiritual sentiment—one closer to James's. (The second letter, alluding to Pragmatism, is discussed further on in connection with that element of James's philosophy.)

Related with the "feel" and using the language of some of the eyewitness reports of religious experience transcribed explicitly in William James's *Varieties of Religious Experience,* Proust's narrator undergoes a series of mystical-like experiences stimulated in the first instance by the "petite madeleine" (which has become an archetype for them in the popular imagination). Mysterious and metaphorical, such inspired revelations of insight and transport are eminently suited to develop and express the permeating affective connections the narrator would "discover" through episodic resurgent memory. These variations allude to a literary tradition of epiphany and serve to structure Proust's novel.

Pericles Lewis asserts that James's term "religious experience" accords with the language modernist novelists used to depict transcendent experience that, like the "petite madeleine," arose in the everyday but launched perception or insight far exceeding anything ordinary.[149] For James, religious experience rests on our heed to an "unseen order" that inspires us.[150]

In *Psychology: Briefer Course,* the 1892 textbook version of *The Principles of Psychology* published in French in 1909 as *Précis de Psychologie,* James introduced sensation in the first chapter. This laid the groundwork for his notion of mind as the "entire conscious states as they are concretely given to us,"[151] the streaming transitions and associative relations with physiological bases in the brain and nervous system. Correspondingly, Proust used sensation as the triggering basis for his narrator's tale of memory and personal conscious experience.

The weary and indifferent narrator, subject like the rest of us to a life of experience come and gone and attended to more or less, returns home on a cold day to his mother's offer of tea and madeleines. After at first rejecting her offer, he acquiesces with no expectations and without knowing the reason for his change of mind. Out of the murky penumbra of his forgotten past comes a sudden insightful memory, resurgent because of the simple taste sensation of the tea and cake. He attempts to decipher the meaning of what he feels, to understand what caused a pleasure so intense, so much like that of love that it makes him shudder and relieves him of all sense of being stifled by daily life, of being mortal.

He endeavors to unravel what he feels to be as overwhelming as any Christian religious convert, practicing shaman, Buddhist, spiritualist, or Hindu might find his own sort of mystical experience.[152] He wants to untangle the threads of meaning the sensation suggests, eventually to *use* it to create and make sense of his world: "Certes, ce qui palpite ainsi au fond de moi, ce doit être l'image, le souvenir visuel, qui, lié à cette saveur, tente de la suivre jusqu'à moi. Mais il se débat trop loin, trop confusément" [Undoubtedly what is thus palpitating in the depths of my being must be the image, the visual memory which, being linked to that taste, is trying to follow it into my conscious mind. But its struggles are too far off, to confused and chaotic].[153] The experience hangs there, opaque and stubborn. And then, just as suddenly as the "spontaneous" revival of a forgotten name[154] that James describes in *The Varieties of Religious Experience*—where voluntary effort comes to naught, but the mental processes once initiated seem automatically to retrieve it[155]—the meaning behind the feeling, the memory lurking beneath the taste, is revealed. "Et tout d'un coup le souvenir m'est apparu. Ce goût c'était celui du petit morceau de madeleine que le dimanche matin à Combray [. . .] quand j'allais dire bonjour dans sa chambre, ma tante Léonie m'offrait après l'avoir trempé dans son infusion de thé ou de tilleul" [And suddenly the memory revealed itself. The taste was that of the little piece of madeleine which on Sunday mornings at Combray . . . when I went to say good morning to her in her bedroom, my aunt Léonie used to give me, dipping it first in her own cup of tea or tisane].[156]

The mechanics and expression used here for a special *Sunday* experience strongly resemble those occurring in real involuntary conversion experiences described in detail by James. Taking place within a self, they are recounted in first-person voice as they felt at the time. These are "sudden and memorable"[157] occasions of grace to which the "spiritual energy" of certain individuals may have predisposed them.[158] James's knowledge of such experience was close and first-hand.

He had written to his wife, Alice, from Keene Valley in the Adirondack Mountains of New York on the morning of July 9, 1898, following a nighttime experience like no other. Surrounded by woods, the variegations of "streaming moonlight" intensifying his field of vision, a *sturm und drang* of feelings takes place in his chest: "it seemed as if the Gods of all the nature-mythologies were holding an indescribable meeting in my breast with the moral Gods of the inner life." Suddenly, he is overtaken by an unanticipated combination of sensory attentiveness and reminiscence, "so that memory and sensation all whirled inexplicably together," coming upon him "unplanned for and unexpected." Of the resulting discovery, he concludes, "I understand now what a poet is. He is a person who can feel the immense complexity of influences that I felt and make some partial tracks in them for verbal statement."[159]

James gropes to express the emotions the experience arouses. A poet would best be able to broach its full force in words, to disclose the layers of perception and shades of meaning, to clarify the core of truth and articulate the dynamic linking of sensation and memory. "It was one of the happiest lonesome nights of my existence [. . .] In point of fact, I can't find a single word for all that significance, & don't know what it was significant of, so there it remains, a mere boulder of *impression*."[160] Some remnant of the experience will be included, he wrote, in his upcoming Edinburgh lectures, basis for *The Varieties of Religious Experience*.

For James, the lonely night in the Adirondacks was the equivalent of a Proustian "moment privilégié." His flash encounter with insight a "triggering, originating, or catalyzing moment" inspiring him with an understanding of the affective underpinnings of religious belief.[161] In *The Varieties of Religious Experience*, genuine religion would be portrayed similarly as a matter of unanticipated (sometimes life-altering) feeling accessible to anyone and evident in personal testimony.[162]

A "boulder" of this sort marks a rift in personal experience, and its expression required the special handling of which only certain temperaments and talents are capable. James used the term "channel" or the word "track" to indicate the intrusion into an individual's life of this kind of life-altering impression. Proust used the term "sillon" for those lasting impressions that like James's demand full focus and effort to capture and explicate: "le petit sillon qu'une phrase musicale ou la vue d'une église a creusé en nous, nous trouvons trop difficile de tâcher de l'apercevoir" [To try to perceive the little furrow which the sight of a hawthorn bush or of a church has traced in us is a task that we find too difficult].[163]

Proust had already recorded moments of feeling comparable to James's; in previous writing and at the earliest stages of preparation of his novel, they had not yet come to fictional fruition: "Années caractérisées par un / rêve sur une couleur, une grappe, un coin du bois, d'autre part / par un désir. Personnes sur / le nom et le pays de qui on / se forge des rêves, comme un / livre non lu"[164] [Years characterized by a dream about a color, a cluster of grapes, a secluded spot in the woods, or else by a desire. People whose names or whose country we forge dreams about, like a book not read]. These are utterly unlike the arid "snapshots" of intellect that do not inspire artistic "enthousiasme" [enthusiasm] or justify literary immortality.[165]

While James would like to repeat the Adirondack experience for the pure pleasure and insight of it, he doubts that its unique and spontaneous aspects can be reproduced deliberately. Proust's narrator repeatedly tastes the tea and cake in an effort to understand its impact. But, subject to sensory desensitization, his efforts are less and less informative.

Proust appears to use the real-world experiences James describes as a framework for developing literary truth and enabling literary invention. Like James, Proust's narrator understands that the experience demands creative work and turns inward:

> Je pose ma tasse et me tourne vers mon esprit. C'est à lui de trouver la vérité. Mais comment? Grave incertitude, toutes les fois que l'esprit se sent dépassé par lui-même; quand lui, le chercheur, est tout ensemble le pays obscur où il doit chercher et où tout son bagage ne lui sera de rien. Chercher? pas seulement: créer. Il est en face de quelque chose qui n'est pas encore et que seul il peut réaliser, puis faire entrer dans sa lumière.[166]
>
> [I put down the cup and examine my own mind. It alone can discover the truth. But how? What an abyss of uncertainty, whenever the mind feels overtaken by itself; when it, the seeker, is at the same time the dark region through which it must go seeking and where all this equipment will avail it of nothing. Seek? More than that: create. It is face to face with something which does not yet exist, which it alone can make actual, which it alone can bring into the light of day.[167]]

James uses Dr. Starbuck's terms to describe the "self-surrender" of involuntary religious conversion, characteristics reprised in Proust's description of his narrator's moments of revelation. They arrive unexpectedly when the mind is on other things or on nothing at all. Something so simple as walking into a church and seeing a dog go by, or reading a book in one's bedroom, and suddenly there occurs "a new inward apprehension."[168] "I felt supremely happy."[169] A shudder and "an explosion of the most ardent joy," "the sense of being in the light as if bindings had been removed from one's eyes."[170] "It all happened in my interior mind."[171]

Temperaments liable to emotional intensity are more prone to religious experience. First-person accounts by individuals subject to "exalted emotional sensibility" or "pathological" abnormal visions and voices would furnish James information about the nature of mystical experience. "Symptoms of nervous instability,"[172] along with superior intellect (attributes of Proust's narrator, too) characterize George Fox, a founder of the Quaker sect whose religious conversion experience included (noteworthy to a reader of Proust) testimony of inspiration by the view of the "three steeple-house spires" of Lichfield.[173]

"There are moments of sentimental and mystical experience [. . .] that carry an enormous sense of inner authority and illumination with them when they come."[174] These infrequent and unsolicited moments—"unreasoned," "immediate," and assured[175]—can carry for an individual the intense import of a divine connection[176] or of a connection with the "core" or inner self. The transformations and conversions that result from irruptions from the subliminal into conscious awareness have gestated until ripe for intrusion. Proust had noted what might be deemed such subconscious incubation in his notebooks: "Escalier, Baldwinn Potocka, / moments où l'on voit la réalité / en vrai avec enthousiasme, dépouillé de l'habitude,/ nouveauté, ivresse, mé / moire. . . . vérité / mystérieuse seule douce / à mes yeux blessés"[177] [Stairway, Baldwinn Potocka / moments when one sees reality / in truth with enthusiasm, stripped of habit / novelty, intoxication, me/mory. . . . truth / mysterious solely sweet / to my stricken eyes].

During one of these moments, an individual may become aware of a particular sensation or thought that leads in him a particular "reaction."[178] Although the experience is psychological in nature, it has a nearly physical basis: "We may now lay it down as certain that in the distinctly religious sphere of experience, many persons [. . .] possess the objects of their belief, not in the form of mere conceptions which their intellect accepts as true, but rather in the form of quasi-sensible realities directly apprehended."[179]

David Brainerd was walking idly in a densely wooded area. After "exhaustion of the anxious emotion hitherto habitual," he says, "unspeakable glory seemed to open the apprehension of my soul." A privileged moment of inner illumination or "regeneration"[180] brought with it a "state of inward joy, peace, and astonishing." Everything looked different.[181]

> Certes / ces moments-là sont rares. / Mais ils dominent toute la / vie. Ajouter pour dire qu' / il faut qu'il y ait presque / hallucination [(donc) apporté par le dehors] car / pour [reconstruire la foi] bien revoir, il faut / croire et pas seulement / imaginer.. [*sic*].[182]
>
> [Certainly / those moments are rare /. But they dominate all of / life. Add to say / that it is necessary almost to have an / hallucination [(therefore) provided by the outside] because / [to reconstruct faith] to see again well, it is necessary / to believe and not only / to imagine.. (*sic*).]

The two ideas bracketed here were crossed out by Proust and emphasize the similarities between Proust and James. Intense emotional experience bordering perhaps on hallucination, inspired by something from outside the individual, and the importance of belief in reconstructing faith suggest that Proust was considering something along the lines of James's terms and conceptions. The construction of faith becomes artistic creation; the source of inspiration metamorphosizes from something external and perhaps divine into a trigger for memory that allows Proust's narrator to create and advance his plot. The combination of an unimportant impression, such as his auto's horn honking to overtake another car, with an earlier similar one creates an atemporal depth or "épaisseur" of experience, basic and general, that carries the sort of joy of divine order that converts experience: ordinary, random daily events acquire a universal quality and new meaning in an individual life.

For Henry Alline, an experience occurred on March 26, 1775, so powerful "that it seemed as if God was praying in, with, and for me" and "redeeming love broke into my soul [. . .] with such power that my whole soul seemed to be melted down with love."[183] Replete with a similar sense of joyful election, Proust's narrator says: "de la même façon qu'opère l'amour, en me remplissant d'une essence précieuse: ou plutôt cette essence n'était pas en moi, elle était moi" [having had the effect that love has, of filling me with a precious essence; or rather this essence was not in me it *was* me].[184]

The intrusions of buried memory into ordinary consciousness, perhaps mystical in nature or caused by nervous activity, are worthy of study,[185] notes James. Beyond our usual awareness (the range where normal daily attention moves from one item of interest to the next) lies the subliminal area of personal and private consciousness. "Our whole past store of memories floats beyond this margin, ready at a touch to come in."[186] This "touch" is a galvanizing sensation in the present that stimulates a resurgent memory of something from our past no longer in our field of awareness but suddenly brought back to life.

When this parallax occurs, as Proust demonstrates repeatedly in the life of his narrator, what James calls "regeneration" can ensue: "The personality is changed, the man is born anew" with a new sense of "assurance and peace." An unwonted ray of awareness or subconscious memory penetrates the grind and cacophony of daily life, sparked by something particular, something similar, psychological or divine.[187] The layers of experience mediating between the past moment and the present are peeled away. The moments are "delicious." "Intellect and senses swoon away in these highest states of ecstasy;"[188] exhilaration results; mortality is irrelevant, wrote James, quoting President Finney: "I had no fear of death."[189] "The deadness with which custom invests the familiar vanishes, and existence as a whole appears transfigured. The state of a mind thus awakened from torpor."[190] A man is called to new feats.[191]

For Proust's narrator, too, this is a moment to savor beyond the taste of cake: "un plaisir délicieux" [an exquisite pleasure][192] and one that once multiplied will empower the narrator to write his book. Quasi-mystical experiences propel the narrator into his vocation as participant, witness, and recorder of his own experience. They integrate disparate moments of the narrator's existence into a coherent story, giving his life meaning and purpose much as a religious quest or conversion might do. Mystical experience and episodes of involuntary memory are both experienced only first-hand and directly; they involve illumination and understanding, truths that are of singular, private, and subjective importance, involving realizations that cannot be derived by logic, like science, or sought by intellectual effort; they arrive unexpectedly, rapidly, are of brief duration, are nonverbal awakenings that demand the individual's immediate and full attention and can be analyzed subsequently at leisure. The experience that the narrator has when he tastes a madeleine resembles the moments of religious conversion and mystical experience cited by James in *The Varieties of Religious Experience* in structure and in terms of the broadened awareness it delivers, the mechanism it provides for freeing the narrator from the ennui and frustrations of an abortive career, allowing him to develop his creative talents the way a more saintly individual might found a church or sect or withdraw from secular life to enter a sphere of existence based entirely upon religion, in a convent or monastery. Here, however, it does not function in a specifically religious way because Proust adapts it to the specific secular devotional activity of his narrator's quest. Proust did not simply copy James's descriptions per se, but rather, using similar language, delved into the psychic states that preceded and surrounded such experience, bending and subordinating them to the fictive exigencies of his own project, as his hero develops into an artist. In *The Varieties of Religious Experience* James has laid the groundwork for Proust's search and his plot. As for James's religious individual, the potent inspiration Proust's narrator receives can only be recorded and relayed in the first-person singular; they have cash-value that is nonnegotiable.

Regardless of whether its role in Proust's fiction should be sourced to literary tradition or to theory and experimentation covered in journals of philosophy and the popular press during the first decade of the twentieth century, James held a major place in the lineage of the passel of psychologists and philosophers who examined and popularized "affective memory." And discussion of the term in the press seemed to end around 1910, the year William James died.

That year, in his article entitled "A Suggestion about Mysticism,"[193] James reported another of his own aberrant experiences. His purpose was to investigate the pathological aspects of sudden "mystical intuition" and to examine further the unexpected intervention into normal conscious awareness of the subliminal or subconscious halo surrounding it. The description echoes what he had written in *Varieties* and is stunningly similar to Proust's narrator's description of his privileged moments, particularly that triggered by the madeleine.

A broadening James likens to the widening beach at low tide reveals "transmarginal" awareness generally ignored.[194] It enhances ordinary sensational experience by infusing it with emotion and a throng of swarming memories, galvanizing it with the psychic vigor typical of what James calls the "mystical paroxysm": the present sensational moment is steeped in "a mass of subconscious memories, conceptions, emotional feelings, and perceptions of relation"[195] that, suddenly perceptible, amplify and elucidate it, much the way "tout Combray" surges out of the taste of tea and madeleine in a Parisian apartment on a cold afternoon.

While in conversation himself, James reports that he was "all at once reminded of a past experience; and this reminiscence [. . .] developed into something further that belonged with it, this in turn into something further still, and so on." His perception was that "knowledge of past [. . .] reality was enlarging pulse by pulse"[196] and mushrooming to intervene into the present, filling it with "distant realities that incomprehensibly belonged to my own life."[197] Past first-person experience is felt again as it did when it was present experience, as it would for Proust's narrator.

Easily comparable is the narrator's discovery of "le livre intérieur" in *Le Temps retrouvé*, the source of his creativity. This "book" lies beyond logic and normal consciousness, its text below ordinary surface discernment, beneath the tide that hides the private pebbles, rocks, and shells of experience. Bringing it to the surface is an ultimate act of individual imaginative invention:

> Quant au livre intérieur des signes inconnus (de signes en relief, semblait-il, que mon attention, explorant mon inconscient, allait chercher, heurtait, contournait, comme un plongeur qui sonde), pour la lecture desquels personne ne pouvait m'aider d'aucune règle, cette lecture consistait en un acte de création où nul ne peut nous suppléer ni même collaborer avec nous.[198]
>
> [As for the inner book of unknown symbols (symbols carved in relief they might have been, which my attention, as it explored my unconscious, groped for and stumbled against and followed the contours of, like a diver exploring the ocean-bed), if I tried to read them no one could help me with any rules, for to read them was an act of creation in which no one can do our work for us or even collaborate with us.[199]]

PROUST PRAGMATISTE, PROUST PLURALISTE, PROUST EMPIRISTE RADICAL

"Pragmatism is willing to take anything, to follow either logic or the senses, and to count the humblest and most personal experiences. She will count mystical experiences if they have practical consequences."[200] Proust's narrator accumulates experience as he searches for a way to transcribe and transmit its meaning. The book recounting his experiences has the same functional duality that William James ascribed to paint: it is pigment, an objective thing in a putative "real world" item on the wall, and at the same time, paradoxically, it is a medium for conveying a personal vision[201]—like the little mental paint tubes out of which bloom sparkling scenes of Proust's narrator's past.[202]

In *Pragmatism* and in *The Essays in Radical Empiricism*, William James constituted a new way of considering experience that would result in a new way of making art in a new century. His message helped to advance the bar of cultural evolution, and Marcel Proust was beneficiary and practitioner of the new theories. James's thinking, coming at the end of the nineteenth century, says John J. McDermott, "changed everything." Life, according to James, is lived in the "trenches"; we are continuously moving forward through this corridor of experience and impression.[203]

In this respect, James's classic, *The Principles of Psychology*, published in 1890 and so widely read during his lifetime—and since—is "of a piece" with his more doctrinal works.[204] As a philosophical stance, radical empiricism pervaded James's writings continuously—from his early response to Spencer in "On Some Omissions of Introspective Psychology" published in 1884—to the end of his life. Announced as a philosophical "attitude" in *The Will to Believe* in 1897, radical empiricism comes into its own full-blown in eight essays published as journal articles in 1904 and 1905. These were collected by Ralph Barton Perry and appeared posthumously in 1912 in the single volume entitled *Essays in Radical Empiricism*. Other writings from the last half of James's last decade, including *Pragmatism* (1907), *The Meaning of Truth*, and *A Pluralistic Universe* (1909), show its imprint as well. *Essays in Radical Empiricism* did not generate the flurry of critical response in Europe that greeted James's *Pragmatism*. Perhaps this was due to James's demise in 1910 before publication of the collected volume, so the essays did not enjoy the added impact of appearing together in a group, or, as McDermott suggests, because of their more technical nature and less florid prose. Whatever the reason, as an ensemble, *Essays in Radical Empiricism* was not translated into French until 2005.[205]

Finding the prevailing philosophies of his day (Idealism, Associationism, Rationalism) to be subject to significant shortcomings in their attempts to interpret human experience, James contrived a theory all his own to contend with the affective richness and continuity of experience and with feelings of relation so often disregarded in formal philosophies. These were considerations, he wrote, that had been omitted by Spencer. In our use of language, the emphasis we place on "names" (which obviate all not named) and on conceptual logic designates specifics of experience at the cost of all the "delicate idiosyncracies"[206] that a radical empiricist could not ignore.

By depicting consciousness as a sensible stream in the *Principles of Psychology*, James is already tending away from a mind-body or thought-thing dualism in favor of something very much like the notion of "pure experience" as it will appear in *Essays in Radical Empiricism*. In his 1895 article "The Knowing of Things Together," we find an early mention of the "identity of object and mental content" that undermines any notion of consciousness as an entity, leading to James's later functional explanation of the experiential process. And the preface to *The Will to Believe* (1897), though not so much the content of the book, contains James's statement declaring his basic philosophical approach to be that of radical empiricism and pluralism.

James's eight essays on radical empiricism were written in only eight months (between July 1904 and February 1905), but it is clear that his thinking on the subject had long percolated. In radical empiricism, James fully embraces the notion of "felt relations" and the importance of transitions and conjunctions in our thought processes. Integrated and additive, radical empiricism highlights the "conjunctive relation of continuous transition." Events and understanding are subject to transition and time; thoughts perform the task of "knowing" or "reporting."

In the condensed form in which James advanced the heart of his argument, entitled "La Notion de Conscience" and presented as a lecture delivered in French in Rome in 1905 and published in the *Archives de Psychologie*, he refutes the existence of "consciousness" as traditionally understood—one half of the Cartesian "dualisme fondamental"[207] comprising subject and object or thought and thing, mental awareness and material object. In its place, "pure experience" connects thought with its objects—inner life with outer world—in a purely functional process that typifies our normal feelings of relation to the concrete pluralistic world around us: "Les attributions sujet et objet, représenté et représentatif, chose et pensée, signifient donc une distinction pratique qui est de la dernière importance, mais qui est d'ordre *fonctionnel* seulement, et nullement ontologique comme le dualisme classique se la représente"[208] [The attributes "subject" and "object," "represented" and "representative," "thing" and "thought," mean, then, a practical destinction of the utmost importance, but a distinction which is of a *functional* order only, and not at all ontological as understood by classical dualism[209]]. "La réalité est l'aperception même"[210] [Reality is apperception itself[211]]—reality is our conscious perception of it, our processing of an object (physical, emotional, or purely mental in the case of memory or imagination, fantasy, dream)—in terms of our past experience.

Cognition, the interpretive relation between "knower" and "known," is, then, a matter of substantiating association through "continuous transition" over time, and the transitions are just as significant as what they connect: "rapports qui sont eux-mêmes des parties essentielles de la trame des expériences"[212] [connections which themselves are essential parts of the fabric of experience].

Attributes or relations we assign to the object are *felt*, having "des rapports à notre sensibilité émotive propre."[213] "[W]e think to be speaking objectively [of a 'frightful storm, a hateful man, a mean action' or 'an arduous road, a sullen sky, a superb sunset'], although in a strict sense these terms express only relations to our own emotive sensibility."[214]

James uses the term *"pure experiences"* to designate the "primary reality" of which we are all aware.[215] These "succeed one another; they enter into infinitely varied relations," and the associated relations are also experienced in the manner of a "web" of "intersection[s]" in which one experience can have a function in more than one "field" simultaneously. The awareness and perception taking place inside our bodies meets the rooms we inhabit at this point of "intersection"—our experience takes place when our mind meets the physical environment in which we live.[216] "Knowledge of sensible realities thus comes to life inside the tissue of experience,"[217] and our memory will store it (Combray experienced live and remembered, for example). In memory, a room no longer must obey the necessary laws of the material world in which we found it; it is part of a field of associates subject to "emotive fancies" or fields of immaterial "psychic" experiences unrelated to it.[218] This aspect of "pure experience"—freed from time and from the contingencies of the tangled, substantive, everyday world that originally surrounded it—will enable Proust's narrator to elucidate his impressions, see his past clearly, and reweave it into the web of his book.

James described radical empiricism as "a philosophy of plural facts"[219] that suffuse one into the next and change over time.[220] Experience extends to "more" by accretion at its margins. Knowledge is not an essential element of things; rather, "[l]a connaissance des choses leur survient"[221] ["knowledge of things *supervenes*"[222]] actively and in an *additive* way by a series of intermediate steps:[223] "une suite d'expériences intermédiaires."[224]

In James's radical empiricism, "pure experience" comprises perceptual encounter that James terms "knowledge-of-acquaintance" as well as our more conceptual and generalizing "knowledge-about" in which past experiences, upon reflection, are viewed afresh in a new context, connected by these tracts of transitional felt experience.

> What is true of the here and the there, is also true of the now and the then. I know of the thing which is present and perceived, but I know also of the thing which yesterday was but is no more, and which I only remember. Both can determine my present conduct, both are parts of reality of which I keep account. . . . The things in the room here which I survey, and those in my long-vanished boyhood, influence and decide me alike, with a reality which my experience of them directly feels.[225]

However, distortions can occur. Memory can play tricks, and the imagination, trying to fill in the blanks, can make a leap of connection wholly in error, thus begging for substantiation in the "cash-value" of the actual. This is where we find Proust at play and his narrator in pursuit of the truth of his experiences.

Near the end of his life, on June 17, 1910, James wrote to Henry Adams that in terms of progress in culture and history, the "rill" that really makes a difference is not quantitative, responding to the amount of energy required for a given effect, but the power of ideas that affect the way the "reservoir" of human effort drains. Men can write, and they can evaluate works of art, and through their thought and effort they cause the events of history to happen. "Human cerebration is the most important rill we know of, and both the 'capacity' and the 'intensity' factor thereof may be treated as infinitesimal."[226]

The artist's impression, Proust's "sillon," may be a tiny "rill," but it acts as signally as James's "boulder." It is a channel for human energy to influence culture.

For Proust's narrator, the artist's impression was an individual glimpse of necessary truth[227] with the pragmatic power to change everything about how we "see" the reality around us. The works by "le nouvel écrivain"[228] [new writer] are at first incomprehensible; they advance culture by upending literary habituation and artistic expectation,[229] expanding the reader's comprehension. Each new artist is a cultural oculist who adjusts our view:

> Et voici que le monde (qui n'a pas été créé une fois, mais aussi souvent qu'un artiste original est survenu) nous apparaît entièrement différent de l'ancien, mais parfaitement clair. [. . .] Tel est l'univers nouveau et périssable qui vient d'être créé. Il durera jusqu'à la prochaine catastrophe géologique que déchaîneront un nouveau peintre ou un nouvel écrivain originaux.[230]

> [And, lo and behold, the world around us (which was not created once and for all, but is created afresh as often as an original artist is born) appears to us entirely different from the old world, but perfectly clear. [. . .] Such is the new and perishable universe which has just been created. It will last until the next geological catastrophe is precipitated by a new painter or writer of original talent.[231]]

In *A Pluralistic Universe*, James cites Fechner's use of the word "threshold," that point in perceptual psychology when we become aware of change. A creative work can "result in a 'change of horizons' through [. . .] raising newly articulated experiences to the level of consciousness."[232]

In response to the Vinteuil sonata, Proust's narrator adopts a Jamesian pragmatic perspective and suggests that works themselves create history, preparing and developing their own posterity by exposing the public to new ways of looking or listening.[233] The Vinteuil sonata, with its special "petite phrase"—so vital to the courtship of Odette and Swann—was difficult to absorb upon first hearing: "Mais souvent on n'entend rien, si c'est une musique un peu compliquée qu'on écoute pour la première fois" [But often one hears nothing when one listens for the first time to a piece of music that is at all complicated].[234] Like any first impression, his was partial, obscured by unfamiliarity and the seeming randomness characteristic of new experience: "je ne la possédais jamais tout entière: elle ressemblait à la vie" [I never possessed it in its entirety: it was like life itself].[235] No musical memory existed to enhance comprehension, to clarify the structure of the piece. Successive hearings reveal that what he appreciated at first were the parts most resembling sounds with which he was already familiar. But the sections at first least accessible were the most beautiful; his ear had to adapt, a type of memory had to build, in order to value them, just as the revolutionary work of an author or philosopher can seed the public's mind for its eventual acceptance.

> Ce temps du reste qu'il faut à un individu [. . .] pour pénétrer une œuvre un peu profonde, n'est que le raccourci et comme le symbole des années, des siècles parfois, qui s'écoulent avant que le public puisse aimer un chef-d'œuvre vraiment nouveau. [. . .] C'est son œuvre elle-même qui en fécondant les rares esprits capables de le comprendre, les fera croître et multiplier.[236]
>
> [The time, moreover, that a person requires [. . .] to penetrate a work of any depth is merely an epitome, a symbol, one might say, of the years, the centuries even that must elapse before the public can begin to cherish a masterpiece that is really new. [. . .] It is his work itself that, by fertilising the rare minds capable of understanding it, will make them increase and multiply.[237]]

"Je me trouvais en pays inconnu," thinks the narrator once again at the opening bars of the Vinteuil septuor he hears at the Verdurins' reception.[238] Soon recognizing elements of the petite phrase from the sonata, now refitted in new musical raiment, he realizes he is hearing another work by Vinteuil for which the earlier sonata had prepared him.

But some new works, those that become classics—and some new philosophies—have a revolutionary effect. Vinteuil's "septuor rouge" [the red septet] cuts a special space in cultural evolution, and prepares—with durable freshness—its own unique channel of long-term appreciation that will *not* become homogenized into the general culture: "La révolution que leur apparition a accomplie ne voit pas ses résultats s'assimiler anonymement aux époques suivantes; elle se déchaine, elle éclate à nouveau, et seulement quand on rejoue les oeuvres du novateur à perpétuité" [The revolution that their apparition has effected does not see its results merge unacknowledged in the work of subsequent generations; it is unleashed, it explodes anew, when, and only when, the works of the once-for-all-times innovator are performed again].[239]

Proust's letter to Jacques Boulenger (November 29, 1921) refers to an appreciative comment by critic Benjamin Crémieux about Proust's own contribution to the French novel. Co-winner of the 1919 Prix Goncourt, he had done something truly new: "mon livre qui 'renouvelait l'évolution du roman'" [my book which renewed the evolution of the novel].[240]

Despite his affectionate friendships with European philosophical colleagues, the reception of James's *Pragmatism* was distorted by misconception in the French philosophical community.[241] James's work, in that moment of immense creative innovation, found greater acceptance in literary circles than among philosophers and had a great impact on European stream of consciousness writers like James Joyce and Virginia Woolf, even painters like Picasso. Artists were willing to experiment in their exploration of human experience and focused on the inner workings of individual consciousness, the mechanics of which had been laid out by James. He advanced the culture to new ways of producing and understanding art, challenging the public mind-set in ways that continue to influence our thinking profoundly.

With the lightest of touches, our emotional and physical environments "wrap" us in a full-body experience; feeling is fleeting and the past intermittently bears upon the present. The links between sensational experience and perception or the ideas and memories it awakens are undetectable, wrote James, asking: "Mais qui peut faire la part, dans la table concrètement aperçue, de ce qui est sensation et ce qui est idée? [. . .] Les coutures et les joints sont imperceptibles" [But who, in the concretely apperceived table, can say what part is sensation and what part is idea? . . . The seams and joinings are imperceptible].[242] How does one disentangle the ambiguity of objective and subjective in the beauty of a statue or sonata? Does the asthetic element reside in the object we experience or in our pleasure experiencing it?[243] Vinteuil's "transposition, dans l'ordre sonore, de la profondeur" [transposition of profundity into terms of sound] depicts forces other than rational and intellectual at work].[244]

"[L]e monde physique objectif et le monde intérieur et personnel de chacun de nous se rencontrent et se fusionnent comme des lignes se fusionnent à leur intersection" [In this full, concrete, and undivided experience, such as it lies before us, as a given, the objective physical world and the personal inner world of each one of us meet and merge as lines merge at their intersection].[245] This is where imagination and memory encounter napkin or cobblestones for Proust's narrator. The secret interior world of Vinteuil enclosed in his music is not analyzed objectively as a thing in itself—notes on a page—but is exposed as experienced, as a living part of the narrator's own life, and as recounted it is infused with the listener's thoughts and observations, his memories of the composer's daughter and her illicit lover.

An answering structure, perhaps, for a world without absolute fixity and certainty lies in concretizing the dynamic vague of an impression or externalizing the surprise connection of an episodic memory capturing time and joyfully linking present and past. When the past has been resuscitated by something linking it to the present, the intermediary stages of experience may well have been "shed." "Union in consciousness must be *made* by something, [. . .] must be brought about [. . .]. *Discriminative knowing-together, in short, involves higher processes of reminiscence*"[246] [italics in original]. For philosopher, poet, or lover, James had written, ordinary external reality gives way to an inner life where insight and illumination reveal what he called "a new centre" and "new perspective," meaning beyond the relentless empiracy of ordinary time and the responsibilities of the everyday.[247]

Experience becomes memory and part of the history of each auditor in James's lecture hall. Knowledge happens and develops. In the effort to expose and understand, Proust's narrator must delve inside his experiencing Self; he must look back to unravel and explore the missing intermediate steps of his story, the learning curve and psychological material of his novel. James describes "the persistent identity [. . .] of the experience continuum."[248] Reliving a "sensible experience" joins it to a later time, highlights the interval, and emphasizes the fictional aspects of the retelling without making of it a totally different experience.[249]

Though a work of art is not the fruit of dry intellectual analysis, nor simply the cinematic display of recorded biography, the artist may not be able to build a novel from epiphanies alone:

> Je sentais pourtant que ces vérités que l'intelligence dégage directement de la réalité ne sont pas à dédaigner entièrement, car elles pourraient enchâsser d'une matière moins pure mais encore pénétrée d'esprit, ces impressions que nous apporte hors du temps l'essence commune aux sensations du passé et du présent, mais qui, plus précieuses, sont aussi trop rares pour que l'oeuvre d'art puisse être composée seulement avec elles.[250]
>
> [I felt, however, that these truths which the intellect educes directly from reality were not altogether to be despised, for they might be able to enshrine within a matter less pure indeed but still imbued with mind those impressions which are conveyed to us outside time by the essences that are common to the sensations of the past and of the present, but which, just because they are more precious, are also too rare for a work of art to be constructed exclusively from them.[251]]

There is room in the artist's representation of experience for keenly observed individual surface tics, accents, and actions that convey the general. In portraying "verité psychologique"[252] [psychological truth] in a novel, sensitive observation and imagination are fungible, and experience may be as useful as the fantasy of imagination.

Without the mature ability to make connections among disparate factors in a complex environment, the naïve young narrator trips and stumbles, guesses and imagines with only imperfect information, suffering misperception and jealousy, as James had described: "Ignorance breeds mistake, curiosity, misfortune, pain, for me; I suffer those consequences."[253] This does not mean, however, that there are no connections to be made, no rationalizing order to be considered. "What pluralists say is that a universe really connected loosely, after the pattern of our daily experience, is possible," wrote James.[254] This is a basic tenet of Proust's story: certain elements of his narrator's experience will turn out to be conjoined: Méséglise and Guermantes are after all simply two alternatives directions on a connected route; Gilberte Swann is Mlle. de Forcheville who becomes the wife of Saint-Loup, their daughter the genetic tie between walking paths and social strata; Mme. Verdurin becomes the Princesse de Guermantes, allying the bourgeois petit clan to the aristocracy's highest reaches. The novel fills the time and topography between childhood and adulthood with events that find connection geographically and within the experience of the narrator; connections at first not evident become so.

Throughout Proust's novel are sprinkled generalizations representing the observations and lessons garnered from the narrator's seemingly random experiences that occur ostensibly without pattern. There is an unspoken tension between originally lived experience "that distributed and strung-along and flowing sort of reality which we finite beings swim in," which James described,[255] and a formulation of it that allows the narrator to understand it.

A unique human talent raising us above the "brutes" is our power to make the connections and envision a rationalizing format for our activity and our understanding.[256] "But all these abstract concepts are but as flowers gathered, they are only moments dipped out from the stream of time, snap-shots taken, as by a kinetoscopic camera, at a life that in its original coming is continuous."[257]

Proust's narrator, searching for the essence of experience, finds it to be elusive. Without maturity developed over time (a suggestion for plot), how can the narrator process and verify the meaning of what he encounters? How can he identify just what it is that accounts for "l'essence particulière à François le champi"[258] or "l'essence des beaux jours,"[259] the essence of asparagus,[260] "l'essence d'une liaison particulière,"[261] "l'essence de la petite phrase,"[262] "l'essence du genie de Giotto,"[263] "l'essence de personnalités,"[264] "l'essence de la ville,"[265] "l'essence unique" des jeunes filles en fleurs,[266] "l'essence sublime de Phèdre par la Berma,"[267] "l'essence de la vie inconnue,"[268] "l'essence de la supériorité militaire,"[269] "l'essence de l'amour,"[270] "l'essence unique d'Isabelle d'Este"[271] [the particular essence of *François le champi*, the essence of beautiful days, of asparagus, of a particular linkage or affair, of the little musical phrase, of Giotto's genius, of personalities, of a city, of the little band of budding young girls, the sublime essence of Phèdre played by La

Berma, of life unknown, of military supremacy, of Isabella d'Este]? To cite such examples is to skim the surface of the narrator's efforts to capture meaning—just as he tried to capture love.

James felt philosophically liberated from the Platonic ideal of derived eternal laws akin to truths unearthed through scientific discovery and intellectual distillation; he was free to gambol in the turbid waters of the real, just as Proust's hero advances through his search through the murky particulars of an individual albeit fictional "life."

Once absolutes of church and monarchy, philosophy and science are loosened from traditional bounds, permanence gives way to moment; uncertainty and change are the new constants in philosophy and in culture. Truth is no longer an abstraction of man's conception bearing little relation to experienceable reality. Truth as an idea about something must be substantiated. It has become a relationship between an object and the idea ("opinion, belief, statement, or what not"[272]) one holds about it. Truth for James is not eternal but instead demonstrates "our subjective relation to realities."[273] Truth is particular and governs action.

James was supremely modern in viewing truth as relative ("truth may vary with the standpoint of the viewer"); he was an early believer in randomness ("the indeterminism of certain futures"), which was the direction physicists were heading, and, as Proust's narrator eventually recognizes, we are free agents who can effect certain outcomes by virtue of belief, will, or effort.[274] Proust's narrator shares these views: different individual viewers would thus hold different opinions:

> Si la réalité était cette espèce de déchet de l'expérience à peu près identique pour chacun, parce que quand nous disons: un mauvais temps, une guerre, une station de voitures, un restaurant éclairé, un jardin en fleurs, tout le monde sait ce que nous voulons dire; si la réalité était cela, sans doute une sorte de film cinématographique de ces choses suffirait et le "style," la "littérature" qui s'écarterait de leurs simples données seraient un hors d'œuvre artificiel. Mais était-ce bien cela, la réalité?[275]
>
> [If reality were indeed a sort of waste product of experience, more or less identical for each one of us, since when we speak of bad weather, a war, a taxi rank, a brightly lit restaurant, a garden full of flowers, everybody knows what we mean, if reality were no more than this, no doubt a sort of cinematograph film of these things would be sufficient and the "style," the "literature" that departed from the simple data that they provide would be superfluous and artificial. But was it true that reality was no more than this?[276]]

Not only are different views of truth evident to different observers, different views of truth occur to a single observer over the course of time. The palimpsest of Self is not a pathological multiple personality but a philosophical posture for James. With its unintentional feelings and recurrent memories, its palimpsest endlessly rewritten, such a fractured Self is an accurate portrayal of character in Proust's novel. The intermittence of emotion, separating a feeling from normal time flow, magnifies its impact. Nothing is "static."[277] Time's force is visible in the abrupt recognition of what had been gradual change. At the Princesse de Guermantes's matinée when Proust's narrator observes the guests and sees Time's passage visibly in their barely recognizable faces, haircolor, gait and demeanor, and in a new social dynamic that James, too, had witnessed as cultural shift:

> Those of us who are sexagenarians have witnessed in our own persons one of those gradual mutations of intellectual climate, due to innumerable influences, that make the thought of a past generation seem as foreign to its successor as if it were the expression of a different race of men.[278]

James uses the image of a dried, shrunken head created by Dyak natives in Borneo to illustrate, in the unrelated danglings of "feathers, leaves, string, beads"[279] that adorn such a skull, the tangle of multiple experiences each individual accumulates. The wizened heads at Proust's Bal de Têtes each have the danglings of their own past personal histories extending behind them, like the brightly glowing debris trailing a comet in James's example, or buttressing them at the present moment on stilts—a pinnacle of past experience—in Proust's.

For James, the blending of past into present is that moment when "our self is riven and its narrow interests fly."[280] Not merely an additive function, like a series of snapshots, nor a patchwork, the mind blends "our sights plus our sounds plus our pains," and once gone from the immediate field of view they continue to mingle elements of our past in mental reliquaries, making connections with our present, creating new patterns and discoveries.[281] This is the adapting, associating neural circuitry of the brain at work.

In an address before the American Psychological Association at Princeton in December 1894, James drew his listeners' attention to experience in the first-person singular, an aggregate in the conscious perception of a single viewer: what we feel, "be it bird or constellation, it is nothing but our vision, nothing but an effect on our sensorium when a lot of things act on it together. It is not realized by any organ or any star, or experienced apart from the consciousness of the onlooker."[282] That consciousness has a history.

Understanding—or truth—for Proust's narrator is generated in dynamic moments when his consciousness connects him with his past, authentic and unchanging. The scent revives the fruit: "sensations of one sense [can] be signs of realities which are objects of another. Smells and tastes make us believe the *visible* cologne-bottle, strawberry, or cheese to be there."[283] Such an intensely affective experience can stimulate whole atmospherics:

> Sans doute, au moment où la raideur de la serviette m'avait rendu Balbec, pendant un instant avait caressé mon imagination, non pas seulement de la vue de la mer telle qu'elle était ce matin-là, mais de l'odeur de la chambre, de la vitesse du vent, du désir de déjeuner, de l'incertitude entre diverses promenades, tout cela attaché à la sensation du linge comme les mille ailes des anges qui font mille tours à la mi nute.[284]
>
> [Naturally, at the moment when the stiffness of the napkin had restored Balbec to me and for an instant caressed my imagination not only with the sight of the sea as it had been that morning but with the smell of my room, the speed of the wind, the sensation of looking forward to lunch, of wondering which of the different walks I should take (all this being attached to the feel of the linen like those thousand wings of the angels which revolve a thousand times in a minute).[285]]

To fix the experience, turning sensation and its encircling field of feeling and memory into thought and text, to "rationalize" meaning and give it permanent form, the narrator will bind it in language in the overlapping spheres of metaphor, the poetic rendering of the plurality of possibilities:

> Une heure n'est pas qu'une heure, c'est un vase rempli de parfums, de sons, de projets et de climats. Ce que nous appelons la réalité est un certain rapport entre ces sensations et ces souvenirs qui nous entourent simultanément [. . .] rapport unique que l'écrivain doit retrouver pour en enchaîner à jamais dans sa phrase les deux termes différents.[286]
>
> [An hour is not merely an hour, it is a vase full of scents and sounds and projects and climates, and what we call reality is a certain connexion between these immediate sensations and the memories which envelop us simultaneously with them [. . .] a unique connexion which the writer has to rediscover in order to link for ever in his phrase the two sets of phenomena which reality joins together.[287]]

What makes Proust's novel so strikingly modern, taking the reader into the first-hand psychological experience of the protagonist in a fiction so authentic, so revealing of the way experience happens for an individual personality that it has often been assumed to be autobiographical, required evolution of viewpoint from Jean to "je." The hero's experience is the author's process of representing it. For the narrator in this "roman" [novel], "the facts of his own subjectivity" create his world.[288] "Pensée et actualité sont faites d'une seule et meme étoffe, qui est l'étoffe de l'expérience en général" [Thought and actuality are made of one and the same stuff, which is the stuff of experience in general].[289]

James illustrates the process Proust uses to resurrect Combray with examples of a dream of a golden mountain, his house far away in America, the very room in which he is speaking, his hat in the cloakroom nearby; all these items are equally real to his attention and equally motivating to his actions. "L'externe et l'interne, l'étendu et l'inétendu, se fusionnent et font un mariage indissoluble" [Outer and inner, extended and unextended, merge into an indissoluble combination].[290] They form a part of his experience. Today the space of the lecture hall in which he speaks is a physical thing—with table, chairs, and walls. It has a construction and financial history as part of a building, but tomorrow with the simple passage of time, it will become a part of individual biographies as memory.

Similarly for Proust's narrator, sensations and events experienced in the present summon and mirror what he felt in the past, his dreams and fantasies, his hunger for lunch, his desire for a particular woman. When, in a virtual affective earthquake, the imagination is shaken and memory roused from its slumber, his experience in full is resurrected in the present as his book. James's "pure experience" is Proust's "idée d'existence" [the concept of "existence"] and is expressed in a Jamesian way as "un peu de temps à l'état pur" [a fragment of time in the pure state].[291] The memory has been freed from the distracting details of daily life that clouded the actual original experience: the people, places, and events that occupied its space are perhaps more *evident* than they were before.

The second of the two letters Proust wrote referring to William James does not mention James by name but does allude to Pragmatism, making it clear that Proust was familiar with the philosophy. Typesetters working on his novel, complains Proust to Gaston Gallimard in September 1920, have substituted Bergson for Bergotte; a reference to Bergotte in *Le Côté de Guermantes*, then in the process of publication, appears twice as "Bergson" in the proofs.[292] The reason, Proust suspects, is the notoriety of the French translation of James's book with its preface by Bergson; in their error, the typesetters have probably wanted to show that they are "au courant." The confusion was not unimaginable, just very annoying.[293] The date of the letter is noteworthy, given that James died in 1910, and the French translation of *Pragmatism* was published one year later (or nine years before Proust's letter to Gallimard).[294] Evidently, James's theory had penetrated the general culture, extending to typesetters who had probably seen the word often in their work, given the boon James's theory and the resulting controversy must have been for the publishing industry. Characterizing the way new theory is accepted into general culture and anticipating frustration at the reception of his pragmatic theory of truth, James had written: "First, you know, a new theory is attacked as absurd; then it is admitted to be true, but obvious and insignificant; finally it is seen to be so important that its adversaries claim that they themselves discovered it."[295] Apparently, by the time of Proust's letter everyone had discovered Pragmatism.

Pragmatism: A New Name for Some Old Ways of Thinking was first published in 1907, based on the series of Lowell lectures James delivered in Boston in November and December 1906, and then again at Columbia University in New York in January 1907. Its roots were in the lecture "Philosophical Conceptions and Practical Results," which James had given before the Philosophical Union at the University of California, Berkeley, in August 1898 (published in French in the *Revue de Philosophie* in 1906[296]). James's talk elaborated on a notion borrowed from (and readily credited to) his friend Charles Peirce, whose article "How to Make Our Ideas Clear"[297] lay ignored since first published in 1878. James felt that by 1898 the time seemed right for the public reintroduction of Peirce's ideas relative to his own views on religion.[298]

An indirect benefit of the thematic recurrence in James's works was the publicity gained: often he delivered his thoughts in lecture form, followed by a journal article, or several, and then gathered his articles on a given topic into a book, likely followed by another in response to criticism and counterargument by colleagues. Central elements of his thought were driven home before a wide public.

Summarizing Peirce, James connects attitude with action: "to develop a thought's meaning, we need only determine what conduct it is fitted to produce [. . .] what conceivable effects of a practical kind the object may involve—what sensations we are to expect from it, and what reactions we must prepare,"[299] a thought closely rephrased in *The Varieties of Religious Experience*.[300]

James's goal was to develop a philosophy that would most closely fit the experiences of life, nothing too abstract or too conceptual to reflect the messy realities or banish the ugly sufferings of human existence. Logic and scientific concepts were too dry and intellectualist to reflect the sway of actuality. He preferred a philosophical method that could accommodate the dynamic change characteristic of a modern view of reality. Philosophy, for James, should not leave life behind but rather take it into the classroom and lecture hall: "The world of concrete personal experience to which the street belongs is multitudinous beyond imagination, tangled, muddy, painful and perplexed"—not "a classic sanctuary."[301]

His argument is best represented in his own colorful terms: to illustrate abstract and intellectualist philosophy, James used the image of a "marble temple shining on a hill" isolated from life and "a clear addition built upon it"[302] serving as a "nobler home for our minds" and "a place of escape from the crassness of reality's surface."[303] James allows for the importance of simplification or plan in the formulation of an individual philosophy, but it must be evocative of so much more—of something "conceived in the cube."[304] He derogates the flat, two-dimensional, "skinny"[305] designs or abstract philosophies that do not reflect the girth of experience. These he differentiates from Pragmatism, which reflects individual temperament and desires[306] and a multidimensional reality, as will the density of Proust's prose style and the textual shape of his book.

The first-person singular is the center of the pragmatic universe; it is "a universe with such as *us* contributing to create its truth, a world delivered to *our* opportunisms and *our* private judgments!"[307] Building a philosophy encapsulates the imprint of the individual as he interprets his environment and shapes the truths he perceives in accord with his own temperament. Like the individual vision of Bergotte or Elstir, this is the lens or ocular instrument through which each of us, each of James's listeners (and Proust's hero) grasps reality. Much like the work of an artist, philosophy can illuminate our outlook like the beam of a lighthouse beacon, or in Proust's book "le pan de lumière" [luminous patch], the telling acumen of human sensibility: "no one of us can get along without the far-flashing beams of light it [philosophy] sends over the world's perspectives."[308]

But given this high degree of individuality and the variations in the situation of the viewer, the result can be a fractured world-view, the mélange of contradictory tendencies implied because multiple temperaments are unlikely to enforce a single centralized stance or assert the "superior discernment or authority" of one over the others.[309] So what determines the meaning of truth? Can it ever have a single absolute—in Proust's narrator's case, "essential"—meaning again? Is there an acceptable common understanding?

James conceives of Pragmatism as a method and as a theory of truth. As method it generalizes from the particular and allows any number of approaches to interpretive endeavor—"no dogmas and no doctrines save its method," states James—serving as "hotel corridor," in the view of the Italian pragmatist Papini.[310] Off this artery lie the rooms of various philosophical explanations of the world that must pass through it. As a method, Pragmatism "interpret[s] each notion by tracing its respective practical consequences."[311] Truth is what agrees with reality: "*True ideas are those that we can assimilate, validate, corroborate and verify*" [italics in original].[312]

Truth and meaning are important if they make a real-life difference: "Truth *happens* to an idea. It *becomes true*, is *made* true by events";[313] it is not a fixed idea accurate as a descriptor of actuality once and for all time. For James, philosophy bears the burden of asking what individual world-view is true at a particular moment for a particular individual's life given the concrete and actionable facts. The resulting events determine the truth of the assumptions—or attitudes or beliefs underlying a particular action: "What experiences will be different from those which would obtain if the belief were false?"[314] In a world of flux, a pragmatic truth is proved by events rather than being "a stagnant property inherent" in an idea.[315] Pragmatic truth corroborates and shapes streaming experience, affecting actions we select to implement on the basis of what we believe to be true at a particular time. Proust's narrator demonstrates this in his various hypotheses, investigations, and tests and in his shifting interpretations, particularly about Albertine's activities and sexual tendencies. Pragmatism is a philosophy of adjustment and a rich source for Proust's novel:

> The individual has a stock of old opinions already, but he meets a new experience that puts them to a strain. Somebody contradicts them; or in a reflective moment he discovers that they contradict each other; or he hears of facts with which they are incompatible; or desires arise in him which they cease to satisfy. The result is an inward trouble to which his mind till then had been a stranger, and from which he seeks to escape by modifying his previous mass of opinions.[316]

Deception actuates Pragmatism's verification process. Throughout *À la recherche du temps perdu* the narrator is faced with observations and situations that do not accord with the facts as he thought he knew them or that do not harmonize with his emotions. Taking a pragmatic approach, he revises what he thought he knew in light of what he now feels or observes: he reconciles Mme. de Guermantes's glorious heritage with her petty social behavior, changes his interpretation of Gilberte's "indecent" gesture when he hears her later explanation, observes that the Baron de Charlus and Saint-Loup have hidden proclivities not initially apparent, that Jupien has double business ventures. He suffers boredom and jealousy, a torrent of contradictory desires, and devises mind-games to toy with her and spice things up as Albertine metamorphosizes from mysterious athletic tease to secretive and devious housecat. The tales of misperception and revision help to define the modernism of Proust's work in ever-shifting reinterpretations as new facts and new truths burst upon experience over time. "To a certain degree, therefore," wrote James, "everything here is plastic."[317] James's truth is plural, and like Proust's narrator's grasp of his world, it is in a perpetual state of becoming, can only be revealed through hindsight.

We know things about material objects in the world by the physical sensations, the "group[ing] of attributes" that account for their "sole cash-value for our experience"[318] (Brichot's memories of the Verdurins' furniture). The names we assign come to represent a summarization, "a definite instrument abstracted from experience," coalesced features recapitulated virtually in language so we can process their "sensible realities" in a way that is meaningful—"experience funded."[319] Seeing an acquaintance groups the attributes we associate with him, Proust's narrator tells us; the operation takes place in our minds, "en partie un acte intellectuel." For the narrator, an individual becomes visible in the features we assign: "Nous remplissons l'apparence physique de l'être que nous voyons de toutes les notions que nous avons sur lui, et dans l'aspect total que nous nous représentons, ces notions ont certainement la plus grand part"

[We pack the physical outline of the person we see with all the notions we have already formed about him, and in the total picture of him which we compose in our minds those notions have certainly the principal place].[320]

If what the name brings to mind is incorrect when compared to the actual facts of what is named, the "fit" is off, and "verification" suffers,[321] a process so central to Proust's fiction of experience.

The Charles Swann Proust's narrator's family knew in Combray is distinctly different from the Swann who circulates easily among the highest of aristocratic society in Paris. The mental image and attributes associated with him differ from one observing group to the other. The local Swann of Tansonville was not included when special guests were coming to dinner, even when he had been consulted about the recipe to be used: "on ne l'invitait pas, ne lui trouvant pas un prestige suffisant" [to which he himself would not be invited, being regarded as insufficiently important].[322] Grandmother, grand-tante, and the rest of the family were ignorant of Swann's link with the Jockey Club and the Prince of Wales; their view was clear but splintered and incomplete based on snapshots of experience.

The family in Combray built their picture of Swann from the "caste" position of his father, an "agent de change" [stockbroker],[323] shutting from view anything discordant with this image. In every sense, they ignored the possibility that he might maintain relations beyond the expected social rank of his parents. And from his reticence about art, the questionable—in their minds—location of his Paris home, the "prosaic" nature of his conversation with them, which he restricted to anecdotes about common acquaintances, they could create "le vague et doux résidu—mi-mémoire, mi-oubli" [a lingering residuum, vague but not unpleasing—half memory and half oblivion]—constructed from their weekly luncheons with him, stuffing him like taxidermists with their own personal experiences of him. He was painted in the same sepia tones as they in the narrator's childhood memories: "parfumé par l'odeur du grand marronnier, des panniers de framboises et d'un brin d'estragon" [fragrant with the scent of the great chestnut-tree, of baskets of raspberries and of a sprig of tarragon]—an entirely different creature from the Swann the narrator later knew in Paris.[324]

In *Le Temps retrouvé* the narrator mentions something quite similar: the face of the passerby, barely glimpsed, is like a canvas on which we paint the features according to our own wishes. Each person we know wears "cent masques" [one hundred masks] in our memory, and even so we sketch them our own way, interpreting their acts and their thoughts according to our own emotional barometer.[325] Similarly, James had written, "We receive in short the block of marble, but we carve the statue ourselves."[326]

This is a technique that will be reprised more darkly when events of the past resound in the narrator's episodic memory. Stinging anguish mingles with the physical attributes of the furnishings in the space now emptied of her presence—and seen differently as a result—haunting the narrator after Albertine's departure. With each wave come unknowns requiring additional revisions of view, a new set of questions, and the possibility of a new round of anguished interpretations. She was never just a single, flat, framed photograph. With Léa, with Bloch's sisters, with Mlle. Vinteuil's friend, with the other "jeunes filles" on the beach, with her aunt, with the laundress, with the narrator's mother, with Françoise, and with the narrator himself, she was a multiplicity of potential and contradictory attributes: "Mais même au point de vue des plus insignifiantes choses de la vie, nous ne sommes pas un tout matériellement constitué, identique pour tout le monde et dont chacun n'a qu'à aller prendre connaissance comme d'un cahier des charges ou d'un testament ; notre personnalité sociale est une création de la pensée des autres" [But then, even in the most insignificant details of our daily life, none of us can be said to constitute a material whole, which is identical for everyone, and need only be turned up like a page in an account-book or the record of a will; our social personality is a creation of the thoughts of other people].[327] Perhaps this is why the creative poet/Self is so different from the biography.

Old assumptions—and past experiences—evolve with new knowledge, wrote James: "Our minds grow in spots; and like grease-spots, the spots spread. [. . .] [W]e keep unaltered as much of our old knowledge, as many of our old prejudices and beliefs as we can. [. . .] [I]t happens relatively seldom that the new fact is added *raw*. More usually it is embedded cooked, as one might say, or stewed in the sauce of the old."[328] Personal history is bubbling on the back burner as ingredients are added and alter the flavor.

In the postscript to a letter he wrote to Jacques de Lacretelle,[329] and echoing James, Prousts uses the word "infusoire" to indicate reality's flow—by budding: "par division comme les infusoires" and "aussi bien par amalgame."[330] "New truths thus are resultants of new experiences and of old truths combined and mutually modifying one another."[331] This is Proust's "amalgame" and James's "stew."

Like persistent nostalgia for "la France d'autrefois," embedded in Françoise's language, James notes that the past is never completely obliterated. We carry aspects of it along with us in our ways of thinking—and in discourse: "very ancient modes of thought may have survived through all the later changes in men's opinions."[332] Hereupon future experience is "grafted."[333] Might the grafting mechanism also be a purpose for the generalizing statements so prominent in *À la recherche du temps perdu*? Are they a way of negotiating new experience, easing its absorption, accommodating it to the old? The ability to summarize and conceptualize in general statements, Proust's "maxims," allows the narrator to anticipate alternatives and outcome, to derive what James calls "lessons from the past" and "possibilities for the future" that will facilitate processing his perceptual experience.[334]

Thus grafting or budding could be random, ambiguous, uncertain, or it could incorporate an adaptive filtering and sorting mechanism with the teleological or utilitarian purpose to help explain experience using inherited mind-sets. What is there to see is a matter of our mind's experience: "Je m'étais rendu compte que seule la perception grossière et erronée place tout dans l'objet, quand tout est dans l'esprit" [I had realised before now that it is only a clumsy and erroneous form of perception which places everything in the object, when really everything is in the mind].[335]

> We plunge forward into the field of fresh experience with the beliefs our ancestors and we have made already; these determine what we notice; what we notice determines what we do; what we do again determines what we experience; so from one thing to another, altho the stubborn fact remains that there is a sensible flux, what is *true of it* seems from first to last to be largely a matter of our own creation.[336]

"Experience," wrote James, "has ways of *boiling over*, and making us correct our present formulas."[337] The facts of the past do not change with time, but the truth does; and new truth determines new action. The cultural evolution that occurs through new artistic production, the advancing threshold of cultural reception, and the adaptations reflected in the narrator's ability to assimilate and appreciate new music, the evolution in political discussion and social groupings in *À la recherche du temps perdu* all result from the grafting mechanism described by James in *Pragmatism*:

> Truth grafts itself on previous truth, modifying it in the process, just as idiom grafts itself on previous idiom, and law on previous law. Given previous law and a novel case, and the judge will twist them into fresh law. Previous idiom; new slang or metaphor or oddity that hits the public taste:—and presto, a new idiom is made. Previous truth; fresh facts:—and our mind finds a new truth. [. . .] Truth, law, and language fairly boil away [. . .] at the least touch of novel fact. These things *make them-selves* as we go. Our rights, wrongs, prohibitions, penalties, words, forms, idioms, beliefs, are so many new creations that add themselves as fast as history proceeds.[338]

The dynamic nature of truth allows it to align with actuality while remaining flexible enough to endlessly readjust. Truth is a means, not an end, and leads to "other vital satisfactions."[339] Proust's narrator benefits from the "meliorist" aspects of Pragmatism that induce a salutary end in which reality acts as stimulant to creativity, an imaginative solution to his lax hesitation and methodological dilemma.

The truth the narrator hunted about Albertine was dynamic. She became boring when static and his relations with her felt irrelevant, stale, and uninteresting without the passionate pungency of jealousy or the emotional stimulation of the active hunt for certainty about her tastes and escapades. If his emotional attachment to her were not affecting his behavior, as we observe later when he has forgotten her, true or not the information about her past would be meaningless to him. The facts would no longer be of use, no longer satisfy a need: "The practical value of true ideas is thus primarily derived from the practical importance of their objects to us,"[340] James had written.

And true ideas do not go stale if saved for later: "We store such extra truths away in our memories. [. . .] Whenever such an extra truth becomes practically relevant to one of our emergencies, it passes from cold-storage to do work in the world and our belief in it grows active."[341] Not only are resurgent episodic memories a fact of psychology, they are useful and adaptive for James and for Proust: they inform the present. They provide aesthetic structure, perspective for understanding the past, and motivation for future action: the writing of the novel. "The present sheds a backward light on the world's previous processes," wrote James as if dictating plot to Proust. "They may have been truth-processes for the actors in them. They are not so for one who knows the later revelations of the story."[342] When Proust's narrator writes the book we read, unlike us his readers following along, he is looking back. He knows the errors and the outcome, and he knows well before we do, in the circularity of the novel's structure, what if anything will constitute the ultimate truth of events. His book is the story of that process happening.

Pragmatism is a world of possibilities. A conceptual view that requires evisceration into inert presentation rather than live incarnation is inappropriate for rendering reality. There is only so much that scientific method can offer when the focus is on productions of the imagination. Taine, in Proust's view, erroneously used methods borrowed from the natural sciences to examine the products of mind like fiction:[343]

Laying the stakes for a fictional structure like the one Proust adopted for his novel, James stated: "We live forward, we understand backward, said a danish [*sic*] writer; and to understand life by concepts is to arrest its moment, cutting it up into bits as if with scissors, and immobilizing these in our logical herbarium."[344] Proust chooses to unroll the vegetative fabric of his narrator's experience in a style that conveys its density and complexity as lived—simultaneously, as if in real time *and* upon reflection.

The world the narrator perceives around him is indefinite and adrift in the lights and shadows of his perception. Events are refracted through the tale he recounts, their truth distilled by his vision: "Et comme l'art recompose exactement la vie, autour des vérités qu'on a atteintes, en soi-même flottera toujours une atmosphere de poésie, la douceur d'un mystère qui n'est que le vestige de la pénombre que nous avond dû traverser, l'indication, marquée exactement comme par un altimètre, de la profondeur d'une oeuvre" [And as art exactly reconstitutes life, around the truths to which we have attained inside ourselves there will always float an atmosphere of poetry, the soft charm of a mystery which is merely a vestige of the shadow which we have had to traverse, the indication, as precise as the markings of an altimeter, of the depth of a work].[345] Subject to the narrator's perspective, the reader is prisoner of his rhetorical stance, his quest to harness truth in a modernist reality of indeterminacy.

Joan Richardson, describing similar uncertainty in "William James's feeling of *if*," fourth chapter of her book *A Natural History of Pragmatism*[346] accentuates the "vague" as the arena in which men stand alone, attempting to determine the source of meaning in their experiences and interacting with it through the medium of language.

Richardson uses very contemporary terms to describe James's understanding of the term "vague," noting the meaning "wave" in French—a scientific phenomenon actively researched during James's lifetime—that has the present-day meaning of "*wave packet*, a probability amplitude composing a range, a scale of *possibles*" [emphasis in original].[347]

Like gravity, Albertine exerts a force field of uncertainty, an arena of potentiality for powerful emotion, and, like Charlus's chains, nearly pleasurable suffering, binding the narrator to her in an orbit of pain. And like a magnet, she is capable of compelling the narrator's emotions to align in a specific pattern. The emotional gray zone surrounding her, the obscurity of factual information keeps the bored, constrained narrator tethered: "Même quand je restais à la maison tout l'après-midi, ma pensée la suivait dans sa promenade, décrivait un horizon lointain, bleuâtre, engendrait autour du centre que j'étais une zone mobile d'incertitude et de vague" [Even when I stayed in the house all the afternoon, my thoughts accompanied her on her drive, traced a distant blue horizon, created round the centre that was myself a fluctuating zone of vague uncertainty].[348] The primary activity of a Jamesian subjective mind, according to Richardson, is to sift through the "vague" and select language to express how an experiencing mind relates to its world.[349]

In their review of her book for the online journal *William James Studies*, Harry Heft and Susan Saegert focus on Joan Richardson's suggestion that the scientific discoveries of James's day obliged his contemporaries to experiment with language and "invent a new relationship between language and perception." Writers contemporary with Proust (although her study does not include him) explored James's stress on feeling "as a vibratory membrane between embodied persons" and they probed "the legacy of linguistically encoded meanings." In their works, "language becomes a tool for perceiving and thinking" used to "transmute" the clash between the advances in science and contemporary cultural clichés. James's insistence on dynamic flux and the use of language "as a tool for rendering what is invisible in experience visible"[350] was fundamental.

Isabelle de Vendeuvre and David Lapoujade[351] identify William James's Pragmatism as a method of assessing choice of idea and action based on utility and determining truth by believing with confidence inspired by communal understanding. Reflecting James's pragmatic methodology and approach to truth, an artist's ideas act as "vectors" (the same term used by Joan Richardson), and their value lies in their ability to help articulate, test, and verify truth, creating a new reality. As such, they are not static objects like accumulated encyclopedic facts or a frozen snapshot; they are "activated" by the artist, and they are able to further "reconsolidate" his reality—and ours—in the telling by recalling (memory) and recasting (writing), like Proust's "nouvel écrivain."

In *Albertine disparue*, written for the most part beginning in 1914, Proust's narrator describes the muse of experience, of ordinarily life, of individual temperament and memory, as the muse of "la sagesse [. . .] des familles" [the wisdom . . . of families],[352] a muse inspiring recognition of certain truths different from stable inalterable truths proffered by philosophy or traditionally conveyed in art. This is the muse of the fortuitous, of the shifting and self-correcting that takes place in experience over time—a muse avoided by the narrator of *Jean Santeuil*, who was thirsty for direct impression, hungry for deep essential meaning, yearning to create an expression of indissoluble truth. The pragmatist's truth, on the other hand, gains its ultimate meaning from the fleeting messiness of the everyday flow of events. It is every bit as serious, but it is a truth in the making; it embraces the acts of individuals faced with the actual, the probable, and the possible: "La Muse qui a recueilli tout ce que les muses plus hautes de la philosophie et de l'art ont rejeté, tout ce qui n'est pas fondé en vérité, tout ce qui n'est que contingent, mais révèle aussi d'autres lois: c'est l'Histoire!" [the Muse who has gathered up everything that the more exalted Muses of philosophy and art have rejected, everything that is merely contingent, but that reveals other laws as well: the Muse of History].[353]

The seemingly unimportant noise surrounding the events of a life, the contradictory, the accidental have value in Proust's pragmatic approach. In a church, where fixtures, liturgy, and decorative iconography manifest permanent truths, like the static aesthetic truth celebrated by Ruskin, there also exists the archival truths of a changing congregation, alterations to the building, refurbishment of furnishings and ritual objects, an evolving historical truth pragmatic in nature. This truth is dependent upon the value its transformations have for the onlooker, the consequences they bear on what he does. Their truth is a truth that works for him and alters his course.

NOTES

1. *Corr.*, XIII, *43*, 98–101, 99.
2. William James, "On a Certain Blindness in Human Beings," *Atlantic Monthly* (1899), repr. *Talks to Teachers on Psychology; and to Students on Some of Life's Ideals* (New York: Holt, 1899 and 1912), 133. Trans. Pidoux (Paris: Alcan, 1900, 2nd ed. 1907). Repr. John J. McDermott, *The Writings of William James* (Chicago: University of Chicago Press, 1977), 629–645, 630. McDermott uses the 1912 edition. Repr. *Talks to Teachers* (Cambridge: Harvard University Press, 1983), 133.
3. James, *Pluralistic*, Appendix A, 348.
4. Marcel Proust, "Réponses à une enquête des Annales," *Les Annales politiques et littéraires*, 26 février 1922, repr. *Essais et Articles, Contre Sainte-Beuve* (Paris: Éditions Gallimard [Bibliiothèque de la Pléiade], 1971), 640–641.
5. Perry, *Thought and Character*, II, 156.
6. James, *Pluralistic*, 212, 213, 217.
7. James, *Pluralistic*, 250–251.
8. See William James, "The Experience of Activity," *Psychological* Review 12 (1905): 1–17, repr. *Essays in Radical Empiricism* (New York: Longmans, Green & Co., 1912) 170, note 1 (168-171), repr. (Cambridge: Harvard University Press, 1976), 86, note 8 (85–86), and cited by John J. McDermott, intro. William James, *Essays in Radical Empiricism* (1976 edition), xxxvii.
9. Marcel Proust, "Dix-sept ans. 11 heures du soir. Octobre in R. Dreyfus, *Souvenirs sur Marcel Proust* (Paris: Grasset, 1926), 58-59.
10. *RTP*, III, 590. Enright, V, 100.
11. William James, "The Place of Affectional Facts in a World of Pure Experience," *Journal of Philosophy, Psychology, and Scientific Methods* 2 (1905): 281–287. repr. *Essays in Radical Empiricism* (New York: Longmans, Green & Co., 1912. repr. Cambridge: Harvard University Press, 1976), 48, 87.
12. See letter to Jacques Riviere, February 6, 1914, *Corr.*, XIII, *43*, 98–101, 99.
13. William James, "Address at the Emerson Centenary in Concord," *Riverside Press for the Social Circle in Concord* (June 1903), 67–77, repr. *Memories and Studies*, ed. Henry James Jr. (New York: Longmans, Green & Co., 1911), 19.
14. William James, "On Some Mental Effects of the Earthquake," *Youth's Companion* 80 (June 7, 1906): 283–284, repr. *Memories and Studies*, ed. Henry James Jr. (New York: Longmans, Green & Co., 1911), IX, 217.
15. James, *Memories and Studies*, 211–212.
16. James, *Pragmatism*, 110.
17. James, *Pragmatism*, 107.
18. James, *Pragmatism*, 108.
19. See Bruce Lowery, 123.
20. Boodin, Intro., xxi and 209, note 19.
21. James, *Pluralistic*, 250–251.
22. James, *Pluralistic*, 269.
23. James, *Pluralistic*, 268, 269.
24. *RTP*, III, 694. Enright, V, 248.
25. James, *Pluralistic*, 279.
26. *RTP*, III, 694. Enright, V, 250.
27. *RTP*, IV, 297. Enright, VI, 40.
28. *RTP*, IV, 296. Enright, VI, 40.
29. James, *Varieties*, 497.
30. James, *Varieties*, 545–546.
31. James in "On the Function of Cognition" (1885) in *MT*, 197.
32. Proust, *Jean Santeuil*, 269.
33. Marcel Proust, "Sur la lecture," *La Renaissance latine* (15 juin 1905), repr. "Journées de lecture," *Pastiches et mélanges. Contre Sainte-Beuve* (Paris: Éditions Gallimard [Bibliothèque de la Pléiade], 1971), 160–194.

34. Proust, "Journées de lecture," *CSB*, 172.
35. Marcel Proust, "Journées de Lecture" (*Le Figaro*, March 20, 1907), in *Essais et Articles* in *Contre Sainte-Beuve* (Éditions Gallimard [Bibliothèque de la Pléiade], 1971), 526–533 and note 2, 924–929.
36. *Le Carnet de 1908*, 95.
37. *RTP*, IV, 462. See also Lambilliotte, who observes that Proust wrote about classifying books by the sensations they evoke for the reader, 84.
38. Wolf, 16.
39. *RTP*, IV, 463. Enright, VI, 284.
40. *RTP*, IV, 457.
41. Enright, VI, 273.
42. *RTP*, I, 39–40. Enright, I, 54.
43. *RTP*, III, 787. Enright, V, 378.
44. James, *Principles*, I, 311.
45. For James, "cash value" is the "concreteness" language provides: "You must bring out of each word its practical cash-value, set it at work within the stream of your experience" (James, *Pragmatism*, 31–32).
46. *RTP*, III, 788–789.
47. Enright V, 379.
48. *RTP*, III, 789. Enright, V, 380.
49. William James, "The Knowing of Things Together," *The Psychological Review* 2 (1895): 105–124, repr. *Collected Essays and* Reviews (New York: Russell & Russell, 1969), repr. *The Writings of William James*, ed. John H. McDermott (Chicago: The University of Chicago Press, 1977), 152–168, 155. Repr. William James, *Essays in Philosophy* (Cambridge, MA: Harvard University Press, 1978), 71–89, 73.
50. *RTP*, IV, 450. Enright VI, 263.
51. *RTP*, IV, 621.
52. Enright, VI, 525.
53. *RTP*, III, 789. Enright, V, 380.
54. James, *Varieties*, 483.
55. James, *Varieties*, 483.
56. James, *ERE*, 45, Longman's edition; Harvard edition, 23–24.
57. James, *Varieties*, 530.
58. James, *Briefer Course*, 18.
59. *RTP*, IV, 622.
60. Enright, VI, 526–527.
61. *RTP*, II, 198.
62. *RTP*, II, 141.
63. *RTP*, I, 221.
64. James, *Varieties*, 168.
65. *RTP*, II, 439.
66. Enright, III, 184.
67. Enright, III, 184.
68. *RTP*, II, 438–440. Enright, III, 185.
69. *RTP*, IV, 153. Enright, V, 774.
70. *RTP*, IV, 451. Enright, VI, 263–264.
71. James, *Varieties*, 419.
72. James, *Briefer Course*, 308.
73. James, *Briefer Course*, 155.
74. James, *Briefer Course*, 308.
75. James, *Briefer Course*, 142.
76. James, *Briefer Course*, 300–301.
77. *RTP*, IV, 457. Enright, VI, 273.
78. *RTP*, IV, 457. Enright, VI, 273.
79. James, "The Knowing of Things Together," in McDermott, 158. James, *Essays in Philosophy*, Harvard edition, 77.

80. *RTP*, IV, 457. Enright, VI, 273.
81. James, "Emerson Centenary," *Memories and Studies*, 19
82. James, *Varieties*, 158.
83. *RTP*, IV, 520. Enright, VI, 368.
84. James, *Varieties*, 159.
85. James, *Varieties*, 163.
86. Boodin, 214.
87. Boodin, 210.
88. James, "Rationality," 32.
89. Descombes, *Proust: Philosophy*, 6.
90. *RTP*, III, 693.
91. James, "Rationality," 32.
92. James, "Rationality," 34.
93. James, "Rationality," 33.
94. *RTP*, III, 696. Enright, V, 248.
95. *RTP*, III, 696. Enright, V, 250.
96. James, "Rationality," 34.
97. *RTP*, IV, 3. Enright, V, 563.
98. *RTP*, IV, 223. Enright, V, 873–874.
99. *Le Carnet de 1908*, 61.
100. James, "Rationality," 33.
101. Ralph Barton Perry uses the term "instrumentalist" in connection with the essay. See Perry, *Annotated Bibliography*, 1879, 7, 10.
102. James, "Rationality," 34.
103. *RTP*, IV, 451.
104. Enright, VI, 264.
105. James, "Rationality," 38.
106. *RTP*, IV, 459. Enright, VI, 276–277.
107. James, "Rationality," 36.
108. James, "Rationality," 36.
109. *RTP*, IV, 458. Enright, VI, 274.
110. *RTP*, IV, 622.
111. James, "Rationality," 38.
112. *RTP*, IV, 464.
113. *RTP*, IV, 622.
114. Gilles Deleuze, *Proust and Signs*, 40: http://books.google.com/books?id=HUZwFDjPL_wC&lpg=PP1&dq=deleuze%20proust%20and%20signs&pg=PA40#v=onepage&q&f=false
115. Descombes, *Proust: Philosophy*, 6.
116. James, "Rationality," 38.
117. James, "Rationality," 45.
118. James, "Rationality," 46.
119. James, "Rationality," 46.
120. James, "Rationality," 48.
121. James, "Rationality," 49.
122. *RTP*, II, 19–21. Enright, 324.
123. James, "Rationality," 50.
124. James, "Rationality," 45.
125. *RTP*, II, 366. Enright, III, 81.
126. James, "Rationality," 55.
127. James, "Rationality," 56.
128. *RTP*, IV, 474. Enright, VI, 299.
129. James's, "Rationality, Activity and Faith" was translated into French for publication in the *Critique philosophique* in 1882, the year of its publication.
130. James, "Rationality, Activity and Faith," 58.
131. James, "Rationality, Activity and Faith," 61.

132. James, "Rationality, Activity and Faith," 61.
133. James, "Rationality, Activity and Faith," 64.
134. James, "Rationality, Activity and Faith," 69.
135. McDermott, *Writings*, xi–xv.
136. James, "Rationality, Activity and Faith," 71.
137. James, "Rationality, Activity and Faith," 71.
138. *CSB*, 303–305.
139. James, "Rationality," 62.
140. James, *Pragmatism*, 138.
141. The "madeleine" is used as an archetype for the narrator's experiences of resurgent memory.
142. *RTP*, III, 693. Enright, V, 245.
143. *RTP*, III, 693. Enright, V, 246.
144. *RTP*, III, 693. Enright, V, 246.
145. *RTP*, III, 693. Enright, V, 245.
146. *RTP*, II, 568. Enright, III, 368.
147. *Corr.*, XVII, 87, 227–231. See Appendix.
148. In 1918, another edition of the French translation of James's *Pragmatism* was published.
149. Pericles Lewis, *Religious Experience and the Modernist Novel* (Cambridge: Cambridge University Press, 2010), 20.
150. James, *The Varieties of Religious Experience: A Study in Human Nature* (New York: The Modern Library, 2002), 61–62.
151. James, *Briefer Course*, 2.
152. See Barbara J. Bucknall, *The Religion of Art in Proust* (Urbana: University of Illinois Press, 1969), 177.
153. *RTP*, I, 45. Enright, I, 62.
154. While suddenly remembering a forgotten name is certainly a common experience for us all, James describes it in detail in *Varieties*, and coincidentally Proust chooses it to structure his plot.
155. James, *Varieties*, 227–228. See also James, *Principles, I*, 243, and *RTP*, IV, 456.
156. *RTP*, I, 46. Enright, I, 62.
157. James, *Varieties*, 239.
158. James, *Varieties*, 226–227.
159. James, *Letters*, II, 75–78.
160. James, *Letters*, II, 77–78.
161. Robert D. Richardson, *Maelstrom*, 375.
162. James, *Varieties*, 367.
163. *RTP*, IV, 470. Enright, VI, 293.
164. *Le Carnet de 1908*, 49.
165. *RTP*, IV, 444. Enright, VI, 253.
166. *RTP*, I, 45.
167. Enright, I, 61.
168. James, *Varieties*, 236.
169. James, *Varieties*, 245.
170. James, *Varieties*, 249.
171. James, *Varieties*, 250.
172. James, *Varieties*, 9.
173. James, *Varieties*, 10.
174. James, *Varieties*, 19.
175. James, *Varieties*, 85.
176. James, *Varieties*, 36.
177. *Le Carnet de 1908*, 62.
178. James, *Varieties*, 61.
179. James, *Varieties*, 73.
180. James, *Varieties*, 264.

181. James, *Varieties*, 236–237.
182. *Le Carnet de 1908*, 124–125.
183. James, *Varieties*, 241–242.
184. *RTP*, I, 44. Enright, I, 60.
185. James, *Varieties*, 259–260 and note 1.
186. James, *Varieties*, 256–257.
187. James, *Varieties*, 266–267.
188. James, *Varieties*, 449.
189. James, *Varieties*, 281.
190. James, *Varieties*, 518.
191. James, *Varieties*, 285.
192. *RTP*, I, 44. Enright, I, 60.
193. James, "Mysticism," 88.
194. James, "Mysticism," 85.
195. James, "Mysticism," 86.
196. James, "Mysticism," 87.
197. James, "Mysticism," 88.
198. *RTP*, IV, 458.
199. Enright, VI, 274.
200. James, *Pragmatism*, 44. All references are to the 1978 edition.
201. James, *ERE*, 9. Published by Ralph Barton Perry after James's death, the title and for the most part the content of this book were selected by James several years earlier. References are to the 1912 edition and/or to the 1976 Harvard University Press edition (HUP) as indicated.
202. *RTP*, II, 311–312.
203. John J. McDermott, Keynote Address, James/Royce Centennial Conference, "William James and Josiah Royce a Century Later: Pragmatism and Idealism in Dialogue." Harvard Divinity School, May 25-27, 2007.
204. McDermott, *Writings*, xxvii.
205. William James, *Essais d'Empirisme Radical*. Traduit de l'anglais et préfacé par Guillaume Garretta et Mathias Girel (Marseille, France: Agone, 2005).
206. James, "Omissions," 5-6.
207. James, *ERE*, HUP, 106.
208. James, *ERE*, HUP, 117.
209. James, *ERE*, 271. James. "La Notion de Conscience," *Essays in Radical Empiricism*, Cambridge: Harvard Universiry Press, 1976), 105–117. Orig. trans. Salvatore Saladine in McDermott, *Writings*, with minor changes for the Harvard edition cited here.
210. James, *ERE*, HUP, 108.
211. James, *ERE*, HUP, 263.
212. James, *ERE*, HUP, 114.
213. James, *ERE*, HUP, 111.
214. James, *ERE*, HUP, 266.
215. James, *ERE*, HUP, 268.
216. James, *ERE*, HUP, 269–270.
217. James, *ERE*, HUP, 29.
218. James, *ERE*, HUP, 270.
219. James, *ERE*, HUP, 22.
220. James, *ERE*, HUP, 35.
221. James, *ERE*, HUP, 116.
222. James, *ERE*, HUP, 270.
223. James, *ERE*, HUP, 271.
224. James, *ERE*, HUP, 117.
225. James, Perry, *ERE*, 31. Dover, 10 (see note 233). HUP, 11.
226. James, *Letters*, II, 345.
227. *RTP*, IV, 458.

228. Luc Fraisse, "'Le Nouvel écrivain': Proust précurseur de Jauss." Talk delivered at the Colloque international de littérature comparée de Tours on the topic of "Originalité de l'oeuvre et notion d'originalité dans la pensée de Marcel Proust," March 5-6, 2009.
229. *RTP*, II, 622–623.
230. *RTP*, II, 623.
231. Enright, III, 445–446.
232. James, *Pluralistic*, 231–232.
233. *RTP*, I, 520–523.
234. *RTP*, I, 520. Enright, II, 140.
235. *RTP*, I, 521. Enright, II, 141.
236. *RTP*, I, 521–522.
237. Enright, II, 142.
238. *RTP*, III, 753.
239. *RTP*, III, 758. Enright, V, 338.
240. *Corr.*, XX, *319*, 543. Crémieux's actual wording was that Proust had brought "une formule nouvelle dans notre littérature" [a new form to our literature].
241. See William James, *Essais d'empirisme radical [1912]*, trans. et préface Mathias Girel et Guillaume Garreta (Marseille: Agone, 2005), rééd. (Paris: Flammarion, Collection Champs, 2007), and remarks by Girel, "The Influence of James and Royce on European Thought Then and Now," James/Royce Centennial Conference, "William James and Josiah Royce a Century Later: Pragmatism and Idealism in Dialogue." Harvard Divinity School, May 25–27, 2007.
242. James, "La Notion," *ERE*, 216, 217. William James, "The Notion of Consciousness," *Essays in Radical Empiricism* (Mineola, NY: Dover Publications, Inc., 2003), 114, 115. HUP, 110.
243. James, *ERE*, 217–218. HUP, 265.
244. *RTP*, III, 761. Enright, V, 342.
245. James, *ERE*, 227. *Essays in Radical Empiricism*, 120. HUP 269.
246. James, "The Knowing of Things Together," *Coll. Essays and Reviews*, 389.
247. James, "Blindness," in McDermott, 634. James, *Talks to Teachers*, HUP,
248. James, "The Thing and Its Relations," Appendix to *Pluralistic*, 356.
249. James, "*Pluralistic*, 356–357.
250. *RTP*, IV, 477.
251. Enright, VI, 303.
252. *RTP*, IV, 479.
253. James, *Pluralistic*, 39.
254. James, *Pluralistic*, 76, 79.
255. James, *Pluralistic*, 213.
256. James, *Pluralistic*, 217.
257. James, *Pluralistic*, 235.
258. *RTP*, I, 41.
259. *RTP*, I, 82.
260. *RTP*, I, 119.
261. *RTP*, I, 216.
262. *RTP*, I, 233.
263. *RTP*, I, 382.
264. *RTP*, I, 539.
265. *RTP*, II, 5.
266. *RTP*, II, 189.
267. *RTP*, II, 345, 347.
268. *RTP*, II, 353.
269. *RTP*, II, 427.
270. *RTP*, II, 492.
271. *RTP*, II, 814.

272. William James, Preface to *The Meaning of Truth*, in *Pragmatism* and *The Meaning of Truth* (Cambridge: Harvard University Press, 1978), [3] 169. (Pagination refers to page 3 in *The Meaning of Truth* section of the book, page 169 of the volume.)
273. James, *Pragm/Meaning*, [89] 255.
274. James, *Pragm/Meaning*, [135] 301.
275. *RTP*, IV, 468.
276. Enright, VI, 290.
277. James, *Pragm/Meaning*, [89] 255.
278. James, *Pluralistic*, 29.
279. James, *ERE*, 46.
280. James, "Blindness," in McDermott, 634. *Talks to Teachers*, HUP, 138.
281. James, *Pluralistic*, 168–171.
282. James, *Pluralistic*, 194.
283. James, *Briefer Course*, 301.
284. *RTP*, IV, 454–455.
285. Enright, VI, 269–270.
286. *RTP*, IV, 467-468.
287. Enright, VI, 289.
288. James, "Moral Philosopher," 614–615.
289. James, *ERE*, 216. James, *Essays in Radical Empiricism*, 114 (HUP, 1976, 110) .
290. James, *ERE*, 216–217. James, *Essays in Radical Empiricism*, 114 (HUP, 1976, 110).
291. *RTP*, IV, 451. Enright, VI, 264.
292. *Corr.*, XIX, *213*, 437–440. See Appendix.
293. In note 7 the editors refer specifically to the French translation of James's book published in 1911 with Bergson's preface.
294. The French edition was republished in 1918.
295. James, *Pragmatism*, 95. References in the text are to the edition of *Pragmatism* published by Harvard University Press 1978.
296. *Revue de Philosophie* 8 (1906): 463-484.
297. Charles Peirce, "How to Make our Ideas Clear," *Popular Science Monthly* 12 (January 1878): 286–302.
298. It has been said that James introduced his thinking on Pragmatism in *The Varieties of Religious Experience*. In the Preface to *Pragmatism*, James lists further reading on Pragmatism, suggesting articles in English by Dewey and Schiller and readings in French including those by G. Milhaud, *Le Rationnel*, 1898; Le Roy in *La Revue de Métaphysique*, vols. 7, 8, and 9; Blondel and de Sailly in *Les Annales de Philosophie Chrétienne*, 4e Série, vols. 2 and 3. He mentions as well a forthcoming book to be published in French by the Italian pragmatist Papini. See James, *Pragmatism*, 6.
299. James, *Pragmatism*, 28–29.
300. James, *Varieties*, 484–485.
301. James, *Pragmatism*, 17–18.
302. James, *Pragmatism*, 18.
303. James, *Pragmatism*, 23.
304. James, *Pragmatism*, 25.
305. James, *Pragmatism*, 25.
306. James, *Pragmatism*, 24.
307. James, *Pragmatism*, 125.
308. James, *Pragmatism*, 10–11.
309. James, *Pragmatism*, 11.
310. James, *Pragmatism*, 32. See also James, *Pragmatism*, 147, note 6.9, citing William James, "G. Papini and the Pragmatist Movement in Italy," *Journal of Philosophy, Psychology, and Scientific Methods* 3 (1906): 337–341.
311. James, *Pragmatism*, 28.
312. James, *Pragmatism*, 96–97.
313. James, *Pragmatism*, 97.
314. James, *Pragmatism*, 97.

315. James, *Pragmatism*, 97.
316. James, *Pragmatism*, 34–35.
317. James, *Pragmatism*, 35.
318. James, *Pragmatism*, 46.
319. James, *Pragmatism*, 127.
320. *RTP*, I, 19. Enright, I, 23.
321. James, *Pragmatism*, 102.
322. *RTP*, I, 18. Enright, I, 22.
323. *RTP*, I, 16. Enright, I, 19.
324. *RTP*, I, 19. Enright, I, 24.
325. *RTP*, IV, 622.
326. James, *Pragmatism*, 119.
327. *RTP*, I, 18–19. Enright, I, 23.
328. James, *Pragmatism*, 83.
329. *Corr.*, XVII, *76*, 193–95.
330. See Nicola Luckhurst, 136.
331. James, *Pragmatism*, 83.
332. James, *Pragmatism*, 83.
333. James, *Pragmatism*, 83.
334. James, *Pragm/Meaning*, [135] 301.
335. *RTP*, IV, 491. Enright, VI, 323.
336. James, *Pragmatism*, 122.
337. James, *Pragmatism*, 106.
338. James, *Pragmatism*, 116.
339. James, *Pragmatism*, 98.
340. James, *Pragmatism*, 98.
341. James, *Pragmatism*, 98.
342. James, *Pragmatism*, 107.
343. Proust, *CSB*, 220: "Il a importé dans l'histoire morale les procédés de l'histoire naturelle" and "sa conception intellectualiste de la réalité ne laissait de vérité que dans la science."
344. James, *Pluralistic*, 244.
345. *RTP*, IV, 476. Enright VI, 302.
346. Joan Richardson, *A Natural History of Pragmatism* (New York: Cambridge University Press, 2007).
347. Joan Richardson, 120.
348. *RTP*, III, 538. Enright, V, 27.
349. Joan Richardson, 127.
350. All quotes in this paragraph are from Harry Heft and Susan Saegert, rev. of *A Natural History of Pragmatism: The Fact of Feeling from Jonathan Edwards to Gertrude Stein* by Joan Richardson, *William James Studies* 2.1 (Summer 2007). http://williamjamesstudies.press.uiuc.edu/2.1/.
351. See Isabelle de Vendeuvre, "Proust et la question du savoir," *Proust et les moyens de la connaissance*, éd. Annick Bouillaguet (Strasbourg: Presses Universitaires de Strasbourg, 2008), 235–245. See also Lapoujade, 142–143.
352. *RTP*, IV, 253. Enright, V, 918.
353. *RTP*, IV, 254. Enright, V, 919.

FIVE

Patterns of Palimpsest

James's Theories and Proust's Prose in the Purview of Neuro-Cognitive Science

"The brain has emerged as the prime vehicle of selfhood—after the soul, and the psyche, even after memory, the locus of identity for Proust [. . .] and many others,"[1] observed Maria Warner. In its examination of the elusive self, cognitive neuroscience not only scans, pictures, and measures the living brain at levels from behavioral to cellular, it looks to literature as well. Art, particularly the art of language, encapsulates the workings of a brain that cannot wriggle out of a machine or refuse permission to subject itself to research. Proust, penultimate observer of the narrative brain at work, nears the top of many a project that also claims a footing in William James's astute descriptions of the process of consciousness.

Experience, noted James, is different for each of us. Neuroscientists attempt to tell us why: the patterns vary, Maria Warner explains, because "the smallest differences in emotional histories and life circumstances will foster distinctions." As new experience overwrites old in patterns of palimpsest, the cultural moment or "l'air du temps" leaves its mark on us as it did on the early twentieth-century's "modernist" writers for whom the very uniqueness, variability, and unpredictability of the self's life in time became a common focus.

> Chaque artiste semble ainsi comme le citoyen d'une patrie inconnue, oubliée de lui- même, différente de celle d'où viendra, appareillant pour la terre, un autre artiste. [. . .] Quand la vision de l'univers se modifie, s'épure, devient plus adéquate au souvenir de la patrie intérieure, il est bien naturel que cela se traduise par une altération géné-

rale, des sonorités chez le musicien comme de la couleur chez le peintre.[2]

[Each artist seems thus to be the native of an unknown country, which he himself has forgotten, and which is different from that whence another great artist, setting sail for the earth, will eventually emerge. [. . .] When his vision of the universe is modified, purified, becomes more adapted to his memory of his inner homeland, it is only natural that this should be expressed by a musician in a general alteration of sonorities, as of colours by a painter.[3]]

Franco Moretti has observed the power of cultural forces to shape novelistic production and the occurrence of precipitating events that contribute to divergence in the prevalent paradigms of narrative content, perspective, and style. A cultural "trigger" will undermine the prevalent intellectual climate and its formal expression in the novel and cue the emergence of a new perspective or taxonomy of literature; a new way of looking at life upends existing literary forms and engenders new ones.[4] The novel, according to Haun Saussy, is a "permeable membrane."[5]

It is in the realm of the imaginary or explanatory narrative that the results of cultural pressures are visible. Moretti undercores the turn in the first years of the twentieth century toward what he calls "the irreducibly singular."[6] In Proust's narrator's "snapshot" or capsule memories of Albertine, his inability to capture her in any epistemological fullness, and the instability of his representations of her despite his attempt to imprison her, we recognize the futility of any attempt to penetrate the brain or fathom the total psychic history of a different discrete self, as described in James's *Principles of Psychology*.

For the generation of novelists classified as "stream of consciousness" writers—beginning with Proust's explosively original metaphorical vitality in the reconstruction of self through memory and the exploration of the fringe of relations and feeling—William James had refocused cultural attention on a comprehensive and beautifully expressed summation of laboratory and theoretical research on individual human psychology to that day. He had laid the basis for research still ongoing in neuro-cognitive science laboratories interested in the same questions. His work itself became a palimpsest for patterns of epistemological, literary, and scientific exploration.

But James has not received the critical attention he deserves as a source for Proust's writing the way others of his generation have. Elizabeth Czoniczer did not credit him as one of the major medical, psychological, or psychiatric sources she calls the "antécédents." Although she does speculate that textbooks by major writers in the field would likely have been present in Proust's home. Justin O'Brien has pointed out that in 1957 Dr. Wilder Penfield used implantation of electrodes in subjects' brains to reproduce affective experience resembling Proust's descriptions, referring to the presence of a "stream of consciousness" recorded in memory but forgotten for purposes of intentional recall. O'Brien notes the term's origin in James's texts without pursuing the comparison. While Penfield suggested that the purpose of forgotten experience was to provide for fuller and "automatic interpretation of the present,"[7] this relational purpose for brain storage of experience, as Proust described it, more complex and substantial than the initial occurrence seemed at the time, is seconded today in much greater detail in the work of Gerald Edelman; substantiated, too, is the fundamental significance of the "fringe of relations" described by James.

Utilizing his training in physiology and his powers of observation and introspection, William James had suggested that the continuously altering stream of conscious awareness had its basis in the combined action of the brain and body,[8] emotions and nerves, as a system working together. Since body and mind act together as this Jamesian "ensemble," notes Edward S. Reed, through our cognitive powers we perceive lived experience in the present, subjective thoughts and feelings about our experiences, and memories of them the same way that we experience space—as a streaming whole.[9] Jonah Lehrer, author of *Proust was a Neuroscientist*, suggested that James discovered the idea of the "ensemble"[10] of mental substance by reading Walt Whitman, a poet James often quoted. Art, posited Lehrer, leads the way and science follows.

However, the idea of this form of art/science connection in cultural evolution is neither new with Lehrer's book, nor is his model of it necessarily accurate. Daniel Engber, like Lehrer, spent time as a graduate student in neuroscience. His experience was filled with "madeleine moments" like that of every other neuroscience student. Proust is quoted so frequently at the beginning of neuroscience lectures and papers that it almost feels "obligatory,"[11] writes Engber.

But the fact that early twentieth-century writers, composers, and painters explored the workings of the mind in areas as diverse as consciousness, experience, memory, free will, taste, adaptation, vision, does not mean they spontaneously and uniquely uncovered the workings of the brain that have ignited today's neuroscientific research. More likely is the fact that William James, among other scientists before and since who researched and deliberated on such questions of human experience and brought them to the public eye, contributed to the coincident artistic exploration. While Engber recognizes Paul Sollier's concurrent work on the reviviscence of affective memory, for the major leaps in the understanding of psychological processes on which Proust and artists contemporary with him based their work, Engber credits William James. What Proust did, according to Engber, that places the madeleine at the beginning of articles, lectures, and textbooks for today's neuroscientists doing the nuts-and-bolts research on how the brain works does not supplant

James's preeminent contributions to the discussion, but earns that position for tea and cake because Proust was able *to express it best*.

In 1999, Jean-Yves Tadié, professor and editor of the most recent Pléiade edition of *À la recherche du temps perdu*, and his brother Marc, also a professor and a neurosurgeon, together published *Le Sens de la mémoire*, in which they characterize memory as a source of individual identity. This notion, however, was certainly not original with them. In *The Varieties of Religious Experience* James suggests that it derives from British sources, including Locke: "What you mean by it ["the question of personal identity"] is just your chain of particular memories, says he."[12] The questions are not new.

The Tadié brothers, in accord with Lehrer and well in advance of his 2007 book, conjecture that literary works may serve as forerunners to subsequent scientific corroboration. Perhaps it is a question of publicizing the issues. Scientific explanations follow as methods and means to explain become available.

The Tadié brothers' historical overview of nineteenth- and twentieth-century work on memory features only Europeans: Taine, Ribot, the physicians Broca, Wernicke and Déjerine, Freud, Ebbinghaus, and Bergson. It then skips to Gerald Edelman's work on the reentry patterns of brain interactivity, completely omitting William James. The only reference to James's work is a quotation comparing memory to a scar left by experience on cerebral tissue. In fact, a quotation they attribute to the 1890 edition of the *Principles of Psychology* omits a page reference (which would have indicated that the authors had actually read James—something that may not be the case).[13] A reviewer in *Sciences Humaines* notes that the brothers Tadié emphasize the importance for Proust of a focused beam of attention in the formation of enduring memories.[14] This notion of a "beam of attention" was already evident in James's writings.

Memory, for the Tadié brothers, rests in large part on the bulwark of the "affect" and on the relational aspects of experience (James's "flights" and "fringe"), which they feel surpasses voluntary effort.[15] Imagination, like sensation and emotion, is for them a critical element of human character better evidenced in the work of artists than in laboratory science. Although their interest is specifically in understanding memory, their method is to use literary sources as the point of departure for subsequent scientific validation. In their view, it is the selectivity of forgetting that permits the individuation of identity, although clearly it must also be an effect of the selectivity of remembering. Creativity, and ultimately individual personality, resides in the "regrouping" of perceptual experience—sensory and emotional memory—that occurs in the brain and that we feel when memories resurface to awareness[16] and mingle with our present moment, our willingness to accept their truth as part of our self (an idea James had clearly articulated in *The Principles of Psychology* in 1890).

In this way, each artist develops his own personal "vision" and a view of the universe rooted in the neuronal web of self, his personal sensibility.

Memory, according to cognitive researchers Bernard J. Baars, Uma Ramamurthy, and Stan Franklin, serves consciousness in the very ways Proust noted: voluntary memories can be summoned at will; spontaneously resurgent memories are stimulated by sensory cues, sometimes flooding the subject with pleasure and exhilaration in Proust's "moments bienheureux." At other times, however, spontaneously arising memories can bring unwanted pain (exactly as described by Proust's narrator in the experience of Albertine's absence after her abrupt and unanticipated departure). These painful memories that arise unexpectedly can be likened to what is now called post-traumatic stress disorder, explored by Proust as "le choc moral imposé" [a spiritual shock that comes from without].[17] This is the nefarious clash with Habit the narrator experiences after Albertine's desertion, when pain floods over him as the objects in the room vibrate with memories when touched by his gaze, his attention flitting and momentarily lingering on the armchair in which Albertine sat and the pedals of the pianola her mule-clad feet played. The ordeal and trauma of suffering so well described by Proust, like a repeating and reverberating bird-call or the substance less repetition of graffiti on a wall, here represent a form of what we now call "flashback," a painful and unwanted obsessively resurgent memory, according to the these three writers.

Their research uses Proust as masthead for their model and James as background reference, just as Engber has warned us would be the case, with theory and method in use here that neither James nor Proust could ever have imagined.[18]

The three authors delineate two types of spontaneous and unsolicited memory, and note the difference between what Proust called "involuntary" memory and what they term "non-voluntary" memory. Because of the potential for spontaneously arising memories that occur not only unwilled but, as in the case of the painful memories of Albertine after she abandons him, most certainly counter to the will of the narrator, researchers Baars, Ramamurthy, and Franklin separately categorize them. Literary research tends to focus on the aesthetic role of the narrator's pleasurable resurgent memories; important, too, in providing depth to the narrator's description of his suffering are the comparably resurgent memories that create the emotional pain only eliminated by forgetting. In their description of the workings of voluntary and the two types of involuntary memory in consciousness, these researchers turn for backdrop to William James's work on habit and the psychology of volition. James's work, they suggest, encapsulates the thinking and depicts the laboratory research of his period. They draw on the same notions of intentional effort to remember and those that occur without intent that James had described and that Proust used to illustrate the waves of torment his narrator felt after Albertine vanished, the misery that recurred unbidden: "la reviviscence intermittente et involontaire d'une impression spécifique, venue du dehors, et que nous n'avons pas choisie" [the intermittent and involuntary reviviscence of a specific impression that has come to us from without and was not chosen by us].[19]

James's exploration of how we voluntarily manage to get out of bed on a freezing morning (in the days before central heating) and that the authors call "an example of making a voluntary decision contrary to one's own desire" was a part of his "ideomotor hypothesis." This would include actions performed without focusing attention on the means or arriving at conscious ends without struggling with the strategy for doing so, the coping mechanisms provided for by memory. This calls to mind Proust's narrator's feckless deliberations on pursuing Albertine directly or waiting for her to return on her own, while comparing his feelings about each possible course of action to how he felt at the end of his relationships, real or imaginary, with Gilberte and Mme. de Guermantes. He wrestles with the active and passive sides of decision-making, delving into the emotional ramifications of each possibility. Action, however, is not part of the initial plan, which is mired in an emotional cloud of cogitation upon alternatives. The seemingly endless reflection so characteristic of Proust's narrator that slows the pace of the novel's action to a muddy crawl to the great frustration of many readers reproduces the density of the lived experience so appealing to neuroscience.

The painful associations that recur unbidden (as memories of Albertine are generated by perceptions of surroundings and habits that once did but no longer include her presence) do not serve the same aesthetic function in *À la recherche du temps perdu* as the joyful resurgences of childhood, Balbec and Venice. Painful memories are explored as example of the intermittence of emotion remembered and reported—the flashback—but they are not used for the same joyful formal resurrective purpose in the novel ("salvationist," as some critics term it) that enables the narrator to frame and structure his creative endeavor. The soothing of forgetting, like the balm of his mother's kiss, will ease the narrator's distress, but the novelist does not see pain as the same generator of a literary aesthetic or fictional structural format as the "moments bienheureux."

As is so often the case, the Baars et al. article begins with Proust, recognizes James, and veers into technical analysis of the mechanisms of episodic memory, association, and conscious attention in the initiation of behavior. A discussion of the "fringe" or "penumbra" of awareness signaled by James and exploited by Proust provides background for the authors' explanation of the way episodic memory revives past experience when a feeling of familiarity is triggered, whether pleasurable or painful. The point to reiterate once again is that James summarized the thinking of his time on these questions, Proust explored them in painstaking detail in his art in ways very reminiscent of James's theory, and neuro-cognitive science now has better tools with which to revisit the same questions and explain the mechanisms.

> "L'impression est pour l'écrivain ce qu'est l'expérimentation pour le savant, avec cette différence que chez le savant le travail de l'intelligence précède et chez l'écrivain vient après. Ce que nous n'avons pas eu à déchiffrer, à éclaircir par notre effort personnel, ce qui était clair avant nous, n'est pas à nous. Ne vient de nous-même que ce que nous tirons de l'obscurité qui est en nous et que ne connaissent pas les autres."[20]
>
> [The impression is for the writer what experiment is for the scientist, with the difference that in the scientist the work of the intelligence precedes the experiment and in the writer it comes after the impression. What we have not had to decipher, to elucidate by our own efforts, what was clear before we looked at it, is not ours. From ourselves comes only that which we drag forthe from the obscurity which lies within us, that which to others is unknown.[21]]

Contemporary neuroscientists, including Gerald Edelman, study the brain with the help of tools listed in a 2004 article on consciousness in time written by Oliver Sacks: functional MRIs and PET scans, computerized neural modeling—all more complicated than anything of James or his contemporaries could ever conceive. Research using these tools substantiates the fact that sense data (that in James's theory of emotion stem initially from a bodily reaction to an outside stimulus) are combined by an adaptive brain into associated conscious experience. Sacks suggests that "population theory" may explain how—by determining the grouping of neurons—experience alters brain operation, "literal[ly] shaping the connectivity and function of the brain."[22]

But neither Whitman nor any other artist is the standard against which Edelman and his colleagues measure their discoveries and examine their theories. They turn to William James as benchmark for their science, as does Sacks. Although they may refer to Proust's elaboration in art of these very phenomena, it is because the questions were raised by science and continue to be interesting scientifically that they are revisited. Thus it is that James's view—that sensory and perceptual inputs blend with remembered experience and other forms of cognitive awareness and do not "displace each other" or "interfere with each other's perception" ("seen things comes at last to be thought of as always having a fringe of *other things possible to be seen* spreading in all directions round about it"[23])—has been supported by current research.

Oliver Sacks reiterates Edelman's view and ultimately James's that perception and memory "interact" in the brain and lead to what he calls "a thematic and personal continuity in the consciousness of every individual." In the background of every person's perception is the network of individual experience, his "reflections, memory, associations" that intervene to flavor those perceptions and his selective attention to stimulation, giving him his unique self. What we see in the environment around us is formulated by who we are and what has come before in our very personal lives. For Proust as for James, Sacks observes, there was no other reality than that of "je," the individual observer/actor, immersed in the multiplicity of flowing moments of a self in time. Included in an artist's personal vision, his individual sensibility, are the many elements of his conscious experience as it develops within the unique neuronal connections of his brain, blending with his unique memory and feeling: "One extraordinary phenomenal feature of conscious experience is that normally it is all of a piece—it is unitary. Any experienced conscious moment simultaneously includes sensory input, consequences of motor activity, imagery, emotions, fleeting memories, bodily sensations, and a peripheral fringe."[24]

When space is too extensive to be perceived at once, and when events are spread over time, we do conceive them successively, notes Edward S. Reed, not in a "smooth" single view but rather with "a certain granularity, being composed of many separate scenes and situations."[25] This multiple view of space and time, described earlier by James, parallels the structure of *À la recherche du temps perdu*, written over time and about time. Although Proust's novel as a written work retains the additive units of experiences remembered, the subject of the work, in the medium of language, is an artist's depiction of an individual's unique feelings of a flowing and clumping conscious personal experience, his beam of attention focusing first here then there, on the spaces inhabited and attended to over time and remembered, to reflect and reverberate, revealing, beyond time and for all time, the interior sensibility and vision of that individual artist.

Given the human mind's ability to discriminate and to associate, certain objects, according to James, can stand in for others, as "signs" for their "reality," and "the feeling of them [. . .] a present sensation, is eclipsed in the glare of the knowledge, which is a merely imagined one."[26] The past, or knowledge of it, is reactivated to affect the present: "a present sensation can at any time become the sign of a represented one judged to be more real."[27] For Proust's narrator that past experience can be "retrouvé" to feel more real than the normal, contingent reality streaming rapidly by. We carry our past, our previous learning, and neural connections with us, just as Proust's narrator will discover; it is always there and colors our reading of our present. Every present moment incorporates what Gerald Edelman calls "the dynamic interaction between memory and ongoing perceptions."[28] This, Edelman refers to as patterns of brain activity that create the panorama we see around us and the rapport with it that our individual "self" maintains based on sensory cues.[29] Thus, the bodily connections of sensation and response that James placed at the core of emotional feeling in his theory of emotion incarnate what individuates the artist's sensibility. Any personal consciousness with its included memory is individual, not commonly shared; it is the property of a particular "je" with all the bodily privacy that implies, as Edelman notes: "Observations from without, or even from within, by a demon that does not have the animal's body cannot fully capture the content of that privacy."[30] Once again, the substance that interested James and Proust is still of interest to neurology. But what makes an artist is not that experience or consciousness alone; it is the expressive ability to give that content form with style. And it is the appeal of his style that accounts for why Proust is so commonly cited as point of departure.

When a past experience is recalled with sufficient strength to garner the attention, its recurrence is not simply an identical repeat. James states that a recurrent memory is not like a clock chime that repeats itself as a totally indistinguishable duplicate.[31] It returns, whole, but known as past, our past. How does the brain do this?

By examining the brain's structure and chemistry to understand the major features of its activities in "perception, memory, action and intention"[32] and in generating its adaptive ability, contemporary neuroscience is attempting to find out: "to account for the Jamesian properties of consciousness requires a much more dynamic picture involving integration of the activities of multiple brain regions."[33] The repetition of a memory is context-dependent and varies because of the "degenerative" nature of brain function: similar results are produced by differing groupings of neurons,[34] and in different individuals the patterns of the regrouping vary. Using techniques of magnetoencephalography, Edelman states: "The data also show that different individuals reporting similar conscious responses have different individual patterns—that is, each case is distinct from the others."[35] James had suggested something like this more than one hundred years before:

> Our earlier chapters have taught us to believe that, whilst we think, our brain changes, and that, like the aurora borealis, its whole internal equilibrium shifts with every pulse of change. The precise nature of the shifting at a given moment is a product of many factors. The accidental state of local nutrition or blood-supply may be among them. But just as one of them certainly is the influence of outward objects on the sense-organs during the moment, so is another certainly the very special susceptibility in which the organ has been left at that moment by all it has gone through in the past. Every brain-state is partly determined by the nature of this entire past succession. Alter the latter in any part, and the brain-state must be somewhat different. Each present brain-state is a record in which the eye of Omniscience might read all the foregone history of its owner.[36]

Edelman restates James's explanation based on current research, saying that in consciousness the brain forms interconnected associations spontaneously, mixing memory and sensory input, imagery, and imagination:

"Because of the degeneracy of the neural circuits that arise dynamically as a result of these selective processes, associative interactions are guaranteed."[37] When James states, as Edelman notes, that for consciousness to exist there is no need for an external witness, because "the thoughts themselves are the thinker," Edelman's science confirms the position of the "je" as the combination sensor, actor, thinker—a "first person [who] is simply present."[38]

For Proust, this is the central and essential axis around and through which all experience floats. The ever-changing range on which Proust's narrator focuses as the beam of his attention wanders from next to next, corresponding to Edelman's description of normal conscious functioning: "Higher-order consciousness that is reflected by qualia [*sic*] in a high-dimensional space, and which is integrated to yield a scene having a focal center with shifting fringes and ongoing changes, can never be focused to just one precise token."[39] As for James (who theorized the "specious present") and like Proust's narrator's search for lost time and his unique personal history of self, the moment of primary consciousness, the ongoing now, is all that exists. The past and the future, according to Edelman, are mental assemblages,[40] fictions, awareness of which is accessible intermittently as the beam of attention focuses on them or as sensory stimulants bring them to mind.

"LES INTERMITTENCES DU COEUR" [THE INTERMITTENCIES OF THE HEART]: THE HEART OF THE SEARCH

Despite his original intention to use "Les Intermittences du coeur" as the overall title of a two-volume work—the first a volume of fiction to be followed by a work of aesthetic theory—because it "fait allusion dans le monde moral à une maladie du corps"[41] [alludes, in the moral world, to a bodily malady], Proust changed his mind.[42] Instead, he decided to restrict the phrase to the heading for a section of *Sodome et Gomorrhe* focusing on the narrator's second visit to Balbec. Its use would signal the irregular, unpredictable occurrence of feelings, memories, past experiences as they come into the spotlight of attention unintentionally and sporadically, spurred into existence by random actions and sensory encounters.

The totality of our experiences is not constantly available to us, Proust narrator realizes. "À n'importe quel moment que nous la considérions, notre âme totale n'a qu'une valeur presque fictive, malgré le nombreux bilan de ses richesses, car tantôt les unes, tantôt les autres sont indisponibles, qu'il s'agisse d'ailleurs de richesses effectives aussi bien que de celles de l'imagination" [No matter at what moment we consider it, our total soul has only a more or less fictitious value, in spite of the rich inventory of its assets, for now some, now others are unrealisable, whether they are real riches or those of the imagination].[43]

The discontinuities of memory and feeling are integral to the patterns of the narrator's psychology. As the brain accesses varying associations, the self is remembered in chunks of interrupted experience. Fiction and life resemble each other in this respect; both are written in sections and made whole for narrative purposes. "Car aux troubles de la mémoire sont liées les intermittences du coeur" [For with the perturbations of memory are linked the intermittencies of the heart].[44]

Intermittence became a key concept in Proust's work because it highlighted his narrator's temerity, "nervosité" [nervous excitability], and his insecure fear of change. The dissolution of the present self into new experience, the fear of his parents' death, the lack of control over his life and legacy haunt the narrator, as they likely did the author. When his grandmother leaves his room on the first night of his first visit to Balbec, he suffers acutely:

> Peut-étre cet effroi que j'avais [. . .] de coucher dans une chambre inconnue, peut-être cet effroi n'est-il que la forme la plus humble, obscure, organique, presque inconsciente, de ce grand refus désespéré qu'opposent les choses qui constituent le meilleur de notre vie présente à ce que nous revêtons mentalement de notre acceptation de la formule d'un avenir où elles ne figurent pas.[45]
>
> [Perhaps this fear I had [. . .] of sleeping in a strange room, perhaps this fear is only the most humble, obscure, organic, al most unconscious form of that great and desperate resistance put up by the things that constitute the better part of our present life against our mentally acknowledging the possibility of a future in which they are to have no part.[46]]

This terror extends to the dissolution of his self, his emotions, his memories: "mes défauts, mon caractère qui ne se résignaient pas à l'idée de ne plus être et ne voulaient pour moi ni du néant, ni d'une éternité où ils ne seraient plus" [my frailties, my character, which did not easily resign themselves to the idea of ceasing to be].[47] He is obsessed by the need to create evidence of his unique existence with its haze of feelings and diaphanous fringes, his personal vision that can only be preserved permanently as a work of art. Although forgetting acts as a soothing balm, this fight with the angel of death entails modifications, even at the cellular level:

> [C]e serait donc une vraie mort de nous-même, mort suivie, il est vrai, de résurrection, mais en un moi différent [. . .] la longue résistance désespéré et quotidienne à la mort fragmentaire et successive telle qu'elle s'insère dans toute la durée de notre vie, détachant de nous à chaque moment des lambeaux de nous-mêmes sur la mortification desquels des cellules nouvelles multiplieront.[48]

> [It would be in a real sense the death of the self, a death followed, it is true, by resurrection, but in a different self [. . .] the long desperate, daily resistance to the fragmentary and continuous death that insinuates itself throughout the whole course of our life, detaching from us at each moment a shred of ourself, dead matter on which new cells will multiply and grow.[49]]

The fact of the body, which supports the conscious mind, hides the detritus of experience in the dark lair of unconscious memory, in a web of associations and a network of neuronal patterning inaccessible most of the time to our conscious attention: "Mais si le cadre de sensations où elles sont conservées est ressaisi, elles ont à leur tour ce même pouvoir d'expulser tout ce qui leur est incompatible, d'installer seul en nous, le moi qui les vécut" [But of the context of sensations in which they are preserved is recaptured, they acquire in turn the same power of expelling everything that is incompatible with them, if installing alone in us the self that originally lived them].[50]

James makes just this point in chapter 25 of *The Principles of Psychology,* which was translated into French by G. Dumas as "La Théorie de l'Émotion" and published by Alcan in 1902:[51] "how much our mental life is knit up with our corporeal frame, in the strictest sense of the term."[52] "The emotion here is nothing but the feeling of a bodily state, and it has a purely bodily cause."[53] Music, a flavor, or a smell can remind us of the past, "due to the arousing of associational trains which reverberate. A flavor may fairly shake us by the ghosts of 'banquet halls deserted,' which it suddenly calls up; or a smell may make us feel almost sick with the waft it brings over our memory of 'gardens that are ruins and pleasure-houses that are dust.'"[54]

The most striking similarity between James's and Proust's descriptions of this phenomenon, however, occurs when the narrator leans over to unfasten his shoes on his second visit to Balbec. He is swept back to the self he was when, on his first visit to Balbec, his grandmother bent down to undo his shoes. The pain of losing her, which he had not felt so deeply at the time of her death, overwhelms him. In the chapter on emotion, James writes that "the mere memory or imagination of the object may suffice to liberate the excitement [. . .] and we melt more over a mother who is dead than we ever did when she was living."[55] As Proust does later, James notes that the revived emotion feels as if we are reliving the original: "This cause is now only an idea, but this idea produces the same organic irradiations, or almost the same, which were produced by its original, so that the emotion is again a reality. We have 'recaptured' it. [. . .] [T]he emotion, to be distinct, must become real again."[56] In a flashback, the moment that was lost (*perdu*) has been regained (*retrouvé*).

Spontaneous but *unhappy* memories elicit various "qualia" or feelings in the history of self that recur unbidden in just the same way as the "moments bienheureux" [blissful moments], as noted by Baars, et al.

The concept of irregularity in emotion experienced over time predates Proust's decision to use involuntary memory as structural underpinning of his novel, according to Antoine Compagnon, and is more emotionally compelling. The multiplicity of the self over time accommodates spontaneous memories that are accompanied by a joyous sense of well-being as well as those that are painful and unwanted. The loss of his grandmother felt long after her passing and the passages in which Albertine's image float in and out of the narrator's emotional awareness bring agony and the pain of loss, pain that will not be sublimated in the joy of artistic creation.[57]

Traumas that return to awareness unbidden, like the stressful memories soldiers have of war, do not serve the same structural aesthetic purpose as happy memories of childhood when the narrator decides to use them to spur his writing, but they are as real and heartfelt and stem from the same psychological process, all described by William James in *The Principles of Psychology*. Proust was determined to explore this process in its positive and negative sides, but decided to exploit, for its greater aesthetic value and his plot's structure, the analogy between joyful memories and the joy of creation.

Proust's use of the concept of intermittence to contrast the fractures and interruptions of remembered experience with the desire for a continuous, integrated sense of self was central to a panel discussion featuring Oliver Sacks, Richard Macksey, and Mary Warnock. "Spontaneous memory" was the solution Proust envisioned to provide "continuity" to the self through memory, they asserted.

Macksey immediately noted the importance of William James's efforts to "describe personal identity and memory."[58]

Warnock remarked on Proust's disparagement of photographic memory and voluntary efforts to recall that do not encompass the affective features of a moment of experience or assist in forming an enduring sense of self or of others. She termed Proust a philosopher (putting him in the same category as James) and highlighted the religious connotations of the language he used to portray "anchor" moments on which his plot and aesthetic were based: "I would only add that although Proust portrays the moments of integration, these visitations of unbidden, spontaneous memory as miracles, as something like the gift of grace or a conversion experience."[59]

Sacks identified elements in Gerald Edelman's work on the "inventive," "imaginative," "innovative" aspects of memory that bring the history of a life lived, including the internal and affective aspects of that history, close to biography or fiction. This is reminiscent of James's idea that memory is a fiction that we believe because it feels warm and real to us, perhaps, then, a blend of science and art.[60]

As Engber notes, for years journals of neurology and cognitive science have included articles mentioning Proust and considering the connections between him and their discipline. Most begin with a reference to William James. But others incorporate ideas James promulgated without noting his part in the discussion.

Among these is Renate Bartsch, a member of the research group working in Logic and Cognitive Science at the University of Amsterdam, whose book *Concept Formation, Remembering, and Understanding: Dynamic Conceptual Semantics and Proust's "À la recherche du temps perdu"*[61] describes memory as a grouping of neurons that acting together produce understanding. Previous experience informs and shapes our understanding of ongoing experience. Processing what goes on around us assists in adaptation and is to some extent hard-wired into the species. She examines Proust's use of memory and, like James but without acknowledging his contributions, underscores the idea that memory is not a static file sitting in a cabinet drawer in the mind but rather something that is fabricated in the act of remembering[62] as ongoing sensory and motor inputs interact[63] with stored "imbedded" experience. She also highlights Jamesian notions of the role in memory of association by similarity and contiguity.[64] Resurgent memory brings the narrator joy because it reveals the patterning without distraction by current experience or voluntary (i.e., purposefully oriented) behavior:[65] "Each time such a remembrance gets unfolded by seeing in its similarity to other episodes, the Narrator reports experiencing an aesthetic or intellectual pleasure."[66]

However, well before Bartsch, and even before 1896 when Bergson (whom Bartsch considers a "model" for Proust's use of memory to organize the narrator's life history and the aesthetic theory underpinning the novel[67]) published *Matière et mémoire,* William James had described the conscious and emotive linkage between mind and body, as well as the changeability and multiple layers of a continuing self that exist in our personal subjective experience over time, whether viewed from within or by others.

Of writers who did recognize James in connection with Proust, examples might include Randy L. Buckner's article in *Neuron* in May 2004 entitled "The Potion's Magic." In it he describes the olfactory effect during remembering. Drawing from William James for the suggestion that "the cortical processes that underlie imagination and sensation are not quite as discrete as one at first is tempted to suppose," Buckner uses Proust's madeleine experience to illustrate the reactivation of memory by means of the sensations of smell and taste. James and Proust are joined here in an effort to understand the olfactory stimulus and memory and to give literary heft to contemporary research.[68]

While James was overshadowed by functional and behavioral psychology as well as by Freudian analysis through the 1960s, cognitive scientists have recently renewed examination of James's theories because they are also interested in understanding subjective experience and the neural machinery that underlies it, and they now have the technological tools to do so.

Utilizing current techniques of brain research, Kirsten Shepherd-Barr and Gordon M. Shepherd examine the neurological apparatus responsible for Proust's narrator's experience of resurgent memory upon tasting the madeleine dipped in tea in their 1998 article, "Madeleines and Neuromodernism: Reassessing Mechanisms of Autobiographical Memory in Proust."[69] Literary scholars, they suggest, increasingly use the tools and research of neurological science to explicate modernist literature. Proust, they write, used resurgent memory in a "salvationist" manner (a term that certainly adds to the religious aura surrounding the revelations of the madeleine). Although they note that Proust credited precursors Chateaubriand, Nerval, Musset [*sic*, but actually Baudelaire, not Musset],[70] who shared the experience of a sensory trigger bringing about a powerful emotional memory, the authors argue that he himself distinguished his experience from that of other authors[71] by using it as aesthetic scaffolding for structuring his work, thereby giving it far greater prominence. The moment brings intense joy but not an immediate grasp of the reason for it. The narrator exerts effort to understand, and perceives the "revelation" and the "quasi-divine grace"—more religious terms—as a means of shaking off habit and the dulling ordinariness of daily life in exchange for the glory of a revitalized memory trace, or engram. The associations engendered return his childhood life in Combray to his full attention. And this the authors attempt to explain using neuroscientific data to describe the eliciting of memory based on a sensory trigger, just as William James had in Proust's day: "In Proust's time, a number of critics began to be aware of the relevance of brain mechanisms to understanding the nature of the memory events that Proust was probing. William James wrote. . . . " The authors note that James's account for the function of memory was based on a neurophysiological approach to memory retention and recall, one that identified brain activity as responsible for it.[72] That James's work might have had an effect on Proust's understanding of the function of memory is not far-fetched for these authors: "Proust's study of contemporary neurology while seeking treatment for asthma, and the internal evidence from the text of his awareness of his search for the 'how' as well as the 'what,' one assumes that a neurological explanation of the sort we seek would have been of keen interest to him."[73]

They describe research into the link between olfactory stimulus and memory, the effort exerted by Proust's narrator to understand the emotive impact of tasting the madeleine, the "gestalt" or wholeness of the memory of Combray eventually perceived by the narrator (James's "streaming whole") through use of "content-addressable memory" in which a small bit of information permits recall of something in entirety, the use of brain-imaging technologies to identify the locus of these effects, as well as listing chemical components responsible for the accompanying emotions.[74] They conclude that a neurological study lifts the madeleine out of the realm of "literary cliché" and bolsters the neuroscientific basis in fact that Proust employed. Given the reference that they, like so many others, make to William James, it is hard not to see his writings as contributory.

In 2000, cognitive and brain scientists Russell Epstein and David Galin examined the neuroscience behind William James's stream of thought. Within a few years Donald Dryden joined them in publishing further work on James's theories of consciousness and the fringe of relations as exemplified in Marcel Proust's aesthetic. Their articles brought these two authors together in a coherent way, looking specifically at consciousness, memory, and aesthetic theory. That some form of relation might exist between James and Proust simply could not be ignored.

In "The Neural-Cognitive Basis of the Jamesian Stream of Thought," Russell Epstein observes the revival of interest in James's theories about thought among neuroscientists in the early 1990s. He analyzes James's descriptions of the "nucleus" or central and attended focus of conscious thought as well as what James termed the "fringe"—the surrounding halo of relational information or vaguely perceived background and prelinguistic non-articulated associated knowledge in our memory that accompanies the thought and acts to aim it in certain specific directions, to alter its focus.[75] Epstein's interest is in explaining the function of the "fringe" and how it is active in the progress of thought.

In drawing the distinction between "nucleus" and "fringe," James used the image of the kaleidoscope in which a momentarily stable pattern is separated from the next by a brief interlude of process to its successor. This brief stability is like the substantive "nucleus" of a thought, often an image or pre-verbal "sensory representation" that holds our attention.[76] The "fringe," on the other hand, has to do with all the unattended associated relations of that thought or of the thought coming next in the streaming sequence that our consciousness elicits from our memory. Voluntary memory seeks—through the encyclopedic reference of associations—to locate the particular piece of information we want, as in situations where we have forgotten a name and have only partial information in our conscious awareness. The "fringe," according to Epstein, also includes elements of expectation, familiarity, intention, summation, satisfactoriness.[77] Feelings could be counted among the associations in the "fringe," as well. In fantasy or dream, the associations receive greater prominence. Epstein distinguishes between associations and the feelings that gauge or measure their appropriateness by proposing that they occur in separate areas of the brain.[78]

Long before current methods of studying brain anatomy and function were available, James presupposed an active set of neuronal memory connections as well as a guidance system in charge and observed that genius encompasses greater awareness of the associative relational network than is visible to others. Epstein delves into specific brain research to explain his view of James's "fringe" and its control mechanisms, made evident with the help of brain-imaging technology only recently in common use. On that basis he assigns specific functions to certain neuronal brain structures and advocates continued research into the behavioral, physical, and linguistic aspects of human consciousness,[79] as William James attempted to do.

Four years later, in "Consciousness, Art and the Brain," Epstein outlines James's interest in exploring "mental life" by the traditional method of introspection and by scientific experiment in an effort to expose the brain's actual neural apparatus for bestowing conscious experience on humans. Proust, Epstein asserts, explored the same turf.[80] In Proust's superb introspective rendition of individual experience, Epstein recognizes the conceptual tools forged by William James with a similar neural basis.[81] James's depiction of the stream of consciousness and the nature of the metaphors he uses to depict it, Epstein maintains, are closely linked to Proust's prose, his observations and assumptions about the way the mind works, his presentations of involuntary memory, and his narrative art. Proust's suppositions about conscious experience and his aesthetic theory descend from James's work on the stream of thought and specifically on the focal and associated relational aspects of conscious thought James termed the "nucleus" and "fringe." Proust's art reflects the associative elements of the "fringe" posited by James that are normally relegated to the background of experience. Surrounding the salient conscious sensory material that "dominates each individual thought" is the "underlying network of associations that controls the transition from one thought to another" and directs its forward movement, confirms or corrects its direction,[82] a network of associations of relation and affect that encloses conscious sensory perception like a halo or web and directs the flow of conscious thought without being evident in the experience itself.

Only randomly occurring involuntary memories triggered by sensory stimulation can, using Epstein's term, "re-instantiate" the affective fullness and substance of past experience as it really was; that is not attainable through voluntarily sought "snapshot" type memories summoned at will. Epstein contrasts a privileged "re-instantiation" experienced by Proust's narrator, a "moment bienheureux," with mere "snap-shot" instances of voluntary recall. The snapshot, according to Epstein, resembles "le passé composé," so to speak, an occasion of intellectual and conceptual reconstruction of a past moment of lived experience extracted from its affective milieu. It is highly conscious, goal-directed, created intentionally for a purpose, akin to James's conception of the "nucleus" of conscious thought, and so lacks the affective tang of an instance of the past that incorporates the larger network of associations that relate to that moment in the individual's history. Involuntary memory, on the other hand, widens the horizons considerably to include not only a specific event or place or person that Epstein terms "perceptual and spatial information," but also "the whole tangled web of sensory, emotional, and appetitive experiences that made up these earlier moments in time *as well as* an appreciation of how all these experiences fit together in a whole."[83] James conceived the "fringe" as the relational part of the stream of consciousness that hints (to introspection) of the surrounding network of memories, potentially germane associations and desires, and some future directional information. It transmits the flavor of an experience that is only available as its internal resonance rather than something that could appear in a photograph.[84] Proust noted the need for distance from an event in order to develop its "fringe." The imagination, or "fantasy" in Epstein's words, can only appreciate the digressive aspects surrounding a specific experience, its entire context of relations and possibilities, other potential courses of action not taken, when it is not faced with a decision or deed demanded by events as they happen[85] and when its immediate emotional rigging has relaxed.[86] Epstein explains this as the need to appear in relief against the ordinary day-to-day of our experience that requires a widely spaced interval—or even forgetting.[87] Epstein's article attempts to relate the elated emotions Proust's narrator feels during moments of involuntary experience to the potential for similar emotions in the creation of art, calling them at base "aesthetic emotions."[88]

Proust's long digressive paragraphs—of potential alternative action and various possible emotional tacks, as well as elements that usually remain unexpressed—illustrate in his art the Jamesian "fringes" engulfing his plot. Unlike flatly descriptive narration, Proust's narrator envelops his plot in what Epstein terms the "savor" that expresses what is unique in an individual artist's sensibility,[89] his multidimensional "vision."

Metaphor, like paint, is a tool that serves to release the associative and emotive potential of the writer's experience, baring it to and reproducing it in the reader.[90] The "essence" the narrator seeks in experience, atemporal and eternal, can only be revealed through the universalizing process that is art and by the linkages of metaphor. Two disparate instantiations of a feeling, two different networks of association, are joined to reveal what is permanent and unchanging about their momentary connection.[91] A work of art reveals an artist's sensibility, the fragile and fleeting aspects of the flowing stream of his personal consciousness, his "internal memory networks"[92] that he could never explain directly and elicits that same "fringe" in the viewer (or the reader according to Maryanne Wolf[93]), creating a connection that exists beyond time:[94] "the importance of the work of art is not that it conveys the emotion, but that a [*sic*] conveys the sensibility of the person who has the emotion."[95]

Epstein points to the parts of the brain involved in producing the neurological underpinnings of James's "stream" and Proust's aesthetic theory.[96] His experimental summary generally reiterates Edelman and other contemporary researchers of brain function.

Imagination, the ability to summon memory and predict the possible outcomes to a given action, Epstein describes as useful in sequence-forward consciousness to differentiate actual from fantasy[97] and to judge the appropriateness of intended action. The parts of the brain where the "fringe" actions are mapped in MRI experiments, those areas that determine the direction of thought by measuring the "fit" of new thought with existing sensory reality, also determine the aesthetic "fit" of parts of a work of art in an unconscious measure of aptness. Epstein tells us that neuroscientists refer to this as the brain's "pattern detector."[98] Imagination is also useful for "re-experience" of past events, the intermittent memories Epstein and others term "episodic"[99] that is characteristic of narrative. James had ascribed to memory an imaginative function—or fictionalizing with the warmth of recognition and belief (something Epstein refers to as "monitoring of the imagined sequence for *autobiographical consistency*"[100])—and had observed the "narrative" emerging from association by contiguity in storytelling. "Proustian art is *narrative* art: when Proust concerns himself with conveying the memory networks that guide his stream of thought, is clear [*sic*] that he is mostly interested in episodic memories—in telling stories,"[101] writes Epstein.

Citing S. Zeki's 1999 study of visual art and the brain,[102] Epstein notes that in addition to his superb use of light and color, Vermeer, one of Proust's favorite painters, used visual clues to represent unchanging "essence" as well as a kind of psychological ambiguity that incorporates the "fringe" or unexpressed associative network. The viewer reads the painting as Proust's reader experiences a book, a story he uncovers in himself that reflects the eloquent but silent patterns of nerve currents that are stimulated in his brain.[103]

The sensations of a given moment and the associative channeling network they summon represent in Proust's art, like the patterns of a palimpsest, James's theory of consciousness. Current research in neuroscience, concludes Epstein, seems to confirm the cognitive machinery underlying the relationship.[104]

Two articles of commentary immediately followed Epstein's in the same journal issue of *Consciousness and Cognition*. The first, by D. Galin, agrees with earlier philosophical writings by Susan K. Langer that an artist produces works in order "to communicate *with himself*, not with an audience."[105] Proust's recalled "collages," in Galin's words, have greater density than voluntary memories; while Galin seems to deduce Proust's style of writing from that density,[106] he is unable to observe the kind of substantive differences in content in them that Epstein finds in voluntary versus involuntary memories. Nucleus and fringe co-exist in all experience, no matter how sifted and selective, asserts Galin.

But contrary to Galin's view, it is difficult not to recognize that something significant and affective has been omitted in the narrator's description of his experience of going up the stairs to bed in Combray, illuminated like a photo or little vignette in a single ray or spotlight, compared to the fullness of his childhood memories after the revelations of the madeleine. It is that welter of highly significant emotional consequence and history he prepares to recount. The difficulty Galin has identifying differences in pre- and post-madeleine description of experience has more to do with James's metaphors than with Proust's prose. James variously uses "flights" and "perchings," "nucleus" and "fringe," and "stream" flowing over and around rocks to describe the stream of thought. Proust utilized all the nuances of James's metaphors for what Galin calls "feature content" and "explicators" to represent consciousness and experience at different points in his narrative.[107]

The second major point of contention between Galin and Epstein has to do with the aesthetic value of a work of art. For Galin, it is the form the artist has given to his subject, rather than simply the nature of its content, that determines its artistic value:[108] the message is in the work, not in some implied relation to the creator.[109] Nonetheless, Galin lauds Epstein's article for connecting neurological advance in understanding art to James's psychology.[110]

The third article appearing in the same issue of *Consciousness and Cognition* adds further commentary. Like the Tadié brothers, D. Dryden focuses his argument on memory and notes that memory is less a straight recovery than a creative restoration project for the mind involving some sort of intellectual or "conceptual" activity.[111] Representations recovered from the past involve the search not only for the experiences that are represented, but also for some form of meaning to be attached to them.[112] The images Proust selects to depict the past experience of his narrator are, in Dryden's view, both "selective and interpretive of the experiences they represent."[113] Art makes visible the "private" in experience and, in Dryden's reading of Langer, "objectifies" it[114] in a way that always carries some conceptual baggage with it. The cacophony of experience is sorted and clarified in a work of art or history or literature and metamorphosized through the individual writer's use of language and composition. It is no longer actual experience but rather narrative or fiction, verisimilitude rather than fact: "Literary art creates an image of lived experience in the mode typified by memory, and this is one reason that memory figures so prominently in Proust's aesthetics."[115] This memory is individual, and reflects through a writer's body of works his personal sensibility.[116] But unlike Epstein, who felt that art evokes the artist's sensibility in the viewer or reader, Dryden notes, based on Langer's work, that art delivers and provokes and takes the active role in creating a reaction not only in the viewer but in the artist himself, as he discovers by means of his formulations truths that he did not anticipate,[117] creating new paradigms.

Langer, in the 1950s and 1960s, according to Dryden, suggested—again, well before Jonah Lehrer—that the arts have much to teach about the psychology of consciousness from its neurological foundations to broad cultural movements. Artists bring to public awareness a certain entrée into the private realms of subjective feeling, a subject that finds a basis of scientific explanation in the work of William James. In the "study of the neurobiology of consciousness" such as Epstein's, Dryden adds, "James is now widely recognized as an ally and as a contemporary"[118] and Langer should be considered one as well.

Proust's relations with the medical world are well documented, given his father's celebrated position as professor of medicine and international expert in public health, and his brother's as noted physician specializing in gynecology. This is well attested to in Donald Wright's study *Du discours medical dans "À la recherche du temps pedu": science et souffrance.*[119] Connections between Proust and the Parisian neurological establishment of his day, his reach into the medical world in an effort to relieve the asthma symptoms first experienced in childhood and suffered throughout his life (thought at the time to be neurological in origin) are reiterated by Julien Bogousslavsky.[120] He remarks in particular on Proust's connections with Paul Sollier, who directed the clinic where Proust spent somewhere between four and six weeks in December 1905, after his mother's death. Sollier, like Edouard Brissaud (introduced to Proust by his father, who wrote the introduction for Brissaud's book on asthma), was pupil and follower of Charcot.

Sollier's "treatment" plan involved complete isolation from the home environment and attempted, through use of techniques to stimulate the affective or emotional memory, to revive previous emotional states, former situations of the personality with all their contextual elements. It was based on his experiences in Sollier's clinic that Proust chose to include *"reviviscences,"* or regeneration of an emotional state in its original entirety through instances of "involuntary memory," in his work, according to Bogousslavsky. But interest in Sollier's methods dimmed in the onrush of interest in Sigmund Freud's theories, and with one exception in a notebook Proust made no mention of Sollier in his work or even in his correspondence.[121] Bogousslavsky refers to a single entry in *Le Carnet de 1908* that appears alongside a notation of involuntary memory regarding "pavés," which he credits second-hand to Edward Bizub's article "Proust et le docteur Sollier: les molécules impressionnées."[122] (In fact, there is more than one reference to Sollier in *Le Carnet de 1908.*[123])

Edward Bizub emphasizes Sollier's medical credential, his role on the borderline between scientific psychology and philosophy (its antiquated scientific parent), and his place in the psychological establishment at the time. He lists a visit to his sanatorium (and lunch) among the activities scheduled for participants during the fourth International Psychological Conference in 1900, as well as the books Sollier published on memory, emotion, and association. He does not propose, however, that these works might have been composed in response to ideas already circulated by others, specifically William James, whose books on similar topics had recently been reviewed or translated.[124]

Sollier dismissed Bergson's ideas on memory, according to Bogousslavsky, just as he had disagreed with William James on emotion. What Bogousslavsky underscores as the "distinction between a simple memory and an 'emotional revival'"—and credits to Sollier—appeared as far back as 1890 in William James's *Principles of Psychology*, where resurgent memory is described as involuntary memory. The fact that Bogousslavsky also credits the stay at Sollier's clinic with providing Proust the "'will' to become a writer" is problematic at best. Yes, his narrator, too, spends time in a sanatorium, but there is no way to be certain that the novel's outcome—or its genesis—had anything to do with the author's very short stay in one. Sollier's method, as Bizub describes it, was a talking cure to revive a past personality state through a process of "regression," much as an archeologist would dig through layers of sediment to unearth an actual relic of a past civilization, or an earthquake would heave up erstwhile hidden layers.[125]

Proust, however, also uses an analogy that describes how, in response to unanticipated triggers, the fringe of association and feelings described by James and captured in language accesses memory that involuntarily bubbles to the surface through gossamer layers of superimposed experience, too gauzy and web-like to be excavated by direct archeological digging:

> De même, rien moins que ces tristes noms faits de sable, d'espace trop aéré et vide, et de sel, au-dessus desquels le mot "ville" s'échappait comme vole dans Pigeon-vole, ne me faisait penser à ces autres noms de Roussainville ou de Martinville qui, parce que je les avais entendu prononcer si souvent par ma grand-tante à table, dans la "salle", avaient acquis un certain charme sombre où s'étaient peut-être mélangés des extraits du goût des confitures, de l'odeur du feu de bois et du papier d'un livre de Bergotte, de la couleur de grès de la maison d'en face, et qui, aujourd'hui encore, quand ils remontent comme une bulle gazeuse du fond de ma mémoire, conservent leur vertu spécifique à travers les couches superposées de milieux différents qu'ils ont à franchir avant d'atteindre jusqu'à la surface.[126]

> [In the same way, nothing could have reminded me less than these dreary names, redolent of sand, of space too airy and empty, and of salt, out of which the suffix "ville" emerged like "fly" in "butterfly"—nothing could have reminded me less of those other names, Roussain-

ville or Martinville, which, because I had heard them pronounced so often by my great-aunt at table, in the dining-room, had acquired a certain sombre charm in which were blended perhaps extracts of the flavour of preserves, the smell of the log fire and of the pages of one of Bergotte's books, or the colour of the sandstone front of the house opposite, and which even today, when they rise like a gaseous bubble from the depths of my memory, preserve their own specific virtue through all the successive layers of different environments which they must traverse before reaching the surface.[127]]

Proust uses diaphanous images of veils, too, to emphasize social exclusivity and to note how the self is cordoned off, keeping its experience private, as it was depicted by James: "les écharpes de celle-ci tendaient devant la petite société comme un voile parfumé et souple, mais qui la séparait du monde" [the latter's scarves hung before the little company a sort of fragrant, flowing veil, but one that kept it apart from the outer world].[128] The billowing sails of another person's experience entice the narrator, and desire stimulates him to attempt to *know* them, to pierce their awareness, their memories, to imaginatively inhale their environments, Mlle. Stermaria in Balbec, and then later and with much greater effort, Albertine:

> Car il me semblait que je ne l'aurais vraiment possédée que là, quand j'aurais traversé ces lieux qui l'enveloppaient de tant de souvenirs—voile que mon désir voulait arracher et de ceux que la nature interpose entre la femme et quelques êtres [. . .] afin que trompés par l'illusion de la posséder ainsi plus entière ils soient forcés de s'emparer d'abord des paysages au milieu desquels elle vit et qui plus utiles pour leur imagination que le plaisir sensuel, n'eussent pas suffi pourtant, sans lui, à les attirer.[129]
>
> [For it seemed to me that I should truly have possessed her only there when I had traversed those regions which enveloped her in so many memories—a veil which my desire longed to tear aside, one of those veils which nature interposes between woman and her pursuers [. . .] in order that, tricked by the illusion of possessing her thus more completely, they may be forced to occupy first the scenes among which she lives and which, of more service to their imagination than sensual pleasure can be, yet would not without that pleasure have sufficed to attract them.[130]]

But this kind of penetration, this kind of knowledge, this kind of archeology or geology, the exploration of other people's private existence can only succeed through imaginative displacement in art.

Despite Bogousslavsky's best efforts to rehabilitate him as "one of the first modern neuropsychologists," until recently Sollier has largely been silenced in the history of his profession. He did write about memory, emotion, mental illness, and association, but so did many others. Bogousslavsky compares Sollier to modern neurophysiologists because he queried general issues of "process," "brain regions," "components," and "mechanisms" in memory and lauds his mechanistic explanations of the brain's "plasticity" in forming memory, but these were not necessarily unique to him, and his methods were denigrated in his own time.

A review of Sollier's 1900 book, *Le Problème de la mémoire: essai de psycho-mécanique*, published by I. M. Bentley in *The Philosophical Review* in 1901,[131] criticized Sollier's "physical" and mechanistic view of memory as ignoring important physiological factors that would come to light as a result of the incipient study of brain physiology just beginning at the time and likely to provide better explanations of the factors responsible for its function. The reviewer observes: "The psychology of memory is plainly undervalued in the work before us." The controversy over the value of Sollier's legacy in his own time, seen from today's perspective when answers to the physiological workings of the brain are more readily available, does not necessarily accurately portray the mark he might have left on his contemporaries. Perhaps Sollier's influence on Proust has been justifiably obscure, dismissed by the patient himself and, more importantly, by the scientific establishment of his time. Many more present-day studies of brain physiology and neurological theory refer to William James as antecedent (and to Proust as illustration) than to Sollier in any capacity.

While artists at the beginning of the twentieth century grappled with questions of sensation, perception and memory, consciousness and the self, language and music, as Jonah Lehrer points out in his book *Proust was a Neuroscientist*, neuro-cognitive scientists have recently developed the microscopy, imaging, and computational tools to examine and understand them. Literary critics, too, are not far behind. Their forays into MRI labs and neuro-cognitive science departments give the discipline of "comparative literature" new meaning, expanding the field beyond incorporation of psychological and linguistic research; the scope of literary theory, now much more importantly, would integrate results of research into brain structure and function to fathom the correlation of brain-to-literary activity. What James had surmised and theorized one hundred years before would be examined experimentally and could be utilized critically.

In his preface to Jorge Luis Borges's short story collection *Labyrinths*, André Maurois writes:

> Kafka *was* a direct precursor of Borges. [. . .] As for Kafka's precursors, Borges's erudition takes pleasure in finding them in Zeno of Elea, Kierkegaard and Robert Browning. In each of these authors there is some Kafka, but if Kafka had not written, nobody would have been able to notice it—whence this very Borgesian paradox: "Every writer creates his own precursors."[132]

Teasing out the hints of precedence entails multiple efforts. Certain views, certain works, seem so appropriate to their moment that they diffuse into and permeate the culture into which they are introduced and become the new paradigm for interpreting reality, for creating new art, for "reading into" as well as reading derivatively. Literature and the science of mind have been drawn together not only by literary critics but also on the scientific side, by the researchers in the laboratory who take it upon themselves to look at this same phenomenon, the brain's role in language utilization—the making of literature—and in textual interpretation—its reception. In the course of their efforts, researchers have elected to examine William James and Marcel Proust, severally and together. Their research applies specifically and blends readily with the search for patterns of palimpsest, for the precursor in James that Proust's book demands we examine.

According to Gerald Edelman, conscious experience is the purview of a self, "tied to an individual body and brain and to their history."[133] Proust's narrator's story as the story of a self in action can only be told by "je" because the qualities of experience, the feelings of "if" or "cold" or "blue" in James's words, or of "greenness" or "warmth," the qualia in Edelman's terms,[134] can only be experienced in the first person and symbolized in language by him. No fringe of relations or fragment of direct experience is visible to a third-person narrator, so to explore it and attempt to represent it in any genuine way requires a first-person speaker.

In the end "Coda" to his book, Jonah Lehrer notes Virginia Woolf's comment that "On or about December, 1910, human nature changed."[135] What is of great interest in Woolf's statement about change, the moment when she noticed something new was in the intellectual air, is the coincidence of timing she attributes to the cultural shift that inspired her work. As we know, William James's death in August of 1910 was a major news story all over the intellectual world. His was not the only influence on culture at the end of 1910, but analysis and discussion of his works was covered in newspapers and journals for many months after his death. It was very difficult, as we have previously indicated, to avoid grappling with his descriptions of human psychology at the end of 1910. His contribution to the change in artistic paradigm was enormous. As Gerald Edelman points out: "For descriptive insight, nothing beats the efforts of William James."[136] The questions James raised, the elements of the human mind that he surveyed, were the questions artists wanted to probe.

It was at that moment and in that atmosphere that Proust was writing. Proust's narrator's somewhat dismissive view of experimental science as subordinate to the formal artistic elaboration of impression is interpreted by Lehrer as privileging Bergson's view of the importance of intuition. Lehrer makes no comment, however, about the crucial role of psychological theory embedded in Proust's narrator's point of view. Lehrer's contention that Proust's "discovery" of memory's fallibility took precedence over similar conclusions by neuro-cognitive researchers also forgets James's basic descriptions of memory as fiction.

The question to consider regarding Jonah Lehrer's view that the artists of the early twentieth century together, as he writes, "looked in the mirror" for subject matter is what could have stirred them to do so? Darwin and Einstein, Ralph Waldo Emerson and psychology constitute his answer. He contends that "what reality *feels* like," "consciousness from the inside," and an "abiding interest in human experience" were the motivating forces for their artistic "acts of exploration."[137] Lehrer contends that it is from the insights of modern artists that the questions about mind and brain only now corroborated in the lab first emerged.

Yet the major role that William James played in promulgating the bases for this avenue of aesthetic examination and creation, the degree to which the formidable content of his research and writings informed artistic works, is touched on only briefly in Lehrer's book, and most specifically in the chapter on Gertrude Stein. The magnitude of James's contribution to the new direction in art is missing. As Daniel Engber has written in his article in *Slate*, "Many of the breakthroughs attributed to the artists profiled in the book seem to have been prefigured—or even stated outright—by contemporary theorists like William James." And, "Midway through the book, I started to wonder if a better title would have been *James Was a Psychologist*."[138]

If the artists' works have supplied contemporary neuroscientists with a fresh reserve of research avenues, it was James's summation of research on similar questions that have often been asked by artists—and many other observant and curious individuals—and his early theories about the way consciousness streams, about the fringe of relations, about the experience of the experiencing self, as well, that scientists in the lab have begun to look at afresh.

> The stream of thought flows on; but most of its segments fall into the bottomless abyss of oblivion. Of some, no memory survives the instant of their passage. Of others, it is confined to a few moments, hours, or days. Others, again, leave vestiges which are indestructible, and by means of which they may be recalled as long as life endures. Can we explain these differences?[139]

Proust's narrator, deemed unreliable as an informant in the discourse of the novel according to Dorrit Cohn, has, according to Lehrer (and just like the rest of us), an unreliable memory. James had noted the fact that "the brain-tracts excited by the event proper, and those excited in its recall, are in part different from each other."[140] Mistakes may be inevitable. The ability of an individual to retain memories varies: "The persistence or permanence of the paths is a physiological property of the brain-tissue of the individual,"[141] noted James. We remember things right, and we remember them incorrectly, too.

While Lehrer identifies the madeleine as "a revelation" (another word for knowledge that once again supports a view of its religious affiliation) for its ability to revive feeling, he sees the experience primarily as representing an instance in which a taste of cake arouses olfactory memory.

Lehrer's conclusion is that Proust wanted us to know that memory fails the test of truth: "the instability and inaccuracy of memory is the moral," he writes, stating with regard to Albertine's moving beauty spot, "[I]n any other novel, such sloppiness would be considered a mistake." He refers to a letter from Proust to Jacques Rivière, in which the author notes that he depicts errors in his works in order to support the fallibility of memory,[142] but Lehrer omits any mention of the fact that the novel depicts experience, and not just the inaccurately repeated location of a facial mole. The errors of experience are errors of naïveté and ignorance, of anticipation and imagination, of fantasy and desire. These are the errors of a fictional "real life." Yes, Lehrer is right, as James's writing corroborates, our memories feel true whether they are or not, but he does not recognize, as James does, that the reason they "feel" true and become part of our history of self is that we believe them: "Memory is then the feeling of belief in a peculiar complex object":[143]

> Memory requires more than mere dating of a fact in the past, It must be dated in *my* past. In other words, I must think that I directly experienced its occurrence. That "warmth and intimacy" which were so often spoken of in the chapter on the Self, as characterizing all experiences "appropriated" by the thinker as his own.[144]

If contemporary scientists investigating that memory find that it is not reliably truthful, it is not simply on the basis of Proust's book. The question goes deeper than Jonah Lehrer's facile though factual Proustian connection. As D. T. Max notes, Lehrer is good at demonstrating that the artist used some psychological phenomenon that the neuroscientist is researching, but it is not clear that the neuroscientist is researching it *because* the artist used it.[145]

This leaves at large the question of the writer's intention. Was the beauty spot wandering on purpose, to demonstrate the fallibility of memory? Or did this happen because the author of so many pages, writing at night and under the influence of so many medical preparations, kept revising in order to approximate more closely his thoughts and feelings, to sharpen his narration, to burnish his style, without close enough review or time enough to revise what he had written before? If scholarly research reveals that Albertine's beauty spot was itself intended to demonstrate the fractures in the narrator's experience of her, beyond the varying episodic memories of his life with her that make her into a Picasso-like model of the experience of "woman," then Lehrer's argument holds true. We certainly know that the brightly glinting shreds of experience that result from perception over time and the random revival of memories are applicable to the Albertine story. The question remains as to how connected the splinters are to the revisions in the particular case of the beauty spot.

Yes, it is true that Proust revised his text to incorporate new aspects of his experience, such as rewriting the scene of Bergotte's death as his own approached, and incorporating the narrator's passionate affair with Albertine and his overwhelming suffering on her death, following the author's own experience with his chauffeur Alfred Agostinelli. But these alterations to the novel were not the results of faulty memory.

Many critics, Dorrit Cohn among them, have discerned that the accuracy or inaccuracy of autobiographical memory is not necessarily the only subject of Proust's book. The book is not just "a poor partial snapshot," as James would say, of a reality that the author actually experienced, and it is not supposed to be. It is so much more than a demonstration of the inaccuracy of remembered fact. It is perhaps a daydream, a work of artistic innovation, replete with a vague halo of feeling surrounding experience, an interior vision like that of Elstir or Vinteuil, described in beautiful metaphorical—poetic and therefore hardly realistic—language that serves as this artist's pigment and medium of choice.

On the other hand, the moments of resurgent memory, when Lehrer assumes Proust felt greater "truthfulness," may in fact be just as much a fictional a device as any other aspect of the novel. Lehrer states: "Proust worshipped these sudden epiphanies of the past because they seemed more truthful, less corrupted by the lies of the remembering process."[146] In fact, it was the narrator, not the author, for whom these moments were "epiphanies." We are still inside the novel, not in correspondence or diary, and so the truthfulness, although similar in language and emotion to the experiences described by actual participants in religious conversion in James's *Varieties of Religious Experience*, cannot be counted upon as truth any more than any other aspect of *À la recherche du temps perdu*.

The "shock" and wonder of these sudden blissful memories that so "obsess" us, according to Lehrer, were never elucidated by what he calls "the old scientific models."[147] This statement has little foundation in fact because William James describes similar phenomena in great detail, using the introspective tools of his day to explain the psychology of human nature's religious epiphanies, revelations, and conversions. At the time he wrote, however, the tools to investigate or observe the actual brain activity he surmised (and the chemistry upon which it was based) had not yet been invented. He did, however, register the phenomenon: "Experiences of bygone date will revive after years of absolute oblivion, often as the result of some cerebral disease or accident which seems to develop latent paths of association, as the photographer's fluid develops the picture sleeping in the collodion film."[148] This sounds very much like the Japanese paper flowers exploding to life in water or Combray and the subsequent biography in all of its felt reality surging like a wave from madeleine dipped in tea.

We have noted that as soon as techniques and tools become available to elucidate these aspects of human experience, it does not take scientists long to put them under the laboratory lamps, microscopes, and magnetic resonance imaging machinery. Lehrer equates Proust's revisions of his text with scientists' revisiting old questions when new methods are available. Perhaps this is coincidental. Writers almost always revise to attain the best expression of their thought in the best possible form. Scientists always attempt to improve their methods and resolve ambiguities or pursue answers to unanswered questions. Artists paint picture after picture to get closer to their interior vision, to explore the possibilities of their technique. Scientists question previous results and build new research models and tools to advance their discipline's pure research and in more goal-directed ways to find cures, built devices, and hopefully improve the quality of daily life.

Some are still engaged in controversial theorizing about why certain memories resurface seemingly unbidden and whole, just as they did in James's day. Today, however, the study of prions and neurochemical transmitters may shed some light on the process. It was in a lab doing just that kind of research on the brain that Lehrer assisted when he began to read Proust[149] and, forgetting about William James, determined that creative artists raised the questions first.

If James served as palimpsest for Proust, in this case at least some of the questions were there before the art.

James recognized the complexity of the phenomenon and knew what had to be researched: "What memory goes with is [. . .] a very complex representation, that of the fact to be recalled plus its associates, the whole forming one 'object' [. . .] known in one integral pulse of consciousness [. . .] and demanding probably a vastly more intricate brain-process than that on which any simple sensorial image depends."[150]

On the cutting edge, the biological laboratories will continue to revisit these questions and further clarify the processes of consciousness and memory, the facts behind the theories. While some scientists whose work we have described here have used Proust's aesthetic experience as subject for research, it is not impossible that Proust used James—among others—upon whom to pattern his own inquiry. We know that the ancient Greeks, Socrates in particular, theorized the "engram" or metaphorical wax tablet upon which memory was encoded to explain the same phenomenon. Plus ça change . . . [The more things change . . .].

In 2000, the *Proceedings of the Royal College of Physicians of Edinburgh, Scotland,* included an article by retired Fellow A. E. Stuart entitled "Proust, Memory and the Engram."[151] The article is one of the many that describe similarities between Proust's view of memory and that of modern neuroscience, reviewing potential scientific explanations for Proust's observations. He indicates that the methodology of introspection was used by both Proust and William James, recognizes Proust's understanding of the "snapshot" nature of voluntary memory, the relationship between memory and "context," recognition by association, erroneous memory, the processes by which short-term memory snaps to life and fades, by which long-term memory is formulated and retained. Stuart also notes Socrates' theory of the block of wax, or engram, on which experience is impressed and can be retained as memory. This is a term often used by neuroscientists to suggest a trace or locus of retained memory, similar to Edward Bizub's notion of the grooves of the phonographic cylinder as the furrows of impression.

Involuntary memory, as used by Proust, however, stands apart for Stuart. It represents dissociation from the mundane and involves entry into a non-temporal sphere where the self of today contemplates the self of the past. Stuart distinguishes it from other types of memory, characterizing it instead as having religious undertones. Involuntary memory, for Stuart, is "preserved in eternity," "invaded by exquisite pleasure, by all-powerful joy," and, using George Painter's words for these moments, is "linked with ecstasies of inexplicable delight, a world without disappointment, without sin and without death."[152] Even the painful flashback to his grandmother unlacing his boots is viewed by Stuart as a moment when the narrator is "filled with a divine presence" that is linked to similar though ecstatic moments of "well-being and detachment from the world."[153] Blending the religious language of conversion experiences with the neuro-cognitive examination of memory, Stuart's analysis joins with other studies to underscore the patterns of palimpsest reflecting James's theory in Proust's prose.

NOTES

1. Maria Warner, review of *An Alchemy of Mind: The Marvel and Mystery of the Brain* by Diane Ackerman (New York: Scribner, 2004) in "Circuits," *New York Times*, August 29, 2004.
2. *RTP*, III, 761.
3. Enright, V, 342.
4. See Moretti's reading of Karl Mannheim, "The Problem of Generations," *Essays on the Sociology of Knowledge* (London: Oxford University Press, 1952), 279, quoted in Franco Moretti, *Graphs, Maps, Trees: Abstract Models for a Literary History* (London: Verso, 2005), 21. See also, Franco Moretti, *The Novel*, 2 vols. (Princeton: Princeton University Press, 2006), 585–592.
5. Comment by H. Saussy, chairman of the Department of Comparative Literature, Yale University, in a lecture delivered at Washington University in St. Louis, October 4, 2007.
6. Moretti, *Graphs*, 88.
7. Justin O'Brien "Proust Confirmed by Neurosurgery," *PMLA* 85.2 (March 1970): 295–297, 296. See Dr. Wilder Penfield (Montreal Neurological Institute), *Proceedings of the National Academy of Sciences*, xliv.ii (February 15, 1958): 65.
8. James, "What is an Emotion?" *Coll. Essays and Reviews*, 247–248.

9. Edward S. Reed, *From Soul to Mind: The Emergence of Psychology from Erasmus Darwin to William James* (New Haven: Yale University Press, 1997), 210.
10. William James, *The Writings of William James, 1878–1899,* ed. Gerald E. Myers (New York: Library of America, 1987), 996. Cited in Jonah Lehrer, *Proust Was a Neuroscientist* (Boston: Houghton Mifflin, 2007), 18.
11. Daniel Engber, "Proust Wasn't a Neuroscientist: How Jonah Lehrer's *Proust was a Neuroscientist* Overstates the Case," *Slate* (November 26, 2007). http://www.slate.com/id/2178584?nav=wp.
12. James, *Varieties*, 483.
13. Jean-Yves et Marc Tadié, *Le Sens de la mémoire* (Paris: Gallimard, 1999), 112–113.
14. Gaëtane Chapelle, rev. of *Le Sens de la mémoire* by Jean-Yves et Marc Tadié (Gallimard, 1999), *Sciences Humaines,* "Livre du mois," 101 (Janvier 2000). http://www.scienceshumaines.com/articleprint2.php?lg=fr&id_article=111.
15. Tadié, *Le Sens de la mémoire*, 111–112.
16. Tadié et Tadié, 297, 322, 330.
17. *RTP*, IV, 13. Enright, V, 578.
18. Bernard J. Baars, Uma Ramamurthy, and Stan Franklin, "How deliberate, spontaneous and unwanted memories emerge in a computational model of consciousness." ccrg.cs.memphis.edu/assets/papers/Chapter%209%20Baars_Ramamurthy_Franklin%20July13.doc.
19. *RTP*, IV, 14. Enright, V, 579.
20. *RTP*, IV, 459.
21. Enright, VI, 276.
22. Oliver Sacks, "In the River of Consciousness," *The New York Review of Books* 51.1 (January 15, 2004).
23. James, *Briefer Course*, 296.
24. Gerald Edelman, *Wider Than the Sky* (New Haven: Yale University Press, 2004), 61.
25. Reed, 210.
26. James, *Briefer Course*, 300.
27. James, *Briefer Course*, 304.
28. Edelman, 55.
29. Edelman, 75.
30. Edelman, 75.
31. James, *Principles*, I, 611.
32. Edelman, 33.
33. Edelman, 31.
34. Edelman, 52.
35. Edelman, 107.
36. James, *Principles*, I, 228.
37. Edelman, 114, 126.
38. Edelman, 134.
39. Edelman, 135.
40. Edelman, 134.
41. *Corr.*, XI, *135*, 257, cited in *RTP*, III, 1226.
42. The ostensible reason, as he wrote to Bernard Grasset in 1913, was a book by M. Binet-Valmer with the title *Le Coeur en désordre*, which touched on a similar mind-body connection in disarray.
43. *RTP*, III, 153. Enright, IV, 211.
44. *RTP*, III, 153. Enright, IV, 211.
45. *RTP*, II, 30–31.
46. Enright, II, 338.
47. *RTP*, II, 31. Enright, II, 338–339.
48. *RTP*, II, 32.
49. Enright, II, 340.
50. *RTP*, III, 154. Enright, IV, 212.

51. Making it available for analysis and refutation by others such as Dr. Sollier and others.
52. James, *Principles,* II, 1082.
53. James, *Principles,* II, 1074.
54. James, *Principles,* II, 1083, note 21.
55. James, *Principles,* II, 1059.
56. James, *Principles,* II, 1088.
57. See *RTP,* III, *Notice,* 1227.
58. Richard Macksey, Oliver Sacks, Mary Warnock, "Discussion: Commentaries by Richard Macksey and Oliver Sacks," (Comparative Literature) *MLN,* 109.5 (December 1994): 950–958, 951.
59. Macksey, Sacks, Warnock, 954.
60. Macksey, Sacks, Warnock, 957–958.
61. Renate Bartsch, *Concept Formation, Remembering, and Understanding: Dynamic Conceptual Semantics and Proust's "À la recherche du temps perdu"* (Philadelphia: J. Benjamins, 2005). References above are to the full text available online at University of Amsterdam Institute for Logic, Language and Computation, Publications, Logic, Philosophy, and Linguistics (LP) Series. http://www.illc.uva.nl: Renate Bartsch The Role of Consciousness and Intentionality in Perception, Semantics, Representations and Rules.
62. Bartsch, 51.
63. Bartsch, 56.
64. Bartsch, 74.
65. Bartsch, 81.
66. Bartsch, 79.
67. Bartsch, 49.
68. Randy L. Buckner, "The Potion's Magic," *Neuron* 42.4 (May 27, 2004): 526–527.
69. Kirsten Shepherd-Barr and Gordon M. Shepherd, "Madeleines and Neuromodernism: Reassessing Mechanisms of Autobiographical Memory in Proust," *Autobiography Studies* 13.1 (Spring 1998): 39–60.
70. Reference to Musset is an error in the Shepherd-Barr and Shepherd article. In fact, Proust acknowledges Baudelaire and not Musset (*RTP,* IV, 498).
71. Shepherd-Barr and Shepherd, 42.
72. Shepherd-Barr and Shepherd, 47.
73. Shepherd-Barr and Shepherd, 49.
74. Shepherd-Barr and Shepherd, 53, 55, 56, 57.
75. Russell Epstein, "The Neural-Cognitive Basis of the Jamesian Stream of Thought," *Consciousness and Cognition* 9 (2000): 550–575, 550.
76. Epstein, "Jamesian Stream," 552.
77. Epstein, "Jamesian Stream," 553–554.
78. Epstein, "Jamesian Stream," 555.
79. See also Russell Epstein, "Substantive Thoughts about Substantive Thoughts: A Reply to Galin," *Consciousness and Cognition* 9 (2002): 584–590. Galin's commentary on Epstein's original article appears in the same journal as "Comments on Epstein's Neurocognitive Interpretation of William James's Model of Consciousness," 576–583.
80. Russell Epstein, "Consciousness, Art, and the Brain: Lessons from Marcel Proust," *Consciousness and Cognition* 13 (2004): 213–240, 214. Previous approaches to the topic cited by Epstein include B. Mangan, "Meaning and the structure of consciousness: An essay in psycho-aesthetics," unpublished Ph.D. thesis: University of California, Berkeley, "Some philosophical and empirical implications of the fringe," *Consciousness and Cognition* 2.2 (1993a): 142–154, and "Taking phenomenology seriously—the fringe and its implications for cognitive research," *Consciousness and Cognition* 2.2 (1993b): 89–108, as well as S. Langer, *Feeling and Form* (New York: Scribner, 1953).
81. Epstein, "Consciousness, Art," 215.
82. Epstein, "Consciousness, Art," 214, 222.
83. Epstein, "Consciousness, Art," 218.

84. Epstein, "Consciousness, Art, " 219.
85. Epstein, "Consciousness, Art," 220–221.
86. Epstein, "Consciousness, Art," 222.
87. Epstein, "Consciousness, Art," 221.
88. Epstein, "Consciousness, Art," 222.
89. Epstein, "Consciousness, Art," 223.
90. Epstein, "Consciousness, Art," 224.
91. Epstein, "Consciousness, Art, " 224–225.
92. Epstein, "Consciousness, Art," 227.
93. Wolf says that for Proust reading provides "a sense of encounter" with different beings, permitting us "to try on, identify with, and ultimately enter for a brief time the wholly different perspective of another's consciousness" (Wolf, 7). It permits us to develop "empathy" for what another individual thinks and feels: "In this process we step outside ourselves for ever-lengthening moments and begin to understand the 'other,' which Marcel Proust wrote lies at the heart of communication through written language" (Wolf, 86).
94. Epstein, "Consciousness, Art," 225–226.
95. Epstein, "Consciousness, Art," 227.
96. Epstein, "Consciousness, Art," 227.
97. Epstein, "Consciousness, Art," 231.
98. Epstein, "Consciousness, Art," 234.
99. Epstein, "Consciousness, Art," 230.
100. Epstein, "Consciousness, Art," 231.
101. Epstein, "Consciousness, Art," 234.
102. See S. Zeki, *Inner Vision: An Exploration of Art and the Brain* (Oxford: Oxford University Press, 1999) and S. Zeki and A. Bartels, "Toward a Theory of Visual Consciousness," *Consciousness and Cognition* 8.2 (June 1999): 225–259.
103. Epstein, "Consciousness, Art," 236.
104. Epstein, "Consciousness, Art," 237.
105. D. Galin, "Aesthetic Experience: Marcel Proust and the Neo-Jamesian Structure of Awareness," *Consciousness and Cognition* 13 (2004): 241–253, 242.
106. Galin, "Aesthetic," 244.
107. Galin, "Aesthetic," 247.
108. Galin, "Aesthetic," 248.
109. Galin, "Aesthetic," 249.
110. Galin, "Aesthetic," 251.
111. D. Dryden, "Memory, Imagination, and the Cognitive Value of the Arts," *Consciousness and Cognition* 13 (2004): 254–267, 255.
112. Dryden, 256.
113. Dryden, 258.
114. Dryden, 259.
115. Dryden, 260.
116. Dryden, 262.
117. Dryden, 263.
118. Dryden, 266.
119. Donald Wright, *Du discours médical dans "À la recherche du temps perdu": science et souffrance* (Paris: Honoré Champion Éditeur, 2007).
120. Julien Bogousslavsky, "Marcel Proust's Lifelong Tour of the Parisian Neurological Intelligentsia: From Brissaud and Dejerine to Sollier and Babinski," *European Neurology* 57 (2007): 129–136, and "Memory after Charcot: Paul Sollier's Visionary Work," *Journal of Neurology, Neurosurgery and Psychiatry* 78 (2007): 1373–1374.
121. This, however, is not the case, as there is mention of Sollier in Proust's correspondence. For example, in the volume of letters written in 1909, there is mention of Sollier as a possible source to contact in order to refer a friend to nursing care.
122. In "Memory after Charcot."

123. In section 5 there is the following notation: "L'intérêt pour petits événements / du régiment, chez Sollier / etc." and a note about Proust's stay at Sollier's sanatorium; in section 11 verso, the following notes of impressions include a reference to Sollier as well and are followed by mention of "pavés": "Sifflets des trains / décrivant la campagne / près des falaises au clair / de lune, dans la nuit froide / à Illiers, Versailles, St. / Germain, [chez] Sollier. Descente / du train. Pavés foulés / avec joie. Pavés scintil / l[an]ts de lune de Félicie" (*Le Carnet de 1908*, 52, 62).

124. Sollier's books on memory were published in 1892 and 1900, after James's *Principles of Psychology*: Paul Sollier, *Les Troubles de la Mémoire* (Paris: J. Rueff, 1892, 1900), and *Le Probème de la Mémoire* (Paris: Alcan, 1900). Chapter 25 from *The Principles* was translated into French for publication in 1902 as *La Théorie de l'Émotion* and much of Sollier's 1905 volume on the topic was devoted to his disagreement with James's ideas: Paul Sollier, *Le Mécanisme des Émotions* (Paris: Alcan, 1905). Sollier's 1907 book on association clearly follows James's publications: Paul Sollier, *Essai critique et théorique sur l'Association en psychologie* (Paris: Alcan, 1907).

125. Bizub, "Proust et le docteur Sollier," 45, 46, 47.

126. *RTP*, II, 22.

127. Enright, II, 326–327.

128. *RTP*, II, 42. Enright, II, 355.

129. *RPT*, II, 50.

130. Enright, II, 365–366.

131. I. M. Bentley, rev. of *Le Problème de la mémoire: Essai de Psycho-Méchanique* by Paul Sollier, *The Philosophical Review* 10.1 (Jan. 1901): 98.

132. André Maurois, preface, trans. Sherry Mangan *Labyrinths* by Jorge Luis Borges (New York: New Directions, 1962), x–xi.

133. Edelman, *Wider*, 63.

134. Edelman, *Wider*, 64.

135. Lehrer, 192.

136. Edelman, *Wider*, 181,

137. Lehrer, x.

138. Engber review in *Slate*.

139. James, *Principles*, I, 605.

140. James, *Principles*, I, 618.

141. James, *Principles*, I, 621.

142. Lehrer, 82.

143. James, *Principles*, I, 613.

144. James, *Principles*, I, 612.

145. See the review of Lehrer's book by D. T. Max, "Swann's Hypothesis," *New York Times* (November 4, 2007).

146. Lehrer, 90.

147. Lehrer, 90–91.

148. James, *Principles*, I, 641.

149. Lehrer, 91–95.

150. James, *Principles*, I, 612.

151. A. E. Stuart, "Proust, Memory and the Engram," *Proceedings of the Royal College of Physicians of Edinburgh* 30 (2000): 172–175.

152. G. D. Painter, *Marcel Proust, A Biography* (Pimlico Editions, 1996), 38, quoted in Stuart, 174.

153. Stuart, 17.

Afterword

What could be more prosaic than a railroad timetable? William James posed the question: "What more deadly uninteresting object can there be than a railroad timetable? Yet where will you find a more interesting object if you are going on a journey, and by its means can find your train? At such times the timetable will absorb a man's entire attention, its interest being borrowed solely from its relation to his personal life."[1]

Proust echoed the thought: "[J]e ne sais s'il est pour moi une lecture qui vaille celle [. . .] des indicateurs de chemin de fer. Ah, la douceur et la caresse de tous ces noms de villages et de villes du P.-L.-M., l'évocation charmante des pays de lumière et de vie où je n'irai jamais"[2] [I do not know if there is any reading that is worth as much to me as train timetables. Ah, the sweet caress of all the village names of the Paris-Lyon-Méditeranée line, the charming evocation of lands filled with light and life that I will never go see].

For Proust, the timetable stimulated creative fantasy. James's psychological observation had become an indispensable tool for the daydreaming inventiveness of the artist. The essence of travel here is the mental trip: the psychological distance discriminated between point of departure and golden glow of the imagined destination. The menial, often uncomfortable process of travel has become "l'opération miraculeuse"[3] [miraculous operation] and "l'acte de l'esprit" [act of the mind][4] that like a work of art issues forth from a personal space unconnected to the actual towns and villages that configure the everyday terrain through which the traveler would actually move. Bewitchingly, it ensnares profound particularities expressible through the sonority of language.

At journey's end in Proust's work of art would appear a thickly pigmented reality,[5] like newfound fields of sensory awareness impregnated with the power of seemingly authentic—near "autobiographical"—personal experience, with shimmering fringe of inchoate feeling and memory that far outweighs the thinner watercolor of anticipation or the prosaic tedium of event, exposing even the affective price of relinquishing home's habitual comfort and emotional stability.

Using the biographer's technique of living forward and remembering looking back as a "witness to happenings in time," Proust's narrator records his observations and reports on the trials and errors involved in creating a life, analyzing the psychological and philosophical substratum of his search for the "Vérités" [truths] of human experience, exploring the conscious mind for whom present sensation entails constant interaction with the "farther facts" that accompany perceptive experience, the strata of affect and resonance.[6] This search would organize his hero's story, connecting the desire to tell it with portrayal of the process of its creation.

William James and Marcel Proust lived during a moment of highly sophisticated worldliness and cultural integration, of "une convergence entre les arts de nature et de patries diverses"[7] [when there existed a convergence among arts of diverse natures and countries of origin]. Despite the fact that Europeans broadly read and embraced James, there since followed a long blank when the importance of James's contribution faded from view in what Kennan Ferguson calls "a conscious historical amnesia on the part of French thinkers."[8]

While James was highly visible in the media when Proust meditated on, made notations for, and began drafts of *À la recherche du temps perdu,* he was significantly less discernable to the public eye by the time all but the first of the novel's volumes were published and critics were attempting to establish from what sources Proust's unique and individual perspective arose. The storm over *Pragmatism* and the fact that James was no longer present to defend himself against his critics in the controversies his thought generated may have contributed to his fading from view. Philosophy, social thought, and psychology evolved into more secular and even existential realms, with Freud and the Behaviorists, Marx and the Fascists taking center stage after the devastation of the war years (1914–1918) and the subsequent social upheavals throughout Europe.

Nevertheless, over an extended number of years, James had been acclaimed in France and closely allied with Émile Boutroux and Henri Bergson, who themselves had ties to Proust and his family. Proust had had the opportunity to have "en main" [in hand], and in French, a number of James's texts. He had ample occasion to become familiar with James's ideas even second-hand from what had circulated in the media, the major journals with which he was familiar, and the newspapers, including *Les Débats,* that he had read for at least the ten years when James was news. When James died in 1910, obituaries were legion in the press; eulogy books summarizing his works were numerous in 1911. That year A. Ménard released his restatement and analysis of *The Principles of Psychology,* and Henri Bergson "presented" the French translation of *Pragmatism*. Letters[9] Proust wrote at the time make it clear he was reading *Les Débats* during this period of the paper's peak coverage of eulogies for James and summaries of his major writings. (In a letter to Robert de Billy written on July 18, 1911, Proust notes he is so exasperated with the paper that he is considering cancelling his subscription. Thus, we can readily suppose he has been reading it.)

Between 1914 and 1922 when Proust died, a few of James's works were published in France,[10] and a few articles mentioning him or topics he had written about continued to appear in French journals. A selection of James's correspondence was published in French by Floris Delattre and Maurice le Breton in 1924 with a preface by Bergson, suggesting that there was still a reading public interested in James. But beyond Jacque-Émile Blanche's notation about reading a letter to William James from his brother, Henry (perhaps in English or from an early draft of this translation), no memory of William James and no connection to Proust penetrated the *NRF's "Hommage"* in 1923.[11]

The Principles of Psychology was so widely read that it was a significant financial success for a struggling professor with a large family. James, writes biographer Linda Simon in a series of observations conspicuously applicable to Proust, saw human identity as accumulated memory actuated intermittently depending on circumstance and analogous in rhythm to the flights and perchings of conscious awareness. While substantives in language have widely accepted meanings, the fringe theorized by James was the locus of the personal and individual, the source of artistic "vision." This funds "l'autre moi créateur" so important to Proust, the private Self so different from the Self in society.[12]

There can be little doubt that James's works inspired Proust's modernity and assist interpretation of his novel. Proust had the highly sensitized temperament and literary talent to create in exhaustive descriptive detail a work exploiting James's scrutiny of human experience. James enabled Proust to focus the beam of attention, allowing thought to cohere[13] amid flights and fringes, to develop as a writer from fragments worth fictionalizing in *Jean Santeuil* to the density of *À la recherche du temps perdu*, and to advance from his notes to a fully formed theoretical aesthetic structured to recount the experience of the process of its creation. His drive to create form led Proust to employ memory, particularly when resurgent, intermittent, and unanticipated, as the schematic element shaping his drama.

When Proust sounds the depths of his narrator's grief and sorrow, the misery of lost love, the precarious flailing of residual memory, and the minute observations of emotional pain might as well have taken place in the laboratory. The narrator's disconsolate cry that suffering teaches more about human psychological behavior than the study of psychology texts is hardly casual. It reveals to the reader the writer's ultimate plan to probe an individual mind from the inside and to make a novel conveying an entire world out of private individual experience. In this, he is a direct descendant of William James.

Proust used an "autobiographical" pretext as a necessary tool to analyze the mundane events of this life observed from the inside. The evolving nature of a personality—not an immutable Self, but a Self that chooses and is created by its accumulating experiences, a Self that responds according to its temperament yet differently at different times with differing interests, dependent in some measure upon contextual learning and developing understanding—characterizes the subject of both psychologist and novelist. James's descriptions of the Self and the "je" of Proust's literary persona demonstrate basics of hard-wired human cognitive perception and behavior. The outlines of the Self delineated in *The Principles of Psychology* enabled Proust to create a first-person narrator, "je," who recounts yet is simultaneously a "moi" with a multifaceted history, surrounded by "others" as eternally impenetrable as they are in real life.

Proust adopted and adapted the structures of streaming conscious life delineated by James, isolating in sharp focus certain emotionally significant moments extracted from the fuzzy daily flow of event and thought. He depicted the relational flights between substantive perchings of concentrated contemplation and the vague unspoken fringes of affect, nebulous and undefined, surrounding objects of thought and embedded in language. Like glass carafes containing water stilled from the stream in which they float, these selected sparkling experimental beakers can be examined at leisure and described at length in the slow-moving detail of Proust's prose. In addition to providing a design for fabricating his fiction, James's theory provided Proust an investigative method for the digressive and exhaustive analysis accompanying the narrator's expeditions through events and his relationships with different individuals, his forays into groups.

Metaphor cross-references two images to expose what James termed the "irradiating" fields or "halo" of feeling or impression at their convergence. Proust was able to translate this into literary discourse. James's illustration of the overlapping petals of association intersecting in and surrounding a pistil-like central sphere graphically expresses Proust's theory of metaphor in which partially superimposed rings of style enclose areas of "essential" commonality in differing image systems. This doubled spatial and temporal experience catalyzes newfound awareness in the narrator and articulates the dramatic system for Proust's book.

James's widely read and much celebrated writings on religious experience furnished specific descriptions Proust could use for his salvational dénouement. James's pragmatist and pluralistic philosophical posture highlighted the importance of attitude, the uncertainties and variability of truth only verified when tested, dislodging the notion of a singular and unchanging essential truth. Instead of a unique core of monadic meaning underlying and coordinating impressions and experience, Proust explored the random and the relative, a flotilla of flavor, feeling and reactive or retrospective interpretation in a world changing so rapidly that memory furnished the only stability.

Like the memoirs of Mme. de Boigne, his narrator's experience included the unchanging concrete sensational "cash-value" of the past (as in Brichot's memories) but also "positioned" it, shaping it intentionally and in depth for effect, creating fictional verisimilitude in the determination to use memories to constitute a revivified consciousness, but not actually autobiographical, not his own.

Contemporary neuroscience corroborates the contention that Proust was the "poet" to express James's "boulder" of impressive experience, and whose exposition is so beautiful and so close to the facts that he is widely cited in neuro-cognitive lecture halls, articles, and books.

Given the richness of references in his text and in his wide correspondence, French critics have tended to look to French sources to explain potential "influences" on Proust's novel. Today, however, comparative literary criticism is as globalist as the intellectual world was in James's and Proust's time. Imagery and "idées reçues" may have been circulating in "l'air du temps" one hundred years ago, such that the similarities between James and Proust are accidental and suggestive rather than determinative. But copious and frequent instances of commonality in their writings are undeniable. Indeed, it is possible that James's presence in Paris was so pervasive during the first decade of the twentieth century that the ideas he generated had become the "idées reçues." And Proust was among the first of the major artists inspired by their energy. Together they account for a good part of modernity's paternity.

NOTES

1. William James, "Interest," chapter 10 in *Talks to Teachers on Psychology; and to Students on Some of Life's Ideals* (New York: Holt, 1899, and London: Longmans, Green & Co., 1899), trans. Pidoux (Paris: Alcan, 1900; 2nd ed., 1907). http://des.emory.edu/mfp/tt10.html.
2. Arnyvelde, 294.
3. *RTP*, II, 5.
4. *RTP*, II, 5. Enright, II, 302.
5. *RTP*, II, 6–7.
6. James, *Principles*, II, 723.
7. Claude-Edmonde Magny, *L'Âge du roman américain* (Paris: Éditions du Seuil, 1948), cited in Lowery, 371.
8. Kennan Ferguson, "La Philosophie Américaine: James, Bergson, and the Century of Intercontinental Pluralism" (Baltimore: Johns Hopkins University Press, 2006), sections 4, 362, 403. http://muse.jhu.edu/journals/theory_and_event/v009/0.1ferguson.html.
9. See Proust's letters to Henry Bordeaux (to congratulate him on being named to the Légion d'Honneur), August 2 or 3, 1910 (Proust, *Corr.* X, *73*, 156); to Robert Dreyfus (on the Portuguese revolution), October 8, 1910 (Proust, *Corr.* X, *86*, 181–184); again to Robert Dreyfus (about Bourdeau's article on Tolstoy), November 21, 1910 (Proust, *Corr.* X, *100*, 211–213); and to Robert de Billy, July 18, 1911 (Proust, *Corr.*, X, *156*, 315–319).
10. William James, *Aux Étudiants*, trans. Henri Marti, préface É. Boutroux (Paris: Payot, 1914); William James, *Causeries pédagogiques*, trans. L.-S. Pidoux (Paris: Payot, 1921).
11. Blanche, "Quelques instantanés," *Hommage*, 53.
12. See L. Simon, *Genuine Reality*, 233–235.
13. See William James, *The Principles of Psychology*, rev. by G. Stanley Hall, *The American Journal of Psychology* 3.4 (February 1891): 578–591, 585, 586, 591.

Appendix

TOME XVII : 1918 227

87

A LIONEL HAUSER

[Le jeudi 2 mai 1918][1]

Mon cher Lionel

Il faut croire que la théosophie donne la divination des actes d'autrui ou les leur suggère. Car quand j'ai reçu ta lettre j'étais en train d'écrire au critique littéraire du *Figaro,* Abel Hermant[2] pour lui recommander ton livre[3]. Je pense en effet qu'un livre qui se flatte à tort ou à raison de régénérer l'humanité, n'est pas destiné à rester dans l'ombre, et veut être propagé. Ce raisonnement m'avait suffi pour écrire la lettre que je vais appuyer de deux autres.

Voici pourquoi. Hermant qui, je le sais, nourrit à l'endroit de mon livre de chaleureux sentiments n'en a jamais parlé. Il a tant de relations dans le monde littéraire, et, ce qui, en ce moment où il est candidat[4], l'intéresse surtout, dans le monde académique, que ne pouvant parler d'un sur mille parmi les livres qu'on lui envoie, il a pris le parti de consacrer son feuilleton[5] à quelque point littéraire qui lui fournisse l'occasion de mettre en valeur quelques-unes de ses théories et d'écrire une jolie page. Cela fait qu'on célèbre d'autant plus sa réputation d'écrivain mais ne satisfait pas ses confrères. Je pense pourtant qu'il obtempérera à ma requête.

Du temps du pauvre Calmette j'aurais eu des moyens plus efficaces. Mais tout en espérant qu'Hermant m'écoutera, comme je connais le Directeur d'un journal qui bien que populaire par son titre est extrêmement littéraire par sa rédaction composée de nos meilleurs écrivains, l'*Intransigeant*[6], je vais lui écrire aussi pour le prier de signaler au moins l'apparition de ton livre.

Enfin il y a en ce moment une Revue qui fait beaucoup parler d'elle. Elle est dirigée par M. Germain[7], fils du directeur du Crédit Lyonnais. Or M. Germain que je ne connais pas, m'a fait indirectement demander des articles pour cette Revue (les *Écrits Nouveaux*)[8]. Je ne

Figure 3. Proust, *Correspondance*, éd. Philip Kolb, Paris: Éditions Plon, 1989, #87 à Lionel Hauser. T.XVII (1918), 227–231. *Correspondance* / Marcel Proust. Text edited and annotated by Philip Kolb and published by Plon, Paris. Copyright © 1989 and 1991. Reprinted by permission of the publisher.

puis leur donner satisfaction à cause du travail excessif que me donne mon livre, mais je vais profiter de la sympathie qu'on veut bien avoir pour moi dans ce groupe pour recommander ton livre à leur attention et leur demander de le désigner à l'attention de leurs lecteurs. Ce sera peut'être un peu plus difficile qu'aux deux journaux précités, parce que cette Revue a une espèce de doctrine qu'à vrai dire je ne connais pas et ne publie que des choses d'un caractère ultra-moderne avec lesquelles tranchera peut'être trop ton ouvrage, futuriste dans son dessein, mais entièrement classique dans sa forme. Je te tiendrai au courant de ces diverses démarches et peut'être d'autres s'il me vient d'autres idées. Mais je suis en mauvais termes avec Prévost [9] *(Revue de Paris)* depuis qu'il a refusé de publier des extraits de mon livre [10]. Peut'être indirectement pourrai-je lui faire remettre le tien.

Tu t'es entièrement mépris sur ma pensée si tu as cru que j'opposais la Science à la Théosophie et croyais à la certitude de la première. J'ai beaucoup plus de sympathie pour la seconde. D'ailleurs mes considérations sur la dégénérescence physique sont assez dans ce sens. Tu n'ignores pas que tous les mystiques ont généralement eu un état physique qui relevait de la pathologie et qu'un monsieur parfaitement normal et heureux (au moins de notre temps et sauf exceptions) pensera fort peu à son union avec le Créateur, à ses incarnations antérieures et s'il interpose entre le golf et son bureau les vêpres à Saint-Augustin le fera d'une façon qui n'a de religieuse que le nom.

Ne sois pas impatient pour mes démarches [11], car je sais par expérience personnelle combien ces choses-là aboutissent lentement, et j'étais convaincu qu'on ne dirait pas un mot de mes livres quand des années après (cela ne sera pas si long pour toi, tranquillise-toi), l'article écrit par un ami, composé etc., finissait tout d'un coup par paraître. Avant la guerre on disait « l'actualité ne nous a pas encore permis, Loti attend depuis trois mois » etc.) et maintenant j'enrage d'avance en pensant qu'Hermant, Bailby *(Intransigeant)* et les *Écrits Nouveaux* vont me parler de la pénurie du

Figure 3 continued.

papier, de la place infime réservée à ce qui n'est pas la guerre etc. Néanmoins je compte aboutir.

Contrairement à toi, je pense que la partie peu importante de ma lettre était celle concernant les valeurs que je dois déclarer. C'est pourquoi étant trop fatigué pour faire tout à la fois, je remets à demain ou après-demain de te faire porter (peut'être sans lettre mais tu comprendras, sachant de quoi il s'agit, ce serait seulement dans le cas où j'aurais trop mal aux yeux) les ordres de vente dont la réalisation a constitué le chèque impayé (le mot ordre de vente n'est pas le mot exact, tu verras toi-même ce que c'est, j'ignore l'expression juste) et le relevé de mes valeurs de Juin. La comparaison, et aussi [12] avec les documents que tu possèdes toi-même, te permettront sans doute de me dire à peu près ce qui me reste encore de valeurs non vendues. Je te demanderai une fois que tu n'auras plus besoin des comptes que je t'enverrai ces jours-ci de me les renvoyer, car ils pourront me servir. Ils sont là à deux pas de moi, et je suis levé. Mais n'ayant pas dormi depuis neuf jours, je n'ai pas le courage de faire ces deux pas, ni d'appeler Céleste. Remettons cela à ces jours-ci [13].

J'ai préféré te dire d'abord la coïncidence de nos idées au sujet de la diffusion de ton livre théosopho-pratique (j'avais bien lu les noms des auteurs que tu cites, ou du moins auxquels tu renvoies le lecteur [14], mais cela n'infirmait en rien ma remarque (qui n'est nullement une critique) sur le ton péremptoire avec lequel tu parles presque entre parenthèses, de nos vies antérieures, comme si c'était un lieu commun admis de tous et qui va de soi. J'aime au contraire assez que la Foi dédaigne ainsi de condescendre aux explications de sens commun ; les prédicateurs qui se mettent trop à la portée de leurs ouailles ne me plaisent pas et je préfère certaines affirmations hautaines qui pour relever du « Le cœur a ses raisons que la raison ne connaît pas » [15] n'ont aucun rapport avec le « *Credo quia absurdum* ») [16]. Comme ta théosophie, le Pragmatisme est à la fois pratique et transcendant et va de William James [17] à Eusapia Paladino [18].

Figure 3 continued.

Crois-moi mon cher Lionel ton bien reconnaissant et dévoué

Marcel PROUST

Tu pourrais peut'être faire déposer chez moi deux exemplaires de ton livre, car je pourrais prêter le mien mais pour *trois* journaux, un ne suffira pas. J'en achèterai volontiers d'autres mais en attendant il vaut mieux ne pas retarder, or je ne peux faute de personnel faire faire de courses lointaines.

1. oφ Coll. U. Ill. Cette lettre se situe entre celles du destinataire datées du *1er mai 1918* (note 3 ci-après) et du *3 mai 1918* (notes 11 et 13). L'allusion à la candidature d'Hermant (note 4) nous permet de dater cette lettre du *jeudi 2 mai 1918*.

2. La plupart des lettres que Proust échangea avec Abel Hermant ne nous sont pas parvenues.

3. Allusion à la lettre du destinataire, du *1er mai 1918*, qui demande s'il y aurait possibilité d'obtenir un article sur son livre dans *Le Figaro*.

4. Abel Hermant était candidat, à l'Académie française, au fauteuil de Jules Lemaître. L'élection eut lieu le jeudi 2 mai 1918. R. Peter, *L'Académie française et le XXe siècle*, p. 114.

5. Ms : *littéraire*, mot barré.

6. Il s'agit de Léon Bailby (voir *Cor* VII, p. 202, note 9). La lettre en question, ainsi que la plupart de celles que Proust échangea avec lui, ne nous sont pas parvenues.

7. André Germain. Voir *Cor* IV, p. 331, note 2.

8. Voir *Cor* XVI, note 2 de la lettre 159.

9. Marcel Prévost. Voir *Cor* V, p. 302, note 7.

10. Voir *Cor* XII, p. 284.

11. Hauser répondra à ce propos dans sa lettre 92, datée du *3 mai 1918*.

12. Ms : *et aussi*, mots ajoutés en interligne.

13. Il semble pourtant que Proust ait envoyé les documents en question avec sa lettre, car Hauser les lui renverra avec la sienne, lettre 91, datée du *3 mai 1918*.

14. Allusion au passage du livre cité que voici : « N'ayant aucunement la prétention de faire ici un cours de Théosophie, nous nous permettons de renvoyer ceux de nos lecteurs qui seraient désireux d'en poursuivre l'étude aux admirables ouvrages d'H.P. Blavatsky, Annie Besant, Leadbeater, etc. [...] » *Op. cit.*, p. 35. — Hélène Petrovna Hahn, dame Blavatsky (1831-1891), théosophe russe. — Annie Besant, née Wood (1847-1933), présidente de la Société théosophique anglaise, auteur de *Réincarnation* (1892). — Charles Webster Leadbeater (1847-1934), collaborateur d'Annie Besant.

Figure 3 continued.

TOME XVII : 1918 231

15. Pascal, *Pensées*. Voir ci-dessus, note 11 de la lettre 41 du même au même.

16. « Je le crois parce que c'est absurde », paroles faussement attribuées à saint Augustin. Il enseignait que le propre de la foi est de croire sans avoir besoin de comprendre. La formule paradoxale est peut-être une transposition de passages de Tertullien sur le baptême et sur la résurrection. « Si tu n'as pas compris, crois. La compréhension est en effet la récompense de la foi. Ne cherche donc pas à comprendre pour croire mais crois afin de comprendre... » Saint Augustin, *Homélies sur l'Évangile de Saint Jean*, homélie XXIX, § 6. *Œuvres de Saint Augustin*. Traduit par M.F. Berrouard, éd. Desclée De Brouwer, 1977, v. 72, p. 607. Ms : parenthèse non refermée ; nous corrigeons.

17. William James (1840-1910), philosophe et psychologue américain qui contribua à la fondation de la philosophie pragmatique.

18. *Sic*. Il s'agit d'Eusapia Palladino (1858 ?-1918), chiromancienne qui eut une certaine notoriété à cause des séances où elle produisait des matérialisations, des empreintes, etc., devant Branly, Bergson, Mme Curie. — Henri Bardac situe en 1918 une anecdote selon laquelle Proust se serait fait mener chez une chiromancienne. *Cah* I, 91. Peut-être était-ce elle ?

Figure 3 continued.

213

A GASTON GALLIMARD

[Le jeudi 2 septembre 1920] [1]

Cher ami

(Et naturellement cela n'a aucun rapport avec ce que je voulais vous dire hier, et vous dirai, je ne sais quand)

Vous voyez un homme au désespoir. Hier, en rentrant, je me suis mis à lire *Le Côté de Guermantes* ; sauf dans certaines parties, les fautes sont tellement nombreuses et rendent les [ph]rases si inintelligibles, que devant mon déshonneur j'ai compris Vatel se perçant de son épée [2].

Je vous avais dit naïvement que pour les fautes grossières [3] le lecteur rétablirait et qu'il valait mieux se borner pour l'erratum aux singularités oubliées qui serviront dans la suite. Mais devant tant de fautes, il vaut mieux les signaler dans un très long erratum (naturellement il serait mille fois mieux de les corriger

Figure 4. Proust, *Correspondance*, éd. Philip Kolb, Paris: Éditons Plon, 1991, #213 à Gaston Gallimard, T. XIX (1920), 437–440. *Correspondance* / Marcel Proust. Text edited and annotated by Philip Kolb and published by Plon, Paris.

438 CORRESPONDANCE DE MARCEL PROUST

dans le texte car personne, à chaque phrase qu'il ne comprendra[4] pas, ne se reportera toutes les trois minutes à l'erratum. Mais puisque vous jugez les corrections impossibles, l'erratum, s'il ne servira guère à faciliter la lecture, palliera au moins le déshonneur)[5]. Je crois que mon tort a été de demander moins d'épreuves que celles auxquelles j'avais droit et de vous dire « Lançons-nous comme cela ! »

Je vais pourtant recommencer cette tactique en beaucoup plus grand puisque pour *Sodome et Gomorrhe I* je crois que je ne vous demanderai pas d'épreuves du tout, ou seulement des premières épreuves. Mais c'est que là, ça marche sur des roulettes.

Pour *Guermantes I* c'est si désastreux que j'ai pensé à vous demander d'attendre février afin que paraissant avec *Guermantes II* et *Sodome I*, on fasse moins attention. Mais j'ai songé qu'au fond, on ne fait pas attention. Monsieur (le charmant dada qui a revu les épreuves et dont le nom m'échappe par une amnésie d'un instant) Breton[6] a cru lire, Jacques Rivière a cru lire. Ils ne se sont pas aperçus que chaque fois que je parle des romans de Bergotte, on a imprimé les romans de Bergson. Erreur sans gravité quoique inexplicable, car les deux *t* de Bergotte devraient prémunir contre toute confusion avec Bergson (mais les protes veulent interpréter, montrer qu'ils sont au courant, que le pragmatisme[7] ne leur est pas inconnu). Mais si ces Bergson pour Bergotte ne sont pas graves, beaucoup d'autres fautes ôtent tout sens à une phrase. Hé bien ces lecteurs avertis ne s'en sont pas aperçus. Comptons sur l'aveuglement des autres. Mais je suis navré. Jamais je n'ai attendu un livre avec tant d'impatience et ne l'ai lu avec tant de désolation.

Cher ami vous feriez bien de ne pas attendre pour m'envoyer les deux volumes brochés (dont une première édition). Je regrette que l'un n'ait pu déjà partir.

Quant à l'erratum (qui naturellement ne sera pas joint à ces deux exemplaires sacrifiés), quand faut-il que vous ayez mes feuilles corrigées ?

En regardant les corrections, vous ferez dresser vous-même l'erratum, dont je sais mal comment il sera rédigé (lire pour...) Malheureusement jusqu'ici tout ce que j'ai

Figure 4 continued.

corrigé l'a été dans la désolation, et sans songer que cela servirait à l'erratum. C'est vous dire que c'est fort illisible. Mais je serai à votre disposition s'il y a des choses qui ne vous paraissent pas claires. D'ailleurs elles vous le paraîtront (claires)[8], à cause de l'évidence de la faute. Je tâcherai de tout corriger. Avec mes yeux ce n'est pas facile. Mais on me dit que le grand oculiste que je dois consulter depuis quatre ans[9] rentre ces jours-ci. Peut'être me découvrira-t-il de meilleurs verres. Si je vous demande la date où vous avez besoin des corrections, c'est pour ne pas retarder la parution au 1er Octobre. Comme on est rentré à Paris plus tôt cette année, à cause du temps[10], on repartira plus tôt pour les villégiatures d'hiver.

Vous savez que si *Sodome I* est presque au net, *Guermantes II* réclame beaucoup d'ajoutages. Que l'imprimeur ne me fasse donc pas attendre trop les épreuves puisque les deux paraîtront ensemble (15 février). J'aurais préféré que ma préface à Morand ne parût qu'après ce *Sodome I* qui est[11] littérairement réhabilitateur, après nos pataugeages de *Guermantes*. Mais sans doute le livre de Morand paraît avant. Et je ne veux pas le retarder pour cela. J'ai été bien heureux de votre visite hier. C'est vous qui avez pris bonne mine, bonne allure, et rajeuni ! Cela fait très grand plaisir à votre très affectueusement dévoué

Marcel PROUST

On me dit que les manuscrits de Claudel sont encore plus difficiles à lire que les miens. Pourtant il n'y a jamais de fautes[12].

Lire jusqu'au bout, très important[13]

1. φ Coll. Archives Gallimard. *MP-GG* 266-268 (n° 169). Cette lettre doit dater du *jeudi 2 septembre 1920* : voir ci-après, note 5.

2. Voir les lettres de Mme de Sévigné des *24* et *26 avril 1671*. Vatel était le maître d'hôtel du Grand Condé.

3. Ms : *on*, mot barré : *le lecteur*, mots ajoutés en interligne.

4. Ms : *pas*, mot ajouté en interligne.

5. Gallimard répondra, le *Vendredi 3 Sept[embre 1920]* : « votre lettre me consterne [...] Je voudrais pouvoir faire refaire toute l'édition. [...] Il est donc entendu que nous ferons un erratum. Il

Figure 4 continued.

faudrait pour être prêt le 1er octobre, que j'aie vos épreuves corrigées le 15 septembre au plus tard. » *MP-GG* 269, lettre 170.

6. Voir ci-dessus, la lettre de Rivière du *29 juin 1920* et sa note 3. — Ms : *Breton*, nom ajouté en interligne.

7. Deux fois, à la p. 200 de l'édition originale, le nom de Bergson paraît alors que le marquis de Norpois et la duchesse de Guermantes parlent des romans de Bergotte. Voir II, 222 de l'édition de 1954. — Bergson avait présenté une traduction de *Le Pragmatisme*, par William James, publiée chez Flammarion en 1911.

8. Ms : la parenthèse est ajoutée en interligne.

9. Voir ci-après, la lettre du *lundi 6 septembre 1920* à Soupault, où Proust se demande s'il ne faut pas qu'il se résigne « après quatre ans d'hésitation à aller voir un oculiste ».

10. *Le Figaro* du 2 septembre 1920, p. 1, *Échos*, parle de « cette saison presque automnale » dont bénéficient les grands restaurants de Paris. — Ms : *à cause du temps*, mots ajoutés en interligne.

11. Ms : *qui est*, mots ajoutés en interligne.

12. Paul Claudel s'était plaint des coquilles dans l'édition du *Pain dur*. *MP-GG* 268, note 1 (archives Gallimard).

13. Ms : phrase ajoutée en tête de la lettre.

Figure 4 continued.

Works Cited or Consulted

PRIMARY SOURCES: MARCEL PROUST

Proust, Marcel. *À la recherche du temps perdu*. 4 vols. Paris: Éditions Gallimard [Bibliothèque de la Pléiade], 1987–1989.

———. "À propos du 'style' de Flaubert." *Essais et articles. Contre Sainte-Beuve*. Éd. Pierre Clarac et Yves Sandre, 586–600. Paris: Éditions Gallimard [Bibliothèque de la Pléiade], 1971.

———. Cahier 59. Manuscript facsimile.

———. *Le Carnet de 1908* [Cahiers Marcel Proust 8]. Éd. Philip Kolb. Paris: Éditions Gallimard, 1976.

———. "Contre l'obscurité." *La Revue blanche* (15 juillet 1896). Repr. *Essais et articles. Contre Sainte-Beuve*. Éd Pierre Clarac et Yves Sandre, 390–395. Paris: Éditions Gallimard [Bibliothèque de la Pléiade], 1971.

———. *Contre Sainte-Beuve* précédé de *Pastiches et Mélanges* suivi d'*Essais et Articles*. Éd. Pierre Clarac et Yves Sandre. Paris: Éditions Gallimard [Bibliothèque de la Pléiade], 1971.

———. *Correspondance*. Éd. Philip Kolb. 21 T. Paris: Librairie Plon, 1970–1993.

———. "Gérard de Nerval." *Contre Sainte-Beuve*. Éd Pierre Clarac et Yves Sandre, 233–42. Paris: Éditions Gallimard [Bibliothèque de la Pléiade], 1971.

———. *In Search of Lost Time*. Trans. C. K. Scott Moncrieff and Terence Kilmartin. Rev. D. J. Enright. 6 vols. New York: The Modern Library, 2003.

———. Interview with André Arnyvelde. "À propos d'un livre récent: L'Oeuvre écrite dans la chambre close. Chez M. Marcel Proust (1913)." [Cahiers Marcel Proust 3]: *Textes retrouvés*. Éd. Philip Kolb, 292–95. Paris: Éditions Gallimard, 1971.

———. Interview with Élie-Joseph Bois. "Swann expliqué par Proust." *Le Temps* (novembre 13, 1913). Repr. *Essais et articles. Contre Sainte-Beuve*. Éd. Pierre Clarac et Yves Sandre, 557–59. Paris: Éditions Gallimard [Bibliothèque de la Pléiade], 1971.

———. *Jean Santeuil*. Paris: Éditions Gallimard [Bibliothèque de la Pléiade], 1971.

———. "Journées de lecture." *Essais et Articles. Contre Sainte-Beuve*. Éd. Pierre Clarac et Yves Sandre, 526–33, note 2, 924–29. Paris: Éditions Gallimard [Bibliothèque de la Pléiade], 1971.

———. *Lettres à Bibesco*. Préface Thierry Maulnier. Lausanne: La Guilde du Livre, 1949.

———. *Lettres à Mme. Scheikévitch*. Intro. René Gillouin. Paris: Librairie des Champs-Élysées, 1928.

———. "La Méthode de Sainte-Beuve." *Contre Sainte-Beuve*. Éd. Pierre Clarac et Yves Sandre, 219–32. Paris: Éditions Gallimard [Bibliothèque de la Pléiade], 1971.

———. "[Projets de Préface]" *Contre Sainte-Beuve*. Éd. Pierre Clarac et Yves Sandre, 211–18. Paris: Éditions Gallimard [Bibliothèque de la Pléiade], 1971.

———. ["Réponses à une enquête des Annales"]. *Les Annales politiques et littéraires*. février 26, 1922. Repr. *Essais et Articles. Contre Sainte-Beuve*. Éd. Pierre Clarac et Yves Sandre, 640–41. Paris: Éditions Gallimard [Bibliiothèque de la Pléiade], 1971.

———. "[Révélations de Proust sur la suite de son roman vers la fin de 1915]." Lettre à Marie Scheikévitch, *Essais et articles, Contre Sainte-Beuve*. Éd. Pierre Clarac et Yves Sandre, 559–64. Paris: Éditions Gallimard [Bibliothèque de la Pléiade], 1971.

———. "Sur la lecture." *La Renaissance latine* (15 juin 1905). Repr. "Journées de lecture." *Pastiches et mélanges. Contre Sainte-Beuve.* . Éd. Pierre Clarac et Yves Sandre, 160–94. Paris: Éditions Gallimard [Bibliothèque de la Pléiade], 1971.
———. *Textes retrouvés.* [Cahiers Marcel Proust 3]. Éd. Philip Kolb. Paris: Éditions Gallimard, 1971.

PRIMARY SOURCES: WILLIAM JAMES

James, William. "Address at the Emerson Centenary in Concord." *Riverside Press for the Social Circle in Concord* (June 1903): 67–77. Repr. *Memories and Studies.* Ed. Henry James, Jr., 17–34. New York: Longmans, Green & Co., 1911.
———. "A Great French Philosopher at Harvard" *Nation* 90 (1910): 312–14.
———. *A Pluralistic Universe: Hibbert Lectures to Manchester College on the Present Situation in Philosophy.* New York and London: Longmans, Green & Co., 1909. Trans. Le Brun and Paris. *La Philosophie de l'Expérience.* Paris: Flammarion, 1910. Repr. Cambridge: Harvard University Press, 1977.
———. "Are We Automata?" *Mind* 4.13 (January 1879): 1–22.
———. "A Suggestion about Mysticism." *Journal of Philosophy, Psychology, and Scientific Methods* 7 (1910): 85–92.
———. "Bain and Renouvier." *Nation* XXII (1876): 367–69.
———. "Bergson and His Critique of Intellectualism." *A Pluralistic Universe,* 223–73. New York: Longmans, Green & Co., 1909.
———. "Brute and Human Intellect." *Journal of Speculative Philosophy* 12 (1878): 236–76. Trans. *Critique Philosophique* 8.1 (1879): 369–76, 394–97. *Critique Philosophique* 8.2 (1879): 17–26, 41–48. Repr. *Essays in Psychology,* 1–37. Cambridge: Harvard University Press, 1983.
———. "The Congress of Physiological Psychology at Paris." *Mind* 14 (October 1889): 614–615.
———. "The Dilemma of Determinism." *Critique Philosophique* 13.2 (1884): 273–80, 305–12. *Critique Philosophique* 13.2 (1885): 353–62.
———. "Does Consciousness Exist?" *The Journal of Philosophy, Psychology, and Scientific Methods* 1.18 (September 1, 1904): 477–91. Trans. *Archives de Psychologie* 5 (1905): 1–12. Repr. *Essays in Radical Empiricism.* New York: Longmans, Green & Co., 1912. 1–38. Repr. Cambridge: Harvard University Press, 1976. Intro. John J. McDermott, 3–20.
———. "The Energies of Men." *Philosophical Review* 16 (1907): 1–20. Trans. *Revue de Philosophie* 10 (1907): 317–39.
———. *Essays in Radical Empiricism.* New York: Longmans, Green & Co., 1912. Repr. Cambridge: Harvard University Press, 1976. Intro. John J. McDermott. *Essais d'empirisme radical [1912].* Mineola, NY: Dover Publications, Inc., 2003. Trans. et Préface Mathias Girel et Guillaume Garreta. Marseille: Agone, 2005. Trad. avec l'aide du C.N.L. Rééd. Paris: Flammarion, Collection Champs, 2007.
———. "The Experience of Activity." *Psychological Review* 12 (1905): 1–17. Repr. *Essays in Radical Empiricism,* 155–89. New York: Longmans, Green & Co., 1912. Repr. Cambridge: Harvard University Press, 1976.
———. "The Feeling of Effort." *Anniversary Memoirs of the Boston Society of Natural History* (1880): 32pp. Trans. *Critique Philosophique* 9.2 (1880): 123–28, 129–35, 145–48, 200–208, 220–24, 225–31, 289–91.
———. "G. Papini and the Pragmatist Movement in Italy." *Journal of Philosophy, Psychology, and Scientific Methods* 3 (1906): 337–41.
———. "Great Men, Great Thoughts and Their Environment." *Critique Philosophique* 9.2 (1881): 396–400, 407–15: *Critique Philosophique* 10.1 (1881): 1–14.
———. "The Hidden Self." *Scribner's Magazine* 7 (1890): 361–73.
———. *Human Immortality: Two Supposed Objections to the Doctrine.* Boston: Houghton Mifflin, 1898.

———. "Interest." *Talks to Teachers on Psychology; and to Students on Some of Life's Ideals.* Ch. 10, 91–99. New York: Holt, 1899, 1900. London: Longmans, Green & Co., 1899. Trans. Pidoux. Paris: Alcan, 1900; 2nd ed., 1907. http://des.emory.edu/mfp/tt10.html.

———. "The Knowing of Things Together." *The Psychological Review* 2 (1895): 105–24. Repr. *Collected Essays and Reviews*, 371–400. New York: Russell & Russell, 1969. Repr. *The Writings of William James*. Ed. John J. McDermott, 152–68. Chicago: University of Chicago Press, 1977. Repr. *Essays in Philosophy*, 71–89. Cambridge: Harvard University Press, 1978.

———. *The Letters of William James*. Ed. by his son Henry James. 2 vols. Boston: The Atlantic Monthly Press, 1920.

———. *The Meaning of Truth: A Sequel to "Pragmatism."* New York: Longmans, Green & Co., 1909. Repr. *Pragmatism and The Meaning of Truth*. Cambridge: Harvard University Press, 1978.

———. *Memories and Studies*. New York: Longmans, Green & Co., 1911.

———. "The Moral Philosopher and the Moral Life. "*International Journal of Ethics* 1 (1891): 330–54. Repr. *The Will to Believe, and Other Essays in Popular Philosophy*, 184–215. New York: Longmans, Green & Co., 1897. *The Writings of William James*. Ed. John J. McDermott, 610–29. Chicago: University of Chicago Press, 1977. Repr. Cambridge, MA and London: Harvard University Press, 1979.

———. "La Notion de Conscience." *Archives de Psychology* V.17 (June 1905): 1–12. Repr. *Essays in Radical Empiricism*, 206–33. New York: Longmans, Green, & Co., 1912. Repr. Cambridge: Harvard University Press, 1976. Trans. Salvatore Saladino. *The Writings of William James*. Ed. John J. McDermott, 184–94. New York: Random House, 1967. Repr. Cambridge: Harvard University Press, 1976.

———."La Notion de Conscience." *Essays in Radical Empiricism*. Ed. Ralph Barton Perry. Repr and Trans. Stanley Appelbaum. New York: Dover Publications, Inc., 2003.

———. "On a Certain Blindness in Human Beings." *Atlantic Monthly* (1899). Repr. *Talks to Teachers on Psychology; and to Students on Some of Life's Ideals*. New York: Holt; 1899. 2nd ed, 1912: 229–64. Trans. Pidoux. Paris: Alcan 1900; 2nd ed., 1907. Repr. John J. McDermott, *The Writings of William James*. Chicago: University of Chicago Press, 1977. Repr. Cambridge: Harvard University Press, 1983.

———. "On Some Mental Effects of the Earthquake." *Youth's Companion* 80 (June 7, 1906). Repr. *Memories and Studies*. Ed. Henry James Jr., 207–26. New York: Longmans, Green & Co., 1911.

———. "On Some Omissions of Introspective Psychology." *Mind* 9.33 (1884): 1–26.

———. "On the Function of Cognition." *Mind* 10 (1885): 27–44. Repr. *The Meaning of Truth*. New York: Longmans, Green & Co., 1909. Repr. *Pragmatism* and *The Meaning of Truth*. Cambridge: Harvard University Press, 1978. [13]179–[32]198.

———. "The Perception of Time." *The Journal of Speculative Philosophy* XX (1886): 374–407.

———. "Personal Idealism." *Mind* 12 (1903): 93–97.

———. "Philosophical Conceptions and Practical Results." *University of California Chronicle* (1898): 24pp. Trans. *Revue de Philosophie* 8 (1906): 463–84.

———. "The Philosophy of Bergson." *Hibbert Journal* 7 (1909): 562–77. Abridged and altered as "Bergson and His Critique of Intellectualism." *A Pluralistic Universe; Hibbert Lectures to Manchester College on the Present Situation in Philosophy*, 223–73. New York: Longmans, Green & Co., 1909.

———. "The Place of Affectional Facts in a World of Pure Experience." *Journal of Philosophy, Psychology, and Scientific Methods* 2 (1905): 281–87. Repr. *Essays in Radical Empiricism*, 137–54. New York: Longmans, Green & Co., 1912. Repr. Cambridge: Harvard University Press, 1976.

———. *Pragmatism: A New Name for Some Old Ways of Thinking*. New York: Longmans, Green and Co., 1907. Repr. *Pragmatism and The Meaning of Truth*. Intro. A. J. Ayer. Cambridge: Harvard University Press, 1978. Trans. E. LeBrun. *Le Pragmatisme*.

Intro. Henri Bergson. Paris: Flammarion, 1911. Trans. Swedish by Algot Ruhe. *Pragmatism; ett nytt namn för nagra gamla tankegangar. Allmänfattliga föreläsningar över filosofi av William James.* Stockholm: A. Bonnier, 1916.

———. *The Principles of Psychology.* 2 vols. New York: Holt, 1890. Repr. 2 Vols. London: Macmillan, 1891. Repr. Intro. Gerald E. Myers. 2 vols. Cambridge, MA: Harvard University Press, 1981.

———. *Psychology: Briefer Course.* New York: Holt, 1892. Repr. Holt, 1920. Repr. Cambridge, MA: Harvard University Press, 1984. Trans. E. Baudin and G. Bertier. Paris: M. Rivière, 1909.

———. "Quelques considérations sur la méthode subjective." *Critique Philosophique* 6.2 (1878): 407–13.

———. "Rationality, Activity and Faith." *The Princeton Review* 2 (1882): 58–86. Trans. *Critique philosophique* 11.2 (1882): 129–40, 161–66.

———. "Reflex Action and Theism." *Critique Philosophique* 10.2 (1882): 385–91, 401–10; *Critique Philosophique* 11.1 (1882): 5–13.

———. "Remarks on Spencer's Definition of Mind as Correspondence" *Journal of Speculative Philosophy* 12.1 (January 1878): 1–18. Repr. *Essays in Philodophy,* 7–22. Cambridge: Harvard University Press, 1978.

———. "Réponse de M. W. James aux Remarques de M. Renouvier sur sa théorie de la volonté." *Critique Philosophique* 4.2 (1888): 401–4.

———. "The Sentiment of Rationality." *Mind* 4 (1879): 317–46. Trans. C. Renouvier. *Critique Philosophique* 8.2 (1879): 72–89, 113–118, 129–138. Repr. *Essays in Philosophy,* 32–64. Cambridge: Harvard University Press, 1978.

———. *Some Problems of Philosophy: A Beginning of an Introduction to Philosophy.* Ed. Henry James Jr. New York: Longmans, Green & Co., 1911. Repr. Cambridge, MA: Harvard University Press, 1979.

———. "The Spatial Quale." *Journal of Speculative Philosophy* 13 (1879): 64–87.

———. *Talks to Teachers on Psychology; and to Students on Some of Life's Ideals.* New York: Holt, 1899. London: Longmans, Green & Co., 1899, 1900. Repr. Cambridge: Harvard University Press, 1983. Trans. Pidoux. Paris: Alcan, 1900; 2nd ed., 1907. http://des.emory.edu/mfp/tt10.html. *Aux Étudiants.* Trans. Henri Marti. Préface É. Boutroux. Paris: Payot, 1914. *Causeries pédagogiques.* Trans. L.-S. Pidoux. Paris: Payot, 1921.

———. "The Thing and Its Relations." *A Pluralistic Universe: Hibbert Lectures to Manchester College on the Present Situation in Philosophy.* Appendix A, 347–369. New York: Longmans, Green & Co., 1909. Repr. Cambridge, MA: Harvard University Press, 1977. *La Philosophie de l'Expérience.* Trans. Le Brun and Paris. Paris: Flammarion, 1910.

———. Unsigned Rev. of *Du Sommeil et des États analogues, considérés surtout au point de vue de l'action du Moral sur le Physique* by A. A. Liébault. *Nation* 7 (1868): 50–52.

———. Unsigned Rev. of *Rapport sur le Progrès et la Marche de la Physiologie générale en France* by Claude Bernard. *North American Review* 107 (1868): 322–328.

———. Unsigned Rev. of *Unüberwindliche Mächte* by Herman Grimm. *Nation* 5 (1867): 432–433.

———. *The Varieties of Religious Experience: A Study in Human Nature.* New York: Longmans, Green and Co., 1902. Repr. 1915. Repr. Cambridge, MA: Harvard University Press, 1985. Repr. New York: The Modern Library, 2002. Excerpted in *Annales de Philosophie Chrétienne,* 1903, *Revue de Philosophie,* 1905. Trans. F. Abauzit. *L'Expérience religieuse: Essai de Psychologie descriptive.* Préface Émile Boutroux. Paris: Alcan, 1905.

———. "The Will to Believe." *New World* 5 (1896): 327–347. Repr. *The Will to Believe and Other Essays in Popular Philosophy,* 1–31. New York: Longmans, Green & Co., 1897. Repr. *The Will to Believe and Other Essays in Popular Philosophy,* 13–33. Cambridge: Harvard University Press, 1979.

———. "What is an Emotion?" *Mind* XXXIV.9 (1884): 188–205. Trans. G. Dumas. *La Théorie de l'émotion*. Paris: Alcan, 1903. Repr. *Collected Essays and Reviews*, 244–275. New York: Russell and Russell, 1920. Repr. 1969.

———. "What Makes a Life Significant." *Talks to Teachers on Psychology; and to Students on Some of Life's Ideals*, 265–301. New York: Henry Holt and Company, 1899, 1900. Repr. 1912. Repr. *The Writings of William James* by John J. McDermott, 629–660. Chicago: University of Chicago Press, 1977. Repr. Cambridge: Harvard University Press, 1983.

———. "What the Will Effects." *Critique Philosophique* 4.1 (1888): 401–420.

James, William, and Théodore Flournoy. *The Letters of William James and Théodore Flournoy*. Ed. Robert C. LeClair. Madison: The University of Wisconsin Press, 1966.

OTHER PRIMARY AND SECONDARY SOURCES

Album Proust, Iconographie réunie et commentée par Pierre Clarac et André Ferré. Paris: Gallimard, 1965.

Alden, Douglas W. "Proust and Ribot." *Modern Language Notes* 58.7 (November 1934): 501–507.

Alexandrov, Vladimir E. "Literature, Literariness, and the Brain" *Comparative Literature* 59.2 (Spring 2007): 97–118.

Arnyvelde, André. "À propos d'un livre récent: L'Oeuvre écrite dans la chambre close. Chez M. Marcel Proust (1913)." [Cahiers Marcel Proust 3]: *Textes retrouvés*. Éd. Philip Kolb, 292–295. Paris: Éditions Gallimard, 1971.

Baars, Bernard J., Uma Ramamurthy, and Stan Franklin, "How deliberate, spontaneous and unwanted memories emerge in a computational model of consciousness." ccrg.cs.memphis.edu/assets/papers/Chapter%209%20Baars_Ramamurthy_Franklin%20July13.doc.

Barthes, Roland. *Barthes par Roland Barthes*. Paris: Éditions du Seuil, 1975.

———. *Le Plaisir du texte*. Paris: Éditions du Seuil, 1973.

———. "Texte (théorie du)." *Encyclopoedia universalis*, 1973.

Bartsch, Renate. *Concept Formation, Remembering, and Understanding: Dynamic Conceptual Symantics and Proust's "À la recherche du temps perdu."* Amsterdam: J. Benjamins, 2005. http://www.illc.uva.nl: Renate Bartsch The Role of Consciousness and Intentionality in Perception, Semantics, Representations and Rules.

Beard, George. *A Practical Treatise on Nervous Exhaustion: Its Causes, Symptoms and Sequences*. New York: 1880.

———. "Neurasthenia or Nervous Exhaustion". *Boston Medical and Surgical Journal* (1869; 80): 217–221.

———. *Sexual Neurasthenia (Nervous Exhaustion, Its Hygiene, Causes, Symptoms and Treatment)*. New York: 1895.

Bédé, Jean-Albert. "Chateaubriand et Marcel Proust." *Modern Language Notes* 49.6 (June 1934): 353–360.

Bentley, I. M. Rev. of *Le Problème de la mémoire: Essai de Psycho-Méchanique* by Paul Sollier. *The Philosophical Review* 10.1 (Jan. 1901): 98.

Bergson, Henri. *Correspondances*. Éd. André Robinet. Paris: Presses Universitaires de France, 2002.

———. *Essai sur les données immédiates de la conscience*. Paris: F. Alcan. 1889.

———. *L'Évolution créatrice*. Paris: F. Alcan, 1907.

———. *Matière et mémoire: Essai sur la relation du corps à l'esprit*. 1896. Librairie Félix Alcan, 1913.

———. *Le Rêve*. Conférence faite en 1901 à l'Institut général Psychologique. Rev. by A. Binet, *L'année psychologique* 8.8 (1901): 518–519. Publ. in *L'énergie spirituelle*. Paris: Alcan, 1919.

———. "Réponse à M. Rageot." *Revue philosophique de la France et de l'Étranger* 60.2 (August 1905): 229–230.

———. "Sur le Pragmatisme de William James, Vérité et Réalité." *La Pensée et le mouvant essais et conférences*. Ch. VIII. Paris: Librairie Félix Alcan, 1934. "On the Pragmatism of William James: Truth and Reality." *The Creative Mind*. Ch. VIII, Trans. Mabelle L. Andison. New York: Philosophical Library, 1946.

Berry, Walter. "Du côté de Guermantes." *Hommage à Marcel Proust (1871–1922). La Nouvelle Revue Française* XX, 10.112 (January 1, 1923): 77–80.

Billy, Robert de. *Marcel Proust, lettres et conversations*. Paris: Éditions des Portiques, 1930.

Binet-Valmer, Jean-August-Gustave. *Le Coeur en désordre*. 1912.

Bizub, Edward. "Proust et le docteur Sollier: les 'molécules impressionnées.'" *Bulletin Marcel Proust* 56 (2006): 41–51.

———. *Proust et le moi divisé: La Recherche: creuset de la psychologie expérimentale (1874–1914)* Genève: Droz, 2006.

———. "Proust et Ribot: l'imagination créatrice" *Bulletin Marcel Proust* 58 (2008): 49–56.

Blanche, Jacques-Émile. *Mes modèles*. Paris: Stock, 1928.

———. "Quelques Instantanés de Marcel Proust." *Hommage à Marcel Proust (1871–1922). La Nouvelle Revue Française* XX, 10.112 (January 1923): 52–61.

Blondel, Charles. *La Psychographie de Marcel Proust*. Paris: J. Vrin, 1932.

Blondel and de Sailly. Articles in *Les Annales de Philosophie Chrétienne*. 4e Série, vols. 2 and 3.

Bloom, Harold. *The Anxiety of Influence: A Theory of Poetry*. 2nd ed. New York: Oxford University Press, 1997.

Bogousslavsky, Julien. "Marcel Proust's Lifelong Tour of the Parisian Neurological Intelligentsia: From Brissaud and Djerine to Sollier and Babinski." *European Neurology* 57 (2007): 129–136.

———. "Memory after Charcot: Paul Sollier's Visionary Work." *Journal of Neurology, Neurosurgery and Psychiatry* 78 (2007): 1373–1374.

Bogousslavsky, Julien, and Olivier Walusinski. "Marcel Proust and Paul Sollier: The Involuntary Memory Connection." *Schweizer Archiv für Neurologie und Psychiatrie* (submitted). http://www.baillement.com/lettres/sollier_english.pdf.

Bois, Élie-Joseph. "Variétés littéraires: *À la recherche du temps perdu* (1913)." *Le Temps* (13 novembre 1913). Repr. [Cahiers Marcel Proust 3]: *Textes retrouvés*. Éd. Philip Kolb, 285–291. Paris: Éditions Gallimard, 1971.

Bonnet, Henri. *Alphonse Darlu*. Paris: A.G. Nizet, 1961.

Boodin, John Elof. "William James as I Knew Him." *Personalist* 23 (1942). Repr. *William James Remembered*. Ed. Linda Simon, 206–232. Lincoln: University of Nebraska Press, 1996.

Bortolussi, Marisa, and Peter Dixon. *Psychonarratology: Foundations for the Empirical Study of Literary Response*. Cambridge: Cambridge University Press, 2003.

Botton, Alain de. *How Proust Can Change Your Life: Not a Novel*. New York: Pantheon, 1997.

Bourdeau, Jean. *Les Maîtres de la pensée contemporaine*. Paris: F. Alcan, 1904.

———. *Pragmatisme et modernism*. Paris: F. Alcan, 1909.

———. "Un dernier mot sur le pragmatisme" (2 parts). *Le Journal des Débats Politiques et Littéraires*(September 30, 1910): 636–638 and (November 4, 1910) 873–875.

Boutroux, Émile. "Décès de M. William James: Paroles de M. Boutroux, Président." *Séances et travaux de l'Académie des sciences morales et politiques, compte rendu* (1910): 487–491.

———. "Les Conférences de M Émile Boutroux en Amérique." *Les Débats politiques et littéraires* (22 avril 1910).

———. *Science et Religion dans la philosophie contemporaine*. Paris: Flammarion, 1908.

———. *William James*. Paris: Librairie Armand Colin, 1911. 2nd ed. trans. Archibald and Barbara Henderson. New York: Longmans, Green & Co., 1912.

———. " William James et l'éxpérience religieuse." *Revue de Métaphysique et de Morale* XVI (1908).

Bowne, Borden Parker. *Metaphysics: A Study in First Principles*. New York: Harper & Brothers, 1882.

Brée, Germaine. *Marcel Proust and Deliverance from Time*. Trans. C. J. Richards and A. D. Truitt. New Brunswick, NJ: Rutgers University Press, 1955.

Brooks, David. "The Behavioral Revolution." *New York Times*, October 27, 2008. http://www.nytimes.com/2008/10/28/opinion/28brooks.html.

Brun, Bernard. "Narrateur (*CSB*)." *Dictionnaire Marcel Proust*. Paris: Honoré Champion, 2004.

Bucknall, Barbara J. *The Religion of Art in Proust*. Urbana: University of Illinois Press, 1969.

Buckner, Randy L. "The Potion's Magic." *Neuron* 42.4 (May 2004): 526–527.

"Bulletin: Les Congrès Scientifiques Internationaux" *Revue de l'Hypnotisme expérimental et thérapeutique* (1889–1890).

Carter, William C. "'Am I a Novelist?' Proust's Search for a Genre." *Proust in Perspective*. Ed. Armine Kotin Mortimer and Katherine Kolb. Urbana: University of Chicago Press, 2002.

———. *Marcel Proust: A Life*. New Haven: Yale University Press, 2000.

"Cartoons and Poetry." Narr. Billy Collins. Commentary Marc Sanchez. *Weekend America*. American Public Media. KWMU, St. Louis. September 20, 2008. Poems originally appeared in "Porkface." 1977. http://weekendamerica.publicradio.org/display/web/2008/09/20/cartoons_poetry/#.

Cary, Benedict. "For the Brain, Remembering is Like Reliving." *New York Times*, September 5, 2008. http://www.nytimes.com/2008/09/05/science/05brain.html.

Chapelle, Gaëtane. Rev. of *Le Sens de la mémoire* by Jean-Yves and Marc Tadié. Paris: Gallimard, 1999. "Livre du mois." *Sciences humaines* 101 (Janvier 2000). http://www.scienceshumaines.com/articleprint2.php?lg=fr&id_article=111.

Clark, Terry. *Gabriel Tarde on Communication and Social Influence*. Chicago: University of Chicago Press, 1969.

Cohn, Dorrit. *The Distinction of Fiction*. Baltimore: The Johns Hopkins University Press, 1999.

———. *Transparent Minds: Narrative Modes for Presenting Consciousness in Fiction*. Princeton: Princeton University Press, 1978.

Coleman, Elliott. "Religious Imagery." *Proust, A Collection f Critical Essays*. Ed. René Girard. Englewood Cliffs, NJ: Prentice-Hall, 1962.

Compagnon, Antoine. *Le Démon de la théorie*. Paris: Éditions du Seuil, 1998.

———. *Proust entre deux siècles*. Paris: Éditions du Seuil, 1989.

———. *La Troisième République des lettres, de Flaubert à Proust*. Paris: Éditions du Seuil, 1983.

Cresson, André. *Bergson: Sa vie, son oeuvre*. Paris: Presses Universitaires de France, 1961.

Czoniczer, Elizabeth. *Quelques antécédents de "À la recherche du temps perdu"; tendances qui peuvent avoir contribué à la cristallisation du roman proustien*. Genève: E. Droz, 1957.

Delattre, Floris. *William James, bergsonien*. Paris: Presses Universitaires de France, 192–?

Delattre, Floris, et Maurice Le Breton. *William James: extraits de correspondance/ choisis et traduits de l'anglais*. Préface Henri Bergson. Paris: Payot, 1924.

Deleuze, Gilles. *Proust and Signs*. http://books.google.com/books?id=HUZwFDjPL_wC&lpg=PP1&dq=deleuze%20proust%20and%20signs&pg=PA40#v=onepage&q&f=false.

Descombes, Vincent. *Proust: Philosophie du roman*. Paris: Les Éditions de Minuit, 1987.

———. *Proust: Philosophy of the Novel*. Trans. Catherine Chance Macksey. Stanford: Stanford University Press, 1992.

Dreyfus, R. *Souvenirs sur Marcel Proust*. Paris: Grasset, 1926.

Dryden, Donald. "Memory, Imagination, and the Cognitive Value of the Arts." *Consciousness and Cognition*, 13 (2004): 254–267.

Durkheim, Émile. Cours inédit d'Émile Durkheim, *Pragmatisme et sociologie*, éd. Armand Cuvillier. Paris: Librairie philosophique J. Vrin, 1955. *Pragmatism and Sociology*. Trans. J. C. Whitehouse. Ed. John B. Allcock. Preface by Armand Cuvillier. Cambridge: Cambridge University Press, 1983.

Edelman, Gerald. *Wider Than the Sky*. New Haven: Yale University Press, 2004.

Ellenberger, Henri F. *The Discovery of the Unconscious: The History and Evolution of Dynamic Psychiatry*. New York: Basic Books, Inc., 1970.

Engber, Daniel. "Proust Wasn't a Neuroscientist: How Jonah Lehrer's *Proust Was a Neuroscientist* Overstates the Case." *Slate*, November 26, 2007. http://www.slate.com/id/2178584?nav=wp.

Epstein, Russell. "Consciousness, Art and the Brain: Lessons from Marcel Proust." *Consciousness and Cognition* 13 (2004): 213–240.

———. "The Neural-Cognitive Basis of the Jamesian Stream of Thought." *Consciousness and Cognition* 9 (2000): 550–575.

———. "Substantive Thoughts about Substantive Thoughts: a Reply to Galin." *Consciousness and Cognition* 9 (2002): 584–590.

Everdell, William R. Rev. of *Einstein's Clocks, Poincaré's Maps* by Peter Galison. New York: W. W. Norton, 2003. "Books." *New York Times* August 17, 2003.

Ferguson, Kennan. "La Philosophie Américaine: James, Bergson, and the Century of Intercontinental Pluralism." Baltimore: Johns Hopkins University Press, 2006. http://muse.jhu.edu/journals/theory_and_event/v009/0.1ferguson.html.

Ferré, André. *Les Années de collège de Marcel Proust*. 4e Éd. NRF: Librairie Gallimard, 1959.

Flournoy, Théodore. *The Philosophy of William James*. Trans. Edwin B. Holt and William James Jr. New York: Henry Holt & Co., 1917.

Fraisse, Luc. "Le Nouvelle écrivain: Proust précurseur de Jauss." Colloque international de littérature comparée de Tours. "Originalité de l'oeuvre et notion d'originalité dans la pensée de Marcel Proust." March 5–6, 2009.

Friedman, Melvin. *Stream of Consciousness: A Study in Literary Method*. New Haven: Yale University Press, 1955.

Galin, David. "Aesthetic Experience: Marcel Proust and the Neo-Jamesian Stucture of Awareness." *Consciousness and Cognition* 13 (2004): 241–253.

———. "Comments on Epstein's Neurocognitive Interpretation of William James's Model of Consciousness." *Consciousness and Cognition* 9 (2002): 576–583.

Gautier, Théophile. *Le Capitaine Fracasse*. Serialized 1861–1863. Full text, Paris: Charpentier, 1863.

Genette, Gérard. *Fiction et diction*. Paris: Édiions du Seuil, 1991.

———. *Figures III*. Paris: Éditions du Seuil, 1972.

———. *Narrative Discourse: An Essay in Method*. Trans. Jane E. Lewin. Ithaca, NY: Cornell University Press, 1980.

———. *Palimpsestes: la littérature au second degré*. Paris: Éditions du Seuil, 1982.

———. "Proust Palimpseste." *Figures of Literary Discourse*. Trans. Alan Sheridan. New York: Columbia University Press, 1982: 203–228.

———. "Rhetoric Restrained." *Figures of Literary Discourse*. Trans. Alan Sheridan. New York: Columbia University Press, 1982: 103–126.

Gillouin, René. *Essais de critique littéraire et philosophique*. Paris: Bernard Grasset, 1913.

Girard. René. *Proust: A Collection of Critical Esays*. Englewood Cliffs, NJ: Prentice-Hall, Inc., 1962.

Girel, Mathias. "The Influence of James and Royce on European Thought Then and Now." James/Royce Centennial Conference. "William James and Josiah Royce a Century Later: Pragmatism and Idealism in Dialogue." Harvard Divinity School. May 25–27, 2007.

Goethe, Johann Wolfgang von. "Toward a General Comparative Theory," 1790–1794. Princeton: *Scientific Studies*, 1995.

Gregh, Fernand. *L'Âge d'Or*. Paris: B. Grasset, 1948.

Gumbrecht, Hans Ulrich. "*Stimmung* as an Element in Literary and Textual Analysis." Washington University in St. Louis, November 19, 2008.

———. "*Stimmung* of Latency: How Are the Literature and Culture from the Decade following 1945 Present to Us?" Washington University in St. Louis, November 18, 2008.

Hacking, Ian. *Mad Travelers: Reflections on the Reality of Transient Mental Illnesses*. Charlottesville: University Press of Virginia, 1998.

Hall, G. Stanley. Rev. of *The Principles of Psychology* by William James. *The American Journal of Psychology* 3.4 (February 1891): 578–591.

Hawthorn and the Heart. http://www.umm.edu/altmed/articles/hawthorn-000256.htm.

Heft, Harry, and Susan Saegert. Rev. of *A Natural History of Pragmatism: The Fact of Feeling from Jonathan Edwards to Gertrude Stein* by Joan Richardson. *William James Studies* 2.1 (Summer 2007). http://williamjamesstudies.press.uiuc.edu/2.1/.

Henry, Anne. *Proust romancier: le tombeau égyptien*. Paris: Flammarion, 1983.

Hodgson, Shadworth H. *Time and Space: A Metaphysical Essay*. London: Longmans, Green, Roberts, 1865.

Holland, Michael. "De l'intertextualité: Métacritique." *Texte: Revue de critique et de theories littéraire: Issue on l'Intertextualité, Intertexte, Autotexte, Intratexte* 2. Toronto, Ont: Trinity College, 1983.

Hommage à Marcel Proust (1871–1922). La Nouvelle Revue Française XX, 10.112 (January 1923).

Hughes, H. Stuart. *Consciousness and Society: The Reorientation of European Social Thought, 1890–1930*. London: McGibbon & Kee, 1967.

Humphrey, Robert. *Stream of Consciousness in the Modern Novel*. Berkeley and Los Angeles: University of California Press, 1954.

Index Général de la Correspondance de Marcel Proust. Éd. Kazuyoshi Yoshikawa. Presses de l'Université de Kyoto, 1998.

Jackson, Elizabeth R. "The Genesis of Involuntary Memory in Proust's Early Works." *PMLA* 76.5 (December 1961): 586–594.

Jakobson, Roman. "Closing Statements: Linguistics and Poetics." In Thomas A. Sebeok, *Style In Language*. Cambridge: MIT Press, 1960. Excerpts: http://docs.ksu.edu.sa/KSU_AFCs/Nugali/Linguistics%20and%20poetics.pdf.

Jauss, Hans Robert. *Towards an Aesthetic of Reception*. Trans. Timothy Bahti. Minneapolis: University of Minnesota Press, 1982.

Le Journal des Débats politiques et littéraires, 1789–1944 (journal hebdomadaire, puis quotidian).

Le Journal des Débats Politiques et Littéraires. Édition hebdomadaire. 17e année (22 avril 1910): 170, and (2 septembre 1910): 440–441.

Kallen, Horace M. *The Philosophy of William James: Selected from His Chief Works*. New York: The Modern Library, 1953.

———. *William James and Henri Bergson*. Chicago: The University of Chicago Press, 1914. Repr. *William James and Henri Bergson: A Study in Contrasting Theories of Life*. Chicago: The University of Chicago Press, 1980.

Karlin, Daniel. *Proust's English*. Oxford: Oxford University Press, 2005.

Kristeva, Julia. *Le Temps sensible*. Paris: Éditions Gallimard, 1994.

———. "Revolution in Poetic Language." *The Kristeva Reader*. Ed. Toril Moi. New York: Columbia University Press, 1986. Published in 1974 as *La Révolution du langage poétique*.

———. *Séméiotikè: Recherches pour une sémanalyse*. Paris: Éditions du Seuil, 1969.

———. *Time and Sense: Proust and the Experience of Literature*. Trans. Ross Guberman. New York: Columbia University Press, 1996.

———. "Word, Dialogue and Novel." *The Kristeva Reader*. Ed. Toril Moi. New York: Columbia University Press, 1986. Originally written in 1966 and included in *Sémiotiké* in 1969.

Lalande, André. "Philosophy in France (1905)." *Philosophical Review* 15.3 (May 1906): 241–266.

———. "Pragmatisme et pragmaticisme." *Revue Philosophique de la France et de l'étranger* 61.2 (February 1906): 121–146.

Lambilliotte, Julie. "La Bibliothèque de Marcel Proust: De la lecture à l'écriture." *Bulletin d'informations Proustiennes* 30 (1999): 81–89.

Langer, Susan. *Feeling and Form.* New York: Scribner, 1953.

Lapoujade, David. *William James. Empirisme et pragmatisme.* Paris: Presses Universitaires de France, 1997. Repr. Paris: Vrin "Les Empêcheurs de penser en rond," 2007.

La Rochefoucauld, Gabriel de. "Souvenirs et Aperçus." *Hommage à Marcel Proust (1871–1922). La Nouvelle Revue Française* XX, 10.112 (January 1923): 69–76.

La Sizeranne, Robert de. *The Genius of J. M. W. Turner, R. A.* New York: John Lane, Offices of the International Studio, 1903.

———. *Ruskin and the Religion of Beauty.* Trans. Countess of Galloway. London: George Allen, 1899.

Lehrer, Jonah. *Proust was a Neuroscientist.* Boston: Houghton Mifflin, 2007.

Lejeune, Philippe. *Le Pacte autobiographique.* Paris: Éditions du Seuil, 1975.

Le Masle, Dr. Robert. *Le Professeur Adrien Proust.* Paris: Lipschutz, 1935.

Leroux, Emmanuel. *Bibliographie méthodique du Pragmatisme Américain, Anglais et Italien.* New York: Burt Franklin, 1968.

Le Roy. Articles in *La Revue de Métaphysique*, vols. 7, 8, and 9.

Lewis, Pericles. *Religious Experience and the Modernist Novel.* Cambridge: Cambridge University Press, 2010.

Lowery, Bruce. *Marcel Proust et Henry James: une confrontation.* Paris: Librairie Plon, 1964.

Luckhurst, Nicola. *Science and Structure in Proust's "À la recherche du temps perdu."* Oxford: Clarendon Press, 2000.

Macé, Marielle. "La narratologie, aujourd'hui." 10 sept. 2003. Séminaire CRAL. http://www.fabula.org/actualites/imprimer/article 64416.

Macksey, Richard, Oliver Sacks, and Mary Warnock. "Discussion: Commentaries by Richard Macksey and Oliver Sacks." *MLN* 109.5 (December 1994): 950–958.

Magny, Claude-Edmonde. *L'Âge du roman américain.* Paris: Éditions du Seuil, 1948.

Mangan, B. "Meaning and the structure of consciousness: An essay in psychoaesthetics." Unpublished Ph.D. thesis, University of California, Berkeley.

———. "Some philosophical and empirical implications of the fringe." *Consciousness and Cognition* 2.2 (1993a): 142–154.

———. "Taking phenomenology seriously—the fringe and its implications for cognitive research." *Consciousness and Cognition* 2.2 (1993b): 89–108.

Mannheim, Karl. "The Problem of Generations." *Essays on the Sociology of Knowledge.* New York: Oxford University Press, 1952.

Marillier, Léon. *Revue Philosophique* XXXIV (1892): 449–470 and 603–627; XXXV (1893): 1–32 and 145–183.

Martin, H. Newell. *The Human Body.* New York: Holt, 1881.

Mathys, Jonathan. "The Paradigm of Consciousness and William James's Conception of the Self." *Streams of William James* 6.3 (Fall 2004): 38–42.

Mauriac, François. *Du côté de chez Proust.* Paris: La Table Ronde, 1947.

Maurois, André. Preface. Trans. Sherry Mangan. *Labyrinths* by Jorge Luis Borges. New York: New Directions, 1962.

Max, D. T. "Swann's Hypothesis." Rev. of *Proust Was a Neuroscientist* by Jonah Lehrer. *New York Times,* (November 4, 2007).

McDermott, John J. Introduction. *Essays in Radical Empiricism.* By William James. Cambridge: Harvard University Press, 1976.

———. Keynote address. James/ Royce Centennial Conference. "William James and Josiah Royce a Century Later: Pragmatism and Idealism in Dialogue." Harvard Divinity School. May 25–27, 2007.

McDermott John J., ed. The Correspondence of William James. 12 vol. Charlottesville: University of Virginia Press, 1992–2004.

———. *The Writings of William James*. Chicago: University of Chicago Press, 1977 (including an *Annotated Bibliography* updated through 1977).

Megay, Joyce N. *Bergson and Proust: Essai de mise au point de la question de l'influence de Bergson sur Proust*. Paris: Librairie Philosophique J. Vrin, 1976.

Ménard, A. *Analyse et critique des "Principes de la psychologie" de William James*. Paris: Alcan, 1911.

Metzidakis, Stamos. *Repetition and Semiotics: Interpreting Prose Poems*. Birmingham, AL: Summa Publications, Inc., 1986.

Milhaud, G. Article in *Le Rationnel*. 1898.

Mill, James. *Analysis of the Phenomena of the Human Mind*. Ed. John Stuart Mill. 2 vols. London: Longmans, Green, Reader, and Dyer, 1869.

Morand, Paul. "Notes." *Hommage à Marcel Proust (1871–1922). La Nouvelle Revue Française* XX, 10.112 (1 January 1923): 91–95.

Moretti, Franco. *Graphs, Maps, Trees: Abstract Models for a Literary History*. London: Verso, 2005.

———. *The Novel*. 2 Vols. Princeton: Princeton University Press, 2006.

Mortimer, Armine Kotin and Katherine Kolb, eds. *Proust in Perspective*. Urbana: University of Illinois Press, 2002.

Muhlstein, Anka. *Monsieur Proust's Library*. New York: Other Press, 2012.

Murphy, Michael. *Proust and America*. Liverpool University Press, 2007.

Myers, Gerald E., ed. *The Writings of William James, 1878–1899*. New York: Library of America, 1987.

Naumann, Manfred. "Remarques sur la Réception littéraire en tant qu'événement historique et social." *Literary Communication and Reception*. Ed. Zoran Konstantinovic, Manfred Naumann, and Hans Robert Jauss. Innsbruck: Verlag des Instituts für Sprachwissenschaft der Universität Innsbruck, 1980.

O'Brien, Justin. "La Mémoire involontaire avant Marcel Proust." *Revue de Littératire Comparée: Modernes et Contemporaines*. 19e année. Paris: Boivin et Cie. (January 1939): 19–36.

———. "Proust Confirmed by Neurosurgery." *PMLA* 85.2 (March 1970): 295–297.

O'Brien, Justin, ed. *The Maxims of Marcel Proust*. New York: Columbia University Press, 1948.

Ortigues, Edmond. *Religions du livre et religions de la coutume*. Paris: Le Sycomore, 1981.

Painter, G. D. *Marcel Proust: A Biography*. Pimlico Editions, 1996.

Peirce, Charles. "How to Make our Ideas Clear." *Popular Science Monthly* 12 (January 1878): 286–302.

Penfield, Dr. Wilder. *Proceedings of the National Academy of Sciences* (February 15, 1958), xliv, ii.

Penzac, Daniel. *Le Docteur Proust: Père méconnu, précurseur oublié*. Paris: L'Harmattan, 2003.

Perry, Ralph Barton. *Annotated Bibliography of the Writings of William James*. New York: Longmans, Green & Co., 1920.

———. *The Thought and Character of William James*. 2 vols. Boston: Little, Brown and Company, 1935.

———. *The Thought and Character of William James: Briefer Version*. Boston: Harvard University Press, 1948.

———. "William James." *Dictionary of American Biography*. Ed. Dumas Malone. Vol. IX. New York: Charles Scribner's Sons, 1932.

Piégay-Gros, Nathalie. *L'Introduction à l'Intertextualité*. Paris: Dunod, 1996.

Pierre-Quint, Léon. *Proust et la stratégie littéraire*. Paris: Corréa, 1954.

Pinker, Stephen. *The Blank Slate: New Sciences of Human Nature*. New York: Penguin, 2003.

Pommier, Jean. *La Mystique de Marcel Proust*. Paris: Librairie E. Droz, 1939.

Poulet, Georges. *Études sur le temps humain*. Paris: Plon, 1950. Trans. Elliott Coleman. *Studies in Human Time*. Baltimore: Johns Hopkins University Press, 1959.

Premier Congrès International de Psychologie Physiologique. Premier Session. Paris, 1890. *Compte rendu présenté par la Société de psychologie physiologique de Paris*. Paris: Bureau des Revues, 1890. Repr. Nedeln/Liechtenstein: Kraus-Thomson Org. Ltd., 1974.

Proust, Adrien. "Automatisme ambulatoire chez un hystérique." *Bulletin Médical* IV (1890) I: 107–108.

———. "Automatisme ambulatoire chez un hystérique." *Revue de l'Hypnotisme expérimental et thérapeutique* (1889–1890): 267–269.

———. "Automatisme ambulatoire chez un hystérique." *Séances et travaux de l'Académie des sciences morales et politiques (France)* 133.2 (1890): 779–787.

Proust, A., and G. Ballet. *L'hygiène du neurasthénique*. (Bibliothèque d'hygiène thérapeutique Dirigé par le professeur Proust). Paris: Éd. Masson et Cie. (Libraires de l'Académie de Médecine), 1897. See also http://expositions.bnf.fr/proust/grand/30.htm.

Quaranta, Jean-Marc. "'Et tout d'un coup le souvenir m'est apparu,' genèse et fonction de la mémoire proustienne." *Travaux et recherches de l'Université de Marne-la-Vallée* No. 0 (1999). http://www.univmlv.fr/fr/index.php?rub=recherche&srub=actupub&ssrub=trvxrechumlv 0.

La Querelle de l'Hystérie, bibliographical summary: http://pierrehenri.castel.free.fr/QH18931914.htm.

Rabau, S. *L'Intertextualité*. Flammarion, GF-Corpus, 2002. Texte III. Fabula.org.

Rageot, G. "5th International Congress of Psychology." *Revue Philosophique de la France et de l'Étranger* 60.1 (1905): 84–85.

Reed, Edward S. *From Soul to Mind: The Emergence of Psychology from Erasmus Darwin to William James*. New Haven: Yale University Press, 1997.

Reilly, Eliza Jane. "Concrete Possibilities: William James and the European Avant-Garde." *Streams of William James* 2.3 (Fall 2000): 22ff. http://williamjamesstudies.org/newsletter/Streams_2.3.pdf.

Renouvier, Charles. *Science de la Morale*. 2 T. Paris: Librairie Philosophique de Ladrange, 1869.

———. *Traité de psychologie rationelle*, 2nd essay of the *Essais de critique générale* (1859).

Revue de l'Hypnotisme expérimental et thérapeutique. Dir. Dr. Edgar Bérillon (1889–1890). *Revue de psychologie physiologique* (added to name in 1890).

Ribot, Théodule. *Les Maladies de la mémoire*. Paris: Librairie Germer Baillière, 1881.

Richardson, Joan. *A Natural History of Pragmatism*. New York: Cambridge University Press, 2007.

Richardson, Robert D. *William James: In the Maelstrom of American Modernism*. Boston: Houghton Mifflin Company, 2006.

Riffaterre, Michael. "Intertextual Representation: On Mimesis as Interpretive Discourse." *Critical Inquiry* 11.1 (September 1984): 141–162.

———. "The Intertextual Unconscious" *Critical Inquiry* 13.2 (Winter 1987): 371–385.

———. "Syllepsis." *Critical Inquiry* 6.4 (Summer 1980): 625–638.

Rivière, Jacques. *Quelques progrès dans l'étude du cœur humain*. Paris: Gallimard [Cahiers Marcel Proust, 13], 1985.

Robert, P.-E. *Marcel Proust Lecteur des Anglo-Saxons*. Paris: A.-G. Nizet, 1976.

Roudinesco, Élisabeth. *La Bataille de cent ans: histoire de la psychanalyse en France*. Vol. I. 1885–1939. Paris: Ramsay, Seuil, 1986 [1982].

Ruskin, John. *La Bible d'Amiens*. Trans. M. Proust. Paris: Mercure de France, 1904.

Sacks, Oliver. "In the River of Consciousness." *The New York Review of Books* 51.1 (January 15, 2004).

———. "Speak, Memory" *New York Review of Books* LX.3 (February 21, 2013): 19–21.

Salomon, Michel. *Portraits et Paysages*. Paris: Perrin et Cie., 1920.

Samoyault, Tiphaine. *L'Intertextualité: mémoire de la littérature*. Paris: Nathan, 2001 (repr. 2004).

Santayana, George. *Character and Opinion in the United States*. New York: Scribner's, 1920.

Saussy, Haun. Lecture delivered at Washington University in St. Louis, October 4, 2007.

Segers, Rien T., Hans Robert Jauss, and Timothy Bahti. "An Interview with Hans Robert Jauss." *New Literary History* 11.1 (Anniversary Issue II). Baltimore: Johns Hopkins University Press (Autumn 1979): 83–95. http://www.jstor.org/pss/468872.

Shattuck, Roger. *Proust's Way: A Field Guide to "In Search of Lost Time."* New York: W. W. Norton & Co., 2000.

———. "The Tortoise and the Hare." *The Origins of Modern Consciousness*. Ed. John Weiss. Wayne State University Press, 1964. Repr. *The Innocent Eye: On Modern Literature & the Arts*, 82–106. New York: Farrar, Strauss, Giroux, 1984.

Shepherd-Barr, Kirsten, and Gordon M. Shepherd. "Madeleines and Neuromodernism: Reassessing Mechanisms of Autobiographical Memory in Proust." *Autobiography Studies* 13.1 (Spring 1998): 39–60.

Shook, John R. *Pragmatism: an Annotated Bibliography 1898–1940*. Amsterdam: Editions Rodopi, 1998. See also www.pragmatism.org and for the history of pragmatism in France, see http://www.pragmatism.org/history/pragmatism_in_france.htm.

Simon, Anne."Essence." *Dictionnaire Marcel Proust*. Éd. Annick Bouillaguet et Brian G. Rogers. Paris: Honoré Champion, Éd., 2004.

———. "Phénoménologie. *Dictionnaire Marcel Proust*. Éd. Annick Bouillaguet et Brian G. Rogers. Paris: Honoré Champion, Éd., 2004.

———. *Proust ou le réel retrouvé: le sensible et son expression dans "À la recherche du temps perdu."* Paris: Presses Universitaires de France, 2000.

Simon, Linda. *Genuine Reality: A Life of William James*. New York: Harcourt Brace & Company, 1998.

Simon, Linda, ed. *William James Remembered*. Lincoln: University of Nebraska Press, 1996.

Skrupskelis, Ignas. "William James." *American National Biography*. Vol. 11. Ed. John Garraty and Mark C. Carnes. New York: Oxford University Press, 1999, vol. 11.

Slegers, Rosa. *Courageous Vulnerability: Ethics and Knowledge in Proust, Bergson, Marcel and James*. Leiden: Brill, 2010.

Sollier, Paul. *Essai critique et théorique sur l'Association en psychologie*. Paris: Félix Alcan, 1907.

———. *Le Mécanisme des émotions*. Paris: Félix Alcan, 1905.

———. *Le Problème de la mémoire*. Paris: Alcan, 1900.

———. *Les Troubles de la mémoire*. Paris: Rueff, 1892, 1900.

Speer, Nicole K., Jeremy R. Reynolds, Khena M. Swallow, and Jeffrey M. Zacks. "Reading Stories Activates Neural Representations of Visual and Motor Experiences." *Psychological Science* 9999.9999 (June 2009).

Spence, Donald P. *Narrative Truth and Historical Truth: Meaning and Interpretation in Psychoanalysis*. New York: W.W. Norton, 1982.

Staël-Holstein, Germaine de. *De la littérature considérée dans ses rapports avec les institutions sociales*. 2 vola. Paris: Maradan, 1800.

Stone, Edward. "The Paving Stones of Paris: Psychometry from Poe to Proust." *American Quarterly* 5.2 (Summer 1953): 121–131.

Stout, G. F. "Mental Activity." *Analytic Psychology*. London: S. Sonnenschein & Co., New York: Macmillan & Co., 1896; repr. 1902.

Strouse, Jean, *Alice James: A Biography*. Boston: Houghton Mifflin, 1980; repr. Cambridge, MA: Harvard University Press, 1999.

Stuart, A. E. "Proust, Memory and the Engram." *Proceedings of the Royal College of Physicians of Edinburgh* 30 (2000): 172–175.

Tadié, Jean-Yves. *Marcel Proust*. Trans. Euan Cameron. New York: Viking, 2000.

Tadié, Jean-Yves, et Marc Tadié. *Le Sens de la mémoire*. Paris: Gallimard, 1999.

Taine, H. *De l'Intelligence*. 2 vols. Paris: Hachette, 1870.

Tel Quel. Founders Philippe Sollers and Jean-Edern Hallier. Paris: Éditions du Seuil, 1960.

"La Théorie du texte." *Encyclopoedia universalis*, 1973. French language encyclopedia. Britannica, Inc.

Thiher, Allen. *Fiction Refract's Science: Modernist Writers from Proust to Borges* Columbia: University of Missouri Press, 2005.

Tukey, Ann. "Notes on Involuntary Memory in Proust." *French Review* XLII.3 (February 1969): 395–402.

Vendeuvre, Isabelle de. "Proust et la question du savoir." *Proust et les moyens de la connaissance*. Éd. Annick Bouillaguet, 235–245. Strasbourg: Presses Universitaires de Strasbourg, 2008.

———. "Proust et l'église: grandeurs d'établissement et pouvoir du verbe." *Revue d'histoire littéraire de la France* 108.2 (2008): 421–431.

Walusinski, O., and J. Bogousslavsky. "À la recherche du neuropsychiatre perdu: Paul Sollier (1861–1933)." *Revue Neurologique FMC* (2008): F239–247. www.baillement.com/lettres/sollier.pdf

Warner, Maria. Rev. of *An Alchemy of Mind: The Marvel and Mystery of the Brain* by Diane Ackerman. New York: Scribner, 2004. "Circuits." *New York Times*, August 29, 2004.

Weber. *Boston Medical Journal*, 1888.

Weinstein, Arnold. "Volume and Community in Proust." *Fiction, Form, Experience*. Ed. Grant Kaiser. Montreal: Éditions France-Québec, 1976.

White, Edmund. "The Making of John Rechy." Rev. of *About My Life and the Kept Woman: A Memoir* by John Rechy. *The New York Review of Books* LV.5 (April 3, 2008): 31.

Wills, Rev. James. "Accidental Association." *Transactions of the Royal Irish Academy* XXI (1848).

Wimmers, Inge Crosman. *Proust and Emotion: The Importance of Affect in "À la recherche du temps perdu."* Toronto: University of Toronto Press, 2003.

Wolf, Maryanne. *Proust and the Squid: The Story and Science of the Reading Brain*. New York: HarperCollins, 2007.

Woo, Tomoko Boongja. "Lecture de Proust, à travers Freud, par les premiers critiques." *Bulletin Marcel Proust* 58 (2008): 69–79.

Woolf, Virginia. "Character in Fiction." Lecture to Cambridge Heretics. May 18, 1924. Repr. "Character in Fiction." *Criterion*. Repr. *Mr. Bennett and Mrs. Brown*. Hogarth Press, 1924.

———. *The Letters of Virginia Woolf*. Nigel Nicolson and Joann Trautmann, eds. 6 vols. New York: Harcourt Brace Jovanovich, 1975–1980.

———. "Phases of Fiction." *The Bookman*, April, May, and June 1929. Rpt. in *Granite and Rainbow*. New York: Harcourt Brace, 1958.

Wright, Donald. *Du discours medical dans "À la recherche du temps perdu": science et souffrance*. Paris: Honoré Champion Éditeur, 2007.

Xingjian, Gao. *the case for literature* [*sic*]. Trans. Mabel Lee. New Haven: Yale University Press, 2006.

Zeki, S. *Inner Vision: An Exploration of Art and the Brain*. Oxford: Oxford University Press, 1999.

Zeki, S., and A. Bartels. "Toward a Theory of Visual Consciousness." *Consciousness and Cognition* 8.2 (June 1999): 225–229.

Index

Abauzit, Frank, 17
abnormal psychology, in France, 12–16
absence, presence in, 179–180
Adams, Henry, 205
Ainslie, Douglas, 30
Albertine disparue (Proust, M.), 83, 222
Allcock, John B., 10, 25, 45n54
Alline, Henry, 199
Alphonse Darlu (Bonnet), 17
American Psychological Association, 211
Angelico, Fra, 146, 168n275
Annales de philosophie chrétienne, 32
Les Annales de Philosophie Chrétienne, 17
L'Année 1867 philosophique, 10
L'Année Philosophique, 10
Archives de Psychologie, 203
"Are We Automata?" (James, W.), 65
art: brain and visual, 111, 249; consciousness and, 92–97; experience as, 174, 184–193, 208, 250; James, William, and influence on, 256; of language, 231; memory preserved in, 148; narrative, 249; Proust, Marcel, and development of, 53–54; reading and, 167n222; science and, 233
artists: consciousness and art as way of seeing for, 92–93, 235, 251; creativity and, 82, 84; culture influenced by, 205, 207, 213, 255; experience and, 231–232; habit and, 120–121; heroic mind of, 163; indirect influence and, xi; influence of, 207; with metaphor, 132–133; presence in absence and, 179; Proust, Marcel, on isolation and originality of, xii, 82; truth and, 171, 205; will to action of, 123–124, 162–163, 252
association, 26, 59; by contiguity, 129; involuntary, 107–108, 137, 235, 243, 247–248, 260; language and, 128–129; metaphor and, 126–138, 248; principles, 129–130; rings of, 131, 132, 268; by similarity, 130, 131; voluntary, 111–112, 135–136, 138, 235
Associationism, 202
asthma, 46n70, 245, 251
The Atlantic Monthly, 5
attention: brain and, 108; discrimination and, 106–114; involuntary, 107–108; music, reading and, 108; obsession and, 113; sleep and diffused, 103–106, 128; visual, 110–111; voluntary, 111–112
aubépines (hawthorne flowers), 196; as heart medicine, 102n208; with sense perception and emotion, 88–89, 175
auditory illusion, 153
autobiography: consciousness, genre and, 54–63; hallmarks of, 54
"Automatisme ambulatoire chez un hystérique" (Proust, A.), 13–14
automatisme ambulatoire [involuntary ambulation], 14
automatisme [unconscious involuntary behavior], 14, 16

Baars, Bernard J., 235–236, 236, 243
Ballet, G., 13, 14
Balthasar (France), 33
Barr, Gordon M., 245–246
Barrès, Maurice, 42
Bartsch, Renate, 244
Baudelaire, Charles, 245
Beard, George, 15, 30
Behaviorists, 266

behaviors: desire as behavioral driver, 55, 65, 89, 104, 112; habits shaping, 115–116, 118
Bergson, Henri, 9, 11, 15, 17, 19, 27, 32, 36, 48n120, 49n167, 75, 100n132, 234, 244, 266; as Boutroux's student, 19; experience and, 32; James, William, and, 19, 21–25, 25; lectures, 25; *Pragmatism* preface written by, 9, 24, 40–42, 51n201, 213; Proust, Marcel, and, 19–21, 22, 24–25
Bergson, Henri-Louis, xiii
Bérillon, Edgar, 13
Berry, Walter, 30, 32
Bibesco, Antoine, 20, 47n114
Bible d'Amiens (Ruskin), 7, 20
Bildungsroman, 62
Billy, Robert de, 29, 266
Binet, Alfred, 73
Binet-Valmer, M., 261n42
Bizub, Edward, 15, 27, 41, 73, 251, 260
Blanche, Jacques-Émile, 27, 57, 267
Blondel, Charles, 21
Blondel, Maurice, 32
Bloom, Harold, xi
Blum, René, 42, 47n114, 57, 58
Blumenthal Prize, 19
body: memory and, 233, 242–243, 244, 255; with nucleus of spiritual me, 66
Bogousslavsky, Julien, 26, 27, 251, 253
Bois, Élie-Joseph, 20, 57
Bonnet, Henri, 17, 29
Boodin, John Elof, 36, 184
books: discrimination and example of, 113–114; eulogies in form of, 9; livre intérieur, 188, 201; novels, 207, 232, 255; with reading as sensorial experience, 176, 177–178, 180, 201–202, 224n37, 263n93; *À la recherche du temps perdu* as lived experience in form of, 57–58, 65, 67. *See also specific books*
Borges, Jorge Luis, 254
Boston Medical Journal, 15
Boulenger, Jacques, 207
Bourdeau, Jean, 34–35, 35, 39–40
Bourdeau, M J., 34, 50n180
Bourget, Paul, 27
Boutroux, Émile, 9, 11, 27, 29, 32, 36, 41, 266; James, William, and, 16–19, 37–38; lectures, 17–18, 34; preface in *The Varieties of Religious Experience*, 17; Proust, Marcel, and, 17, 18–19
brain: with attention, 108; with breaking bad habits, 124–125; consciousness, experience and, xi, xiv; with creativity and individual personality, 234; disease, 14; experiments with electrodes and experience, 232; with fringe of relations, 85, 87; with habits, 114, 124–125, 126; with imagination, 151; James, William, neurobiology and, x, 239, 246–247, 251; memory and, 145, 238–239; MRI, 237, 249, 254; neurocognitive science and, 231, 234, 249; PET scans, 237; physiology of, xi; reading and influence on, 71; resurgent memory and, 245; sense data and, 237–240; visual art and, 111, 249; visual stimulus and, 110–111
Brainerd, David, 198
Brancovan, Constantin de, 34
Breton, Maurice le, 267
Brissaud, Edouard, 251
Broca, Paul, 234
Browning, Robert, 254
Brun, Bernard, 59
Brun, Louis, 57
Brunschvicg, Léon, 11, 23, 32
Buckner, Randy L., 244

Cahier 59 (Proust, M.), xiii, 21
Cahier de 1908 (Proust, M.), 25
Le Capitaine Fracasse (Gautier), 6, 28
Carlyle, Thomas, 4, 31
Carter, William, 7, 60, 65
cash value, experience and, 180, 200, 205, 216, 224n45, 268
Chantavoine, Henri, 33
Charcot, Jean-Martin, 12–13, 13, 14, 15, 16, 26, 251
Chateaubriand, François-René, 245
children, 100n148; involuntary attention in, 107; with sensation and perception of space-world, 148–149

church towers, 124
Clark, Terry, 45n55
Le Coeur en désordre (Binet-Valmer), 261n42
Cohn, Dorrit, 3, 63, 256, 258
Collins, Billy, xi
comets, 75, 115, 162, 211
Compagnon, Antoine, 1, 243
Concept Formation, Remembering, and Understanding: Dynamic Conceptual Semantics and Proust's "À la recherche du temps perdu" (Bartsch), 244
Congress of Criminal Anthropology, 13
Congress of Experimental and Therapeutic Hypnotism, 13
consciousness: art and, 92–97; with art as way of seeing for artists, 92–93, 235, 251; brain, experience and, xi, xiv; flights and perchings of, 76–84, 267; fringe of relations and, 84–92; genre and, 54–63; James, William, and, 2, 3, 12, 15–16, 55, 59, 66, 73, 77, 92–97, 203; with me (myself) and I, 61–62, 64, 65–76; mental activity of, 63–65; "La Notion de Conscience", 11; Proust, Marcel and, 2; stream of, 54, 55, 59, 62, 63, 68, 232, 233, 247; structures of, 65, 76–92; time and changes in, 74–75
"Consciousness, Art and the Brain" (Epstein), 247
Consciousness and Cognition, 249, 250
contiguity, association by, 129
Contre Sainte-Beuve (Proust, M.), xii, xiii, 44n35
Correspondance (Proust, M.), 18, 20, 29, 32, 33, 34, 40
Correspondances (Bergson), 9, 100n132
Du côté de chez Swann (Proust, M.), ix, 20, 33, 42, 75, 158; échos and, 57; fringe of relations and, 87, 87–88; publishing history, 58; time experienced through memory in, 140–141
Le Côté de Guermantes (Proust, M.), 119–120

Courbet, Gustave, 1
creativity: artists and, 82, 84; brain, individual personality and, 234
Crémieux, Benjamin, 207, 228n240
criminality, multiple personalities and, 14
La Critique Philosophique, 10, 184
Cruelle Énigme (Bourget), 27
culture: artists influencing, 205, 207, 213, 255; novels and narratives influenced by, 232, 255; uncertainty and change influencing, 210; Woolf and, 255
Czoniczer, Elizabeth, xii–xiii, 232

Darlu, Alphonse, 11, 19, 23, 28, 29, 60, 176
Darwin, Charles, 256
de Boigne (Mme), 177
deception: misperception and, 153–155, 156; truth and, 216–218
de Flers, Robert, 43n7
Déjerine, Joseph Jules, 234
Delattre, Floris, 267
deliberation, effort and, 159
Demange, Charles, 42
depression, 6, 10
Descartes, René, 29, 203
Descombes, Vincent, 57, 184–185, 188
desire, xiv, 157; as behavioral driver, 55, 65, 89, 104, 112; effort, will and, 159–163; emotions and, 29, 33, 92; habit and, 124; in *À la recherche du temps perdu*, 89–90
Dessoulavy, C., 32
d'Humières, Robert, 30
Du discours medical dans "À la recherche du temps perdu": science et souffrance (Wright), 251
discrimination: attention and, 106–114; with book example, 113–114; habit and, 114, 115
dissociation, 16, 55, 105, 260
Dreyfus, Robert, 35
Dryden, Donald, 246, 250–251
Du Bos, Charles, 30
Dujardin, Edouard, 2, 64
Dumas, G., 26, 242
durée réelle [duration and change], 21–22, 75, 78, 100n132, 139

Durkheim, Emile, 8, 25, 31

earthquakes: emotional, 65, 252; in San Francisco, 65, 173
Ebbinghaus, Hermann, 234
échos [editorial product placements], 57
Edelman, Gerald, 233, 234, 237, 238, 239–240, 243, 255
education: of James, William, 4–5, 7, 10; Proust, Marcel, with literary interests and philosophical, xii, 27–31, 35; of Proust, Marcel, 6, 17, 28
effort, 65; deliberation and, 159; will, desire and, 159–163. *See also* will
Egger (prof.), 17
Einstein, Albert, 119, 256
electrodes, brain and, 232
Eliot, Charles William, 16
Ellenberger, Henri, 15–16, 46n70
Emerson, Ralph Waldo, 4, 30, 31, 173, 256
emotions: aubépines with sense perception and, 88–89, 175; desire and, 29, 32, 92; with emotional earthquakes, 65, 252; with emotional habit, 122; with emotional thunder, 76–77; irregularity in, 243; memory and, 26; reading and evoked, 123, 128–129, 169n322, 176; theory of, 26, 60; three trees with sense perception and, 85, 175
empiricism. *See* radical empiricism
Engber, Daniel, 233, 235, 244, 256
English language, 30
envy, originality and, xi
epigram, didactic, 158
epilepsy, 14
Epstein, Russell, 246–248, 249–251
Essais (Renouvier), 10
Essai critique et théorique sur l'Association en psychologie (Sollier), 26
Essai sur les données immédiates de la conscience [*Time and Free Will*] (Bergson), 21
Essays in Radical Empiricism (James, W.), 40, 51n202, 202, 203
eulogies, as books, 9
Europe: James, William, in, 4–9, 10, 11, 12, 16, 24, 31, 36, 40, 202, 266; philosophy in, 31; U.S. and influence in, 30; war in, 24, 266
Everdell, William R., 119
L'Évolution créatrice (Bergson), 23
experience, 171–172; artists and, 231–232; art made from, 174, 184–193, 208, 250; Bergson and, 32; brain, consciousness and, xi, xiv; brain experiments with, 232; cash value and, 180, 200, 205, 216, 224n45, 268; James, William, and, 2–3, 62, 74–75, 195–196, 231; mystical, 195–196, 198–200; neurocognitive science and, 231–232; poor partial snapshot or first-person, 173–184; Proust, Marcel, and, 2, 27; with Proust, Marcel, and aesthetic variations on religious theme by James, William, 193–201, 257; with Proust, Marcel, Pragmatism, pluralism and radical empiricism, 201–222; pure, 204; reading and language translating, 176, 177–178, 180, 201–202, 224n37, 263n93; *À la recherche du temps perdu* as book of lived, 57–58, 65, 67; religious, 194; truth, grafting and future, 218–219
L'Expérience religieuse: Essai de Psychologie descriptive (James, W.), 17

Fechner, Gustav, 205
Ferguson, Kennan, 266
Ferré, André, 28, 29
fiction: consciousness, genre and, 54–63; hallmarks of, 56; James, William, and, 59, 243; with life and narratives, 241; memory and, 71, 243; mental activity and, 54
Le Figaro, 177
Figures III (Genette), 86–87
Finney, 199
first-person experience: James, William, and, 173, 174; past, 198–201; poor partial snapshot or,

173–184; Proust, Marcel, and, 172
flights and perchings, 100n132, 101n159; of consciousness, 76–84, 267; narrators with, 79; *À la recherche du temps perdu* and, 81–84
Flournoy, Théodore, 9, 16–17
forgetting: with habit, 118, 125; identity and selectivity of, 234; importance of, 147, 148, 185, 248; memory and, 56, 71, 72, 73, 96, 147, 148, 241; as normal state, 97, 156, 176, 185; pain lessened by, 185, 235, 236; resurgent memory and, 148. *See also* memory
Fox, George, 197
France, 30; abnormal psychology in, 12–16; James, William, and Renouvier in, 9–11; Pragmatism in, 31–33
France, Anatole, 33
François le champi (Sand), 178
Franklin, Stan, 235–236, 236
free will, 10, 38, 161, 233
Freud, Sigmund, x, 15, 16, 234, 245, 251, 266
Friedman, Melvin, 59–60
fringe of relations: brain and, 85, 87; consciousness and, 84–92; imagery and, 85–86; James, William, and, 84–92, 233, 246; language and, 86–87, 102n223; narrators and, 84–92, 93–94; nucleus of thought and, 246, 247, 249–250; Proust, Marcel, and, 86, 87–92, 252–253

Galin, David, 246, 249–250
Gallimard, Gaston, 213
gaps, in memory, 73
Gautier, Théophile, 6, 28
Genette, Gérard, 56, 62, 86–87, 105, 119, 126–127
genius, 112, 157
genre, consciousness and, 54–63
Ghéon, Henri, 20, 97
Gibbens, Alice. *See* James, Alice
Gifford lectures, 9, 16, 50n187
Gillouin, René, 42
Girel, Mathias, 9
grafting, truth, experience and, 218–219
Grasset, Bernard, ix, 42, 261n42
"A Great French Philosopher at Harvard" (James, W.), 18
Gregh, Fernand, 20
Grimm, Herman, 6
group habits, 119
Gurney, Edmund, 12

habit(s), 235; artists and, 120–121; behaviors shaped by, 115–116, 118; brain and breaking bad, 122, 124–125; brain with, 114, 126; desire and, 124; discrimination and, 114, 115; double-edged comfort of, 114–126; emotional, 122; forgetting with, 118, 125; group, 119; with habitual inhibitions, 162; law of neural, 126; literary, 183; novelty and, 116, 118, 121; professional, 122–124
Hacking, Ian, 13
Hahn, Reynaldo, 30, 34
Halévy, Daniel, 33
Halévy, Élie, 11
Haley's Comet, 75
Hardy, Thomas, 27
Harvard University, 5, 18, 51n203
Hauser, Lionel, 193–194
hawthorne flowers. *See* aubépines
Heath, Willy, 30
Heft, Harry, 221
heroic mind, 163
Hibbert Lectures, 9, 24, 34
historical memory, 140, 177, 180
Hodgson, Richard, 50n185, 133
Hommage à Marcel Proust (*NRF*), 27, 267
Houghton Library, 51n203
"How to Make Our Ideas Clear" (Peirce), 214
"Human Immortality" (James, W.), 22
Human Immortality: Two Supposed Objections to the Doctrine (James, W.), 23
Hume, David, 58–59
Hyde lectures, 18
L'Hygiène du neurasthénique (Ballet and Proust, A.), 13
hypnotism, 13; Charcot and, 12, 14; hysteria and, 12, 13; James, William,

and, 12, 16, 71; Janet and, 13, 165n88; as multiple personalities cure, 14; Proust, Adrien, and, 46n81; Salpêtrière and Nancy schools on, 46n72
hysteria, 12, 13, 14, 16, 26, 31

I. *See* me (myself), and I
Idealism, 202
ideas, thought and, 26, 59
identity, forgetting and, 234
ideomotor hypothesis, 235
illusion: auditory, 153; misperception and, 152–153
imagery, 85–86
imagination: brain with, 151; genius and, 157; James, William, on vision and, xiv; with magic lantern of narrator, 79–81, 93–94, 117; mental trip and, 265; metaphor with, 127; "the popular imagination", ix; representative nouns and, 79; sensation, perception, misperception and, 148–157
impression. *See* sillon
impressions, writers and, 237
influences: artists and indirect, xi; writers with envy, originality and direct literary, xi
inhibitions, habitual, 162
Institut Psychologique Internationale, 16
intentional recall, 144–145
interior monologues, 3
intermittence: with dissolution of self, 241–242; Proust, Marcel, with, 241, 243
"Les Intermittences du coeur", 240
International Congress of Physiological Psychology, 13, 17
International Congress of Psychology, 2, 21, 43n10
interpretations: influence and role in, xi; reasoning and multiple, 158–159
involuntary association, 107–108, 137, 235, 243, 247–248, 260
involuntary attention, 107–108
isolation, artists and, xii

James, Alice (sister), 43n20
James, Alice Gibbens (wife), 40, 42, 195
James, Henry (brother), ix, 6, 9, 27, 30, 174, 267
James, Henry (father), 4, 31
James, Henry (son), 22, 24
James, William, 50n176, 50n187; abnormal psychology in France and, 12–16; on art made from experience, 184; with association and metaphor, 126–138; attention, discrimination and, 106–114; Bergson and, 19, 21–25, 25; Boutroux and, 16–19, 37–38; with brain and consciousness, xi, xiv; cash value and, 224n45; consciousness and, 2, 3, 12, 15–16, 55, 66, 73, 77, 203; on consciousness and art, 92–97; death, 9, 35–37, 50n185, 200, 227n201, 255, 266; depression and, 6, 10; with double-edged comfort of habit, 114–126; early life and education, 4–5, 7; education of, 10; with effort, will and desire, 159–163; in Europe, 4–9, 10, 11, 12, 16, 24, 31, 36, 40, 202, 266; experience and, 2–3, 62, 74–75, 195–196, 231; fiction and, 59, 233, 243; first-person experience and, 173, 174; free will and, 10, 38; fringe of relations and, 84–92, 233, 246; hypnotism and, 12, 16, 71; influence of, x, xii–xiii, xiv–xv, 3, 7, 31–33, 202, 207, 213–214, 232, 234, 237, 256; influences on, 6, 50n178; lectures, 2, 4, 5, 7, 9, 11, 16, 23, 24, 34, 35, 50n187, 196, 203, 212, 214; legacy of, x, xii, xiii, xiv, 4, 7–8, 9, 11, 32, 35–38, 45n61, 50n185, 202, 266, 267; with me (myself) and I, 68, 71, 73; media connections between Proust, Marcel, and, 31–40; memory and, 96–97, 142–143, 173, 234, 243; with mental activity of consciousness, 63–65; metaphor and, 107; mind stuff and, 3; mystical experience and, 195–196; neurasthenia and, 5; neurobiology and, x, 239, 247, 251; neurocognitive science and,

237–240, 245, 246–249; on perception, 109; philosophy and influence of, 31, 214–215; Pragmatism and, xii, xvn14, 8, 9, 23, 31–33, 50n180, 229n298; Proust, Marcel, and aesthetic variations on religious theme by, 193–201, 257; Proust, Marcel, and connection to, 1, 12–27, 27–31; Proust, Marcel, and influence of, xii–xiii, xiv–xv, 3, 8, 21, 28, 29, 193–194, 213–214, 267–269; Proust, Marcel, and similarities to, 6; Proust, Marcel, compared to, ix–xv; publishing history, 5–6, 6–7, 8, 10, 11, 16–17, 34, 51n201, 213–214, 242, 266–267; pure experiences and, 204; radical empiricism and, 9, 40, 51n202, 202, 202–204; reading and literary interests of, 5, 6, 10, 23; with reasoning and multiple interpretations, 158–159; Renouvier in France with, 9–11; with sensation, imagination, perception and misperception, 148–157; with sleep and diffused attention, 103, 104, 105; Society for Psychical Research and, 12; Sollier and, 25, 26; stream of consciousness and, 54, 55, 59, 62, 63, 68, 232, 233, 247; stream of thought and, 21, 59, 60, 63–64, 78–79, 250; time experienced through memory and, 138–148; truth and, 174, 210; on vision and imagination, xiv. *See also* "Are We Automata?"; *Essays in Radical Empiricism*; *L'Expérience religieuse: Essai de Psychologie descriptive*; "A Great French Philosopher at Harvard"; "Human Immortality"; *Human Immortality: Two Supposed Objections to the Doctrine*; "The Knowing of Things Together"; *The Letters of William James*; *The Meaning of Truth*; "La Notion de Conscience"; "On Some Omissions of Introspective Psychology"; *A Pluralistic Universe*; *Pragmatism: A New Name for Some Old Ways of Thinking*; *The Principles of Psychology*; *The Principles of Psychology: Briefer Course*; *Rationality, Activity and Faith*; "The Sentiment of Rationality"; *Some Problems of Philosophy*; "A Suggestion about Mysticism"; *Talks to Teachers on Psychology: and to Students on Some of Life's Ideals*; "Theory of Emotions"; *The Varieties of Religious Experience*; *The Will to Believe and other Essays in Popular Philosophy*; "A World of Pure Experience"

Janet, Pierre, 7, 12, 13, 16, 73, 165n88

Jean Santeuil (Proust, M.), xv, 6, 55, 58, 60, 62–63, 65, 81, 90–91, 176, 184, 222, 267; involuntary attention in, 107–108

Journal de Genève, 17

Le Journal des Débats Politiques et Littéraires, 11, 18, 33–35

Joyce, James, 3, 64, 207

Kafka, Franz, 254

Kallen, Horace, 3, 5, 97

Kant, Immanuel, 59

Karlin, Daniel, 30

Kierkegaard, Søren, 254

kinetoscope, 128, 175

Kipling, Rudyard, 30

"The Knowing of Things Together" (James, W.), 203

Kolb, Katherine, ix

Kolb, Philip, 47n114

Labyrinths (Borges), 254

Lacretelle, Jacques de, 218

Lalande, André, 22, 32–33, 35

Lambilliotte, Julie, xii

Lange, Carl, 26, 60

Langer, Susan K., 249, 250–251

language: art of, 231; association and, 128–129; with fringe of relations, 86–87, 102n223; perception and, 183, 221–222; Proust, Marcel, and English, 30; reading and experience translated into, 176, 177–178, 180, 201–202, 224n37, 263n93; slang, 30; stream of thought and, 77

Lapoujade, David, 9, 222

La Rochefoucauld, Gabriel de, 158
Lauris, Georges de, 20, 28, 31
law of neural habit, 126
lectures, x, 26; Bergson's, 25; Boutroux's, 17–18, 34; Charcot's, 12, 14, 15; Durkheim's, 31; James, William and, 2, 4, 5, 7, 9, 11, 16, 23, 24, 34, 35, 50n187, 196, 203, 212, 214; Proust, Marcel, and, 20, 233
Lehrer, Jonah, 233, 234, 251, 254, 255–256, 257, 258–259
Léon, Xavier, 11
Léonie (Janet's patient), 165n88
Aunt Léonie, 115, 120, 142, 195
The Letters of William James (James, W.), 24
Lewis, Pericles, 194
life: mental, 247; narratives with fiction and, 241; with *À la recherche du temps perdu* as book of experiential, 57–58, 65, 67
literary interests: of James, William, 5, 6, 10, 23; of Proust, Marcel, xii, 27–31, 35
literary style, vision, voice of Proust, Marcel, xiii–xiv, 28
De la littérature (Staël-Holstein), 1
livre intérieur [inner book], 188, 201
Locke, John, 234
Lowell lectures, 16, 214
Lowery, Bruce, ix, 27, 28
Luys, J., 14

Macksey, Richard, 243
madeleine, 186, 233, 258; olfactory stimulus, memory with, 127, 146, 244, 245–246; Proust, Marcel, with aesthetic variations on religious theme by James, William, and mystical, 193–201, 257; resurgent memory and, 54, 81, 142, 147, 192–193, 226n141, 233, 244, 245–246; retrospective time and, 141, 250
"Madeleines and Neuromodernism: Reassessing Mechanisms of Autobiographical Memory in Proust" (Shepherd-Barr and Barr), 245
magic lanterns, and imagination, 79–81, 93–94, 117
Magnetic resonance imaging. *See* MRI
Manet, Édouard, 1
Marcel Proust, lecteur des Anglo-saxons (Robert), 29
Marillier, Léon, 8
Marx, Karl, 266
Massis, H., 75, 100n132
masturbation, 46n70
Matière et mémoire (Bergson), 21, 22, 244
Mauriac, François, 70
Maurois, André, 254
Max, D. T., 257
The Maxims of Marcel Proust (O'Brien), 158
McDermott, John J., 12, 191–192, 202
me, spiritual, 66, 67
me (myself), and I, 267–268; James, William, and, 68, 71, 73; Proust, Marcel, with, 61–62, 64, 65–76
The Meaning of Truth (James, W.), 50n178, 202
Le Mécanisme des émotions (Sollier), 26
media: Pragmatism in, 31–33; Proust, Marcel, and James, William, connected through, 31–40
Megay, Joyce, 21
memory, 69; body and, 233, 242–243, 244, 255; brain, 145, 238–239; emotion and, 26; false, 72; fiction and, 71, 243; forgetting and, 56, 71, 72, 73, 96, 147, 148, 241; gaps, 73, 135; historical, 140, 177, 180; intentional recall of, 144–145; involuntary, 107–108, 137, 235, 243, 247–248, 260; James, William, and, 96–97, 142–143, 173, 234, 243; misperception and, 156; as neuron grouping to produce understanding, 244; olfactory stimulus and, 244, 245–246; painful, 235, 236; with partial recall, 133; personality reactivated by, 74; photographic, 145, 181–182, 243; as preserved in art, 148; Proust, Marcel, and, 56, 58, 72–73, 267; resurgent, 54, 81, 142, 147, 148, 192–193, 226n141, 233, 244, 245, 258;

sense data and, 237–240; snapshot of, 106, 151, 209, 211, 217, 232, 247, 260; time experienced through, 106, 138–148; voluntary, 111–112, 135–136, 138, 235
Ménard, A., 266
mental activity, 175; of consciousness, 63–65; fiction and, 54
mental life, 247
mental peace, 185
mental trip, 265
Mentré, M., 39
Meredith, George, 27
Mes modèles (Blanche), 27
metaphor: artists with, 132–133; association and, 126–138, 248; with imagination, 127; James, William, and, 107; Proust, Marcel, and functions of, 131
"La Méthode de Sainte-Beuve" (Proust, M.), 175
microscopes, 84, 142, 159, 174, 188, 254, 259
Mill, James, 143
mind, 96; heroic, 163. *See also* memory; stream of consciousness with body and, 233; stuff and interior monologues, 3; brain
Mind, 8, 14, 44n39, 65, 184
misperception: deception and, 153–155, 156; illusion and, 152–153; memory and, 156; music of, 155–156; sensation, imagination, perception and, 148–157
monologues, interior, 3
Montesquiou, Robert de, 30
Morand, Paul, 1
Moréas, Jean, 42
Moretti, Franco, 232
Mortimer, Armine Kotin, ix
MRI (Magnetic resonance imaging), 237, 249, 254
Muhlstein, Anka, xii
multiple personalities, 14, 15, 16, 73
Murphy, Michael, 30
music: attention and, 108; as communication, 83, 94; discrimination and, 113; of misperception, 155–156; sonate de Vinteuil, 93, 205–206, 207; unfamiliar, 81; unique voice of the artist and, xi
Musset, Alfred de, 245
Myers, Frederick, 12
mystical experience, 195–196, 198–200

Nancy School, 13, 46n72
narratives: art, 249; cultural forces influencing, 232, 255; with fiction and life, 241
narrators: with association and metaphor, 126–138; with attention and discrimination, 109–110; with flights and perchings, 79; with fringe of relations, 84–92, 93–94; imagination with magic lantern of, 79–81, 93–94, 117; interior monologues and mind stuff of, 3; with me (myself) and I, 61–62, 64, 65–76; old-fogyism and, 157; Proust, Marcel, as, 54; with sensation, imagination, perception and misperception, 150–151, 151; with sleep and diffused awareness, 103–104, 104–106, 128; with structures of consciousness, 76–92; of "Sur la lecture", 76–77; unreliable, 256
The Nation, 5, 6, 18
A Natural History of Pragmatism (Richardson, J.), 221
Nerval, Gérard de, 245
nervous exhaustion. *See* neurasthenia
Neuberger, Louise, 19
"The Neural-Cognitive Basis of the Jamesian Stream of Thought" (Epstein), 246
neurasthenia (nervous exhaustion), 15; James, William, and, 5; Proust, Adrien, and, 14, 46n70, 46n81
neurobiology, James, William, and, x, 239, 247, 251
neurocognitive science: advances in, 254; brain and, 231, 234; experience and, 231–232; James, William, and, 237–240, 245, 246–249; Proust, Marcel, and, 233, 240–260; sense data and, 237–240; visual art and

brain with, 249. *See also* memory
Neuron, 244
New York Public Library, 8
Noailles, Anna de, xiii, 42
Nordlinger, Marie, 30
The North American Review, 5
"La Notion de Conscience" (James, W.), 11, 203
nouns, representative, 79
Nouvelle Revue Française (NRF), x, 27, 267
novels: cultural forces and, 232, 255; Proust, Marcel and influence on, 207. *See also* books
NRF. *See Nouvelle Revue Française*
nucleus: of conscious thought, 246, 247, 249–250; of spiritual me and body, 66

O'Brien, Justin, 158, 232–233
obsession, attention and, 113
old-fogyism, 157
olfactory stimulus, memory and, 127, 146, 244, 245–246
À l'ombre des jeunes filles en fleurs (Proust, M.), 34
"On Some Omissions of Introspective Psychology" (James, W.), 202
originality: authentic, xiii; Proust, Marcel, on artists, isolation and, xii, 82; Proust, Marcel, on painters and, 1; of Proust, Marcel, xii–xiii, xiii; writers with direct literary influence, envy and, xi

pain: forgetting and lessening of, 185, 235, 236; memory and, 235, 236
paint, 202
Painter, George, 260
painters: James, William and influence on, x; Proust, Marcel, on originality and, 1. *See also specific painters*
Papini, G., 215
paranormal psychology, 12
partial recall, 133
past, 177; first-person experience, 198–201; pastness and conceived time, 138, 210–211
peace, mental, 185
Peirce, Charles, 32, 35, 214
Penfield, Wilder, 232–233
pénombre [penumbra], 104–105
perception: aubépines with emotion and sense, 88–89, 175; false, 157; James, William, on, 109; language and, 183, 221–222; sensation, imagination, misperception and, 148–157. *See also* attention
perchings. *See* flights and perchings
Perry, Ralph Barton, 5, 8, 10, 16, 43n18, 50n176, 51n202, 202, 225n101, 227n201
Perry, Thomas Sargeant, 50n178
personality: brain, creativity and individual, 234; memory reactivating, 74
PET scans, 237
"Phases of Fiction" (Woolf), 92
The Philosophical Review, 32
philosophy: in Europe, 31; James, William, and influence on, 31, 214–215; philosophical education and literary interests of Proust, Marcel, xii, 27–31, 35; uncertainty and change influencing, 210
"Philosophy in France" (Lalande), 32
photographic memory, 145, 181–182, 243
Picasso, Pablo, 207
Pierre-Quint, Léon, 57–58
Pillon, François, 10, 50n187
Les Plaisirs et les Jours (Proust, M.), 154
Plato, 210
pluralism: Proust, Marcel, with Pragmatism, radical empiricism and, 201–222; rationalizing order with, 208–209
A Pluralistic Universe (James, W.), xiv, 9, 24, 34, 172, 202, 205
Poe, Edgar Allen, 30
Poincaré, Henri, 119
"the popular imagination", ix
population theory, 237
"The Potion's Magic" (Buckner), 244
Poulet, Georges, 105
Pragmatism: Bergson, 40–42; James, William, and, xii, xvn14, 8, 9, 23, 31–33, 50n180, 229n298; in media,

31–33; in letters of Proust, Marcel, 272–279; Proust, Marcel, and, 193–194, 201–222; truth and, 215–216
Pragmatism and Sociology (Durkheim), 25
Pragmatism: A New Name for Some Old Ways of Thinking (James, W.), 7, 18, 23, 25, 192–193, 266; Bergson's preface in, 9, 24, 40–42, 51n201, 213; influence, 31–33, 202, 207; publishing history, 213–214
presence, in absence, 179–180
present, specious, 138–140
principle of association, 129–130
The Principles of Psychology (James, W.), xi, 4, 6, 21, 22, 23, 184, 243, 266; association by similarity in, 131; Boutroux and preface in, 17; influence, 106, 202; legacy of, 8, 11, 59–60, 267; multiple personality in, 16; publishing history, 8, 16–17, 242; rings of association, 131, 132, 268
The Principles of Psychology: Briefer Course (James, W.), 7, 23, 194
Prix Goncourt, x, 207
Le Problème de la mémoire: essai de psycho-mécanique (Sollier), 253–254
professional habits, 122–124
Proust (Mme) (mother), 28
Proust, Adrien (father), 13–16, 16, 18, 28, 33, 46n70, 46n81, 251
Proust, Marcel: art as developed by, 53–54; asthma and, 46n70, 245, 251; Bergson and, 19–21, 22, 24–25; Boutroux as link between James, William, and, 17, 18–19; consciousness and, 2; death of, 27, 266; education of, 6, 17, 28; English-language abilities of, 30; experience and, 2, 27; first-person experience and, 172; fringe of relations and, 86, 87–92, 252–253; influence of, ix; influences on, xii–xiii, 15; intermittence and, 241, 243; on isolation and originality of artists, xii, 82; James, William, and connection to, 1, 12–27, 27–31; James, William, and influence on, xii–xiii, xiv–xv, 3, 8, 21, 28, 29, 193–194, 213–214, 267–269; James, William, compared to, ix–xv; James, William, with similarities to, 6; La Rochefoucauld and, 158; lectures and, 20, 233; legacy of, x, xiv; literary style and, xiii–xiv, 28; with me (myself) and I, 61–62, 64, 65–76; media connections between James, William and, 31–40; memory and, 56, 58, 72–73, 267; as narrator, 54; neurocognitive science and, 233, 240–260; novels and influence of, 207; originality of, xii–xiii, xiii; on painters and originality, 1; philosophical education and literary interests of, xii, 27–31, 35; with Pragmatism, pluralism and radical empiricism, 201–222; Pragmatism and, 193–194, 201–222; Pragmatism in letters of, 272–279; with preface to *Sésame et les Lys*, 76–77; publishing history, 6–7, 42, 57–58, 213; reading and, 263n93; religious theme by James, William, and aesthetic variations by, 193–201, 257; with sleep and diffused attention, 103–104, 104–106; Sollier and, 25–26, 26–27, 251, 264n123–264n124; truth and, 175, 210, 211–212, 218, 258; with will to become writer, 162–163, 252. *See also Albertine disparue*; Cahier 59; *Cahier de 1908*; *Contre Sainte-Beuve*; *Correspondance*; *Du côté de chez Swann*; *Le Côté de Guermantes*; *Jean Santeuil*; "La Méthode de Sainte-Beuve"; *À l'ombre des jeunes filles en fleurs*; *Les Plaisirs et les Jours*; *À la recherche du temps perdu*; *Sodome et Gomorrhe II*; "Sur la lecture"; *Le Temps retrouvé*
Proust, Robert (brother), 18–19, 28
Proust and America (Murphy), 30
"Proust et le docteur Sollier: les molécules impressionnées" (Bizub), 251
Proust et le moi divisé (Bizub), 73
Proust in Perspective (Kolb and Mortimer), ix

Proust's English (Karlin), 30
Proust was a Neuroscientist (Lehrer), 233, 254
psychology. *See* abnormal psychology, in France; paranormal psychology
psychopathology, 16
publishing history: James, William, 5–6, 6–7, 8, 10, 11, 16–17, 34, 51n201, 213–214, 242, 266–267; Proust, Marcel, 6–7, 42, 57–58, 213; Sollier, 251–252, 264n124
pure experiences, 204. *See also* "A World of Pure Experience"

Quaker, and George Fox, 197–198
Quelques progrès dans l'étude du coeur humain [*Current Advances in the Study of the Human Heart*], x

radical empiricism: James, William, and, 9, 40, 51n202, 202, 202–204; Proust, Marcel, with Pragmatism, pluralism and, 201–222
Rageot, G., 21
railroad timetable, 265
Ramamurthy, Uma, 235–236, 236
Rationalism, 39, 202
Rationality, Activity and Faith (James, W.), 184
reading, 53, 98n17; art and, 167n222; books with experience translated into language, 176, 177–178, 180, 201–202, 224n37, 263n93; brain when, 71; emotions evoked when, 123, 128–129, 169n322, 176; James, William, with literary interests and, 5, 6, 10, 23; music, attention and, 108; Proust, Marcel, with literary interests and, xii, 27–31, 35; Wolf, Maryanne, on, 59, 61, 71, 98n17, 100n143, 177, 294
reasoning, with multiple interpretations, 158–159
recall: intentional, 144–145; partial, 133. *See also* memory
À la recherche du temps perdu (Proust, M.), ix, xi, 1, 29; association and metaphor in, 126–138; attention and discrimination in, 106–114; as autobiography or fiction, 54–63; Boutroux reference in, 19; desire in, 89–90; double-edged comfort of habit and, 114–126; effort, will and desire in, 159–163; English-language slang in, 30; flights and perchings in, 81–84; format, 44n35; James, William, and influence on, 21; *Le Journal des Débats Politiques et Littéraires* in, 33–34; as lived experience in book form, 57–58, 65; medical backdrop influencing thematic material in, 15; novels influenced by, 207; publishing history, 57–58, 213; reading with experience translated into language in, 177–178; with reasoning and multiple interpretations, 158–159; sensation, imagination, perception and misperception in, 148–157; sleep and diffused attention in, 103, 103–104, 104–106, 128; with time experienced through memory, 138–148
Reed, Edward S., 233, 238
Reilly, Eliza Jane, 7, 8
relations, consciousness and fringe of, 84–92
religious conversions, 197–198
religious experience, 194
Renoir, Pierre-Auguste, 1
Renouvier, Charles, 9–11, 184
representative nouns, 79
resurgent memory: brain and, 245; forgetting and, 148; madeleine and, 54, 81, 142, 147, 192–193, 226n141, 233, 244, 245–246
retrospective time, 141, 250
Le Rêve (Bergson), 19
Revue de l'Hypnotisme expérimental et thérapeutique, 13
Revue de philosophie, 17, 32
Revue de psychologie physiologique, 13
La Revue de Métaphysique et de Morale, 11, 17–18, 23, 28
Revue Lilas, 172
Revue Philosophique de la France et de l'Étranger, 8, 11, 17, 21

Ribot, Théodule, 11, 12–13, 13, 15, 27, 35, 56, 147, 234
Richardson, Dorothy, 3, 64
Richardson, Joan, 221, 222
Richardson, Robert D., 12, 43n18
Richet, Charles Robert, 16, 26
Riffaterre, Michael, 86
Rivière, Jacques, x, 56, 171
Robert, P.-E., 29–30
Roosevelt, Franklin, 24
Ruhe, Algot, 19
Ruskin, John, 7, 20, 29, 29–30, 65, 76–77, 176

Sacks, Oliver, 72, 237–238, 243
Saegert, Susan, 221
Salomon, Michel, 38, 51n193
Salpêtrière school of thought, 13–14, 15, 16, 46n72
Sand, George, 6, 178
San Francisco, earthquake in, 65, 173
Santayana, George, 9
Saussy, Haun, 232
Scheikévitch (Mme), 42, 54
Schiff, 30
science: art and, 233; neurocognitive, 231, 233–254, 234, 237–260
Science et religion dans la philosophie contemporaine (Boutroux), 18
Sciences Humaines, 234
séances de spiritisme [séance to commune with spirits], 19
self: intermittence with dissolution of, 241–242; time and multiplicity of, 243. *See also* me (myself), and I
sensations, 95; from books, 176, 177–178, 180, 201–202, 224n37, 263n93; with children's perception of space-world, 148–149; imagination, perception, misperception and, 148–157
sense data, brain and, 237–240
sense perception, emotion and: aubépines, 88–89, 175; olfactory stimulus and, 127, 146, 244, 245–246; three trees, 85, 175
Le Sens de la mémoire (Tadié, J.-Y. and Tadié, M.), 234
"The Sentiment of Rationality" (James, W.), 184, 185, 189, 192
separation anxiety, 102n212
Sésame et les Lys (Ruskin), 29, 65, 76–77, 176
Shattuck, Roger, 56, 62, 101n159
Shepherd-Barr, Kirsten, 245–246
Shook, John R., 31, 32
Sidgwick, Henry, 12
sillon (imprint), 27, 125, 177, 196, 205
similarity, association by, 130, 131
Simon, Linda, 43n18, 267
Sizeranne, Robert de la, 102n237
Skrupskelis, Ignas, 8
slang, 30
Slate, 256
sleep: with diffused attention, 103–106, 128; sleepwalking, 73; time and, 104
snapshots: Epstein on, 247; explanation of, 182; first-person experience or poor partial, 173–184; of memory, 106, 152, 211, 217, 232, 247, 260; truth as snapshot of momentary accuracy, 174
Société de psychologie physiologique, 12, 13
Société française de philosophie [French Philosophical Society], 31
Society for Psychical Research, 12, 36, 50n185
Socrates, 259, 260
Sodome et Gomorrhe II (Proust, M.), 19, 240
Sollier, Paul, 32, 262n51, 263n121; influence of, 233; James, William, and, 25, 26; as neurophysiologist, 253–254; Proust, Marcel, and, 25–26, 26–27, 251, 264n123–264n124; publishing history, 251–252, 264n124
Some Problems of Philosophy (James, W.), 40, 97
Souday, Paul, 53, 58
space, time and, 238
specious present, 138–140
Spencer, Herbert, 63, 202
spiritual me, 66, 67
Staël-Holstein, Germaine de, 1
Stein, Gertrude, 256

stereoscope, 175
Straus (Mme), 30
stream of consciousness: James, William, and, 54, 55, 59, 62, 63, 68, 233, 247; mind, body and, 233; writers, 64, 232
stream of thought: durée réelle [duration and change] and, 21–22; James, William, and, 21, 59, 60, 63–64, 78–79, 250; language and, 77
Stuart, A. E., 259, 260
Stumpf, Carl, 7, 16
style. *See* literary style
"A Suggestion about Mysticism" (James, W.), 25, 200
"Sur la lecture" (Proust, M.), 76–77, 80–81

Tadié, Jean-Yves, 234, 250
Tadié, Marc, 234, 250
Taine, H., 234
Talks to Teachers on Psychology: and to Students on Some of Life's Ideals (James, W.), 23, 37
telescope, 174
Le Temps retrouvé (Proust, M.): reading with experience translated into language in, 177–178. *See also À la recherche du temps perdu*
"Theory of Emotions" (James, W.), 6, 26
Theosophy, 194
thought, 58; flights and perchings of, 76–84; ideas and, 26, 59; nucleus of conscious, 246, 247, 249–250; with reasoning and multiple interpretations, 158–159; Salpêtrière school of, 13–14, 15, 16, 46n72; stream of, 21, 21–22, 59, 60, 63–64, 77, 78–79, 250
threshold, 205
time: consciousness and passing, 74–75; different rates of, 119, 141–142; durée réelle and, 21–22, 75, 100n132, 139; ephemeral and personal captured in language, 124; madeleine and retrospective, 141, 250; memory and experience of, 106, 138–148; multiple views of space and, 238; with multiplicity of self, 243; pastness and conceived, 138, 210–211; railroad timetable, 265; sleep and, 104; with specious present, 138–140
Time and Space (Hodgson), 133
Tolstoï, Leo, 35
trees, three, 85, 175
truth: artists and, 171, 205; deception and, 216–218; dynamic fluidity of, 176; with grafting and future experience, 218–219; James, William, and, 174, 210; as mutable, 193, 215, 219–220; pragmatic, 215–216; Proust, Marcel, and, 175, 210, 211–212, 218, 258; as snapshot of momentary accuracy, 174
Turner, William, 102n237
Tyrrell, George, 32

The Varieties of Religious Experience (James, W.), 7, 9, 16, 17, 22, 23, 32, 37, 192, 194, 195, 196, 200, 214, 258; Locke and influence on, 234
Vendeuvre, Isabelle de, 222
Vermeer, Johannes, 93, 95–96, 109, 185
View of Delft, 95–96, 109
Villeparisis (Mme), 42
Vinteuil, sonate de, 93, 205–206, 207
vision: of artists with consciousness and art, 92–93, 235; James, William, on imagination and, xiv
visual attention, 109–110
visual stimulus, brain and, 110–111
voluntary association, 111–112, 135–136, 137, 235
voluntary attention, 111–112

Walusinski, O., 26, 27
war, in Europe, 24, 266
Warner, Maria, 231
Warnock, Mary, 243
Weber, 15
Wernicke, Carl, 234
What Maisie Knew (James, H.), 30
Whistler, James McNeill, 30
Whitman, Walt, 233, 237
Wilde, Oscar, 30

will: with artists and will to action, 123–124, 162–163, 252; effort, desire and, 159–163; free, 10, 38, 161, 233; heroic mind and, 163
William James Studies, 221
The Will to Believe and other Essays in Popular Philosophy (James, W.), 23, 184, 202, 203
Willy, Colette, 42
Wolf, Maryanne, 59, 71, 100n143, 177–178, 263n93
Woolf, Virginia, 3, 64, 92, 207, 255
"A World of Pure Experience" (James, W.), 172–173
Wright, Donald, 251
writers: with envy and direct literary influence, xi; impressions and, 237; James, William and influence on, x; with rewriting, 257–258, 259; stream of consciousness, 64, 232; with will to write, 123–124, 162–163, 252. *See also specific writers*

Zeki, S., 249
Zeno of Elea, 254

About the Author

Marilyn Sachs holds a doctorate in French literature. She is an independent scholar living in St. Louis, Missouri.

CPSIA information can be obtained at www.ICGtesting.com
Printed in the USA
BVOW08*0128251113

337105BV00002B/2/P

9 780739 181621